BEGINNING WITH CHRIST

TIMELESS WISDOM FOR COMPLICATED TIMES

E. STANLEY JONES

COMPILED BY ANNE MATHEWS-YOUNES

ABINGDON PRESS
NASHVILLE

BEGINNING WITH CHRIST:
TIMELESS WISDOM FOR COMPLICATED TIMES

This book is printed on acid-free paper.

Library of Congress Cataloging-in-Publication Data has been requested.

ISBN: 978-1501-85871-0 (PRINT)
ISBN: 978-1501-85872-7 (E-PUB)

This volume includes selections, used by permission, from the following books by E. Stanley Jones:

Victorious Living. Copyright © 1936 by Whitmore & Stone, renewed 1964 by E. Stanley Jones, updated edition published 2015 by Abingdon Press.

Abundant Living. Copyright © 1942 by Whitmore & Stone, renewed 1970 by E. Stanley Jones, published 1990 as an Abingdon Classic by Abingdon Press, updated edition published 2014 by Abingdon Press.

The Way. Copyright © 1946 by Stone & Pierce, renewed 1974 by Mabel Lossing Jones, published 1984 as a Festival edition by Abingdon Press.

The Way to Power and Poise. Copyright © 1949 by Abingdon Press, published 1978 as a Festival edition by Abingdon Press.

How to Be a Transformed Person. Copyright © 1951 by Pierce and Smith, published 1978 as a Festival edition by Abingdon Press.

Growing Spiritually. Copyright © 1953 by Pierce & Washabaugh.

Mastery. Copyright © 1955 by Pierce & Washabaugh, renewed 1983 by Mrs. Eunice Mathews, published 1992 as an Abingdon Classic by Abingdon Press, updated edition published 2017 by Abingdon Press.

Christian Maturity. Copyright © 1957 by Abingdon Press, renewed 1985 by Eunice T. Mathews, published 1992 as an Abingdon Classic by Abingdon Press.

In Christ. Original copyright © 1961 by Abingdon Press. New edition copyright © 2017 by E. Stanley Jones Foundation. Published 2017 by Seedbed Publishing, Franklin TN. Used by permission.

The Word Became Flesh. Copyright © 1963 by Abingdon Press, published 1979 as a Festival edition by Abingdon Press, updated edition published 2006 by Abingdon Press.

Unless otherwise noted, scripture quotations are from the Revised Standard Version of the Bible. Copyright 1946 and 1952 by the Division of Christian Education of the National Council of the churches of Christ in the U.S.A.

Scripture quotations marked CEB are taken from the Common English Bible (CEB), copyright 2011. Used by permission. All rights reserved.

Scripture quotations marked Weymouth are taken from the *The New Testament in Modern Speech*, by Richard Francis Weymouth (London: James Clarke & Co., 1903).

Scripture quotations marked Moffatt are from *The Bible: A New Translation*, by James Moffatt. Copyright 1922, 1935,1950 by Harper & Bros. Used by permission.

Scripture quotations marked KJV are from the King James or Authorized Version of the Bible.

Scripture quotations marked NEB are from *The New English Bible.* © The Delegates of the Oxford University Press and The Syndics of the Cambridge University Press 1961, 1970. Reprinted by permission

Scripture quotations marked PHILLIPS are from The New Testament in Modern English by J.B Phillips copyright © 1960, 1972 J. B. Phillips. Administered by The Archbishops' Council of the Church of England. Used by Permission.

18 19 20 21 22 23 24 25 26 27—10 9 8 7 6 5 4 3 2 1

MANUFACTURED IN THE UNITED STATES OF AMERICA

CONTENTS

FOREWORD

I see E. Stanley Jones almost every day. In the sanctuary of the Church of the Resurrection, he sits next to a river, gazing up at the risen Christ, part of the Resurrection Window. When people ask me who this man is, I respond, "He is one of the most remarkable Methodists I've ever known."

I was in seminary when I first came to know of E. Stanley Jones. Dick Schaefer, with whom I worked, gave me a copy of Jones's *A Song of Ascents*. I had just joined The United Methodist Church a few years before, and Schaefer said, "You must get to know this man." Jones published the book when he was eighty-four years old, calling it his "spiritual autobiography." As I read of his amazing journey, he became, and remains, among my heroes of the faith.

I think many who have claimed Jones as a theological hero might be surprised by some of the things that he penned in his books. He was evangelical, to be sure, but of a different sort from many who use that name today. He was described to me while I was in seminary as a "liberal evangelical." He became for me a pattern of what a United Methodist looked like, a pattern that still shapes my life and ministry to this day.

Preparing to write this foreword led me back to Jones's other books in my library. I reached for *The Christ of the Indian Road*, first published in 1925 (my copy is a sixth edition, published in 1927, when Abingdon Press was still located in New York). The book sold more than a million copies and inspired people around the world. Jones offered a thoughtful critique of Western Christianity, and of many Christian missionaries and evangelists who had come to India only to repel rather than draw the Indian people to Christ.

When it came to his ministry among the Hindus of India, Jones demonstrated humility and love. He pointed out places where he believed Hinduism and Christianity shared common ground. He preached Christ with words and concepts Hindus were familiar with. He did not believe Indian Christianity would look like Western Christianity, nor should it. He wrote that the most important spiritual ideas in Hinduism might be reinterpreted in the light of Christ, and would form a deep Christian spirituality that would, in turn, have something to teach Western Christians. What a remarkable insight born of a humble spirit!

I reach for another of Jones's books, my copy of his 1931 book, *The Christ on the Mount*. It is a powerful exposition of the Sermon on the Mount, which speaks just as clearly to twenty-first–century readers as it did to those for whom it was first written. It is clear that his passion for inviting others to consider the claims of Christ was no mere invitation to "ask him into your heart," or to have a personal relationship with him—as important as these are—but to actually follow Jesus and to put into practice the ethics he taught.

There's another Jones book I grasp. Inside its front cover is a note that it is a wartime book, and thus printed on thinner paper. It is *The Christ of the American Road*, published in 1944. I'm reminded that Jones served as a go-between with President Roosevelt and a Japanese delegation just before the Japanese bombing of Pearl Harbor. It is a fascinating little book, written in the midst of World War II, with prescient reflections on world events. He anticipated a world with two superpowers when the war was over, atheist Russia and the United States, a nation whose population largely claimed to be Christian. In the book, he called Americans to live up to the faith they professed. Speaking of what would become the postwar economy, he warned that America would need to choose between "a dog-eat-dog economy, or a brother-help-brother economy." In his chapter on "The Seven Hesitations of Democracy," he wrote a scathing critique of America's treatment of "Negroes." Jones penned these words ten years before the young Martin Luther King Jr., broke onto the scene to lead the Civil Rights Movement.

Among my favorite of Jones's books was his last, *The Divine Yes*, which I have quoted and preached about in several sermons. When he was eighty-seven, Jones had a stroke that left him partially paralyzed. He chose this as the opportunity to write one more book, a final testimony to his faith in the face of adversity. In it he writes,

> I cannot afford to be anything but grateful that he thought enough of me to give me this period at the end of my life to be a proof that what I've spoken about all my life—the unshakable Kingdom and the unchanging Person—is true because I'm showing it to be true by his Grace.

Before he died, he traveled back to his beloved India one last time, and there died among the people he loved. Reading that book, I thought to myself what I thought when I read my first E. Stanley Jones book thirty-three years ago: I want to be like this man.

—Adam Hamilton
Senior Pastor
The United Methodist Church
of the Resurrection, Leawood, Kansas

INTRODUCTION

In 1971, my parents, Eunice Jones Mathews and James K. Mathews, compiled *Selections from E. Stanley Jones: Christ and Human Need*, drawing upon passages from Jones's sixteen non-devotional books. My parents fully intended to create a companion book using material from my grandfather's ten devotionals, and wrote in their introduction to *Selections from E. Stanley Jones* that "the devotionals require separate treatment and at a later time we intend to compile a selection of the best passages from them." However, they were not able to complete that task, and I have stepped in to finish it for them.

This book is organized into chapters that focus on deep matters of faith and on the "how" of living a life following Jesus. *Beginning with Christ* includes topics relating to *The Faith Journey*, with selections from Jones addressing belief, faith, and surrender; *Christian Practices*, about love, prayer, forgiveness, witness and evangelism; *Theology*, which shares Jones's thoughts about God, Jesus, the Holy Spirit, and the kingdom of God; *Challenges*, exploring Jones's writings on evil, human suffering, war, and worry; and *Engaging with Our World*, including his writing on the relationship between faith and science, freedom, health, justice, and poverty, to name just a few.

My parents realized an introduction to the life and writings of E. Stanley Jones would benefit a new generation and so created their *Selections from E. Stanley Jones* in the hope of engaging new readers in Jones' unique ministry and timeless message. They wrote:

> In rereading his non-devotional books we were constantly amazed by their continuing vitality and freshness. For the most part Jones reads with an astonishingly contemporary flavor. The themes are in no sense passé; rather the church has not yet caught up with some of his perspectives. Hardly a topic of current interest fails to find expression in one fashion or another. Jones was ecumenical before most people had heard of the term. Race relations is a theme of most of his books and war and peace is repeatedly and inescapably dealt with. Jones' topics cluster around deep matters of faith—including the meaning of Christ today, the kingdom of God, evangelism, discipleship and the inner life. It is all here.

Those observations were written fifty years ago and still ring true in this new volume. Jones's words continue to be used in the spiritual awakening and nurture of literally thousands of persons. His insights bring hope and refreshment to multitudes all over the world—as ordinary persons become extraordinary as they are transformed into new persons through Jesus Christ.

During his long career, Stanley Jones was a witness: an evangelist—the bearer of good news. Very early in Jones's ministry, a wise friend told him: "You are not a theologian; you are a dowsing rod. You tell us where there is water beneath—remember your function." The all-embracing compass of the gospel has been set forth unwaveringly in a more effective manner by Jones than by another evangelist, past or present.

My experience in selecting passages was similar to that of my parents. We both came to understand that choosing one passage meant leaving another out, one that was also meaningful and addressed an important human need. I hope the selections in this volume will be invitations to the reader, rather than mere instructions. Jones-the-evangelist spent his life inviting response, participation, and involvement in new life in Christ.

The ten devotionals that provide the material for this book were published by Abingdon Press over a twenty-seven year period. Selections appearing in *Beginning with Christ* are arranged in chronological order according to publication date: *Victorious Living* (1936); *Abundant Living* (1941); *The Way* (1946); *The Way to Power and Poise* (1949); *How to Be a Transformed Person* (1951); *Growing Spiritually* (1953); *Mastery* (1955); *Christian Maturity* (1957); *In Christ* (1961); and *The Word Became Flesh* (1963). Several of these books are available in updated editions.

I am grateful to Adam Hamilton for the beautiful foreword to this book. I am also grateful to Abingdon Press and in particular to the late Mary Catherine Dean for her support on a range of efforts to introduce E. Stanley Jones to a new generation of readers and for a plan between Abingdon Press and the E. Stanley Jones Foundation to have all of Jones's writings back in print by 2025. Jones's first book, *The Christ of the Indian Road*, was published by the Methodist Publishing House in 1925. In 2025, Abingdon Press will have had books by E. Stanley Jones continually in print for a century. Surely they will remain an invitation to new generations to experience the transforming power of a life lived in Jesus Christ.

—Anne Mathews-Younes
President, E. Stanley Jones Foundation

1
THE FAITH JOURNEY

CHRISTIAN MATURITY

Nothing could be clearer: the aim and purpose of the whole impact of the Christian faith is to produce maturity. And nothing is more gloriously breathtaking than the pattern of that maturity; the measure of the stature of the fullness of Christ....

If I write of maturity from an experience stretching across half a century, learned among all nations of the world, I know that maturity does not come by accumulated experiences. It comes through basic responses to grace. I am as mature as my basic responses to grace. And no more mature....

So maturity is not a matter of age but of attitudes. And these changed attitudes can be sudden and lasting. But they may also be gradual. But in either case you become mature to the degree that you relate yourself to God, respond to God's grace, and work it out in life. Receptivity to grace is the secret of maturity.

Christian Maturity
(Introduction, viii, xi)

BELIEF

The Question That Halts Our Quest
Job 11:7-9; 21:15; 23:3-9; John 14:8

The facts of life are too much for us—the unemployment, the hunger of little children, the underlying strife in modern life, the exploitation of the weak and incapacitation of them by the strong, the apparently unmerited suffering around us, the heartlessness of nature, the discoveries of science which seems to render the hypothesis of God unnecessary—all these things, and more, seem to shatter our belief in God. We do not reject that belief; it simply fades away and becomes unreal.

Victorious Living
(Week 1, January 1)

Having Our Being in God
Hebrews 4:16; 6:9-12; 10:39

Belief is the habit of your life; you have to believe in order to live.

Abundant Living
(Week 6, Saturday)

Cease from Struggling
Philippians 4:6-7

It is quite clear. This new birth (John 1:12-13), which leads to a new life, is a gift accepted by faith, by those who "*believed* in his name." But that belief is not mere intellectual assent; it is believing with your life, self-committal to Another. It means letting down the barriers of your inmost being and letting him come in and take over, take over as Sole Owner.

The Way
(Week 11, Friday)

Finding the Good in the Evil
John 4:10-1

Jesus believes in people when they can't believe in themselves. So they have faith in his faith in them. Paul says, "I live by the faith of the Son of God" (Gal 2:20 KJV). One would have thought it was "faith *in* the Son of God," but it is "of." The faith that Jesus had in Paul made him respond with faith in him. Jesus faiths faith out of the faithless, believes belief out of the beliefless, and loves love out of the loveless. We must have faith in people if we are to influence them. Those who believe in us most influence us most. If we become cynical about people, we become powerless to help people.

How to Be a Transformed Person
(Week 39, Monday)

The Wicked Walk in Circles
Romans 5:1-5

For the Christian faith believes in progress, an eternal progress.

The non-Christian faiths never have believed in progress. It is interesting that the chakra, or circle, was developed in Greece, India, and China about the same time, as representing the belief that life is a circle, turning around on itself endlessly. In such a scheme, hope could have no place, for life perpetually turned back on itself, coming back to where it had been. In fact, hope was looked on as an evil.

Then comes the Christian faith with its belief in progress for the individual and for society. This brought to birth a new thing—hope....Augustine translates Psalm 12:8, "The wicked walk in circles." They do. They get nowhere. But a great many Christians "walk in circle"; they too do not get anywhere.

Growing Spiritually
(Week 14, Thursday)

The Simple Art of Drinking
John 7:37-39

Jesus said: "All who believe in me should drink" (John 7:38 CEB)!

The difference between believers is this: some just believe, and some believe and drink; they know how to take, to receive, to drink. Hence they never thirst. Some are always thirsty, for they just believe. They assent to Jesus, but they don't assimilate Jesus. Their minds believe, but their hearts do not receive.

Mastery
(Week 24, Sunday)

A Mature Faith: First Necessity
Ephesians 4:4-6

If we are to be mature we must get hold of a mature faith, or better, it must get hold of us. For the immaturities of our faith will soon show themselves in immaturities in our actions and our attitudes. The creed of today becomes the deed of tomorrow. Nothing can be more immature than the oft-repeated statement: "It doesn't matter what you believe just so you live right." For belief is literally by-lief—by-life, the thing you live by. And if your belief is wrong, your life will be wrong.

Don't misunderstand me. I don't mean to say that if you have a correct belief you'll necessarily have a correct life. That doesn't follow. The creed, to be a creed, must be a vital rather than a verbal one. For the only thing we really believe in is the thing we believe in enough to act upon. Your deed is your creed. But it does matter what you hold as the basic assumptions of your life.

Christian Maturity
(Week 1, Tuesday)

In Christ—Paul's Phrase?

[What happens when] Christianity becomes correct belief about Christ instead of a surrender to Christ, which puts you in him. This is the Great Substitute—the in has become about. Christianity becomes a theological system instead of a way of life—becomes good views, instead of good news.

In Christ
(Week 13, Sunday)

The Gift Creates Initiative
John 4:13-15

Your belief is your life. And your life is your belief. You believe in a thing enough to act on it, to live it. So you are what you believe, and you believe what you are. Your deed is your creed. And your creed is your deed.

The Word Became Flesh
(Week 5, Friday)

CONVERSION

What Is Conversion?
Psalm 86:11; Acts 2:37-38; 3:19; Romans 8:1-2

Jesus puts [conversion] within the content of the moral and spiritual as well as the psychological.... [Conversion is the unifying] of the personality and bringing harmony into the center of life. All life says we must undergo a change.

Victorious Living
(Week 7, Monday)

The Social Order Converts the Individual
Hosea 4:1-3; Amos 8:4-7

In the interest of individual conversion, I am committed to the necessity of social conversion. If a person shows no interest in converting an unchristian social order, then by that very fact that person has little interest in individual conversion, for, apart from the Holy Spirit, the greatest single power to change the individual is the social order.

Abundant Living
(Week 26, Monday)

What Is Conversion?
John 3:3-8

Conversion is that change, gradual or sudden, by which we pass from the kingdom of self to the kingdom of God by the grace and power of Christ.

The Way
(Week 10, Tuesday)

On Pruning for Power and Poise
Hebrews 12:5-8

Conversion is the grafting of the divine life within us. We are made partakers of the divine nature. But this pruning process provides for a continuous conversion: a conversion from the irrelevant to the relevant, from the marginal to the central, from being just busy to being fruitful. There is a cartoon of a girl getting out of her car, walking up to a policeman, and saying: "Can you please tell me where I want to go?" She was going, but didn't know where! A man stood up in a meeting and asked: "Is there anybody going anywhere in a car?" This living without plan and purpose and streamlined intentions results in a lot of running around in circles and getting nowhere.

The Way to Power and Poise
(Week 49, Sunday)

Gradual or Sudden Conversions
Matthew 19:13-15

Some conversions are gradual and some are sudden. Some fold like a flower to the sun, the gradual type. Others take a sudden leap to the breast of God. Some children who are brought up in a Christian home "can testify that 'from their childhood' they knew, not Scriptures, but God." They cannot tell how they came to know God, but they did, just as they knew the blue sky and a mother's love. They knew God before they could understand any name by which our imperfect human speech endeavors to affirm God's goodness, power, or glory.

Most of us need a definite and decisive round-about-face resulting in an unfolding or a sudden conversion. However, even in the decisive type there may be a gradualness; or there may be a suddenness in the gradual type of conversion. They blend into each other. Every Christian knows about Paul's sudden conversion on the Damascus Road, but who can date with any certainty the supreme crisis in the life of Peter? He heard the call "Follow me," and followed, and that following became a flowering. Not the phenomena that surround conversion, but the facts that flow from it are the criteria. "You will know them by their fruits" (Matt 7:16). Both types are valid if they are vital.

How to Be a Transformed Person
(Week 7, Thursday)

We Retreat before We Advance
Romans 6:5-11

Conversion brings freedom from the past and the present, and freedom to grow in the future.

Growing Spiritually
(Week 2, Saturday)

We Have Heard for Ourselves
John 4:39-42

The greatest necessity of the church today is the conversion of secondhand Christians into firsthand Christians, the conversion of people who are walking in half-lights to people who walk in full light. "Whoever follows me won't walk in darkness," said Jesus (John 8:12 CEB); and he might have added, "or in half-lights either." They can be "in the light, as he is in the light" (1 John 1:7 CEB).

Mastery
(Week 34, Friday)

God Is Light on Four Things
Romans 1:19-20

God is light on conversion. If God is light on character, when I look at my character and see God's character in Jesus, then I know my character has to be changed. But how? In Jesus, I see the door, the only door, through conversion. He said, "Except ye be converted...ye shall not enter into the kingdom of heaven" (Matt 18:3 KJV). There are just two classes of people: the converted and the unconverted, a division that really divides and the only division that really divides. And through Jesus, God provides all the resources for conversion, a total conversion of the total person.

Christian Maturity
(Week 7, Wednesday)

"In Him All the Fullness of God"

There is no record or hint that Jesus went from a once broken life through conversion into wholeness. All of us have to go through that; Jesus didn't.

In Christ
(Week 39, Monday)

"Man Is Made for Conversion"
John 3:3-10

We come this week to something inherent in the Christian faith and inherent in us: conversion, new birth. When the Christian faith says: "You must be born anew" (John 3:7), and "Unless you turn and become like children" (Matt 18:3), many think that this "must" and this "unless" are imposed from above arbitrarily; God laid down the condition for entrance into the kingdom, and you can take it or leave it. God as ruler of the universe has the right and the power to impose those conditions. But as we work from Revelation down and from the facts up, both are saying: "You must be born anew."

Humans find themselves incomplete persons in an incomplete world. God apparently created the world incomplete. God left it imperfect so we, in helping the creator to complete the creation, would help to complete ourselves in the process. After creation, God looked upon the universe and saw "it was good"—not perfect, but "good"—for the purpose God had in creation, namely, to make beings who would grow in God's likeness and be perfect as created beings, as God is perfect as Creator God. So to grow into that likeness, we would have to be converted, converted from what we are to what we ought to be.

The Word Became Flesh
(Week 10, Sunday)

FAITH

First Steps out of the Old Life
Luke 19:1-10; John 1:35-42

[How does faith grow? A story]

A [man] sat down with me and abruptly said: "What are you going to do with me? I am a man without any religion. The old is dead and I haven't anything new to take its place. In America no church would take me, for I cannot believe in the divinity of Christ."

I could almost see him inwardly stiffen to meet my arguments to prove Christ divine. So I used none. Instead I asked: "What do you believe? How far along are you?"

"Well," he said, "I believe that Christ was the best of men."

"Then let us begin where you can. If he is the best of men, then he is your ideal. Are you prepared to act according to that ideal? To cut out of your life everything that Christ would not approve?"

He was startled, and said, "But that is not easy."

"I never said the way of Christ is easy. Are you prepared to let go everything he will not approve?"

"If I am honest, I must," he quietly replied, "and I will."

"Then, whoever Christ turns out to be, man or more than man, wouldn't you be stronger and better if he were living with you, in you, all the time?"

"Of course, I would be different."

"Then will you let him into your life?"

"I don't know how."

"Then pray this prayer after me, sentence by sentence."

He did. "This is different," he said as we arose, "for they always told me I had to believe first. Now at least here is something for me to begin on."

The next day he came again, his face radiant. "I didn't know a man could be as happy as I have been today. All my questions and doubts as to who Christ is have gone. And, moreover, I have been talking to my wife and she wants it too."

Christ had verified himself. He does, when we give him a chance.

Victorious Living
(Week 7, Sunday)

God Guides through Opening Providences and the Natural Order
1 Corinthians 2:9; 12:8; 2 Corinthians 2:12; Revelation 3:8

God guides through natural law and its discoveries through science. We have a primary faith in revelation and a secondary faith in science. But in a sense science is revelation: God speaking to us through the natural order. That natural order is God's order. It is dependable because God is dependable. God works by law and order rather than by whim and notion and fancy. There was a time when we tried to put God in the unexplained gaps in nature; we said God must be there, for these gaps are mysterious and unexplainable. But when science began to fill up these gaps, God was pushed out. To have relegated God to those gaps was a mistake, for God reveals the divine self in the very law and order and the explainable facts of nature, and not merely in the unexplainable and the mysterious. The law and order express God far more than the unexplainable and mysterious. For this very law and order is of God. God is in it, is the author of it, works through it, but is not strait-jacketed by it. For this law and order is full of surprises and of freedoms. A closed system of nature is now unscientific. God guides through science. Accept that fact.

Abundant Living
(Week 37, Friday)

Further Steps in Corporate Living
Proverbs 25:8-11; Matthew 5:25; 7:1-5; 1 John 2:8-10

Look on others, not as they are, but as they can be. That was the secret of Jesus' influence on people. He believed in them when they couldn't believe in themselves, for he saw them, not as they were, but as they could be by his help. That attitude will give you, not a querulous mood of dissatisfaction with others, but a constructive mood of expectancy of possibilities. I find myself responding to Jesus' faith in me when I have no faith in myself. I have faith in his faith!

Abundant Living
(Week 39, Monday)

A Center of Moral and Spiritual Contagion
Psalm 42:5-8

Those who are in contact with Christ find a constant quickening of faith in life, in one's self, and in others. I know that Christ believes in me when I can't believe in myself. So I have to respond to his faith in me. "I live by faith in the Son of God" (Gal 2:20), not by my faith in him alone, but by his faith in me.

The Way to Power and Poise
(Week 42, Saturday)

Shock Treatment or a New Faith
Acts 15:37-39

A new faith is a gentle shock treatment that sends the life force into new channels of constructive life and activity. A new faith gets our eyes off ourselves and puts them on Christ, and we find adequacy and power in him.

How to Be a Transformed Person
(Week 29, Tuesday)

9

Being Christian Is the Triumph
Hebrews 12:1-2

Every day you can take hold of life by the handle of fear or the handle of faith. If you take hold of it by the handle of faith, you can find something to rejoice in everything. If nothing in the thing itself, then you can rejoice over the fact that you can rejoice—over everything and nothing. The rejoicing is the victory. Being Christian is the triumph.

How to Be a Transformed Person
(Week 36, Thursday)

The Word of Christianity Become Flesh
1 John 1:1-4

The very center of the Christian faith is the Incarnation, in which the Divine Word becomes flesh; the idea becomes fact. All other faiths are the word become word, the idea projected as an idea. In Jesus, the idea walked. It spoke in human life and manifested in human relationships. It transformed religion from idealism to realism.

Where this faith is sincerely tried, it becomes incarnate as fact. It works in human relationships. And wherever it is tried, it produces something so exquisitely beautiful that we stand "lost in wonder, love, and praise" (Charles Wesley, "Love Divine, All Loves Excelling").

Growing Spiritually
(Week 30, Sunday)

Growth in Freedom
John 8:31-36

There is nothing more fallacious than saying, "Any faith is good, provided you are sincere." You may sincerely follow the wrong thing to a wrong destination. Sincerely sitting in a railway train, believing you are on the right train, won't get you to your destination if it is actually the wrong train.

Growing Spiritually
(Week 50 Sunday)

I Endorse This with All My Heart
John 7:37-39

Faith is receptivity toward God. Faith is not a talisman that brings certain things because of the faith. Faith is an attitude toward God which makes it possible for God to work. If God gave to us without our faith, it would mean imposing something on us without our cooperation. Faith is cooperating with God. It is saying yes to God's yes, affirming God's affirmations.

Mastery
(Week 51, Tuesday)

Joy Is the Christian Word
Philippians 1:25-26

Yesterday we said that there is something deeper than happiness, and that is joy. Happiness comes from happenings, but joy may be within, in spite of happenings. Happiness is the world's word; joy is the Christian's word. The New Testament does not use or promise the word happiness; it uses the word joy. And for a reason.

Many people are expecting happiness from following the Christian faith: "God will arrange the things that happen to me so they will all add up to happiness." When the things that happen to them do not mean happiness, such people are dismayed and feel God has let them down: "Why should this happen to me?" They expect to be protected from happenings that make them unhappy. This is a false view and leads to a lot of disillusionment. For the Christian is not necessarily protected from things that make people unhappy.

Was Jesus protected from happenings that make people unhappy? Was Paul? Their Christian faith got them into opposition, into persecution, into death. How could a faith that has a cross at its center promise exemption from happenings that ordinarily bring unhappiness? Then what is the answer? The Christian faith offers joy in the midst of happenings that make people without that faith unhappy. When Christians don't find joy on account of their happenings, they can always find joy in spite of them.

Christian Maturity
(Week 37, Wednesday)

11

All the Good That Is Ours in Christ

To be in Christ is to share one's faith, for you cannot have a share in Christ unless you share him with others. Nothing is ours until we share it. The sharing of the faith makes it possible to share in the faith. Otherwise not; if you are not winning others, Christ has not really won you.

When you share your faith then you "promote the knowledge of all the good that is ours in Christ" (Phlm 6). "All the good that is ours in Christ"! That is what sharing your faith means; it means telling people around all the good that you have found in Christ.

In Christ
(Week 44, Saturday)

Introduction

The Christian faith is not just a little better than other faiths—a little more moral, more free from contradictory elements, more lofty in its conceptions. It is that, but it is more; it is different in kind. Religions are our search for God. The gospel is God's search for us. Therefore, there are many religions, but only one gospel. Religions are the Word become word; the gospel is the Word become flesh.

This verse, "And the Word became flesh" (John 1:14) sets the gospel off in a class by itself. And yet while it is in a class by itself, a sui generis, nevertheless it relates it to everything—God, life, the material everything. For it is planted in life—spiritual, material, social. But planted in life, it is different, apart, unique.

The gospel quietly says: "And the Word became flesh." It reversed everything and revealed Everything.

Without this verse the Christian faith is the Word become word—an idea, a philosophy, a moralism; with it the Christian faith is the Word become flesh, a fact—a redemptive fact, the supreme fact.

Compared with this, the differences between the Christian way and other ways are marginal and indecisive, but this is central and decisive. And compared with this, the questions of the manifestations of the Christian faith are marginal and indecisive. If the manifestation of the Christian faith is not the Word become flesh—a decision—then it is the Word become word—a discussion—hence sub-Christian.

The Word Became Flesh

A Person to Be Followed
John 21:18-19

So the Christian faith is not a set of propositions to be accepted; it is a Person to be followed. That Person is manifest reality, so to follow Jesus is to follow Reality, manifested as the Word become flesh. So to follow Jesus is not assent to truths, but the acceptance of Truth, embodied in a Person and reembodied in my person.

The Word Became Flesh
(Week 3, Thursday)

The Christian Faith Is Secular Through and Through
Matthew 15:32-38

The Christian faith is secular without being secularized. It is the spiritual working in and through the material. The sacred is secular and the secular is sacred. Unless our religion functions in material terms, it does not function. We are not ghosts; we are embodied beings and we must function in and through the body or we do not function.

The Word Became Flesh
(Week 6, Tuesday)

All the Ideas Are Guaranteed by the Fact of Jesus
John 14:10-11

All the principles of the Christian faith have been verified in the life of Jesus; they work and have produced the character of Jesus. And in any battle of ideas the victory will go to those ideas guaranteed by the facts. In the Christian faith all its ideas have been guaranteed by the fact of Jesus. So the final victory goes to him. For you will never get better ideas than Jesus held until you live a better life than Jesus lived. That can't be done. He is standard.

The Word Became Flesh
(Week 18, Wednesday)

Four Suggestions from Gandhi
Matthew 12:38-42

We pause today to look at what the greatest Hindu of modern times says to the Christians about their faith. I asked Mahatma Gandhi, in the early days when he had just come from South Africa to begin his work of gaining freedom for India, "What would you suggest to us as Christians that we do to make Christianity more naturalized in India, not a foreign thing, identified with a foreign people and a foreign government, but a part of the life of the people and making its contribution to the remaking of India?" He replied without a moment's hesitation:

> I would suggest four things: First, that all of you Christians, missionaries and all, must begin to live more like Jesus Christ. [He needn't have said anything more!] Second, I would suggest that you practice your religion without adulterating it or toning it down—practice it as it is. Third, I would suggest that you emphasize love and make it your working force, for love is central in Christianity. Fourth, I suggest that you study the non-Christian faiths more sympathetically to find a more sympathetic approach to the people.

Here was the leading Hindu telling the Christians that they should live more like Jesus Christ, the central figure of our faith; to practice our faith without adulterating it or toning it down. A representative of the most syncretic religion in the world, Hinduism, suggests that we be Christians in the deepest sense of that word; that will make us universal. That we use love as our working force, for Jesus came armed with no weapons save the weapon of love. And that we discover any truths in the non-Christian faiths we can, for Gandhi implied that that will lead you on then to the Truth, the Incarnate Truth. A great commission from a great Hindu.

The Word Became Flesh
(Week 18, Thursday)

14

The Word Continues to Be Flesh
Acts 2:32-33

Is this Word become flesh a once-and-for-all event, never repeated? Or is it a continuing principle inherent in the Christian faith? Does it pass over into the lives of the followers of Jesus as continuing fact? Did they become the Word become flesh? Imperfectly, of course, but nevertheless, was it the divine intention that they be a continuing incarnation of the life and spirit of Jesus? And did that happen? And does it happen now when we are in line with the reality of the Christian faith?

I am persuaded that the Word became flesh is not only an event in the time of Jesus; it is a continuing principle, a fact that is inherent in the Christian faith. And this is seen and realized in the coming of the Holy Spirit. The coming of the Holy Spirit was the Word become flesh in receptive and obedient believers. Here the historical passed into the experimental. The Word became flesh, not only in "the body of Christ"—the church—but in the bodies of believers as individuals and persons. There was a collective manifestation of the Word become flesh in the new community and an individual manifestation in the new person.

The Word Became Flesh
(Week 26, Sunday)

What a Tragedy When Christianity Broke with Christ
Galatians 1:6-9

A Hindu said at the close of one of my meetings, "As the speaker has gone on, two thoughts have been going through my mind. One was, what a tragedy it was when Christianity broke with Christ. And the other was, what a world awakening would come if Christianity and Christ should come together again." Is the Hindu right? Has there been a break between Christianity and Christ?

I am persuaded that the real point of departure is at the point of turning the Christian faith into the Word become *word* instead of the Word become *flesh*. That is the real point of departure with real results in the consequent effectiveness of the Christian faith in the world. The Christian faith is organized for the most part around the conception of the Word become *word*. Its "services" are verbal services, ritual; its preaching is not practicing but proclaiming; its religious education is learning about, instead of living out.

The Word Became Flesh
(Week 37, Sunday)

15

GUIDANCE

Does God Guide Our Lives?
Psalms 25:9; 31:3; 32:8; 93:24; Isaiah 58:11

Every Christian should live a God-guided life. For if God is, God should be in everything that concerns us—directing, controlling, inspiring. The Christian who doesn't know this sense of guidance is missing something vital. For, mind you, if you are not guided by God, you are guided by something else. Perhaps yourself. But we all know that to be self-managed is to be self-damaged. And we are not good enough, and we don't know enough to guide our lives. God must guide them.

Victorious Living
(Week 36, Monday)

How Does God Guide Us?
Genesis 50:20; Isaiah 54:17; Romans 8:28; Philippians 1:12

God guides us in many ways, not one, but many. Among these are five outstanding ways: (1) circumstances, (2) enlightened Christian intelligence, (3) the spoken or written words of others, (4) an intimate group, (5) the Inner Voice.

Sometimes God guides by (1) circumstances, or shall we call them providences? Something opens before us, perhaps unexpectedly, just when we are in perplexity. That open door is matched against our perplexity, we walk through it, and find it has been God's way.

Or God may close something before us, and that closing of the door proves to be God's preventive guidance.

Victorious Living
(Week 36, Tuesday)

Guidance through Enlightened Intelligence
Acts 6:2-5; 1 Timothy 1:7; 2 Timothy 2:7; Hebrews 8:10

God guides through (2) enlightened Christian intelligence. The development of Christian discernment is a necessary part of Christian development. Hebrews 5:14 says, "But solid food is for adults—that is, for those who through constant practice have their spiritual faculties carefully trained to distinguish good from evil" (Weymouth).

God wants us to love God with the whole of our being, including our minds: "You shall love the Lord your God with...all your mind" (Matt 22:37). Any scheme of guidance that neglects the mind by underemphasis is, to that degree, not Christian. For the whole person is to be perfected.

God's problem is how to guide us but not override us. For in the guidance, God must not merely make us do a certain thing; God must make us free, upstanding, discerning. I question any scheme of guidance that insists only or largely on the blank-sheet method; God is to write on it, as it were, what God wants us to do. Now I believe that God does guide us by the Inner Voice, but to make that the only method and to depend on that to dictate the minute details of our lives would be to weaken us.

Suppose a father or mother should undertake to dictate the minute things in the child's life, asking only for implicit obedience, leaving little room for intelligent weighing of moral issues and free decision. Would that be guiding or overriding? Wouldn't the child's personality remain undeveloped? Moreover, if we ask for dictated guidance in every little thing, we shall be tempted to manufacture it if we don't get it. This makes for unreality. No, we must not take one method alone and practically exclude others. God will guide our mental processes, if we are inwardly honest.

Victorious Living
(Week 36, Wednesday)

God's Guidance through Others
1 Samuel 3:9; Acts 9:11-17; Philemon 5-17

Sometimes God guides us through (3) the written or spoken word of others. Some passage in a book becomes luminous and speaks directly to our need. It is the very voice of God to us. Some word in a sermon seems to have in it more than the word of the speaker; it is God speaking. Or it may be a quiet word with a friend that opens the door to the solution of a problem or relief from a grief.

Victorious Living
(Week 36, Thursday)

Guidance through a Group
Acts 13:1-3; 15:25-28

I cannot help but feel that God's Spirit has been raising up these groups to meet particular needs. Not that I think that any one of them has the complete truth, but each does seem to have some particular phase of truth that is partly neglected by others. The difficulty comes when each becomes exclusive and self-righteous. Then the lilies that fester smell worse than common ordinary weeds.

But God is speaking to and guiding this generation through (4) intimate groups. God spoke to the first generation through groups. The fact is that Jesus formed a group movement when he and his disciples fellowshiped and worked together. It was out of that fellowship that the New Testament came.

Today God guides the individual through the closely knit fellowships of groups. Each individual needs the correction and sustenance of some such group. For the group checks up and tends to keep the individual guidance from going astray. So God often guides through a group.

Victorious Living
(Week 36, Friday)

Guidance through the Inner Voice
Matthew 13:11; Luke 10:21; 12:12; John 16:13-15; Acts 16:7-8

By the (6) Inner Voice, I do not mean the voice of conscience, for the Inner Voice gives guidance, not merely where a matter of right and wrong is involved as in conscience, but where one is taking life directions, deciding perplexities, and where one is bidden to take up tasks and assume responsibilities. The Inner Voice is not contradictory to an enlightened conscience, but is in addition to it and beyond it. It is the Spirit of God speaking to one directly and authentically.

Victorious Living
(Week 36, Saturday)

Guidance Then and Now
Exodus 33:13-15; Psalm 25:5, 9; Isaiah 30:21; 40:11; Acts 8:31

God will not guide us in one way only but in many ways. Perhaps the highest guidance is in the verse, "It seemed good to the Holy Spirit and to us"—we were thinking God's thoughts and coming to the same conclusions. That is cooperative spiritual living.

Victorious Living
(Week 37, Sundy)

Are We Circumstance-Directed?
Matthew 5:43-48; 1 Corinthians 15:33; Galatians 2:11-12

We come now to the matter of guidance. If life is to be at its best we must have the sense of instrumentation, of carrying out purposes not our own, of fulfilling a Will that is ultimate. We must "regain the sense of being led," as one pastor urges. Without that sense of being led, life hangs at loose ends, lacks goal and dynamic to move on to that goal.

If we lose the sense of being led, we become victims of our circumstances....A great many people simply throw their minds into neutral and go where circumstances push them. They have no sense of being led.

Or they allow other people's actions to determine their conduct. They are circumstance-directed instead of Christ-directed. Jesus warned us against allowing others to determine our conduct. "If people slap you on your right cheek,"—don't use their weapons; keep your own—"turn the left cheek to them as well" (Matt 5:39 CEB). The best revenge you can have on enemies is not to be like them.

Abundant Living
(Week 36, Tuesday)

18

Be Silent to God
Isaiah 30:20-21; Jeremiah 1:4-10; Acts 15:28; 16:6-10

God has three things in mind in reference to us: purpose, plan, and person. God has a purpose to make you the best that you can be. God has a plan that embodies that purpose. God has a plan for every life. The next step is for you to be the person for carrying out that purpose and that plan. In the silence you listen for the unfolding of that purpose and that plan. You literally become the plan and purpose of God, an embodied thought of God, the word made flesh.

Abundant Living
(Week 37, Sunday)

The Sevens Ways of God's Guidance
Psalms 25:9; 32:8; 73:24; Isaiah 58:11

God will guide us in one or more or all of these ways:

(1) God gives general guidance through the character and person of Christ. Christ lets us know what God is like, and, therefore, what we must be like.

(2) God guides us through the collective experience of the church, the corporate wisdom gathered through the ages.

(3) God guides us through the counsel of good people.

(4) God guides through opening providences, matching us against some opening opportunity or need.

(5) God guides through natural law and its discoveries through science.

(6) God guides through a heightened moral intelligence and insight; we become personalities who are capable of exercising sound moral judgments.

(7) God guides us through the direct voice of the Spirit within us; God speaks to us in unmistakable terms in the depths of our being.

The probabilities are that God will guide us in more than one of these ways, lest one method narrow us.

Abundant Living
(Week 37, Tuesday)

God Guides through Opening Opportunities
Acts 16:9-10; 1 Corinthians 16:8-9

God guides through opening opportunities and needs. You are now a Christian, and "a Christian is one who cares." As you get into closer touch with Christ, you will "care" more and more for everybody, everywhere. You will now see needs not hitherto seen. Your sympathetic imagination will be quickened. You will project yourself into other people's situations, and you will see and feel from their standpoint....You will be guided to see needs to which the unguided are blind or obtuse. The Spirit will create "a concern" where others are unconcerned.

The Way
(Week 41, Wednesday)

The Guidance of the Spirit
Acts 8:29-31

To cultivate the guidance of the Spirit by the inner voice, one must learn the art of lowly listening. And when the inner voice speaks, test it by the other methods of guidance. In general, it will be in harmony with the other ways. For God does not speak with contradictory voices. God will not speak one thing through the revelation in Christ and another thing through the inner voice. They will morally coincide.

And don't get discouraged if occasionally guidance turns out wrong. Go back and examine to see where the wires were crossed so that the wrong message got through. As a friend put it, "I cannot always trust my own guidance, but I can always trust my Guide." Don't lose faith in God if guidance goes wrong; lose faith in your method of guidance and reexamine it.

But if we are honest, basically honest, the guidance will seldom go wrong. Then tune yourself to hear God's voice, the voice of the God who speaks.

The Way to Power and Poise
(Week 22, Friday)

Corrected by Group Guidance
Acts 13: 2-3

Individual guidance has to be corrected by group guidance. If individual guidance is uncorrected and unchecked by group guidance, it may go off on a tangent and get tangled up in its own subjective states.

Every religious leader needs a group in which to subject himself or herself to a group discipline. For many years as an evangelist, I had no group discipline. I was telling others what to do, but no one told me what to do. I was the poorer for it. Then I found the discipline of an Ashram group, where we pledge to one another not to have inward criticism that we do not bring up. If there is no outward criticism, then we know there is no inward criticism. There is a relaxed fellowship.

But the group life is not for mere correction; it is for contribution as well. If we don't get group correction, we don't get group contribution. In the give-and-take of a group, it is often more take than give....

God guides through the group, and guides especially. The group not only corrects you; it contributes to you as well. The partial idea is filled out by the idea of another. The sparks that fly from the clash of thought upon thought illuminate a subject, and you.

How to Be a Transformed Person
(Week 43, Monday)

20

God's Problem: To Guide but Not Override
Psalms 25:9, 12, 15

Many individuals, though Christian, know little about God's guidance. Hence they have little sense of accountability to God and little sense of God's guidance in their lives. Hence their impact upon life is feeble. Only people who have a sense of mission and who are under God's guidance accomplish things.

How does God guide us? God's problem, I suppose, is to guide us and not override us; to guide us, but not too much. For God must guide us and create initiative in us at one and the same time. This is not easy....

Jesus said to his disciples, "Why even of yourselves judge ye not what is right?" (Luke 12:57 KJV). He wanted them to be morally capable of judging for themselves. So the dictation method of guidance is out, the method that dictates what we are to do for the day. The parent who did that for the child, dictating every least thing he or she should do for the day, would weaken the child.

Growing Spiritually
(Week 40, Tuesday)

The Widow's Mite
Mark 12:41-44

We are dealing with the mastery of perfectionism. We have seen that the way to overcome perfectionism is to be willing to do the next thing at hand and do it well. This passage expresses that attitude: "Do whatever you would like to do, because God is with you" (1 Sam 10:7 CEB). In other words, don't wait for special guidance to do special things; but do the thing at hand and do it in God's name, for God is with you. For whatever you do, you'll do it under divine guidance; for God is with you, guiding you to do the little things in a big way.

Mastery
(Week 49, Wednesday)

We Don't Begin with God, but Jesus
1 Timothy 6:13-16

I was with a group, obviously sincere and dedicated, but in their services they read an essay on religion and then added what they desired from their own thinking. Hence they got their spiritual guidance from the thoughts of others—the essays they read—and from their own sharing of thoughts with one another. It was weak at the place of God's self-revelation in Jesus, and hence weakness at the place of God.

Christian Maturity
(Week 7, Sunday)

The Paralysis of Looking at the Stars

We are thinking about the power from on high that can separate us from the love of God in Christ Jesus. We fastened on astrology as that power that can separate us, and does. When people lose the guidance of God, they will turn to anything for guidance. Of all the things, people turn to for guidance, astrology is the most devastating, for it means that moral considerations have been abandoned, and the position of the stars decides....Any nation or any individual who adopts that method of guidance will decay, has already decayed. Yet we are told that five million people in America decide their daily lives on the basis of astrology. The newspapers that publish these daily charts are contributing to this moral and intellectual decay....

The stars, which the love of God has made can separate us from that love if we make the stars our guide instead of letting the Creator revealed in Christ guide us. It is the sin of idolatry. It is paganism, pure and simple.

In Christ
(Week 10, Monday)

Damning Others Instead of Rescuing the Damned
Jude 19-21

Any movement that suggests guidance from God without reference to the revelation of God in Jesus Christ is bypassing the Incarnation. Apart from Jesus we know little about God and what we know is wrong. You see the Father in the Son, or you don't see God. You substitute your ideas of God for God's revelation, and thus make yourself and your ideas the mediator. "There is one mediator between God and men, the man Christ Jesus" (1 Tim 2:5). You don't go directly to God if you bypass Jesus; you substitute yourself and your ideas as the mediator. That, says John, is antichrist.

Perhaps the most serious tendency, because it is the most widespread, is the tendency of the emphasis of finding guidance from God within. If you do not have the corrective of the revelation of God in Jesus Christ, you are liable to listen to the voice of the subconscious and call it God's guidance.

The Word Became Flesh
(Week 32, Tuesday)

Collective Guidance
Luke 3:1-3

The church [at Antioch] was sufficiently united so the group as a group could get collective guidance. "While they were worshiping the Lord and fasting, the Holy Spirit said, 'Set apart for me Barnabas and Saul for the work to which I have called them'" (Acts 13:2). Here was a group so attuned to God and so attuned to one another that the Holy Spirit could give them a united guidance. We would have thrown it open to debate, then have taken a vote, and the majority would have ruled. This would have left a disgruntled minority. But their method of guidance was different, they desired to come a common mind—and did—under the guidance of the Holy Spirit. "It has seemed good to the Holy Spirit and to us" (Acts 15:28); that was the classic phrase that characterized the early church.

The Word Became Flesh
(Week 35, Friday)

MATURITY

Introduction

I have begun at the lowest rung of the ladder, and have tried to go step by step to the full implications of victorious living. Mature souls must be patient with the first steps, remembering that many are not able to live a victorious life because they do not know how to link up with God's power.

Victorious Living

Who Can Find God?
Luke 11:9-13

There are those, especially in India, who feel that one has to be mature, even old, to find God. But the Christian way is different. At question time one day, I asked, "Where is God?" A little fellow of five excitedly whispered to his mother: "Why, I can answer that. He is in my heart." He was right!

Victorious Living
(Week 4, Thursday)

The Ladder for Old Age
Psalm 92:14; Acts 2:17

Gracious Lord, help me to grow old gracefully and beautifully, to come to maturity majestically. Let me fill my mind and soul with you, so that when physical beauty fades, spiritual beauty may take its place. Physical beauty is an endowment; spiritual beauty an achievement—help me to achieve it by constant companionship with you. Amen.

Abundant Living
(Week 42, Saturday)

The Three Stages of Life
Hebrews 5:11-14

But after independence is gained, one finds that independence isn't what it is cracked up to be. You long to be interdependent, to relate yourself helpfully to other people, to establish right relationships. This is maturity. In maturity you lose your life to find it again.

The Way
(Week 18, Thursday)

The Therapeutic Value of Self-Surrender
2 Corinthians 4:8-12

But let us clear the debris of wrong thought from around self-surrender....It is not weak to surrender to Another. The adolescent attitude is insistence on independence; the mature attitude is to take one's independence and delegate it, or surrender it, to a higher entity.

The Way to Power and Poise
(Week 11, Tuesday)

Through Wheeling into a New Center
Luke 9:23-24

[If] you are to enjoy your own maturity, as the goal of "the mature mind,"...you won't have maturity, but infantilism, for infantilism is preoccupation with oneself. Maturity is a byproduct of a mature purpose attached to a mature object, God, and working out a mature plan: the kingdom of God.

How to Be a Transformed Person
(Week 6, Monday)

Introduction

Spiritual maturity is no longer a luxury for a few; it is a necessity for us all....

But we must not leave readers feeling the club of necessity to be spiritually mature hanging over their heads. We cannot be scared or clubbed into maturity. It must be a beckoning instead of a bludgeoning. We must feel the call. Fortunately that call comes from above and from within. God wills our maturity. God has arranged the world and us with one thing in view, namely, our maturity. And fortunately we are made for maturity: for growth, for development, for perfection. Everything within us works toward that end, everything except one thing: sin, or evil. This is the unnatural intrusion throwing monkey wrenches into the machinery of human living. Except for this, all else—I repeat, all else—is made for spiritual maturity. We are destined to be mature, to be perfect.

Growing Spiritually
(pp. vi–vii)

MENTAL HEALTH

The Kingdom Written Within
Jeremiah 31:33; Romans 2:14-16; 2 Corinthians 3:1-8

What does the psychologist mean by saying, "To be frank and honest in all relations, but especially in relations with oneself, is the first law of mental hygiene." Doesn't that mean that the universe and you and I are built for truth, that the universe won't back a lie, that all lies sooner or later break themselves upon the facts of things? Since the kingdom stands for absolute truth, and our own mental makeup demands the same thing, then are not the laws of the kingdom written within us?

Victorious Living
(Week 2, Thursday)

How Can We Arrive at the Goal of Inward Unity?
Matthew 6:22; Ephesians 4:1-6; James 4:8

If there is one thing that both modern psychology and the way of Christ agree on, it is this: Apart from inward unity there can be no personal happiness and no effective living....

So we toil in rowing, trying to get to the land of inward unity. We are tossed by many a wind and many a wave. And it gets very dark. Then Jesus quietly comes. We more easily let him in this time, for there seems no other alternative. The soul seems instinctively to feel, "The Master has come." He gathers up the inward distinctions, cleanses away the points of conflict, and unifies life around himself. We have arrived.

Victorious Living
(Week 3, Saturday)

"It Will Spring Up Out of the Earth"
Psalm 139:14-16; Proverbs 17:22; Luke 19:40; Ephesians 6:1-3

Dr. Henry Link, in his study of psychology, gave up Christianity as an outmoded superstition. When, however, he began to try to untangle snarled-up lives, he found he had to give them something outside themselves to love. The only thing permanent he could give them was God; and soon he found he was talking himself back into being a Christian. Life wouldn't come out right in any other way. He became a Christian, and wrote two great books on the Christian way, led back to it by the very pressures of life (see, for example, Henry C. Link, *Return to Religion* [New York: Macmillan, 1936]).

Abundant Living
(Week 46, Monday)

Intellectually Mature, Emotionally Immature
1 Corinthians 2:10-12

The church today is, in large measure, halfway between Easter and Pentecost, and is behind closed doors in fear. The grandest good news that ever broke upon human ears had broken freshly upon them: Jesus was alive, yet that didn't free them; they were still locked behind closed doors.

One of the greatest fallacies of this age of intellectual progress is the fallacy that knowledge in itself is necessarily freeing. It may free you, it may not. Many intellectually mature people are emotionally immature. That accounts for the fact that many psychologists and psychiatrists are not integrated. They know, but they don't know freedom. Emotionally they are still bound by old fears and frustrations. That is the basic reason we need some powerful impulse within that will free us from our unreasoning fears and anxieties. That impulse within can be supplied only by the Holy Spirit.

Mastery
(Week 4, Saturday)

God-Salvation or Self-Salvation
Ephesians 2:7-8

Since maturity cannot be found unless we have a faith that is mature, it is all-important to fasten our loyalty and our love upon the maturest faith that can be found. Where is that faith? [I] have no hesitancy in pointing straight to the heart of the matter; the center of that faith is a Person, and that Person is Jesus.

Christian Maturity
(Week 1, Thursday)

Maturity in Spiritual Contagion
Acts 4:18-20

To be able and willing to share Christ with others is the highest and most mature sign of maturity. It shows that we are mature enough to have a surplus, an exportable surplus.

Christian Maturity
(Week 45, Sunday)

Share in Christ

His all for our all. It is all there for the taking. I can be strong in his strength, pure in his purity, loving in his love, and mature in his maturity. I share in the highest there is.

In Christ
(Week 45, Thursday)

The Five Steps in Following Christ
Joshua 24:15; Psalm 55:17; Matthew 6:22; John 6:67-69

Make up your mind: "All who want to come after me" [see Luke 9:23 CEB]. Here is the great decision that decides all decisions. It is what they call in psychology "a major choice"—a choice that you do not have to make over again each day; a choice into which the lesser choices of life fit, and not a choice that fits into them; it is the choice that organizes everything around itself.

Abundant Living
(Week 47, Thursday)

Is the Way Impersonal?
1 Corinthians 13:1-3

The Christian way is not only sanctity; it is sanity. Take any way you will and pursue it, and you will come out to one of two things: if it is not-the-way, you will come to a dead end; if it is the way, you will come to the Way. All the right ways lead to the Way.

The Way
(Week 7, Sunday)

Roads with Dead Ends
Matthew 14:29-31; 1 John 4:18

The first road with a dead end is Fear....Fear harnessed to constructive ends may be constructive. When we use fear and control it, then it is good. When fear uses us and controls us, then it is bad. When fear becomes Fear, then it becomes master and runs us into roads with dead ends.

The Way
(Week 13, Sunday)

Don't Fight Your Fears; Surrender Them
John 6:20-21; 12:15

Don't fight your fears; surrender them to God. If you fight your fears, your mind will be upon those fears, and it cannot be repeated too often that "whatever gets your attention gets you." If your fears get your attention, even though it be a fighting attention, they will get you. A struggle will ensue between the imagination and the will, and in any such struggle the imagination always wins. You must not fight your fears, but surrender them into the hands of God.

The Way
(Week 14, Thursday)

28

Keep Your Sense of Humor
Psalm 4:8; Isaiah 54:10

When you get too tense and begin to take yourself and your troubles too seriously, walk to the mirror and burst out laughing. I often do it; it lets down tensions. As you stand there before the mirror, repeat these words: "O fool, to carry yourself upon your own shoulders! O beggar, to come to beg at your own door!" And then burst out laughing—at yourself.

The Way
(Week 14, Friday)

The Steps out of Negativism
Acts 5:20-21; 18:9-11

Will to be positive. This is important, for you have been willing to be negative, perhaps unconsciously....

The first thing to decide is: Do I will to be well? To be positive? To go out and meet life and master it? When you decide this affirmatively, then all the resources of God are behind that decision. In the inner quietness of your heart throw your will on the side of freedom.

Remember that you are made in the inner structure of your being for creative activity. You are fulfilling yourself when you are creative and positive. You are frustrating yourself when you are noncreative and negative....

Remember that your happiness does not come through what happens to you, but through what you make happen to others....

Happiness doesn't come to you; you join happiness on the way to doing something for others.

The Way
(Week 17, Tuesday)

I Can Do All Things through Christ
Colossians 1:11; 2 Timothy 4:5; 1 Peter 1:13

Keep repeating to yourself, "I can do all things through Christ which strengtheneth me" (Phil 4:13 KJV). Say it the last thing before you drop off to sleep, for the subconscious mind is susceptible then.

The Way
(Week 17, Wednesday)

Conscious and Subconscious Unified
Ephesians 4:1-7

O living Spirit, I want my whole being to be redeemed. Your work is in the area of the subconscious, an area I can't control. So I turn it over to you, for you to cleanse and control and redirect. I thank you. Amen.

The Way
(Week 40, Tuesday)

Self-Cultivation: Another Attempt
Psalm 17:1-5

To leave you concentrated on your self is unhealthy and bad psychology....Any system that leaves you occupied with yourself is wrong, however learned it may be.

This is the essential wrong in the cults of self-cultivation. Self-cultivation means self-concentration, and self-concentration means self-deterioration—inevitably. It may bring an initial inner boost to begin to cultivate yourself, but it will mean an inevitable letdown. Gordon Allport, professor of psychology at Harvard, says: "Paradoxically 'self-expression' requires the capacity to transcend oneself in the pursuit of objectives not primarily referred to the self." [No published source found.] Here psychology and Christian faith coincide: "He who finds his life will lose it, and he who loses his life for my sake will find it" (Matt 10:39). Self-cultivation is all right and very necessary, provided the self has been surrendered to God. Then it can be cultivated, for it is God-centered and not self-centered.

The Way to Power and Poise
(Week 2, Saturday)

The Holy Spirit Is Power: Where It Counts
Ephesians 3:14-21

The modern emphasis on psychology in the remaking of personality is good, but not good enough. Psychology lays bare our problems and our motives. But it lacks power to solve those problems and to unify those motives. It lacks central dynamic. Psychology is successful only where it is combined with religious faith that provides dynamic: one provides information; the other transformation....

Psychology can explain; religion as precepts can exhort; the Holy Spirit makes us exult. For the Spirit gives above "all that we ask [religion] or think [psychology]" (Eph 3:20).

The Way to Power and Poise
(Week 17, Thursday)

30

Free at the Center
Luke 14:26-2

No one is free until free at the center. When we let go, there and then we are free indeed. When the self is renounced, then we stands utterly disillusioned, apart, asking for nothing. We anticipate the buffeting, the slights, the separations, the disappointments of life by their acceptance in one great renunciation. It is life's supreme strategic retreat. You can say to life, "What can you do to me? I want nothing." You can say to death, "What can you do to me? I have already died." Then we are truly free. In the bath of renunciation we have washed our souls clean from a thousand clamoring, conflicting desires. Asking for nothing, if anything comes to us, it is all sheer gain. Then life becomes one constant surprise.

Everything belongs to the person who wants nothing. Having nothing, that person possesses all things in life, including life itself. Nothing will be denied the person who denies self. Having chosen to be utterly solitary, that person comes into possession of the most utterly social fact of the universe, the kingdom of God. He or she wants nothing of people and matter. He or she has God. That is enough. Now the person is ready to go back into the world. Washed clean of desires, now the person can form new ones, from a new center and with a new motive. This detachment is necessary to a new attachment. The fullest and most complete life comes out of most completely empty life.

Would the best in psychology agree? Listen to Anton T. Boisen: "To be at one with that which is supreme in our hierarchy of loyalties, that to which men generally give the name of God, is ever essential to mental health; to be isolated or estranged through the consciousness that there is that within which we cannot acknowledge without being condemned means mental disorder and spiritual death" (*The Exploration of the Inner World* [Philadelphia: University of Pennsylvania Press, 1936], 173). Self-adjustment through self-surrender to God equals mental health.

How to Be a Transformed Person
(Week 19, Wednesday)

Come...Take...Learn
Luke 18:9-12

In reading books on counseling, I have been amazed at the way this question of self-surrender to God is sidestepped and bypassed. Advice is given about every question, but this central question is skirted. And this by Christian leaders. They seem to hesitate to confront the persons counseled with the supreme need of getting off their own hands into the hands of God by self-surrender. They name their method "nondirective counseling." They do not direct the counselees; they allow them to do it themselves. Suppose Jesus had used this nondirective method. Suppose in the Sermon on the Mount he had gathered afflicted humanity about himself and had said to them, "Now talk about yourself. I'll throw in a question now and then." No. He directed people, for he knew the direction, and they didn't. He directed them through presenting truth, which was self-verifying, and for which they were made.

Growing Spiritually
(Week 10, Thursday)

31

Faith and Love That Jesus Christ Inspire
1 John 5:1-5

This passage depicts Jesus' impact: "Faith and love that Christ inspires" (1 Tim 1:14 Moffatt). Now, interestingly enough, psychology is more and more emphasizing...faith and love, as centrally necessary to mental health. If you do not have faith, you become cynical; and if you do not have love, you become self-centered; and if you are cynical and self-centered, you are on the road to inner disruption. Only those who have faith in others and faith in themselves have the basis for mental and spiritual, and hence physical soundness. And only those who have love—genuine, outgoing love for others—are themselves healthy personalities.

But you cannot have faith in and love for others unless they are rooted in faith in and love for some center other than a human center: God. So Jesus, by producing faith in and love for God, by making God worthy of faith and lovable, stimulates in people the two things essential to mental and spiritual, and hence physical health. The impact of Jesus upon human nature has stimulated more growth than any other single influence.

Growing Spiritually
(Week 15, Tuesday)

Right Thinking and Right Emotions
Philippians 4:8-9

I mentioned yesterday two things necessary to health: work and love. Karl Menninger, head of the famous Topeka Clinic, gives four things necessary to mental and physical health: creative work, creative play, creative worship, and creative love. He adds to Cabot's list the word creative (see Richard C. Cabot, *What Men Live By: Work, Play, Love, Worship* [Houghton Mifflin, 1929]). This is important; for if the work, play, worship, and love are not creative, producing something constructive outside self, they bring disease instead of health. It is the element of self-losing and self-transcending that produces health. If any of these leave you in a state of self-reference or self-preoccupation, they are not fruitful—they are festering.

Mastery
(Week 30, Wednesday)

Psychotherapy Does Not Create Saints
1 Corinthians 1:22-24

The Holy Spirit brings new power into life: power to change thought and emotion, power to change the total life.

Christian Maturity
(Week 42, Saturday)

Rejoice in the Lord Always

Psychology is stressing the health of joyfulness. The joyless person is on the skids—physically. Nothing tones up the system as much as a constant flow of joy. Nothing tones down the system as much as a constant flow of depression and sadness.

In Christ
(Week 37, Thursday)

Peace...in Christ Jesus

Is there a peace called "my peace"? Is it different, profoundly different, from the psychological peace called "peace of mind"? Yes.

In Christ
(Week 46, Wednesday)

Is Science Coming Out to the Supremacy of Love?
1 Corinthians 13:8-133

In one of my books, *Christian Maturity,* I took the position that the human personality is as mature as it is mature in love, and no more. One may be mature in culture and knowledge and in ability, but if one is immature in love, that person is an immature personality. And the psychologists are increasingly agreeing.

Dr. Carl Menninger wrote a book on *Love Against Hate*. He took the position that love is the constructive element; love builds up and hate tears down. When he came to the conclusion that people are in his institution because they had not loved or been loved, it was an epoch in his thinking. For psychiatry had been founded on the idea that insight is the cure-all for human personality problems. Give patients insight as to their troubles, and they are automatically cured. Mental institutions are filled with people who have insight as to what is the matter with them, but they are still there. Insight is not necessarily curative. When the diagnosis shifted, the technique had to shift. These people were there because they hadn't loved or been loved. They must be loved into loving.

The Word Became Flesh
(Week 11, Wednesday)

SURRENDER

In Which I Make the Surrender
Matthew 13:44-46; Acts 2:37-42

I have now come to the place in my quest for victorious living where I see that I cannot go on until I make the great decision. I must break down every barrier that stands between me and God; and I must do it withholding no part of the price. But I see I must go further. Not only must I give up every barrier; I must give up myself. I need somebody to master me.

I know that something or other will master me. In the shrine of my heart, I am bound to bend the knee to something. I may bow before myself and take orders from myself, so that self is my ruler. Or I may let sex, passion or money have the final say. Or I may bow before the fear of society and let it dominate me. Or—and this seems my best alternative—I can let Christ master me. I have the choice as to who shall have the final say in my life. I deliberately make the decision: Christ shall have me. There is nothing that is weighed out or measured, nothing that the eye can see; but heart has been given to Heart, will has been given to Will, life has been given to Life. It is done.

As I walked up the aisle of the cathedral in Copenhagen to see the wonderful statue, Bertel Thorvaldsen's "Christ," I was almost overcome with awe as I saw the figure with the soft light upon it dominating the whole cathedral. But as I walked along a Danish friend whispered: "You will not be able to see his face unless you kneel at his feet." It was true, for he was standing with outstretched arms looking at those at his feet. So I knelt at his feet and, lo, his face was looking into mine.

You cannot really see Christ until you bend the knee to him, until you surrender to him. Those who stand far off, surveying him, never really see his face. So bend the knee. Be conquered by him.

Victorious Living
(Week 6, Wednesday)

How Shall I Enter?
Acts 2:37-39; Romans 7:18-20; 8:13

The most delicate moment for many of us now comes as we approach the question of how we may enter the victorious life. We must approach it with a prayer upon our lips and in our hearts.

First of all, there is a difference now in your coming. At first, you came as a stranger and a penitent rebel, knocking at the door for admission. Now you are a child within that home, seeking a deeper and fuller correspondence to the Spirit of the home. You are not asking for admission, but for adjustment. You are asking that everything may be taken out of you that clashes with the Spirit of the home. You can now come with a sense of confidence and assurance, born out of contact with the Lord, that if you meet the conditions, God will meet you more than halfway. The barriers are all within us, not in God.

Victorious Living
(Week 15, Sunday)

Letting That Last Thing Go
Matthew 10:37-39; Acts 5:1-2

The last thing we want to let go is just ourselves. It is the one and only thing we really own. And now Christ with imperious demand asks for that last one thing. It is at this place that the real battle is joined. All else have been skirmishes.

Jesus said with awful decisiveness, "Whoever comes to me and doesn't hate father and mother, spouse and children, and brothers and sisters—yes, and one's own life—cannot be my disciple" (Luke 14:26 CEB). Our families and ourselves must be placed on the altar. This does not mean that we should necessarily leave the family. Here, to "hate" means to "love less," according to the parallel passage in Matthew 10:37.

A lighted candle casts a shadow when it is put before an electric light. Thus the lesser loves, while really light, cast a shadow when this all-consuming Love makes its demand upon the human spirit. These loves are not to be abandoned; they are to be surrendered. You still live with yourself even after you surrender yourself, so you may still live with your family after you surrender them.

Victorious Living
(Week 15, Friday)

The Fourth Step
Luke 9:23-24; Romans 12:1; 1 Thessalonians 5:23

We come now to the most important step of all: (4) Turn over to Christ yourself and all you have. This is the crucial point, and if you bungle this you block the process. Between two persons there is no love without an inward self-surrender to each other. If either one withholds the essential self from the other, love is blocked; it will not spring up no matter how hard you try to love around and past that core of an unsurrendered self. So between you and God there can be no love without an inward self-surrender. Not the surrender of this thing or that thing, but the surrender of you, the essential you.

Abundant Living
(Week 4, Wednesday)

The Basis of Resentments: An Unsurrendered Self
Matthew 14:3-12; Acts 7:59-60

Remember that at the basis of most resentments is a touchy, unsurrendered self. The fact that we have been able to hold the resentment shows that there is a self that is oversensitive because our will has not surrendered to the will of God. When surrendered to the will of God we throw off resentments as a healthy skin throws off disease germs. Unless there is inner disease or an abrasion of the skin, the disease germs can get no foothold. So, when resentments have gained a footing, it shows that there is a raw, sensitive self underneath that has become a culture for the rooting and growth of resentments. Suspect a self that can grow resentments; it is probably diseased with self-centeredness.

Abundant Living
(Week 9, Wednesday)

The Kingdoms of Class and Money
Romans 1:14; 1 Corinthians 1:20, 26; 1 Timothy 6:8-11

Nor can any enter the kingdom of God unless they surrender the kingdom of class.

When we lose our petty class consciousness, we find a human consciousness and with it a God-consciousness. The class must lose its life to find it again.

The kingdom of money must also bend the knee to the kingdom of God. In our acquisitive society money is god. You succeed in terms of accumulation. Our wealth is measured by wealth. People are "worth" the amount they accumulate. These values are false and must be surrendered. Following the god of money leads into a road with a dead end....

When money is surrendered as an end and offered to be a means to the ends of the kingdom, it is found again. Only those who surrender it enjoy it. To surrender it means to surrender it to God to be used for kingdom purposes.

Abundant Living
(Week 32, Thursday)

Further Steps
1 John 5:13-15

Surrender is important, for there can be no love between persons unless there is mutual self-surrender. If either one withholds the self, then love simply will not spring up. It cannot spring up, for love by its very nature is mutual self-surrender.

The Way
(Week 12, Saturday)

The Word Become Flesh
John 1:14-18

Note that the cults that emphasize self-cultivation, discovering the divine within you, are all based on the universal Christ, not on the incarnate Jesus. Why? Because the universal Christ does not demand self-surrender, but the incarnate Jesus does. The universal Christ is an idea to be accepted; the incarnate Jesus is a fact to be surrendered to and followed. The one appeals to the intellectual conceptions, the other to you—to the whole you.

Do not misunderstand me. I believe in that universal Christ; but, I repeat, you cannot say "Christ" before you have said "Jesus," for the universal Christ is defined by the historical Jesus. You cannot say "God" or the "Holy Spirit" or "Christ" until you have first said "Jesus." The gospel begins at Jesus. In him you are confronted with God's offer and demand, an offer of redemption and a demand to take sides.

There are many religions; there is but one gospel. So the gospel does not stand alongside other religions and philosophies; it confronts all religions, all philosophies, all life, with the good news.

The Way to Power and Poise
(Monday, Week 9)

The Therapeutic Value of Self Surrender
2 Corinthians 4:8-12

The process by which we pass from belonging to ourselves to belonging to Jesus Christ is self-surrender. A great many shy [away] at this term. A young man wrote, "I don't like your word self-surrender. Seems to me to be weak—an escapist mentality. You turn over your life to Another because you haven't enough nerve to face life yourself."

When we turn to the New Testament, we do not find the term self-surrender. But the idea is profoundly there. It is central. And it is becoming central in life as a working way to live....

Let us clear the debris of wrong thought from around self-surrender. It is not weak to surrender to another. The adolescent attitude is an insistence on independence; the mature attitude is to take one's independence and delegate it, or surrender it, to a higher entity. The individual surrenders sovereignty to the union in marriage; loses his or her life and finds it again in the fellowship of the union. The citizen surrenders sovereignty to the nation and finds a larger fellowship in the community. The individual surrenders sovereignty to God—seeks first the kingdom of God—and all these things are added again, including the self.

When you most belong to God, you most belong to yourself. Lowest at God's feet you stand straightest before everything else. Bound to God you walk the earth free. Fearing God you are afraid of nothing else. You bow to God, but you do not bow to anything else. You are God's free person, for you are God's slave. The strongest persons are those most surrendered to themselves. This works with a mathematical precision, and there are no exceptions. If you are centered in yourself, you are a problem; if you are centered in God, you are a person.

The Way to Power and Poise
(Week 11, Tuesday)

Steps out of Egocentricity
Luke 14:26-27

First, decide once and for all that you are not God, that God is God, and that you will surrender your life completely to God. The basis of your life now is fundamentally changed from yourself to God. You are no longer a self-centered person; you are from this moment a God-centered person. In the ordering of your life, you are going to listen to God instead of listening to yourself.

How to Be a Transformed Person
(Week 28, Thursday)

Unbreakably Given to Each Other
Philippians 2:1-2

For the Christian demand is twofold: "Unreservedly given to God and unbreakably given to each other." A double surrender is inherent to God and the fellowship. Many are ready to give themselves to God, but they are not ready to give themselves to the fellowship. For look what we are giving ourselves to: these streaky, imperfect people! There we hesitate to let our weight down. So we stand off, superior and aloof.

I said to a missionary who was troubled over the appointment she was getting, "You trust God in this matter?" "Yes," she replied, "I can trust God, but I can't trust the bishop and the district superintendent." It is a big demand, isn't it, to trust the fellowship? And yet, if we pull apart from that fellowship, we pull apart from Christ. If we deny the fellowship, we will soon, like Peter, deny Christ.

How to Be a Transformed Person
(Week 37, Wednesday)

A Dart Straight to the Heart of Our Problem
Matthew 19:13-15

The center of the Christian redemption is to save you from yourself. Not that the self in itself is evil, but it is evil if the self becomes the center of itself and becomes God. The first commandment strikes at this: "You shall have no other gods before me" (Exod 20:3). And the biggest and most persistent of the rival gods is the self.

So the first Beatitude, in the opening verse of the Sermon on the Mount, begins with: "Blessed are the poor in spirit: for theirs is the kingdom of heaven" (Matt 5:3). The word poor here is "anav," "poor by choice." So it could be translated: "Blessed are the renounced in spirit" or "the surrendered in spirit." The first thing Jesus struck at in opening his Sermon was self-centered self-sufficiency. Shift the basis of your life from your self to God by self-surrender. Be a God-centered person instead of a self-centered person. God sends a dart straight to the heart of our problem, the problem of the self. That must be laid down before we can go on.

Growing Spiritually
(Week 3, Sunday)

38

The Cross Breaks Us
1 Corinthians 2:1-5

We are meditating on the need for a central deliverance, the deliverance from the self. The self needs correction, of course, for you cannot wipe out the self. Put out at the door, the self comes back by the window in various disguises.

But what is the freeing power? It is the cross. The cross silently confronts this self with a demand: surrender! It does it powerfully and pervasively. For instance, here was a boy who had been adopted by a headmaster, who afterward became a bishop in India. The boy was increasingly wayward and rebellious and defiant. The headmaster was compelled to punish him one day after an especially flagrant act of disobedience. He took the rod and told the boy to stretch out his hand. The boy defiantly did so with bravado. The headmaster, instead of laying the rod on the boy's hand, laid it on his own hand and laid it on hard. The boy, seeing what was happening, cried out with an inner pain, fell at the master's feet, and with streaming tears begged him to desist and to forgive him. He did so. From that moment the boy was changed. The tyranny of his self-interest was broken. He was forever attached to the headmaster in love. The center was shifted....

The cross conquers the self without violating it. It frees the self from itself and then attaches that self-love to the One who hung on the cross. Deliverance has come.

Growing Spiritually
(Week 3, Friday)

This Serene Assurance
1 Thessalonians 1:2-5

When we are planted in Christ by surrender, then this verse is fulfilled: "Grow out of him as a plant grows out of the soil it is planted in, becoming more and more sure of the faith as you were taught it, and your lives will overflow with joy and thankfulness" (Col 2:6-7 PHILLIPS). When we are rooted in Christ and see our effortless growth, we are more and more sure of our faith. We know that we are made for this; it is our native "soil"; we and the soil are made for each other, and there is a deep affinity. Out of this self-verifying assurance that this is our "soil," we begin to overflow with joy and thanksgiving. Not a joy and thanksgiving over this or that event, but over the fact that our lives are planted in that which can sustain us now and forever. It is a life joy, not an event joy.

Growing Spiritually
(Week 8, Friday)

39

The Center of Our Problem: The Unsurrendered Ego
Genesis 4:9; Zechariah 7:6

The things we have been studying as blocks to growth are all pushing us nearer and nearer to the center of our problems: the unsurrendered ego. We now turn to it. For all else is fruit; this is root.

I say "unsurrendered ego," not the ego. I am sure that the ego is God-created and as such is God-approved and is to be developed. It is not to be canceled or suppressed; it is to be expressed in God's ways. When the ego has found its place, it has found its place of growth and consequent happiness.

Then just what is its place? Its place is not on the throne of the universe. When Swinburne, replacing God, said, "Glory to Man in the highest" (Algernon C. Swinburne, "Hymn of Man," 1871), he made humanity ridiculous, for events since have laughed at the statement. Humanity has shown an infinite capacity to trip over itself and to sprawl in the dust of humiliation when we make ourselves into a little tin god.

Growing Spiritually
(Week 10, Wednesday)

Come…Take…Learn
Luke 18:9-12

So Jesus said, "Come…take…learn" (Matt 11:28, 29 Moffatt). Note the order: the first thing is our relationship to him—"Come to me." Settle that, and you settle everything. But you don't come by just coming; you come by taking his yoke. "Take my yoke"—surrender to his sway. Then you learn—"Learn of me," for Jesus can teach only those under his yoke, surrendered to him. Religious education, for the most part, with some exceptions, reverses this process and says, "Learn….Take….Come." Often the process doesn't get as far as take or come; it stops at the learn. Insofar as it does so, it ends at sterile knowledge.

No, Jesus insisted that we surrender the self, the center of our problems. If we don't surrender that, the center, we have no right to ask him to solve our marginal problems as they come day by day.

Growing Spiritually
(Week 10, Thursday)

I Am Not a Fool
2 Corinthians 10:17-18

It makes us nervous to get close to the center of our problems, to self-surrender. We shy away from it and promise to do anything, anything except that. And the results are not the heaven of self-possession, but the hell of self-losing. A barrenness sets in. This is how one who has tried it describes it, "Two verses describe my condition: 'Ever learning, and never able to come to the knowledge of the truth' and 'Having a form of godliness, but denying the power thereof' (2 Tim 3:7, 5). I hate this dominance of myself that has made my life a hell." The dominion of Christ makes life a heaven, and the dominion of self makes life a hell. That's all there is to it. Everything else is commentary. And there are no exceptions—none....

The strangest thing on this planet is our fear of surrendering to the one safe place in the universe: God. We hug our present delusions, knowing deep down that they are delusions; but they are present, and we hug them for fear of the unknown. But that unknown is love.

The earth, when it runs away from the sun, simply runs into the dark. When we run away from God, refuse to surrender ourselves, then we get one thing: the dark.

Growing Spiritually
(Week 10, Friday)

A Self You Can't Live With
Isaiah 14:13; Luke 12:18

If we center ourselves on ourselves, we won't like ourselves. The penalty is to live with a self you can't live with. This passage expresses it: "Destruction and misery are in their ways" (Rom 3:16 PHILLIPS), not as a result of their ways, but inherently "in their ways." So the penalty for an unsurrendered self is a self that you surrender to.

If instead of God you choose yourself, you lose yourself. Life is made that way, and there is no use kicking against the goad, as Paul did and hurt himself. But when you become dependent on God, you become independent of others, and of yourself—strangely enough, independent of your own self. Your self is freed from itself only as it surrenders to Another. This cannot be explained. It must be experienced.

Amazing authority and power come to the self-surrendered. This passage tells of it: "The conqueror I will allow to sit beside me on my throne, as I myself have conquered and sat down beside my Father on his throne" (Rev 3:21 Moffatt). Here is the amazing possibility of sharing the authority and power of Christ, of sitting beside him on his throne. But the secret is in the second portion: "as I myself have conquered." And how did he conquer? He "emptied himself" (Phil 2:7). The self-emptying became a fullness that "fills the universe entirely" (Eph 1:23 Moffatt). Giving all, he received all, even a throne. And we share that throne; we rule without wanting to rule. We naturally go to the place of authority. It is inherent.

Growing Spiritually
(Week 10, Saturday)

The Seven Road Blocks
Matthew 17:14-20

The first step in [the disciples'] mastery of the world around them and within them was that they should be mastered. But how? It must all be entirely voluntary. There must be no compulsion except love. They had given up a good deal to follow Jesus—fishing nets, boats, parents, home, occupation—everything except themselves. They had never really surrendered the center, the citadel. They gave the marginal things but not the center. The unsurrendered self was the central block keeping redemption from flooding them. Everything was ready except the receptacle, which was still in their hands, not God's. Their inmost selves had not been surrendered. So for ten days they waited in prayer in an upper room, asking God for something God was aching to give, if only they would let the last barrier down. It took them ten days to get to the end of themselves. At the end of themselves was the beginning of God. God took over when they turned over themselves. They offered their all, and that cleared the way for God's all. God can give marginal blessings, but God can't give the divine self—the Holy Spirit—until we give ourselves unconditionally and absolutely.

Mastery
(Week 3, Thursday)

The First Need: To Belong
Romans 1:1-6

The group [the disciples] in that upper room decided to belong, to make Jesus Lord, to bank their all upon him, to surrender to him. The consequence was that, when they surrendered to him, they didn't surrender to anything else—everything else surrendered to them! Low at his feet, they stood straight before everything else. Bound to him, they walked the earth free! Belonging to him, everything belonged to them. They were mastered, and as a result became masterful....

Self-surrender was the key. Not world-surrender, as some think, but something deeper—self-surrender. It is possible to give up the world and not give up yourself.

Mastery
(Week 3, Saturday)

Surrender Is a Catharsis
John 16:32-33

I was awake at night with a heavy burden upon me. I have learned to turn the wakeful period at night into a listening post; I ask if the Lord has anything to say to me? And in this instance God said, "Yes, I automatically take upon myself everything that falls on you. My love does that. So I've got your burden. There is no reason for both of us to carry it. I can do it better than you. So you release it to me." I did, and fell asleep. And when daylight came, God and I solved it together; I supplied willingness and God supplied power.

Surrender is a catharsis. Instead of "blowing your top" to get rid of the tension, as is sometimes advised by people who don't have any other remedy, you surrender it to God. The blowing-the-top method is only a temporary release of tension. Resentments pile up again and another blowup is necessary. The unsurrendered self is still there, the cause of the tension.

Christian Maturity
(Week 36, Saturday)

I Am God's and Forever
Galatians 6:14-17

This surrender of the self is a once-and-for-all business, even when a daily surrender is involved. The daily surrender is not really a surrender of the self, but an unfolding of the once-and-for-all surrender. It is an application to a specific thing of a surrender once made. A friend writes of her victory: "When I said, 'I am God's and forever,' it was the 'and forever' that did it." No surrender is really surrender unless it is "and forever." That takes our hands off the gift. We don't give a book to another person, at the same time holding on to one corner. We give it, and we let it go—hands off.

Christian Maturity
(Week 39, Friday)

Rigor of Devotion
Galatians 3:2-5

The Christian faith does not demand rigor of devotion, as if God were a spiritual taskmaster, whipping slaves to bend lower and to be more ardent in self-abasement....And the Christian faith does not demand self-abasement. For you can abase yourself, and all the while be saying deep down, "Look how wonderful I am to abase myself in this way." You can be proud of your humility.

Attempts to gain salvation through lopping off here and lopping off there, giving up here and giving up there, humiliating yourself here and there are vain attempts at getting rid of yourself through self-abasement. Christianity does not teach self-abasement. But self-surrender does not leave the self intact. Self-surrender is the self moving out of the center and letting God take the center, with the self on the margin, with God in control and the self in obedience. That puts God and you where both ought to be.

Christian Maturity
(Week 40, Thursday)

Place for Ambitious Persons in Christ?

The first thing Christianity demands is self-surrender. The ego, trying to be God, must be renounced and surrendered. Once that surrender is made, however, there is a place in Christianity for the ambitious. The ambition now has a new motive and goal—we are ambitious to serve.

In Christ
(Week 43, Thursday)

To Walk in the Same Way

[Jesus] made a full surrender to God: "not my will, but thine be done" (Luke 22:42). We can apply that principle: a full surrender of the will.

In Christ
(Week 47, Sunday)

Grace upon Grace
Galatians 2:19-21

Grace has law in it, and the law is the law of self-surrender. The gift of grace is a very expensive gift, for if you take the gift, you belong forever to the giver. The giver binds you with cords of love that hold you forever, but you wouldn't have it otherwise for worlds. So accepting grace is not a mental assent, it is a life response. Jesus gives all, and you cannot give less in return. It is my all for his all and his all for my all. It is mutuality, but not equality, for his all is infinitely greater than my all. But it is my all, and therefore not cheap.

The Word Became Flesh
(Week 4, Thursday)

The "This-ness" of the Gospel
1 John 4:13, 17

The Holy Spirit did exactly what Jesus said the Spirit would do, guided [the disciples] into all Truth. For ten days—the ten days that shook and shaped the world—they were guided to surrender this, that, and the other until they came to themselves and they surrendered that last barrier. And the Holy Spirit, the Spirit of Truth, flooded them as if the Spirit had been pent up for ages. This [Pentecost] was the moment. God was to rule persons from within, by their consent, according to a pattern fixed in Jesus and according to a power supplied by the Holy Spirit—from within.

This was the greatest leap forward in the moral and spiritual history of humanity. The Divine Word was becoming flesh in ordinary humanity, very ordinary humanity. Infinite possibilities opened to anybody, everybody, provided they surrendered and cooperated with this divine process. And it was not to be imparted to the learned, but to the willing. That opened the gates to all. No one was barred, except the unwilling.

The Word Became Flesh
(Week 29, Monday)

TRANSFORMATION

Sublimation of the Instincts
Romans 6:13; 1 Corinthians 15:9-10; 2 Corinthians 5:16-17

Being "in Christ"…[means] identification with his purposes so that his victories become our victories. We must now see some of the results of being "in Christ." Paul says, "Therefore, if any man be in Christ, he is a new creature: old things are passed away; behold, all things are become new" (2 Cor 5:17 KJV). This translation says, "old things are passed away," and yet they have not passed away, they "are become new."

There was a sense in which old things had completely passed away, and yet there was a sense in which they had come back again completely transformed and new. This "new creature" is entirely different from the old creature, and yet fundamentally the same, only new.

Victorious Living
(Week 20, May 13)

The Moral and Spiritual Bases of Disease
Psalms 31:9-10; 32:1-5; Isaiah 1:4-6

One lady put her case this way, "…The Lord is truly transforming our home from a morgue to a sanctuary."

"From a morgue to a sanctuary!" Not only are many homes morgues; many bodies are; they harbor death cells of anger, fear, self-centeredness, and guilt. Many a person, instead of having a living vibrant body, awake in every cell and harmonious in every relationship, has a body of death. That body of death can become a sanctuary.

Abundant Living
(Week 24, Saturday)

One Greater Than the Temple Is Here
Revelation 1:17-18; 3:7

We have been studying the naturalness of the Christian way. If we get hold of that, it will transform our attitudes toward the Christian way. We will no longer tend to be afraid of it. It will be easier to surrender to it, for in doing so we find ourselves and our own way.

The Way
(Week 8, Sunday)

The Ten Steps to Victory
Isaiah 1:18-20

Now we are seeking transformation. That involves throwing the will on the side of transformation. That can be done only in an atmosphere of inner prayer. Inwardly commit yourself to follow simply and humbly the steps to the Way.

The Way
(Week 11, Sunday)

In Which We Share Our Victory
Psalm 66:16-20

When people expressed these needs, did anything happen? Did release come? To some, no. They couldn't get beyond themselves. But they were very few. For the most part, those who honestly faced their needs and turned them over to God found release and power and were transformed.

The Way
(Week 27, Tuesday)

The Way of Transformation
Psalm 139:7-12

Transformation...is the only workable way [to deal with life]. By transformation we mean facing life as it comes day by day and transforming it into something else. Life will come to us as justice and injustice, pleasure and pain, compliment and criticism. We must be ready to take hold of it as it comes and make something else out of it. In that way, we face life with no subterfuges, no dodging out of difficulties, no rationalization; we face life honestly and simply and masterfully.

Look at Jesus. He refused an escape into Israel's glorious past, refused to escape into the glorious future of the kingdom of God on earth, refused to retreat into detachment (as the Pharisees who were the Separatists did). He marched straight into life and took everything into his hands and made something else out of it. He took the job of a carpenter, and as he made yokes and plows, made himself ready for the great mission when he would be the architect of a new humanity. He met temptation in the wilderness and made temptation strengthen him; he transformed temptation into a tempering of his soul. He took hold of the ordinary, garden variety of humanity, chose twelve uneducated people, and made them into the teachers of humanity and the transformers of the destiny of the race. He sat by a well with a fallen woman, led her into a new experience, and then made her an evangelist to her village. He touched everything and transformed everything. That is mastery.

The Way to Power and Poise
(Week 29, Thursday)

46

Taking the Worse and Turning It into the Best
2 Corinthians 10:3-5

We look again at Jesus using the method of transformation. He was criticized for eating with publicans and sinners. Jesus took that criticism and transformed it into the three parables of the lost sheep, the lost coin, and the lost son—the most beautiful parables ever uttered—showing the heart of the seeking, redemptive God. He transformed a reviling into a revelation.

He took the ordinary facts of nature: the man sowing seed, the fisherman casting his net, the woman kneading her dough, the shepherd attending his sheep, the man building his house, the gardener planting his vines and pruning them, the children playing in the marketplace, the merchant seeking pearls, the women grinding the meal, the watchman watching his goods, the man threshing his wheat. He took everything commonplace and made it uncommonplace. He glorified everything he touched, and he touched everything.

Sin put him on a cross, and he used that cross to save us from sin. Hate nailed Jesus, and through that nailing, he showed love, the hate producing love. The cross was humanity at our worst, and through it Jesus shows God at God's redemptive best.

Jesus transformed the world's darkest hour into the world's brightest spot. He took a tomb and made it glow with light and hope.

Light looked down and beheld Darkness.
"Thither will I go," said Light.
Peace looked down and beheld War.
"Thither will I go," said Peace.
Love looked down and beheld Hatred.
"Thither will I go," said Love.

. . . .

And the Word was made flesh and dwelt among us.
(Laurence Housman, *Little Plays of St. Francis* [London: Sidgwick & Jackson, 1922], 202)

And as the Word was made flesh, so the flesh became Word and showed and spoke the Divine Word. Everything is different now, since he came. He transforms our dead souls, our dead hopes, even our dead; he makes everything live.

The Way to Power and Poise
(Week 29, Friday)

Life Makes Sense
Romans 8:39; 1 Corinthians 2:10

The central thing in the transformation of the mind is the ability to "make out what the will of God is" (Rom 12:2 Moffat). When your mind and God's mind come together, then all things in heaven and earth fall into their place. Life makes sense.

How to Be a Transformed Person
(Week 21, Sunday)

My Powers Heightened
Isaiah 41:10

The four steps that constitute the life climb of the universe are these: (a) Faith in the higher life; (b) leading to a surrender to the higher life; (c) leading to cooperation with that higher life; (d) the lower life taking these steps is transformed into the image of the higher life and partakes of that higher life. You are no longer inferior; you are a part of a superior Life.

This is transformation: "For thou hast saved my life from death, my feet from stumbling, that I may live, ever mindful of God, in the sunshine of life" (Ps 56:13 Moffatt). "Life from death" (past); "free from stumbling" (present); "that I may live, ever mindful of God, in the sunshine of life" (future). Here is something that covers the past, the present, and the future; it is a total transformation. Accept it; it is yours for the acceptance.

How to Be a Transformed Person
(Week 29, Friday)

World Transformation
Mark 1:14-15; Luke 9:2

We come now in our study of transformation to the question of world transformation. Many people are convinced that the Christian way is the way of transformation, but question whether it can transform the world except incidentally through transformed individuals. Its influence is indirect; it has no head-on proposal or plan for world transformation. Secular forces must control the collective life of humankind.

Well, the control of secular forces has led us to the collective mess we are in: two world wars in one generation, and now we tremble on the brink of a third. Does Christianity let us down in the area where direction and control is most needed, the collective?

Not the Christianity of Christ. For Christ presented something that is a head-on and all-inclusive proposal for the control of the individual and collective life. That proposal was the kingdom of God. The kingdom of God on earth is the most astonishing and radical proposal ever presented to humanity. It is nothing less than that the whole of life shall be organized around one center: the will of God.

How to Be a Transformed Person
(Week 49, Sunday)

Continuous Transformation
Ephesians 4:13-14

We now turn this week to look at continuous transformation. Our main stress has been upon the crisis in transformation, and I believe this emphasis has been sound, for the soul gets on by a series of crises. The crisis precipitates decision, the decision precipitates acceptance of grace, and acceptance of grace precipitates transformation.

But while transformation comes through crisis, it also comes through process—a continuing transformation. This passage gives that continuing process better perhaps than any in Scripture: "But we all mirror the glory of the Lord with face unveiled, and so we are being transformed into the same likeness as himself, passing from one glory to another—for this comes of the Lord the Spirit" (2 Cor 3:18 Moffatt). The phrase "we are being transformed" depicts that continuous process of transformation, a process, I believe, that has no end. It will continue for eternity.

Here then is the figure the apostle uses: We stand with unveiled face continuously gazing at the face of Christ as the center of our attention and love, and we are gradually and continuously changed into the likeness of Christ, thus proceeding from one degree of glory to another, the Spirit within us being the silent Artist who makes us into the divine image. It is a breathtaking conception and so simple! And yet how profound!

How to Be a Transformed Person
(Week 50, Sunday)

A Perfected Individual in a Perfected Society
Colossians 1:11-14

The Christian faith…turns its redemptive energy into transforming the individual unto perfection and into transforming the present world order into the kingdom of God. The end of life is not negation, but affirmation. And affirmation where it counts, in the character of the individual and society.

Growing Spiritually
(Week 1, Saturday)

Jesus the Redeemer of Waste Material
Ephesians 5:3-10

Jesus took his greatest persecutor, Saul, transformed him into the man who could write the most beautiful thing on love that has ever been written—the thirteenth chapter of 1 Corinthians—and thus made love the greatest thing in the world. The man of hate set love at the center of virtues and illustrated it in himself. Jesus was the redeemer of waste materials.

Mastery
(Week 40, Friday)

Round-the-Clock Tutelage of the Spirit
1 Thesssalonians 1:2-4

In the school of the Spirit there are four steps: (1) confession; (2) self-and sin-surrender to God, the Spirit; (3) acceptance by faith of forgiveness and reconciliation to God, the Spirit; (4) transformation. For in confession everything is brought up and out—complete honesty; in self-and sin-surrender there is a transfer of the central allegiance from self and sin to God—complete recentering; in acceptance by faith of forgiveness and reconciliation there is a wiping out of all barriers between the soul and God, and hence, there is transformation. God's power, now free to operate, transforms the honest, the surrendered, and the receptive soul.

Christian Maturity
(Week 43, Thursday)

The Redeemed Become the Redeeming

Yesterday I met a completely transformed woman. She and her husband had kept a gambling house with all the accoutrements in Louisiana for two and a half years. She became an alcoholic to escape from herself —and her past. Now she is a radiant person, her home the center of youth, and her touch on life a creative touch.... Her touch on life was destructive, now it is constructive. She is not absorbed into the divine—she is absorbing the divine into the human and making that human creative. Yet she knows where she belongs—at his feet. Being at his feet she stands straight before everything. She is being created, and she is creative.

In Christ
(Week 15, Saturday)

Fundamental Tendencies: Forgiveness and a Second Chance
1 Corinthians 1:26-30

[One] fundamental tendency [is] toward a new birth, a new beginning. There is a fundamental tendency in the universe to give the second chance, a recovery, a new start. This comes to its supreme manifestation in Jesus; he took the nobodies and turned them into the somebodies, made a new world beginning out of cast-off material, threw open the gates of possibility to the impossible. Recovery and transformation are the twin words written across the whole of the life and purpose of Jesus.

The Word Became Flesh
(Week 50, Friday)

2
CHRISTIAN PRACTICES

Amid all this gloom and uncertainty there is one bright spot—the Christian way. Here life lights up. It regains a sparkle, takes on meaning, goal. Here there seems to be promise of a way out. But the difficulty is that the Christian way has been presented as a way. It is an alternative alongside many others. It deals with the reclaiming and regenerating of the soul now, and heaven hereafter. It lacks total meanings for the total life—individual and collective. This does not grip us, for our faith must be everything or nothing. It must control the whole of life or none of it. It must not merely be a way; it must be the Way. And it must be the Way for everything and everybody, everywhere and in every circumstance.

The Way
(Preface)

CHARACTER

Is Forgiveness the Best We Can Expect?
Romans 6:1-7

Many Christians do not expect anything beyond repeated forgiveness for constantly repeated sins. They do not expect victory over sins. Thus in Christianity the most beautiful thing, namely the forgiving grace of God, is turned into the most baneful, for it actually turns out to be something that encourages evil. What a cross that must be on the heart of God! And what a travesty it is on our Christian faith!

This expectancy of constant forgiveness for constantly repeated sin is weakening to character, and is one reason for so much weak character within the Christian church. Under this idea, life turns flabby.

Victorious Living
(Week 10, Wednesday)

Don't Worry About Your Reputation
Matthew 5:11; Luke 6:22; 1 Corinthians 4:13; Philippians 2:5-11

One who is living victoriously has gained victory over nervous concern about reputation. You don't have look after it. Look after your character and your reputation can look after itself.

Victorious Living
(Week 32, Saturday)

How God Reveals God
Psalm 19:1-6; Hebrews 1:10-12; 2:6-9

The highest thing in our moral universe is moral character. If God can be found anywhere, it ought to be here. The highest illustration of moral character ever seen on our planet is Christ. If God can be found anywhere, it ought to be in the highest thing in our moral universe—the character of Christ. How could God show us the divine character except through perfect a moral character?

The character of God matters. For what God is like we must be like; God's character determines ours. Just what is God like in character? I look up through nature, and I come to the conclusion that God is law. I am grateful for that, but I want something beyond law. I am not a subject asking for a law; I am a child asking for a Parent. Nature cannot tell me of my Parent, not clearly. Nor could the perfect revelation come through prophets or teachers, for the revelation, in going through them, becomes limited, sometimes distorted, because of the human medium. Nor could the revelation come perfectly through a book, for literature cannot rise higher than life; the life that surrounds the literature puts content into the literature. So the book would be pulled to the level of our highest experience. The only complete way of revelation is through a Life, a Character who would show us what God's character is like. That Character is Christ— the human life of God, that part of God we have been able to see. The Bible, then, is not the revelation of God; it is the inspired record of the revelation. The revelation is seen in the face of Jesus Christ. Is God then Christlike? He is! I can say nothing higher. I can be content with nothing less.

Abundant Living
(Week 3, Thursday)

General Guidance through the Revelation in Christ
John 13:15; 14:6-9; Peter 2:21

God gives general guidance through the character and person of Christ. Christ has revealed to us the nature of God, has shown us what God is like; the Lord has lifted up into bold relief the laws that underlie our moral universe, and the laws that underlie our own spiritual, intellectual, and physical beings. In short, God has revealed to us the nature of Reality. Then Christ is our "general guidance." If we want to live according to the nature of Reality, then we must live according to Christ.

Abundant Living
(Week 37, Wednesday)

Witnessing before Dull Ignorance
Acts 3:12-21; 17:22-34; Romans 10:1-4; 1 Timothy 1:12-15

Grasp the truth in these words: "We triumph even in our troubles, knowing that trouble produces endurance, endurance produces character, and character produces hope" (Rom 5:3-4, Moffatt). Note the steps: trouble, endurance, character, hope. The hope is based on the solid reality of tested character, and verse 5 adds: "a hope which never disappoints us." With a hope based on that solid reality, we can wait, for that hope never, never disappoints us.

Abundant Living
(Week 52, Wednesday)

The Christian Way Is Sense
James 3:13-18

The real Christian is the most universalized person on earth, the most natural. A great many people think they have to be less Christian to be more universal. That is a mistake. The more Christian you are, the more universal you are. You are at home in everything, everywhere except in one thing—evil. For in evil, life turns unnatural and lives against itself.

The Way
(Week 6, Saturday)

Our Code Is a Character
Hebrews 12:1-3

One greater than the commandments is here. Our code is not a commandment but a Character.

The Way
(Week 8, Wednesday)

Christianize Your Relationships
Acts 16:14-15; 1 Timothy 3:12-13

[Your] daily occupation can be the extension of your spiritual life, your spiritual life become incarnate in material things. The head of a great foundry told me that the defects of character in the individual workman sooner or later become revealed in the castings. If the character goes wrong, the casting goes wrong. The opposite of that can be true. Your Christian character can be registered in the work you are doing. God and we make people and things in our own image.

The Way
(Week 12, Tuesday)

Going Where We Are Pushed
Philippians 3:7-14

Inner division produces indecision, and indecision produces weakness of character.
...Jesus said to the disciples: "You have a saying, have you not, 'Four months yet, then harvest'?" (John 4:35 Moffatt). In other words, "There is plenty of time—four months yet—then harvest." Then he added: "The fields are right for harvesting!"—now. He was correcting the attitude of being unwilling to face things now, the attitude of indecision. We have a saying that "procrastination is the thief of time." It is worse than that; it is the thief of character. For character is decision....

Then there are those who, after they decide, are always undeciding. They go over their decisions and undecide them by continuously worrying over whether they have made the right decisions. That indecision regarding one's decisions is as weakening to character as no decision. Decisions must be decisive in order to develop character.

The Way
(Week 20, Friday)

Evangelism the Life Blood of the Church
Daniel 12:3; 2 Timothy 4:1-5; Revelation 12:10-11

Two things characterize the real Christian: we listen to God, and we talk to people. Many reverse that: they listen to people, and they talk to God. It was said of John the Baptist: "He came for the purpose of witnessing" (John 1:7 Moffatt). That is psychologically sound. The center was outside himself; he was not talking about himself. That made him a healthy-minded person, and effective.

The Way
(Week 46, Saturday)

Study, Obey, Teach
2 Timothy 2:15, 24-26

Character is caught not taught.

The Way
(Week 52, Wednesday)

Jesus Was No Miracle Monger
Philippians 2:5-11

This is why the Incarnation had to take place before the Indwelling, for the Incarnation fixed the character and nature of the Indwelling.

The Way to Power and Poise
(Week 5, Saturday)

The Silent but Ultimate Forces of God
Acts 10:38; Isaiah 42:1

The ultimate character and the ultimate power are at work in the recesses of our beings, making us into the image of Jesus. We can ask for nothing higher; we can be content with nothing less. This is it: ultimate power produces ultimate character.

The Way to Power and Poise
(Week 7, Friday)

Just Turn the Doorknob
Matthew 9:20-21

Jesus says, "Whatever you pray for and ask, believe you have got it, and you shall have it" (Matt 11:24 Moffatt). Note: "have got it." The word of Jesus is accomplishment, and when I take his word as accomplishment, then it is accomplishment. For behind that word is the character of Jesus, and behind the character of Jesus is the character of the universe. The nature of reality backs it.

How to Be a Transformed Person
(Week 7, Wednesday)

Growth in Balanced Virtues
2 Peter 1:3-8

If our God is unbalanced in character, we become unbalanced. We can be grateful, very grateful, that the center of our faith and our loyalty was the most balanced Character ever seen on our planet.

Growing Spiritually
(Week 48, Sunday)

The Eternal Cry Is "More"
Colossians 2:20-23; 3:1-8

A religion founded on rules comes up against two inexorable alternatives: Either the people in growing break the rules, or the rules are so strong they break the people. A religion founded on rules produces a resistance from the growing, or a restriction of the growing. But not so in the Christian faith. For here the Character, who is our code, is infinitely unfolding.

Growing Spiritually
(Week 50, Thursday)

Any Prods to Perfection There?
Revelation 21:22-26

To overcome [a] tendency to soft flabbiness, [fishermen] introduced huge catfish among the herring [they had caught]. The herring were always running away from the catfish, so they kept in firm condition until the end of the voyage. Life provides us with many "catfish" that prod us into firmness of character.

Growing Spiritually
(Week 52, Friday)

Everything Anchored to Jesus
Hebrews 2:7-9

The whole Christian faith is anchored to Jesus. God is anchored to Jesus. For we know little or nothing about God except through Jesus. Apart from Jesus we look up to God through our own conceptions, but these are usually misconceptions. Through them we arrive at something other than God. But through Jesus we see the Lord, "He that hath seen me hath seen the Father" (John 14:9 KJV). The character of God is none other than the character of Jesus.

Christ was anchored to Jesus. Apart from Jesus, the Christ—the Anointed One, the Messiah—has been misconceived, often as a nationalistic hero or a mystic. "I am the Messiah, Christ reincarnated," said a Hindu in the hearing of a British sea captain. The blunt reply was, "Well, if you are, then I'm changing my religion."

The Holy Spirit is anchored to Jesus. We know little or nothing about the Spirit's character unless we see it in the character of Jesus: "[I] will send another Companion" (John 14:16 CEB)—"another" like me; "the Holy Spirit . . . will remind you of everything I told you" (v. 26); "he will take what is mine and proclaim it to you" (16:14). The Holy Spirit is a Jesus-like Spirit.

The Kingdom of God is anchored to Jesus. He fixes in his own person the character of the kingdom. The kingdom is the spirit of Jesus universalized.

Mastery
(Week 25, Wednesday)

God Is Light on Four Things
Romans 1:19-20

When you see God in the face of Jesus, then "God is light," light on everything. When you lose God you lose everything, and when you find God you find everything....

God is light on character. In Jesus we see the character of God. God couldn't do an un-Christlike thing and still be God. So Jesus is the key to the character of God and humanity. In him we see what God is like and what we can be like. He sets the pattern of character for God and for us. You can transfer to God every single quality of character in Jesus without lowering your idea of God. Lower your idea of God? You heighten it! For if God isn't like Jesus, God isn't good. You ask me my definition of goodness. I do not add virtue to virtue; I point to Jesus. He is goodness. If God isn't like Jesus I'm not interested in God. If God is like Jesus, then God can have my heart without qualification or reservation.

Christian Maturity
(Week 7, Wednesday)

Whatever You Ask in My Name

To respond rightly to the requests and expectations of others is a high test of character. Jesus said that the Father was glorified in what Jesus granted. He would never answer or refuse a request unless the Father too would have answered or refused that request. He and the Father were one in prayer requests.

Yet Jesus seems to leave the matter wide open: "Whatever you ask in my name" (John 14:13). The important portion is "in my name." "In my name" would mean "in my spirit, in my character." It doesn't mean just repeating the name of Jesus at the end of the prayer, but putting into the request the very spirit and character of Jesus: "Pray the prayer that [Jesus] would pray." If you do that, then God is glorified.

In Christ
(Week 14, Wednesday)

The Name and the Spirit

Only in the name or character of Jesus Christ is reality revealed. Therefore God can't give in any other name or character, for if God did so, God would be backing unreality and falsity.

In Christ
(Week 23, Saturday)

In Him the Whole Fullness of Deity

There is nothing in God that isn't in Jesus Christ—at least in character and essence.

In Christ
(Week 40, Tuesday)

57

The Quest for the Perfect Revelation
Matthew 13:16-17

If God isn't like Jesus, I am not interested in God. For the highest I know in the realm of character is to be Christlike. I said that in India, and a Hindu wrote to me: "You took my breath away. This is Bhakti [devotion] par excellence. You said you wouldn't be interested in God if he were not like your Guru [Master]." But my guru is no human guru; my guru is God's authentic self-revelation. When the disciples said, "Lord, show us the Father; that will be enough for us." Jesus quietly said: "Whoever as seen me has seen the Father" (John 14:8-9), and it was one of the greatest moments in human history.

The Word Became Flesh
(Week 1, Friday)

The Silence of Eternity Has Been Broken
1 Corinthians 2:9-10

There was, and is, no other way for God to be revealed except in understandable terms, human terms. God had to show the divine character where your character and mine are wrought out, namely, in the stream of human history. The Word had to become flesh, or else not be the Word; it would be something else—words!

The Word Became Flesh
(Week 1, Saturday)

"He Has Visited and Redeemed"
Luke 1:67-68; 76-79

God dwelt among us from the cradle of the manger to the grave of the tomb. . . . God met life as you and I meet it—as a person, Jesus. Jesus called on no power not at our disposal for his own moral battle. He performed no miracle to extricate himself from any difficulty. If Jesus had power, he had power to restrain power, holding it only for the meeting of human need in others. He never performed a miracle just to show power or to confound an enemy. Jesus lived a normal life, so normal that it became the norm. He dwelt among us as one of us.

The Word Became Flesh
(Week 3, Monday)

A Person to Be Followed
John 21:18-19

God is like Jesus in character. Transfer every characteristic of character from Jesus to God, and you do not lower your estimate of God, you heighten it. For there is nothing higher for God or a person than to be Christlike. Jesus is God simplified, God approachable, God understandable, God lovable. When I say God, I think Jesus. And nothing higher can be thought or said! Jesus is the last word that can be said about God.

The Word Became Flesh
(Week 3, Thursday)

The Perfect Becomes the Progressive
Hebrews 6:1-3

In the realm of character there has been revealed an ultimate character, the Word of character has become flesh. The adjective Christlike is the highest descriptive adjective of character for both God and humans in any language. Beyond that revelation we will never progress. Does that stop character progress? It begins it. For now we know what the norm is. Now we know where to head; we know the goal. That fixed goal is the starting point for infinite progress.

The Word Became Flesh
(Week 4, Monday)

What Do I Want to Know About God?
Philippians 2:5-10

I want to know what God is like in character. For what God is like in character, I must be like. I cannot be at cross purposes with reality and not get hurt. So Jesus makes "known" (John 1:18) the character of God, makes it known in the only possible way God's character can be made known, namely through another character—Jesus' own.

And Jesus reveals the central thing in God's character—Love!

The Word Became Flesh
(Week 5, Sunday)

An Unfinished World a Good World
Colossians 1:28-29

The purpose of God, our Parent, seems to be to produce character in God's children. Not their ease, not their happiness (except as a byproduct), but their character. This means that this life would seem to be a vale of character-making. If this be the end, then God could not create a perfect environment. For character is produced out of overcoming oppositions, obstacles, and impediments. So God had to create a world unfinished. God's purpose seems to have been to leave creation unfinished so that we could help finish it. God left just enough challenges on which to sharpen our wits and our characters. If God had made us perfect beings in a perfect world, we would never have developed. There would be nothing to sharpen us on. Perfect beings in a perfect world would lack one thing: growth!

The Word Became Flesh
(Week 15, Thursday)

God Is Not a Cosmic Signpost
1 Corinthians 10:31; 11:1

The whole fifth chapter of Matthew is not a collection of sayings, but a connected and organic whole, beginning at the sounding of the standard note, "Blessed are the pure [or undivided] in heart, for they shall see God" (v. 8) and ending in the final crescendo, "You, therefore, must be perfect, as your heavenly Father is perfect" (v. 48). If you are undivided in heart, then you not only see God, you become like God, perfect in character and life as a child of God, as God is perfect as God. Nothing could be more ethically and spiritually sound than this. Our code of conduct is not based on ethical principles—the Word become word, or upon the will of God—again the Word become word, but upon the very character and conduct of God—the Word become flesh.

The Word Became Flesh
(Week 22, Wednesday)

Reliance on Character and Authority from Within
Romans 11:34-36

[A] fundamental tendency of the universe [is] to make character the basis of leadership and survival. Among the lower forms of life, the secret of leadership and survival is strength of physical character; among the higher forms of life, mental and moral character. In Jesus this comes to its highest form in moral and spiritual character. Here we see the highest moral and spiritual character ever seen upon our planet. You can transfer every moral and spiritual characteristic of Jesus to God without lowering your estimate of God. Lowering? You heighten your estimate of God when you think of God in terms of Jesus Christ. You simply know nothing higher to say about God or people than to say, "Like Jesus Christ." Jesus is the ultimate character.

The Word Became Flesh
(Week 50, Saturday)

"BEING CHRISTIAN"

Facing the Issues
Luke 11:33-36

People have honest doubts, and I have spent many years in meeting those doubts, perhaps too many years, for I now see that the problem is usually deeper. Not always, but usually.

For instance, a young man came puzzled about the Trinity. I replied that the emphasis in Christianity was not upon the Trinity but upon the Incarnation. The doctrine of the Trinity was rather overheard than heard in the New Testament, but still I could see why the Trinity is reasonable.

Victorious Living
(Week 4, Friday)

Victorious Living and Temptation
Psalm 74:17; Mark 9:43-47; 14:37-38; 1 Peter 1:6-7

We have just been studying the fact that victorious living means to say "yes" to something—the will of God—but that implies that we are to say "no" to something—temptation. Christianity is not a prohibition; it is a privilege, but it does have a prohibition in it.

Victorious Living
(Week 41, Sunday)

The Four Steps in Helping Others to Christ
Mark 13:11; John 1:43-49; 4:6-42

In presenting the Christian way to people, you will have to answer [these] four questions [(1) What is it? (2) What will it do (for you)? (3) Who says so? (4) How can you get it?]. First: What is it? Perhaps you will have to tell the person what it is not, in order to clear away misconceptions. It is not a mere set of beliefs to be believed, an organization to be joined, a rite or ceremony to be undergone. It may and does involve these, but it is much more than these things. It is a personal relationship with God, which involves a change, gradual or sudden, from the kingdom of self to the kingdom of God through the grace and power of Christ. The basis of life is shifted from self to God: you live in a state, not of self-reference, but of God-reference. God's will becomes supreme in your life. That will is interpreted to us in Christ. To be a Christian is to be a Christian—to be committed, with all you have, to Christ in surrender and obedience.

Abundant Living
(Week 47, Tuesday)

The Five Steps in Following Christ
Joshua 24:15; Psalm 55:17; Matthew 6:22; John 6:67-69

(1) Make up your mind: "All who want to come after me." ...
(2) Give up yourself: "say no to themselves." ...
(3) Take up your cross: "Take up their cross!" ...
(4) Keep up your cultivation: "daily." ...
(5) Gather up your loyalties: ... "follow me" (Luke 9:23 CEB).

Abundant Living
(Week 47, Thursday)

The Attitude and Its Outcome or Reward
Numbers 12:3-15; 2 Corinthians 10:1; Philippians 4:13;
Colossians 3:12-17; Titus 3:1-7

The earth belongs to the meek because it won't respond to the proud, the boasting. The earth is made in its inner constitution to work in the Christian way, and hence none but the Christian meek can inherit it.

Abundant Living
(Week 48, Tuesday)

The Aim of the Christian Discipline
2 Timothy 1:7-8; 2:1-5; 4:2, 5

The "Christian discipline": The Christian way is a discipline and not merely a doctrine. The doctrine gives direction and content to the discipline. Doctrine that does not discipline is dead. Christianity is therefore not merely something that you believe, but something that you believe in enough to act upon. Your deed is your creed, the thing you believe in enough to put into practice. You do not believe in what you do not practice. Theory and practice are one. Your theory is your practice.

Abundant Living
(Week 50, Sunday)

My Will and God's Will—Alien?
Psalms 119:37, 103, 130

The Christian way is the way that conforms to nature, real nature. Anything else is doomed.

The Way
(Week 5, Thursday)

Finding God—and Ourselves
Psalm 51:7-12

This passage may well sum up our week's study of the naturalness of the Christian way: "All things have been created by him and for him" (Col 1:16 Moffatt). Note: We are made not only "by" him but also "for" him. That is, life works in Christ's way and in no other way. Look at everything in your life—every organ, every relationship—and you can see, if you have eyes to see, this written in everything, "Made for him."

The Way
(Week 5, Saturday)

The God of Life and the God of Religion
John 1:4; 10:10; 12:50

To be a Christian you may have to give up some things, but not to be a Christian you have to give up everything, everything worthwhile. In giving up things for Christ, I gave up nothing but what subtracted from me, and when I got him, I got everything that added to me.

The Way
(Week 6, Monday)

The Two Pillars of Our Peace
John 14:1-3

The Christian peace is based not only on what Christ does for us but also on what we do for him.

The Way to Power and Poise
(Week 44, Saturday)

The Tongue and the Heart Coordinated
Acts 13:2-3

The Christian way teaches, not withdrawal, but witnessing as the way to poise and power. If we do not create, we cut across our own nature and are frustrated.

The Way to Power and Poise
(Week 45, Thursday)

On Opening the Door to Victory
Acts 16:28-34

I have a Christian stomach. I'm eating everything.

The Way to Power and Poise
(Week 48, Friday)

Turned Only Halfway On
Acts 2:46-47

We are looking at the necessity of being transformed from gloom to gladness. It is a sin against God to be gloomy. It says to the world that God is a gloomy God and produces gloomy followers. A complete reversal of the facts! For there is more joy to the square inch in being a Christian than there is to the square mile outside [of being a Christian]....

There are two great reasons for not being happy, radiant Christians. One is a halfwayness about the whole business of being Christian. We are only tentatively Christian....A lot of Christians have lives that are squeaky and noisy, and they can't hold happiness and joy for long—they leak. Why? Turned only halfway on! Many Christians have just enough religion to set up a conflict, but not enough to set up a concord. A half-Christianity is a problem instead of a power.

The second reason for gloomy Christianity is not realizing our resources....Many of us [take from] current pessimisms and fears instead of [taking from] the green fields of God's grace and power. We should realize our resources and possess our possessions.

How to Be a Transformed Person
(Week 43, Friday)

They Believed in His Beliefs
1 Corinthians 15:54-57

The Christian faith is the only faith that lights up that dark area of life—death. And it lights it up, not with word, but with a Word made flesh.

How to Be a Transformed Person
(Week 44, Wednesday)

The Eternal Cry Is "More"
Colossians 2:20-23; 3:1-8

The definition of a Christian grows the more you see of Christ, who is the standard of what a Christian is.

Growing Spiritually
(Week 50, Thursday)

Jesus, the Perfect but Unfolding Revelation
Matthew 5:17; Romans 10:3-4; Galatians 6:14

The Old Testament, which [tells of] the period of preparation for Christianity, is not Christianity. It is pre-Christian....Christianity is Christ. Christians are people who believe in God and humanity and life through Jesus Christ.

Growing Spiritually
(Week 51, Tuesday)

The Kingdom Written into Us
Acts 9:2; 19:23; 22:22

The Christian Way is the natural way to live. I am convinced that sin and evil and every other way are unnatural ways to live. Iniquity is literally "missing the mark." The "mark" is the kingdom, the way. So all living against that way is a living against yourself. For the kingdom is the "mark" within us, the way we are made to live. To live against yourself is impossible, not only foolish but impossible. So sin and evil break down the self. The self disintegrates under it; "perish" is the word Jesus uses (see John 10:28).

Growing Spiritually
(Week 51, Wednesday)

The Christian Way Works
John 3:5-36; 5:22-24

The Christian way ... will work to the degree that we work it. I know of no other way that does work. All alternatives to the Christian way turn out to be alternative ways to ruin. There are many wrong ways; there is only one right way. And Jesus always turns out to be that way, always. Life to me is one long corroboration of that fact.

Growing Spiritually
(Week 51, Saturday)

If We Walk in the Light
Acts 19:18-20

You do not have to be always right. We are all only Christians in the making. We blunder and stumble. But when we stumble, we stumble forward. When we fall, we fall on our knees.

Mastery
(Week 50, Friday)

Responsible for All We Know and All We Might Know
Romans 8:1-8

A Christian is one who is responding to all the meanings found in Jesus; walking in all the light to be found in him. The moment we refuse to walk in the light as seen in Jesus, then the light ceases. We begin to walk in darkness. Only the person who is living up to the light that he or she has is getting more light.

Mastery
(Week 50, Saturday)

I Endorse This with All My Heart
John 7:37-39

Most Christians are canceled out, not because they don't give, but because they don't give all. They give, but they don't give up. Yet how gladly we should offer our all in exchange for God's all!

Mastery
(Week 51, Tuesday)

Their Problems Turned to Possibilities
John 16:7-11

Mastery began with the Christians themselves; they were mastered by the Master. And that was the right place; it all began within them and then moved out in concentric circles to the total life.

Mastery
(Week 52, Tuesday)

Bodily Health and Healing
Daniel 8:27:10:8

The first thing in Christianity is reconciliation with God; God is the center. When you are reconciled to God you become reconciled to yourself and hence reconciled to your body. The healing of that reconciliation with God is passed on to the body.

Christian Maturity
(Week 47, Sunday)

Maturity Open to "All"
Acts 10:42-45

We are to be adjusted to nothing this side of the highest—the highest in heaven and earth—Jesus Christ. In Christianity sin is *amartia* (literally, "missing the mark"). Applied, it means that sin is missing the mark—Jesus Christ. All departure from his mind and spirit is sin. That is not a legal definition of sin but a life definition.

Christian Maturity
(Week 50, Tuesday)

With Unveiled Face
Proverbs 28:12-13

Just what does "with unveiled face" mean? If it means anything, it means that we must be completely honest with God, with ourselves, with others, with life. We must come clear, absolutely clear.... Christianity begins at...: confession, sin- and self-surrender, acceptance of the grace of God, and transformation. [It begins] with confession, the "unveiled face."

Christian Maturity
(Week 51, Tuesday)

Do More and More

The eternal cry of the Christian is, "More." The Christian's attitude is, "I've seen so much, I want to see more"; "I've tasted so much I want to taste more"; "I've become so much I want to become more." This "more and more" will stretch beyond the grave and forever, for the finite will forever approach the infinite, but will never arrive. That growth will be our eternal joy, and there is no joy greater than the joy of creative growth. There is room for infinite growth in Christ.

In Christ
(Week 52, Monday)

Place for Ambitious Person in Christ

Christianity demands self-surrender. The ego, trying to be God, must be renounced and surrendered. Once that surrender is made, however, there is a place in Christianity for the ambitious. The ambition now has a new motive and goal—we are ambitious to serve.

In Christ
(Week 43, Thursday)

Divine and Human Self-Surrender
Luke 9:23-25

At the very center of the conception of the Word become flesh is the fact of the divine self-surrender. The Christian faith demands of us as its deepest demand, self-surrender. And the Word become flesh shows God doing the same thing, the divine self-surrender.

This is an essential difference between the Christian faith and other faiths: in the Christian faith the divine practices everything God asks us to practice, especially in regard to self-surrender. A prominent Hindu philosopher said to me, "Self-surrender is everything." But in saying this he departed from his Vedantism, for in it Brahma is impersonal. You cannot surrender to an It.

The Word Became Flesh
(Week 47, Sunday)

A Novel Way to End a Strike
Colossians 1:12-14

Goodness is natural. The truly Christian person is the truly natural person. That person is not living against the grain of the universe, but with it. Christians do not hit their shins on the system of things. They know their way about in a universe of this kind; they know how to live. I know exactly how I feel when I sin: I am orphaned, estranged, and everything within me cries, "This is not the way." I also know exactly how I feel when I live the Christian way: I am universalized, at home. Everything within me cries, "This is the way!" Christ's way is my way.

The Word Became Flesh
(Week 49, Tuesday)

I Felt I Was Holding in My Hand a Key
1 John 4:13-15

Someone has said that "Christians are very ordinary people making very extraordinary claims." Not about themselves, but about their Redeemer. They know they are very imperfect followers of a very perfect Lord. So they say, "Glance at me, but gaze at Christ. Don't follow me, follow him. "We preach not ourselves, but Jesus Christ as Lord."

The Word Became Flesh
(Week 50, Monday)

EVANGELISM

Getting the Message Through
John 4:3-42; Acts 28:30-31; Philippians 1:12-14; 2 Timothy 2:9

There are certain things in your life and mine that are inevitable. We have to go to office, to school, to workshop, to home duties; or we may be compelled by circumstance to sit on a park bench, unemployed. Evangelize that inevitable thing; find your opportunity in the ordinary contacts of the day. Then that day will no longer be ordinary, for the contacts are redemptive. You are turning the commonplace into the consequential. The little things of life become the big things, big with destiny. Life-contacts become life-changing. Nothing, absolutely nothing bigger under heaven than just that.

Victorious Living
(Week 39, Tuesday)

The Goal
Matthew 10:8; Mark 5:19; John 1:35-37; 20:28, 31; Colossians 1:18

The end of evangelism is to produce an evangelist. We must not be satisfied to get somebody "in"; we must be Satisfied only when they are getting someone else "in." Then we have really started something that knows no end.

Victorious Living
(Week 40, Tuesday)

A Ladder to a Contagious Life
Psalm 51:12-13; Daniel 12:3; John 15:5, 16; Acts 8:26-39

To have the qualities of Jesus branded into our beings will not be enough unless we have the quality of contagion. For contagion makes these qualities outgoing and places them at the disposal of others. "No heart is pure that is not passionate; no virtue is safe that is not enthusiastic" (Sir John Robert Seeley, *Ecce Homo* [Boston: Roberts Brothers, 1868], 14). No life is Christian that is not Christianizing. If there is no outflow, the inflow automatically stops.

We must deliberately set ourselves to be spiritually creative. Perhaps [this step] will help you toward a contagious life....

I shall have the will to evangelize. Hitherto the desire to evangelize has been in my mind and emotion; now it gets into my will. I have decided to share with others what has been shared with me.

Abundant Living
(Week 47, Monday)

69

Making the Secular into the Perfect
1 Thessalonians 4:7-12; 2 Thessalonians 3:6, 10-11

Our greatest need is laypeople on fire with evangelism.

The Way
(Week 44, Thursday)

The Way Is the Way to Creative Contagion
1 Thessalonians 1:2-8

Evangelism is not something specially connected with an occupation, certain people set aside for it by vocation and occupation. It is not an occupation but an outcome. It is the outcome of the nature of the life itself. Inherent in all life is the impulse to create; life produces life. If it doesn't create, it dies.

The Way
(Week 46, Sunday)

The Way Is the Way of Reconciliation
Ephesians 2:14-22

Second, Philip went beyond the apostles in his reconciling impact. His evangelism was what all evangelism should be—reconciliation. Through everything he did reconciliation runs. And that is the heart of evangelism.

The Way
(Week 46, Monday)

Evangelism the Life Blood of the Church
2 Timothy 4:1-5; Revelation 12:10-11; Daniel 12:3

As soon as one finds Christ, there is an impulse to find another and bring that person to Christ. In the first chapter of John are three "finds": Andrew "finds" Peter, Jesus "finds" Philip, and Philip "finds" Nathaniel. The gospel is a gospel of "finding."

As Jesse M. Bader says: "We have been ringing church bells when we should be ringing doorbells.... We have been doing by proxy what we should do by proximity... by purse what we should be doing in person (Jesse Moren Bader, *Evangelism in a Changing America* [St. Louis: Bethany Press, 1957], 99)...."

O Christ, you hast given me the greatest work in the world, the work of bringing others to you. Help me here and now to dedicate myself to that simple task, and help me to be faithful to that dedication. For nothing counts so much as this. In your name. Amen.

The Way
(Week 46, Saturday)

That's Still in the Pencil
Acts 16:22-25

The very end of the atonement is to get us out of ourselves and released in loving service to others: "And he died for all, that those who live might live no longer for themselves" (2 Cor 5:15), a saving of one from the self. This is the central release. The end of evangelism is to produce an evangelist. We all propagate something. When people see us, they get a dominant impression: an impression of self-preoccupation, or an impression of serenity and poise, or an impression of conflict, or an impression of impurity. The dominant impression that we leave is our evangelism. So we are all evangelists, of something. If this be true, then I choose; I choose Christ. He shall be my evangelism. And this shall be not merely by act but by tongue as well. For if I act and do not speak, then I am a half-witness; just as I am a half-witness if I speak and do not act. To be a whole witness I must witness with my total life—deeds and tongue.

The Way to Power and Poise
(Week 45, Friday)

Not Proselytism, but Conversion
John 4:1-4

Find your evangelistic opportunity in the inevitable contacts you have to have day by day. Evangelism isn't something imported into special weeks and special occasions; it must be the breath of the life....

O God, give me the alert heart and the responsive will to find my evangelistic opportunity everywhere in my daily contacts. Help me to make it a natural part of my natural contacts. Amen.

How to Be a Transformed Person
(Week 38, Friday)

Not in Till They Go Out
John 4:27-38

The end of evangelism is to produce an evangelist. A law of the mind is this: that which is not expressed dies.

How to Be a Transformed Person
(Week 39, Friday)

Mending the Seamless Robe
1 Corinthians 12:15-21

Philip, to whom a secular task was assigned, made the secular and the sacred parts of one whole. For he put evangelism through the tableserving, and made tableserving a part of evangelism. All life spoke one message: the good news.

How to Be a Transformed Person
(Week 42, Tuesday)

71

Growth in Spiritual Contagion
Matthew 28:18-20

Christianity is not merely a conception; it is also a contagion. And when the contagion is lost, then the conception too is lost. For you cannot long be evangelical if you are not evangelistic. It is a law of the mind that that which is not expressed dies. And if our Christianity is not expressed in evangelism, it soon dies as a fact within us. Nothing is really ours unless we share it. For the moment someone else shares our faith, then that faith means something more to us.

Evangelism is not then an imposition into particular days and weeks; it is part and parcel of our Christian faith. . . .

Evangelism, then, isn't something that we can take or leave and nothing happens; it is something that, if we don't take it, we lose the very faith itself. For the expression of the faith is of the essence of the faith.

Growing Spiritually
(Week 46, Sunday)

The Creative Spirit
Ephesians 3:7-9

If the church is reaching out in evangelism at home and missions abroad, there the Holy Spirit is at work in some measure. When the church ceases to lay its hands on its members to send them forth, then the hand of the Lord is not laid on the church in blessing and grace.

Mastery
(Week 21, Sunday)

They Have an Enthusiasm among Themselves
Colossians 1:3-7

The story goes that one time [the Rev. James Alexander Bryan, "Brother Bryan" of Birmingham, Alabama] sat listening to a speaker who was expounding how to do evangelism effectively. Brother Bryan grew restive under the flow of words and ideas; he went out of the meeting, across the street, and sat down with a workman who was eating his noonday lunch, and led him to Christ on the spot. He felt that the way to do evangelism was to do it. The theory was the practice. The fact is that the thing we believe in is the thing we practice. If we don't believe in a thing enough to practice it, then we just don't believe in it. The only way to do evangelism is to do it.

Mastery
(Week 37, Thursday)

An Old Tattooed Woman Won a Thousand
Acts 8:4-8

In [East Asia], I was told that... a grandmother, a member of the head-hunters, was converted and immediately began to convert others....

If an [elderly person] can do [evangelism], then a child can do it too. A little boy of ten said, "Mother, I think I saved the soul of a policeman today." "How?" asked the mother. "Well, he was so nice to me in taking me across the street that I said, 'You're so kind, you're like a Christian. Are you one?'" Whether or not the policeman became a Christian, the little boy was more of a Christian by sharing his faith.

Mastery
(Week 37, Friday)

Three Cardinal Urges
Acts 2:46-47

There are three cardinal signs of the new life in Christ: (1) the desire to pray, (2) the urge to join with others in worship, (3) the desire to bring others to Christ. Without the last-named, there is no new life. For Christianity is a contagion as well as a conception. And if there is no contagion, there will soon be no conception. If a church or individual Christian loses its power to convert it has lost its right to be called Christian. If we cease to be evangelistic, we will soon cease to be evangelical, for it is a law of the mind that that which is not expressed dies.

Christian Maturity
(Week 45, Monday)

73

All of Us: Evangelists of Something
1 Timothy 4:1-2, 5

There are no private worlds; we belong to one another for good or ill. And we are all propagating something. Out of the abundance of our hearts, our mouths speaks, speak something. Some propagate a grouch; they spill over on those whom they meet and douse them with their grouches. That is their evangelism. Others propagate their sex. They play up their sex appeal—the low-cut dress, the silent yet clamorous invitations to look—sex is their evangelism. Others propagate themselves. They introduce the self into every conversation and into every situation....

All of us are evangelists of something. Then I choose Jesus! You are as mature as the thing you propagate. The only way to be really mature is to propagate the highest Maturity—Jesus; then you become what you give out. You, as a person, are born of the qualities you habitually give out.

You don't have to be a saint to make Jesus your evangelism. You are not proclaiming a perfect proclaimer, but a perfect Savior. You are pointing to him, not to you. And the Savior is presented as the Savior of the proclaimer...as well as the Savior of those to whom you proclaim the Savior. The Evangel evangelizes the evangelists in the process of evangelization. Inwardly you go to people on your knees.

You don't have to be a saint to share Jesus, but you do have to be sincere. We are all imperfect proclaimers of a perfect Savior. But in proclaiming the perfect we tend to become more perfect.

Christian Maturity
(Week 45, Tuesday)

Not in Until They Get Out

The only real proof of being in Christ is that we are getting others into Christ. The only proof of our being alive is that we are creating life. Nothing is ours until we share it. The end of evangelism is to produce evangelists. We really haven't got people "in" unless they immediately begin to bring others in. They are not "in" until they go "out."

In Christ
(Week 23, Sunday)

Damning Others Instead of Rescuing the Damned
Jude 19:21

Often evangelicalism itself, instead of propagating itself by evangelism and producing changed lives, makes its stock in trade, criticism, not conversion; damning others instead of rescuing the damned.

The Word Became Flesh
(Week 32, Tuesday)

"It Is Inherent for the Christian to Propagate His Faith"
Matthew 10:7-8

We now come to the consideration of the Word become flesh and evangelism. An interesting incident took place when India's new constitution was being passed in the National Legislature. In the portion where it says that each individual has "the right to profess, practice, and propagate his faith," that word "propagate" was a question mark to many. In the midst of it, a Hindu said this, "To the Christian it is inherent to propagate his faith. If he is faithful to his faith he must propagate his faith. So if you do not allow him to propagate his faith you do not allow him to profess and practice his faith." That argument swung the situation and it was adopted. The Hindu saw clearly that to propagate our faith is inherent in being Christian. Then why don't all Christians do it? I can only testify.

I underwent a half-conversion and joined the church. A revival came on. I was urged to win someone. I tried but was rebuffed by my own lack of having anything to give. It was my first and my last attempt to win someone, until I had found something for myself. What I said was the Word become word. Then came the real thing; I found a conversion for myself, the real thing. The word of conversion became flesh. Then conversions began to happen right and left....

When I tried to win others with the word of conversion become word, it was a failure. When the Word became flesh, it was a success.

The Word Became Flesh
(Week 43, Sunday)

I Know That My Redeemer Liveth
Acts 5:40-42

We are looking at the motive for missions and evangelism. The only adequate motive is based on what God has done. God went on a mission, was the first missionary; God came to us to redeem us. Then when we do the same, we are in line with what God has done and is doing. God is still coming; God is still a missionary and an evangelist. God asks us to do only what God has done and is still doing. When God stops missionary activities so will I. Until then I keep on, not specially elated by success nor depressed by failure; they are irrelevant. To be true to what I see God doing in Jesus Christ is the only relevancy.

The Word Became Flesh
(Week 44, Wednesday)

FORGIVENESS

Untangling Our Lives
Matthew 5:9-15, 23-26; Romans 12:18

Whether sinned against or sinning, the Christian is under obligations to take the initiative in settling the dispute.

But you say, "I can't forgive." Then may I say it very quietly, but very solemnly: You can never, never be forgiven. "But if you don't forgive others, neither will your Father forgive your sins" (Matt 6:15). Do you not remember that in the Lord's Prayer we pray, "Forgive us of our trespasses, as we forgive those who trespass against us"? So if you do not forgive, you ask not to be forgiven. In refusing forgiveness to others you have broken down the bridge over which you yourself must pass, namely, forgiveness.

Victorious Living
(Week 6, Sunday)

The Mark of Jesus: Forgiveness of Injuries
Mark 11:25-26; Luke 11:4; Ephesians 4:32; Colossians 3:13

The sublimest prayer that was ever prayed, for it embodied the sublimest spirit ever shown, was the prayer, "Father, forgive them; for they know not what they do" (Luke 23:34). Sir John Seeley says that the outstanding distinguishing mark of a Christian is willingness to forgive injuries (see Sir John Robert Seeley, *Ecco Homo* [Boston: Roberts Brothers, 1968])....

Now you are to be branded—branded, mind you, with the spirit of forgiveness of injuries. It is going deep, deep; never again will you retaliate or harbor resentments.

Retaliation and harboring of resentments belong to a dead past—gone forever!

Abundant Living
(Week 46, Wednesday)

Cleanse Your Past
Luke 19:9-10

God forgives you; you must forgive yourself. Bury it all at the foot of the cross, and put "No Resurrection" over it. The past is buried. Its effects may carry over into the present, but it, itself, is buried. God can help you counteract and cancel even those continuing effects by starting new redemptive influences. God restores the years that the caterpillar and the locusts have eaten.

The Way
(Week 12, Sunday)

God Forgives You; You Forgive Others
Philippians 2:1-5

Since God forgives you, you can forgive others. But if you shut off others from your forgiveness, then you shut off yourself from God's forgiveness. The wonder of God's forgiveness to us should send us out joyously to forgive others.

The Way
(Week 16, Saturday)

For Thine Is the Kingdom
Luke 11:20; 1 Corinthians 15:25; Jude 24-25

We are to ask God to forgive us on condition that we forgive others [see Matt 6:9-13]. If we do not forgive others, then we can never, never be forgiven. We have broken down the "forgiveness" bridge over which we must pass. This necessity for giving forgiveness if you are to get it is the only portion of the prayer upon which Jesus turns and comments. He thus showed the importance he attached to this matter, vital importance. And note that the forgiveness we are to give others is past, not future—as we "ourselves have forgiven" (v. 12 Moffatt). The basis of expectancy of forgiveness is the fact that we have already forgiven others.

The Way
(Week 30, Monday)

The Seven Pillars of the Christian Faith
John 1:1-5

[Jesus] did not come to announce the forgiveness of God; he was the forgiveness of God. The word of forgiveness became flesh in him. He did not come to announce God's love to humanity; he was that Love.

The Way to Power and Poise
(Week 9, Sunday)

Outer Assurances of Forgiveness
Luke 15:20-24

And now the drama of redemption shifts from the [prodigal] son to the father: "But when he was still far away, his father saw him and felt pity for him and ran to fall upon his neck and kiss him" (Luke 15:20 Moffatt). He saw him "when he was still far away," for, day by day, he had watched that road, early and late, believing that the son would come back. He didn't go after him; there must be no compulsion. The son went on his own and would have to return on his own. But oh, the infinite sympathy; sympathy in its root meaning, "suffering with"!

The father couldn't go into the far country, but he could go a long way down that road when once he was assured that the son was through with the far country. And the old man running down the road with his beard flying and the tears falling down his face like the summer rain is the most touching scene in history. Jesus looks up, in repeating the story, as much as to say "That's God." And it is!

The father let the prodigal repeat his confession, for that confession was catharsis. It had to get up and out. But the father never allowed him to finish it: "Make me as one of thy hired servants" (v. 21); that was choked off. There must be no unreal talk of being a servant: This is my son, my son still! "Quick," he said, "bring the best robe"—the outer sign befitting a son; "give him a ring for his hand"—the ring as the sign of authority; "and sandals for his feet"—only slaves went with bare feet, a son, no; "and bring the fatted calf"—saved for a special guest on a special occasion. And this was it!

Why these outer signs of the father's forgiveness and restoration? Would his word of forgiveness not be enough? No, the sense of guilt and inferiority and shame had gone so deep that, in addition to the word of forgiveness, there had to be these outer signs to assure him. So when we come to God in real repentance, we get outer signs of forgiveness: the robe of self-respect, the ring of authority, and the wiping out of the slave relationship. The emotions God gives are not forgiveness; they are the outer assurances of forgiveness.

How to Be a Transformed Person
(Week 17, Thursday)

Forgiveness Is Power
1 John 4:7, 11

After surrendering these resentments to God, now actively forgive those against whom you have the resentments. Not only forgive them, but tell them so. The telling them so will be the catharsis, the cleansing.

A pastor was in charge of a USO group during World War I. A woman who was jealous of his position and unspeakably nasty to him backed him in a corner and in public struck him on the cheek. He turned the other, and said, "That too, please." Said it three times. The woman was dumbfounded. She stood there helpless. The whole community was won to him and revolted against her by this simple act of forgiveness. Forgiveness is power....

Many people feel that if they don't stand up and retaliate, they will become everybody's doormat. Everybody's doormat, or everybody's temple of refuge? The chamomile plant grows fastest when it is walked on. The soul grows fastest when it has learned to give back love for hate and light for darkness. For you become what you give back.

How to Be a Transformed Person
(Week 26, Friday)

It Is for Sinners
Psalm 51:9-13

A young man in Japan leaned over the back of the bench on which I was seated and whispered, "Are you sure I am forgiven?" I assured him on the authority of the character of God in Christ that he was forgiven. A few minutes later he asked again, "Are you sure I am forgiven." I assured him that he was. A third time he asked the same question, "Are you sure I am forgiven?" The last time he really accepted my assurance. There is nothing, absolutely nothing that we want to know as much as to know whether our sins are forgiven. And there is nothing, absolutely nothing that we can say with greater assurance than that God does forgive, and that God forgives graciously and fully and finally. "Scarlet your sins may be, but they can become as snow" (Isa 1:18 Moffatt). Your very sins become white, for when you look at them, you no longer see sins, you see grace, the whiteness of grace. That indeed is deliverance.

How to Be a Transformed Person
(Week 32, Friday)

The Highest Statement of Morality
Proverbs 19:11; 24:17

[How do we move] out of resentments? Forgive others as Christ forgives you. As you stand in need of forgiveness, so give it to others. For if you refuse it to others, this blocks the forgiveness toward you. God cannot forgive the unforgiving. God's hands are tied. So if we refuse forgiveness, we break down the bridge over which we must pass, the bridge of forgiveness.

The highest statement of morality ever given on this planet of ours is this one: "Treat one another with the same spirit as you experience in Christ Jesus" (Phil 2:5 Moffatt). This transcends all Ten Commandments and goes beyond all moral codes; treat others the way Christ treats you! He forgives and forgives freely, and he forgets and forgets wholly, and he buries and buries completely....

O forgiving God, help me to forgive as freely and fully as you forgive. I do, for Jesus' sake. Amen.

Growing Spiritually
(Week 9, Friday)

Guilt Upsets the Body
Jeremiah 33:6; Malachi 4:2

So if the body is to be at its best, the soul must be clear of all haunting guilt. The most blessed fact of the Christian gospel is the offer of divine forgiveness. This is the most healing fact that can steal into the depths of personality. It pervades one as a sense of release and well-being....

When the blinded Saul heard the word of divine forgiveness, "immediately something like scales fell from his eyes and he regained his sight" (Acts 9:18). The physical symptom dropped away when the spiritual tension was released. As long as he couldn't see spiritually, he couldn't see physically. The "scales" dropped from his eyes when the guilt dropped from his soul.

Growing Spiritually
(Week 34, Thursday)

The Gospel Is God's Search for Humanity
John 1:9-13

Jesus didn't come to bring the forgiveness of God—he was the forgiveness of God.

Mastery
(Week 1, Thursday)

They Did the Most Incredible Things
Luke 9:28-31

When he [Jesus] prayed, "Father, forgive them," God could forgive because Jesus was dying for them that they might be forgiven. He answered his own prayer by making it possible for God to forgive.

Mastery
(Week 42, Monday)

Responsible for All We Know and All We Might Know
Romans 8:1-8

When we refuse to walk in the light, [Jesus] automatically shuts off the cleansing and the fellowship. But the person who is honestly walking in the light has fellowship and cleansing even though that person blunders and sins while walking in the light. If God sees the central intentions are right, God forgives and cleanses marginal mistakes and sins. God is not a mote picker; God is a maker of men and women.

Mastery
(Week 50, Saturday)

A Cleansed Conscience
John 8:10-11

The mature Christian conscience is a conscience that has been cleansed once and for all from all we have done and have been. When Christ authoritatively says, "Your sins are forgiven," the conscience accepts it and ceases to trouble us about those sins any longer. If conscience is the voice of God in the soul, then what God accepts the conscience accepts, what God forgives is forgiven by conscience, what God buries the conscience buries, and what God wipes out of the book of God's remembrance the conscience wipes out of remembrance too.

Paul puts it forcefully: "There is therefore now no condemnation for those who are in Christ Jesus" (Rom 8:1). If you are in Christ you are not in condemnation. To keep on condemning yourself for something that God has forgiven and buried is disloyalty to God.

Christian Maturity
(Week 41, Thursday)

When God Forgives, We Should Also Forgive
Romans 8:31-34

When forgiveness comes, it comes, and there is no mistaking of it. And where God is, there is forgiveness and peace.

Christian Maturity
(Week 41, Friday)

There Is No Emptiness in Love
Matthew 12:43-45

What Christ forgives, we must not dig up again. It is gone forever.

Christian Maturity
(Week 42, Sunday)

He Breaks the Power of Cancelled Sin

Forgiveness was not condoning sin, but cancelling sin by forgiveness and power. The sins are actually gone as condemnation and as present fact. They are gone! He forgives and gives—forgives the past and gives power for the present and the future.

In Christ
(Week 7, Sunday)

"In Him We Have Redemption"

Now God can forgive, for the forgiveness God offers is no longer a cheap forgiveness. It costs God to forgive. The cross is the price God pays to get to us in spite of our sins, "according to the riches of his grace which he lavished upon us" (Eph 1:7-8). This verse says "lavished." The wonder and surprise of being forgiven could only be described by the grateful heart in terms such as "freely bestowed," or "lavished." It seems incredible to everyone who receives it! Divine forgiveness is a surprise. "How could God be so generous?" "God took me—even me!" It all seems so incredible, so undeserved. Of course it is! I find myself saying to myself after fifty-seven years, "This is too good for a ransomed sinner."...All this and forgiveness and heaven too—it seems too good to be true!

In Christ
(Week 30, Wednesday)

Take Heed to Your Reactions
Luke 15:25-30

"Take heed to yourselves; if your brother sins, rebuke him, and if he repents, forgive him." (Luke 17:3). The emphasis here is upon the reactions, what you do when someone sins against you. For your reaction may color and corrode your whole life. The temptation will be to note and emphasize the person's action, the sin against you. But Jesus said your reactions are more important to you than the other's action. Your reactions can harm you, but others' actions cannot harm you unless you let them. So the reactions are more important than the other person's action. Be the Word of forgiveness and reconciliation become flesh and you are therefore unhurt by another's actions.

The Word Became Flesh
(Week 30, Friday)

Inward Conflict Chief Cause of Illness
Galatians 5:16-17

Blessed are the merciful, for they shall obtain mercy. At the heart of mercy is forgiveness. We forgive everybody for everything. And we ask forgiveness. A mission college in India was on strike for twenty-one days and the college closed. An official in the college said a rude thing to a student. The student union, which the student represented, demanded that he apologize to not only the one student but the whole student union. Over that incident, the college was closed for twenty-one days. Ask for forgiveness and give forgiveness to everybody.

The Word Became Flesh
(Week 42, Saturday)

82

Fundamental Tendencies: Forgiveness and Second Chance
1 Corinthians 1:26-30

There is a redemptive strain running through the universe. If a hillside is scarred by torrential rains, nature sets to work to cover the scars with trees and flowers. If a bone is broken, nature makes the broken place far stronger than before. Said a woman to a doctor, "With all these germs I don't see how anybody could be well"; and got the reply, "Knowing the body with all its provisions toward warding off disease and to recover when diseased, I don't see why anybody should ever be sick." There is a fundamental tendency in the universe toward forgiveness and recovery, toward redemption. That fundamental tendency came to its highest manifestation in the cross, where God identifies with our sin, takes it, and offers us forgiveness in a nail-pierced hand. As God forgives, so we are to forgive. "Treat one another as you are treated in Christ" (see Luke 6:31).

The Word Became Flesh
(Week 50, Friday)

LOVE

Growth in Love
Ephesians 3:17; Philippians 1:9; 1 Timothy 1:5; 1 John 2:5

In all our growth, we must grow in love. Unless we are growing in love, we are not growing at all.

Victorious Living
(Week 46, Friday)

Growth in the Social Application of Love
Luke 10:25-37; Ephesians 4:15; 1 John 3:17

The real test of spiritual growth is whether or not we are growing in love.

Victorious Living
(Week 46, Saturday)

The Love Motive: A Rejected Stone
1 Corinthians 13:1-3; James 1:27; 1 John 4:7, 11-12, 20-21

The demand of present day life is that love be built into the social structure. Not practicable? Then living is not practicable, for living demands love....

Only love can provide the ultimate motive for society, for it would include within itself the satisfaction of the hunger motive. For people who love one another will, if their love is real—that is to say if it is a motive determining action—cooperate for the satisfaction of one another's distinct and individual needs.

Victorious Living
(Week 50, Tuesday)

The Self-Centered and the Self-Disrupted
Romans 12:3; 10, 16; 13:9-10; James 2:8-9

There are those who think that Christianity teaches that they must love others, but not themselves. This is a mistake. Christianity teaches self-love: "You shall love your neighbor as yourself" (Matt 22:39). If you do not love yourself, you will not develop yourself. So all attempts to eliminate the "self" end in hypocrisy and disaster. If you put yourself out of the door, it will come back through the window, probably in disguise. Frankly and honestly you must love yourself—not as a master, but as a servant—for the self is a glorious servant, but a gruesome master. Those who love others and not themselves, allowing others to sap the life out of them, end in disaster.

Abundant Living
(Week 7, Monday)

Resentments Resulting in Self-Pity
Jeremiah 31:15-16; Luke 23:28; Acts 21:13

Structurally, you are made for positive good will, in other words, for the Christian way of love. When you try the other way, then the machinery of life breaks down, or at least works so badly that it leaves you exhausted and ineffective. Hate is sand in the machinery of life; love is oil, and life works better with oil than with sand. The lovers love others and themselves; the haters hate others and themselves.

Abundant Living
(Week 8, Saturday)

God Rules in Terms of Christ
John 1:1-5; 10:38; 14:7-11

In Christ, the kingdom is given not only character content, but also personal content. In him, the kingdom is no longer merely an impersonal order. When I give myself to the kingdom, I give myself to the Person who embodies that kingdom. That makes my relationships with the kingdom warm and tender and personal. I can be loyal to an order, but I cannot love it. But in Christ, it is possible both to be loyal to and to love the kingdom. For in him, the kingdom looks out at me with tender eyes, loves me with warm love, and touches me with strong, redemptive hands—it is personal.

Christ is the kingdom personalized.

Abundant Living
(Week 30, Monday)

Good Friday Meditation
John 15:13; Rom. 5:6-11, John 19:16-18

Why did Good Friday have to happen? Did it just happen or was it inevitable—inevitable in a world of this kind? It was inevitable.

It was not an accidental, marginal type of happening; it grew out of the nature of the facts. It had to happen. For it is a law of life that where love meets sin in the loved one, at the junction of that sin and that love a cross of pain is set up. It is the nature of love to insinuate itself into the sins and sorrows of the loved one and make them its own. If it does not do that, then it is not love. All love has the doom of bleeding upon it whenever the object of its love goes wrong. You may say that the guilty alone should bleed, and not the innocent—it is unjust. But, just or unjust, it is a fact.

If you would say to a mother whose son is breaking his own heart and hers by his waywardness: "Mother, it is unjust for you to suffer in this way. You are innocent; your son is guilty," would that mother not say in reply: "Suffer for my son, unjust? It is the very thing that motherhood within me demands that I should do." In the name of a legal justice would you deny that mother the privilege of being noble, of being a mother?

There is a justice higher than legal justice—a justice in which it is right for the strong, at cost to itself, to save the weak; it is right for the holy to save the unholy. This is the law of higher justice. If God is love, then, when that love meets sin in us, the loved ones, that love is bound to wear on its heart a cross of pain. It is inevitable. Good Friday is the outer cross telling us of the inner cross on the heart of God. There is a Christ picture painted in Germany during the famine days after the first World War, and the Christ is famine-stricken too. That is authentic. Christ is hungry with the hungry. He is guilty in the sinful. He makes all these "sufferings" his own. That is atonement.

In South America I was given a stone which had a cross at its center; nature formed that cross there. The cross is at the heart of our relationships; it is built into things. It is "the ground plan of the universe." Everywhere that love meets sin, love suffers. That is the meaning of the cross.

Abundant Living
Good Friday

Made for Each Other?
John 4:13-14; Galatians 5:14

You must love others in order to be able to love yourself. Apparently God has us hooked; if you don't love others, you cannot get on with others or yourself.

The Way
(Week 5, Friday)

Liking People and Loving People
Matthew 18:21-22; 35

Christians are people who love people whom they do not like. Impossible? Oh no, for they love them for what they might be when they cannot love them for what they are. They see in every person another person, the person who might become. That very love and faith helps to create that person.

The Way
(Week 16, Wednesday)

Steps out of Self-Centeredness
2 Chronicles 7:14; 26:16

Don't act as though you have no love for yourself. You do. You are bound to. The Way teaches that you are to love yourself: "You must love your neighbor as you love yourself" (Matt 22:39). A healthy self-love is legitimate and right. If you try to act as though you have no love of yourself, then self-love will dress itself up in other guises and come back again. Love yourself, healthily.

The Way
(Week 18, Friday)

The Seeking for Signs
1 Corinthians 12:4-11

We must not confound the gift of the Spirit with the gifts of the Spirit. The gift of the Spirit is for all, but the gifts of the Spirit are divided "severally as he will" (1 Cor 12:11 KJV); they are not for all. Paul makes this plain: "Are all apostles? Are all prophets? Are all teachers? Do all work miracles? Do all possess gifts of healing? Do all speak with tongues? Do all interpret?" (1 Cor 12:29-30). The answer is no!

Paul urges, "But earnestly desire the higher gifts" (v. 31). And then he goes on in the thirteenth chapter, and expounds on the higher gift of love, and adds to it this: "Make love your aim, and earnestly desire the spiritual gifts, especially that you may prophesy" (14:1). Prophecy here is not foretelling events, but forthtelling the good news. So the power to love and to share the divine love in speech, these are the gifts to desire earnestly.

The Way to Power and Poise
(Week 12, Friday)

Unity with the Unbrotherly, Even with Enemies
Romans 12:17-20

The idea that we are to be "brotherly" only to brothers and sisters runs counter to the Christian concept. Jesus said: "If you love those who love you, what reward have you?... If you salute only your brethren, what more are you doing than others?" (Matt 5:46-47). We are to give out love and only love, no matter what the other person does. If the person takes it, well and good; but if not, then love like "peace... shall return to you." You will be made loving, for you are born of the qualities that you habitually give out. The loving become lovely.

The Way to Power and Poise
(Week 20, Saturday)

I Am Nothing
John 15:12-17

Years ago, at my first meeting with Mahatma Gandhi, I read the thirteenth chapter of 1 Corinthians to him from Moffatt's translation. When I got through, there were tears in his eyes, and he exclaimed: "How beautiful, how beautiful." He organized love into a national movement for independence and made it a working force. And as we look at Gandhi's corporate translation of love in terms of a national movement for freedom, and see it in its higher manifestations, we exclaim: "How beautiful, how beautiful, and how powerful, how powerful." For this love chapter is the power chapter, a description of the only abiding power on earth. All else fades and fails; love alone abides and holds the field.

The Way to Power and Poise
(Week 24, Monday)

Singing Out of the Heart of Pain
1 John 2:9-11

To get the background of [the] thirteenth chapter of 1 Corinthians, we must be reminded that this letter was written out of pain.... This chapter is pain set to music. The heartstrings are drawn so tight by pain that they are thus tuned to the higher notes of love.

But before love can sing, it has to be cut. So it cut in the first three verses—cut away all fancy speaking in tongues of humans and of angels as a sign of the Spirit of God, cut away all boastful claims to prophetic powers and secret knowledge, cut away emphasis on miracles such as removing mountains, cut away all secret boasting about special zeal in giving and sacrificing—cut these all away unless at their basis was love. Where love is not, the Spirit is not. If the first fruit of the Spirit is not love, then the other fruits are rotten to the core. Love makes all the other fruits sound. So if the joy is not a loving joy, the peace not a loving peace, the patience not a loving patience, the kindness not a loving kindness, the goodness not a loving goodness, the faithfulness not a loving faithfulness, the gentleness not a loving gentleness, and the self-control not a loving self-control [see Gal 5:22-23], they are sterile virtues, springing from self instead of the Spirit. Love is creative and makes all the other fruits creative: the joy a contagious joy, the peace a contagious peace, and so on. Love must be the soul of every virtue, or that very virtue turns to a vice.

The Way to Power and Poise
(Week 24, Wednesday)

Love Is Always More Positive Than Negative
1 John 3:1-3

The first thing Paul says about love is that it is patient: "Love is patient" (1 Cor 13:4). The dictionary definition of patience is: "The suffering of afflictions, pain, toil, calamity, provocation, or other evil, with a calm unruffled temper; endurance without murmuring or fretfulness." The root of patience is pati (suffer). The first emphasis, then, is that love can suffer, can take it. Since love is outgoing, and since, by its very nature, it insinuates itself into the sins and sufferings of the loved ones, its very first capacity must be to be patient, to have a capacity to take suffering and sorrow patiently. The very first step takes us to the cross at once, where, in a supreme way, love showed its capacity to take on itself everything that would fall upon the loved one. So if love can go to the cross straight off, it can go anywhere. It meets the supreme test, and all the other tests have been met in this initial test.

The Way to Power and Poise
(Week 24, Thursday)

Love Has No Inferiority Complex
1 John 4:7-9

Love, being power and poise, saves you from the depths and from the false heights that drop you into the depths. For the person who loves another cannot, by the nature of things, be jealous of the other. And the person who loves himself as he loves his neighbor, can neither despise himself nor attempt to put undue value on himself. For the love of the Spirit within makes that person know that he or she is not worthless, but worthwhile; and that same love of the Spirit gives a sense of deep humility that precludes all boastfulness. Maimonides, a noted, twelfth-century Jewish rabbi, said: "Humility is the mean between arrogance and self-abasement." Love is humility, so it is neither up nor down; it is even.

The Way to Power and Poise
(Week 25, Sunday)

A Christian Pulse Beat
Matthew 22:36-40

When Jesus says that the supreme thing in life is to love God and others, human relationships say the same thing. You would expect them to say that the Second Commandment—"You shall love your neighbor as thyself"—is obviously right; but the first—"You shall love the Lord your God"—is not so obvious (Matt 22:37, 39). But it is becoming increasingly obvious, for one of the first things in life is to break the tyranny of self-preoccupation; a self-preoccupied with itself is unhappy and disrupted. And there are no exceptions, even if it is a religious preoccupation. Something must lift you out of yourself and make you love something beyond yourself. Only love to God can do that. That is as necessary for human nature as breathing. If you don't love something beyond yourself supremely, you will be suffocated by yourself. Then, unless you give love to your neighbor, you can't get along with yourself or your neighbor....

The psychologists who love God and people are integrated and happy people; but the psychologists who are fundamentally pagan are, on the whole, disrupted and peculiar. They get caught in the meshes of a method and don't get to the message of the Man, Christ! There is no new center of attachment, nothing eternal to tie to. In spite of all learning, you have to love God and neighbor or you cannot get along with yourself or anybody else. Science is gaining faith through its fingertips. Life works in one way— God's way—or not at all.

How to Be a Transformed Person
(Week 15, Tuesday)

89

Life-Affirming and World-Affirming
1 John 4:9-10

"God so loved the world": that is important, for if the world is the object of God's love, then it is the object of God's redemption. Salvation is not redemption from the world of people and things; the world of people and things are to be redeemed. This sets the love of God at the place where it is most needed, at the heart of the world of people and things. This turns the dynamic of religion into redemption of the world, instead of release from the world.

How to Be a Transformed Person
(Week 18, Tuesday)

Love Yourself—in God
1 Peter 1:8-9

We come now to [another] step in our gaining freedom from ourselves. . . . Now that you have surrendered yourself to God, you can love yourself in God. A great many are afflicted with self-hate, and to hate yourself is as bad as to hate others. Now self-loathing must give way to self-acceptance, which is permitting oneself to be loved by God. You accept yourself and love yourself just as you love your neighbor. C. G. Jung, the psychiatrist, puts it this way: "The acceptance of oneself is the essence of the moral problem and the epitome of a whole outlook upon life" (*Modern Man in Search of a Soul* [London: Routledge, 2001], 240). That I feed the hungry, that I forgive an insult, or that I love my enemy in the name of Christ; all these are undoubtedly great virtues. What I do to the least of my brothers and sisters, I do to Christ. But what if I should discover that the least among them all—the poorest of all the beggars, the most impudent of all the offenders, the very enemy itself—that these are within me, and that I myself stand in need of the alms of my own kindness—that I myself am the enemy who must be loved—what then?"

Now since you are able to live with God, you are able to live with yourself, to be at home with yourself and rather like yourself. For loving Someone beyond yourself, and more than yourself, you are now free to love yourself.

How to Be a Transformed Person
(Week 28, Saturday)

I'm Going to Do Something About It
Ephesians 5:5-6

The unveiled face means that you surrender yourself, transfer the center from yourself to Christ. Christ uses you. You are the recipient of grace. And grace touches the springs of love within you. You love in return. Now you can say, with the little boy who said to his father, "Daddy, I love you and I'm going to do something about it." So you can say, "Jesus, I love you and I'm going to do something about it." The doing springs out of the loving and the loving springs out of surrender. For you don't love a person until you inwardly surrender to that person. You don't love Christ until you completely surrender to him.

How to Be a Transformed Person
(Week 50, Friday)

The Word of Love Made Flesh
1 John 4:11-12

The transforming power of love is not only the most effective way of transforming men and situations; it is also beneficial to the person doing the transforming. It is psychologically sound.

All the problems of psychology revolve around the problem of self preoccupation. Love, by taking you out of yourself, is therefore the best therapeutic that could be devised by divine wisdom. Paul says: "If I am in distress, it is in the interests of your comfort and salvation; if I am comforted, it is in the interests of your comfort" (2 Cor 1:6 Moffatt). Here was a "distress" "in the interests of," and a "comfort" "in the interests of"; both of them—distress and comfort—lifting him outside himself. Distress might have left him in self-centered misery, a miserable man; comfort might have left him in smug self-centered satisfaction; but now whatever happened to him left him with the right center—something outside himself.

Here is the blessing and the blight of some modern movements centered around broadcasting love to everybody. Meetings in which love is mentally broadcast to everybody are popular.

This is psychologically helpful up to a certain point, in that you are thinking in terms of others. But it can leave a subtle blight, in that this may take the place of loving people in concrete situations and providing help in concrete situations. It may and does produce a sentimental type of spirituality that loves everybody in general and nobody in particular. The word of love broadcast remains a word, not the Word become flesh. Jesus did not sit on a hillside broadcasting love to everybody. That would have been the Word become word. He loved people with concrete acts of healing, of feeding, of teaching, and of dying for men. That was the Word become flesh.

Broadcasting love to everybody doesn't produce movements, except movements for further emotion. Creative movements come out of creative thinking, and creative praying resulting in concrete acts in concrete situations for actual people. Loving in the air may leave you up in the air without roots.

How to Be a Transformed Person
(Week 51, Friday)

Perfect Love Casteth Out Fear
1 John 4:17-18

Getting rid of fears and anxieties:...

Keep repeating to yourself this verse: "There is no fear in love; but perfect love casteth out fear" (1 John 18 KJV).

This verse is important—very important—for if there is no fear in love, then the obvious thing for me to do is to love, to love everybody and everything. Fear can come only where love is not. Where love is, fear is not. Fear turns the doors inward, narrows the soul and its contacts, and thus feeds on itself. Love turns the doors outward, broadens the soul and its contacts, and thus feeds on itself. The more loving you become, the more love you get back.

Growing Spiritually
(Week 7, Monday)

Working Out Techniques
Proverbs 25:21; Matthew 5:7, 39-41

Work out techniques for keeping resentments out of your heart and out of your relationships....

Open your heart each day to the invading spirit of love. A man writes, "Resentments come as a result of resisting the wooing of grace." Grace is always ready to invade and pervade you. Let it in.

Melt people; don't maul them. It is easier to melt a block of ice than to break it up by smiting it with a hammer.

If a little bit of love isn't effective, increase the dose. The remedy for the ineffectiveness of a little love is more love. The Chinese have a saying: "Don't try to put out the fire of a load of hay with a cup of water." Increase the dose!

When you think of someone against whom you are tempted to be resentful, breathe a prayer for that person and send your love to him or her.

The victory is in your being loving, even if the other person does not receive it. You are more loving for having loved; that is the victory. Rejoice in it.

Growing Spiritually
(Week 9, Saturday)

Everything for the Love of God
1 Corinthians. 13:1-3

Do everything you do for the love of God. You have been doing everything for the love of self; now do everything for the love of God. This changed motive will glorify everything. The menial task now becomes the meaningful task, for it is done for the love of God....

This is the deepest discipline of self I know: do everything you do for the love of God. Then you are not struggling to keep the self under [control]; you are expressing the self on another level with another motive. Then the self partakes of the glorifying of the task; the self itself is also glorified.

Growing Spiritually
(Week 11, Saturday)

The First Fruit Is Love
Psalm 73:25-26

Having the Spirit within results in qualities of being with [many] characteristics. And the first one is "love." This emphasis on the prime significance of love fits in with Paul's emphasis in 1 Cor 13:13 (Moffatt): "Thus faith and hope and love last on, these three, but the greatest of all is love. Make love your aim, and then set your heart on spiritual gifts." The primacy of love in the spiritual life is not an arbitrary, imposed condition; it is inherent. If you have the Spirit, you have love, and if you do not have love, you do not have the Spirit. And this love is not an occasional attitude manifested toward those who love you, but a characteristic attitude of life. Love is the first outcome of the Spirit within, and if it is lacking, everything is lacking.

To grow spiritually is to grow in love. Without love all other growth is a cancer growth, consuming instead of constructing.

Growing Spiritually
(Week 18, Monday)

Smashing and Melting
John 15:9; Romans 5:6

According to the Christian faith, all motives of life, if they are to be sound, are reduced to one motive: love. And this love must not be love in general; it must be love of a specific kind—the love of Christ. The greatest of Christians said, "I am controlled by the love of Christ." This cuts deep. It is possible to be controlled by the love of achievement, of success, of a cause, of one's fight. To be controlled by the love of Christ is different in not only degree but kind and quality.

Growing Spiritually
(Week 18, Thursday)

The Love of God Is upon All Flesh
Ephesians 5:2; 1 Thessalonians 4:9

The pattern for your loving is God's loving. God loves us, not merely for what we are, but for what God sees we can be. God loves that potential person into being. God, therefore, can love the unlovable, for God sees the possible lovable. We can love the same way. We can love people not for what they are, but for what we see they can be. And by our love we tend to produce the person we see; we love it into being....Jesus looked at the inwardly clashing, tempestuous Saul and loved into being the dedicated and harmonious Paul. Love is creative; it faiths faith out of the faithless, believes belief out of the beliefessness, and loves love out of the loveless.

The love of a man is upon his friends, but the love of God is upon all flesh. For the love of God turns flesh into spirit and turns spirit into creative spirit. Then love all, despair of none; and if we are let down, we are not let down, for we end up more loving.

Growing Spiritually
(Week 19, Monday)

One Remedy: Self Surrender
Matthew 22:34-40

Surrender yourself completely to God, for without this surrender there is no love. A woman came up to me at the close of a meeting, and said: "I've found you out. You've got only one remedy: self-surrender." I laughed and told her that she was right, for I had found myself out; I did have only one remedy....If you understand the meaning of the attitude of losing yourself in the interests of others, you know how to live. Life takes on rhythm, harmony. If you don't know this self-losing, then life gets tangled in the flypaper of its own self-interest.

Love can take place only where there is self-surrender. Between persons no love can spring up unless there is mutual self-surrender. If either one withholds the self, then love cannot come into being. It is automatically blocked. If this is true between persons, it is also true between the divine and the human. You cannot love God unless you surrender to God. And you cannot love God perfectly unless you surrender to God perfectly.

Growing Spiritually
(Week 19, Friday)

First Bind the Strong Man
2 Corinthians 2:14-16

How does the Holy Spirit bind the strong man? By stout ropes of increased inner resolution? No, by the silken cords of love. When we surrender the self to God, the Holy Spirit gently unfastens the cords of love, which the self had entwined around itself, and fastens them upon Jesus. The Holy Spirit makes us love Jesus. And in loving him, the self is freed from self-preoccupation. Really free to love, to serve, to create, and to fulfill its destiny.

Mastery
(Week 14, Sunday)

Two Methods of Binding the Strong Man
Colossians 3:12-15

When we allow the Holy Spirit to bind the strong man by the cords of love to Jesus, then his goods may be taken easily. Then temper, pride, covetousness, irritability, and rampant sex drop away as irrelevant. A consuming love for Christ takes possession of us, and by the "expulsive power of a new affection" (Thomas Chalmers, 1857), these lesser loves are cast out. We love something, Someone, better.

Mastery
(Week 14, Monday)

I Do Not Frustrate the Grace of God
Romans 12:19-21

I was about to go into a situation that had baffled me. It was all tied up with resentments and clashes. As I sat writing in a plane, the Lord said, "Lay aside the writing; I want to talk to you about this situation. You are to go into it with love and nothing but love, no matter what happens." I promised I would. To my surprise, two members of the group came to me beforehand and asked forgiveness for their attitudes. Barriers began to fall. Difficulties cleared up, and there were no problems. Love dissolved them.

Mastery
(Week 33, Wednesday)

Jesus the Redeemer of Waste Material
Ephesians 5:3-10

Jesus took his greatest persecutor, Saul, transformed him into the man who could write the most beautiful thing on love that has ever been written—the thirteenth chapter of 1 Corinthians—and thus made love the greatest thing in the world. The man of hate set love at the center of virtues and illustrated it in himself. Jesus was the redeemer of waste materials.

Mastery
(Week 40, Friday)

The Mastery of Criticism and Critical Attitudes
Matthew 7:1-5

When love gets low, criticism gets high. I find in myself, whenever I get out of touch with Christ, I begin to be critical of others. But when I am in living touch with Christ and therefore filled with love, then that love hides a multitude of sins. I feel sorry for people rather than critical of them.

Mastery
(Week 41, Sunday)

Prosecutor's Stand or Witness Box?
Romans 2:17-23

We have such partial knowledge of people and their motives that we are in no position to judge them. A little boy looked through the keyhole of an operating room and saw a doctor cutting a patient. He said to the son of the doctor, "Your father is a very bad man; I saw him cutting up people." We don't know the why of people's actions, so we are in no position to judge them. Only God knows that. So we must go out to love up the good in people and love down the bad. If we fail, we are better for having tried, for we give out love and become love.

Mastery
(Week 41 Monday)

You Have Me Doing Everything
John 21:15-22

In living contact with Jesus the mood of life changes. You find yourself going out in love to everybody. The critical attitude toward life and people is dissolved when we get into living fellowship with Christ. Where there is communion with Christ, there are no critical attitudes toward others. We don't become blind to their faults, but love sees why the faults are there and pities and longs to help. Love makes you understanding. As "Mary" puts it, "I don't want to be understood as much as I want to be understanding." Then she adds to someone who had helped her, "You have been like a catalytic agent to me. You have me doing everything without you doing anything but believing in me." That last phrase is the secret of helping people: "believing in me." Those who believe in Christ believe in people and in believing in them "have [them] doing everything." [NOTE: "Mary" was a woman whose conversion and life were a great source of inspiration to E. Stanley Jones. He often quoted her in illustrations.]

Mastery
(Week 41, Tuesday)

His Word Final in Scripture
James 3:14-18; 4:1

The early Christians were simple and direct: We refuse to hate. We have been loved by God when we were enemies, and we will love our enemies into friends. If not, we are the better for loving. If we are killed, so what? We don't have to live; we can die. And dying we live forevermore. It worked, and won! They were invincible as long as they kept to their principles.

Mastery
(Week 45, Wednesday)

Nobody but Me and Jesus
John 16:31-33

I can testify; I know Jesus better than I know any other person in the world. And he knows me better than anyone else in the world knows me, and he still loves me.

Mastery
(Week 50, Monday)

Jesus in a Cosmic Setting
Hebrews 1:1-3

The Incarnation is the incredible...love. If love is at the heart of God, then you can expect God to do anything, anything that love would do. And love did this: he who was the Cosmic became the Carpenter.

Christian Maturity
(Week 2, Thursday)

God Is Light on Four Things
Romans 1:19-20

Since God is love, it is the nature of love to create. For love wants beings with whom it can share that love. Parents create because they want children upon whom they can lavish their love and from whom they can receive love in return. God, the Heavenly Parent, is love, and therefore wants children upon whom God can lavish love and receive love in return.

Christian Maturity
(Week 7, Wednesday)

Self-Abasement
1 Corinthians 4:1-4

If you love God supremely, you can love yourself subordinately. Love yourself and like yourself and enjoy yourself. For it is a self accepted by God and therefore accepted by you. The renounced self becomes, strangely enough, the realized self.

Christian Maturity
(Week 8, Wednesday)

Perfection, Not in Character but in Love
John 21:15-17

The Christian position is the only mature position. It is free from perfectionism and from pessimism. It offers a perfection that is possible, namely, a perfection in love. Not a perfection in character. We are only Christians-in-the-making. But we can be perfect in love. And a maturity in love is possible and consistent with a great deal of imperfection in character. You can love God with all your heart, with all your mind, with all your soul, and with all your strength, and yet manifest that love imperfectly.

Christian Maturity
(Week 12, Saturday)

We Could Reap What God Sowed
Isaiah 53:4-6

The One that made love, shall that One not love? And the One that put the deep principle—that all love suffers when there is sin in the loved one—shall that One not suffer when love comes into contact with the sin in us, the loved ones? At the junction of that love and that sin would not a cross of pain be set up, inevitably?

Christian Maturity
(Week 14, Wednesday)

The Cross Lights Up the Nature of God
Romans 5:9-11

If God is love and it is the nature of love to take on itself the burdens and sorrows and sins of the loved ones, would God's love not crimson into suffering as that love meets sin in us, the loved ones? Would there not be an unseen cross upon the heart of God, God being what God is and we being what we are?

But God is a spirit and I am bounded by my flesh. How could I know that there is an unseen cross upon the heart of God? How could I know it, except God show me, show me by an outer cross that there is an inner cross upon God's heart? Has that happened? Yes. The outer cross lifted up on a hilltop called Calvary is the outer cross through which I see the inner cross upon the heart of God. The cross lights up the nature of God as love. Through it, I see that at very center of the universe is redeeming love. No greater discovery could be made, or will be made, than that. That is the ultimate in discoveries.

Christian Maturity
(Week 14, Thursday)

Lack Love and You Lack Maturity
Luke 10:25-28

We are as mature as we are mature in love, and no more mature. We may be mature in knowledge, but if we are not mature in love, we are immature human beings. We may be mature in religious practices and outlook, but if we are immature in love we are immature. Our maturity is maturity in love, or it is immaturity.

This is the central and consistent message of the New Testament. Its message is consistent from Jesus, through Paul, through Peter, through John. The finality of love as the highest characteristic of character is the same through all four of these men. There is no wavering, no equivocation, no hesitation; love is central in God and must be central in people. There is nothing, absolutely nothing, that can take its place. Lack love and you lack maturity, no matter what else you may have beside. Nothing can atone for that lack.

Jesus, God's final Word to humanity, made love the final thing in character. When a scribe asked Jesus: "Which commandment is the first of all?" the ages and all heaven must have bent over to listen to his reply, for his answer would fix in the mind of all humanity the chief quality in character. A misstep here, and all the ages would go wrong with him, and go wrong in the most important thing in living, the main emphasis in character. But Jesus did not go wrong. He unerringly picked out two commandments from among the thirty-six hundred that the Jewish law prescribed for conduct, and those two emphasize the same thing: "You shall love" (Matt 22:36-39). Suppose he had picked out some good thing instead of the best thing, for instance: "You shall be just"; "You shall be merciful"; "You shall be kind." Suppose he had chosen any good thing instead of this highest thing. Then the history of humanity would have been different, and humanity itself would have been impoverished. He sounded a clarion note, "You shall love," and all the ages, whether they have obeyed it or not, have echoed a deep "Amen."

Christian Maturity
(Week 15, Sunday)

First Commandment: Love!
Matthew 5:43-46

We have considered Jesus' emphasis on the primacy of love. We must look further and see not only the primacy of love, but the sweep of this love. It is not only primary, it embraces the total person, loving God totally and neighbor and self equally. Never was love so complete in its sweep and so deep in its depths as here defined in a few swift words: "You shall love the Lord your God with all your heart, and with all your soul, and with all your mind, and with all your strength" (Mark 12:30). Note that the total person is to love God totally "with all your heart"—the affectional nature; "with all your soul"—the volitional, deciding nature; "with all your mind"—the intellectual nature; "with all your strength"—the physical nature. The whole person is to love God wholly—no part left out.

Note that Jesus put in "with all your mind." It was not in the quotation from Deuteronomy 6:5. That addition was important. It annexed the whole world of science, philosophy, and psychology in a single phrase. Had that phrase been left out, Christianity would have been on the edges of the modern world looking wistfully in, but not at home. Now it is at home in the world of science and investigation.

Christian Maturity
(Week 15, Monday)

Perfect Standard and Perfect Content
Philippians 2:5-11

"Love one another as I have loved you" (John 15:12) is the high-water mark of human conduct in the ethical history of humankind. What philosophers, moralists, and religious thinkers have reached after through the ages, Jesus distilled in a sentence. They cannot utter that sentence, because the sentence isn't a verbal sentence, it is a vital sentence. The content of the most beautiful life that has ever been lived has gone into it. No one else can utter it, for it can't be uttered, it has to be lived. That sentence is vascular. Cut it and it will bleed, will bleed with the lifeblood of the Son of God. Thirty-three years of unstained living and loving have come into it. And more, the cross has gone into it. And more still, the resurrection has gone into it. It is suffering love, but it is also triumphant love. That love won out in the end. And it will win out—in the end. It is the purest and most potent power in the universe, the love of Christ.

Christian Maturity
(Week 16, Sunday)

The Love Is the Victory
John 15:17-19

James, with his intense interest in pragmatic values, picks out one law as the "royal law," the law that governs all laws: "You shall love your neighbor as yourself" (Jas 2:8). He fails to put in the moral royal law: "You shall love the Lord your God with all your heart..."; hence his epistle lacks height as well as depth. It is more horizontal than vertical. It is not "an epistle of straw," as Martin Luther said, for there is much grain here. But failing to include love to God as the supreme impulse, thereby creating faith as the working force, James puts in works toward others as the working force. His social passion is needed, but it lacks the reinforcement and motive of a supreme love to God.

Christian Maturity
(Week 17, Thursday)

Taste of Love in Fruits of Spirit
Ephesians 5:1-2

All the fruits of the Spirit (Gal 5:22-23) have the taste of love in them: joy is the joy of love; peace is love grown quiet; patience is love stretched out; kindness is love with hands outstretched; goodness is love relating itself to the moral law; faithfulness is love holding steady amid everything; gentleness is love expressing itself in relationships; self-control is love in charge within.

Christian Maturity
(Week 17, Saturday)

Love—the Alpha and the Omega
1 Thessalonians 5:9-10

The incarnation was an incarnation of love. And that incarnation revealed something that lay back in the nature of things, in God. Jesus showed us that by revealing love in himself, he was revealing love as the very heart of reality. It was not a chance note; it was the dominant note in the music of the spheres.

The "thisness" of the discussion and description of love [in 1 John] makes love take shoes and walk, and walk where we walk, along the dusty roads of life. You cannot get into a single situation where "this" does not apply. For "this" scattered twenty-nine times [throughout the epistle] is saying that "this" is that which lies back in reality.

Christian Maturity
(Week 18, Sunday)

Is Agape Too High?
Luke 7:44-48

We are certain that according to the Christian revelation God is agape. Jesus Christ is incarnate agape. He also made agape the first and second commandments. Paul, Peter, and John made agape supreme; the cross, which is the center of that revelation, is a revelation of agape, the first fruit of the Spirit of love. There is nothing more certain than that agape love is at the center of the Christian faith. If love turns out not to be central in life, then Christianity turns out marginal.

The question then arises, is love central in us? Is it in the very make-up of our being? Are we made by love for love, and can we live without it? Is the demand for love written not merely in the Scriptures but also in us? Do the texts of Scripture and the textures of our lives speak the same thing? And is that same thing a demand—an insistent demand—for love? If so, we are on solid ground in this business of human living. If Christianity and the inmost basic demands of human nature are at cross-purposes, demanding opposite things, then we are in trouble—deep trouble, life trouble. But if they turn out to be the same, then we can be all-out Christians.

Christian Maturity
(Week 22, Thursday)

To Love and Be Loved: Basic Urge
1 Thessalonians 4:9-10

We purse the thought that the urge to love and be loved is the basic urge in human nature. We can readily see that this is so. For if the self has no love as its basic outlook and drive, it is a disrupted self. Every loveless self is an unhappy, unfulfilled self. And this does not work here and there; it works everywhere: in all nations, in all ages, in all sexes, and in all situations. And it works with an almost mathematical precision. Without love the self withers; with love the self blooms. Then love is the sine qua non for the self.

Christian Maturity
(Week 22, Saturday)

Made in the Image of Love
Genesis 1:26-27

Christianity teaches us that God made us in God own image. According to that same Christian faith, God is love. Not that God loves, but that God is basically love and would violate his the divine nature acting in any way contrary to love. When God made us in God's image, would God not make us in the image of love? Would God not stamp love as the deepest thing in human nature? God, being love, would have to make love basic in any created beings. It could not be otherwise.

Christian Maturity
(Week 23, Sunday)

102

The Self-Urge Decides
2 Peter 1:3-8

We have been saying that the Christian faith, as well as the psychiatric and the humanistic approaches, all converge upon the fact that love is the basic urge and the basic need in life. If so, the question arises: Why don't we live by love? Why is there so much hate and resentment among human beings? When we give vent to our natures, why doesn't love come out? When we do give vent, don't selfishness and hate come out more often than not?

This brings us to the crux of our problem. The answer seems to be that the self-urge can decide in which direction the deeper and more basic urges can go. Love is that deepest urge, but self is the deciding urge. The freedom of the personality lies in the self-urge. The self is free to choose. It can direct the love urge. It can entwine this love urge around itself. In that case self-love becomes dominant; the personality becomes self-centered. In that case agape becomes eros and is prostituted to lower ends. An unhappy, self-centered person results.

Christian Maturity
(Week 23, Friday)

Faith Working through Love
2 Corinthians 5:14-15

The Christian faith does not need protection; it needs proclamation. It is its own defense. You don't have to protect the sun because someone throws mud at it. The sun shines and is its own protection. But [some] nervous souls are always trying to steady the ark. If they would go out and love everybody, that would be a protection of the Christian faith for it would be a proclamation of that faith.

Our faith must work by love. Love is the applied edge of that faith. It is faith in shoes; faith going out to serve the least, the last, the lost. When our faith works by love, then that shows that we have faith in love. If we perish loving, we perish; we have no other way. It is love or nothing. We will not call in hate and force to fill in where we feel that love will fail. For love never fails. Everything that has no love in it is doomed to failure; love never fails.

Christian Maturity
(Week 32, Friday)

Love in Shoes
1 John 4:20-21

To see whether our love is mature love, agape love, put I in the place of love in a portion of Paul's description of love in 1 Cor 13:4-7: "I am patient and kind; I am not jealous or boastful; I am not arrogant or rude. I do not insist on my own way; I am not irritable or resentful; I do not rejoice at wrong, but rejoice in the right. I bear all things, believe all things, hope all things, endure all things." How do I come out? Are I and love identical? Our growth in maturity is a growth in that very identification.

Christian Maturity
(Week 49, Monday)

Running Away from Life

Can life separate us [from the love of Christ]? Life can be a more effective separator than death. You can become afraid of life, step out of it, retreat into yourself, and disintegrate. If you become a self-preoccupied person, you will be separated from the love of God in Christ Jesus our Lord. Life can separate you from that love, if life can induce you to attempt to live life in yourself.

This retreat from life into yourself can easily be accomplished. Fear of life and failure can induce you to do it....

If we stay in the love of God in Christ we have learned to face up to life; we are afraid of nothing, for in Christ we are adequate for anything. As long as we stay in him, life cannot separate us.

In Christ
(Week 8, Saturday)

In Me...in You

I can understand why I should abide in [Christ], for he is divine. He is the center of authority and power and redemption. I was made by him and for him, so he is my home. To abide in him is where I ought to be. But for him to abide in me—that's different. Why should He? What does he get out of it? What? Except problems and heartaches? With some occasional satisfactions from our response and development in the new life. Then why should he do it and do it, not as occasional whim of wanting to drop in to see how we are getting along, but with a settled intention of abiding in us through thick and thin, abiding in us forever? The only answer seems to be that being love it is the nature of love to want to create and develop and to be with the loved one.

Evidently God wants to recreate and develop us into God's own divine image, and Christ can do that only from within. He wants to create strong persons who can talk with him face to face, can work with him shoulder to shoulder, and can share the same life and outlook and dreams.

In Christ
(Week 14, Friday)

Abiding in Love

If we are not manifesting our abiding in [Christ] by being a loving person, we are not abiding in him. If our contacts with people are not love contacts, then we have no contact with Christ. It is a simple test, but very profound and important. Some hold that we are abiding in Christ if we have correct views about Christ—if we are orthodox; some hold that we are abiding in Christ if we have correct conduct—if we are orthoprax. Neither of these, though both are important, is the supreme test. The supreme test is: Do I manifest love in all the manifestations of my life? If not, then to the degree that I do not, I am not in him, I am in something else.

Even this must be further qualified: it is not enough to be in love; we must be in a certain kind of love: "This is my commandment, that you love one another as I have loved you." (John 15:12.)

In Christ
(Week 17, Saturday)

Someone Who Is Mad after Jesus

There is ... an indeed freedom that leads you to an indeed bondage. A Muslim said to me one day, "You Christians are too free. We have to pray five times a day, but you don't have to. You are too free." I replied, "But after you pray your five times, you are off duty. I'm never off duty, for I pray without ceasing. And interestingly enough, I want to pray without ceasing. This is a sweet bondage."

This freedom in Christ is a freedom to choose a deeper and deeper bondage. Love is never off duty. There are no moral holidays in being a Christian. You surrender your all to Christ.

In Christ
(Week 28, Monday)

Seeing God through Imperfect Media
Hebrews 1:1-2

A life came among us and lived publicly for thirty-three years. We no longer see the word love in the light of our poor, partial love, but in the light of a Love that prayed for enemies upon a cross: "Father, forgive them; for they know not what they do" (Luke 23:34). The Word of love became flesh.

The Word Became Flesh
(Week 1, Thursday)

The Principle of Motherhood
John 5:39-40

Take the statement: "A new commandment I give to you, that you love one another; even as I have loved you." (John 13:34). Without the last portion, "even as I have loved you," there would have been nothing new in the commandment. The old content— the content gathered from contemporaneous life—would have remained. That content would have been eros—possessive love, and not agape—sacrificial love. Jesus put the agape content into love by his illustration of agape love. But even agape love is not the norm now; the norm is Christ-like love, which is a norm all its own, *sui generis.*

The Word Became Flesh
(Week 2, Friday)

Full of Grace and Truth
Titus 3:3-7

"And the Word became flesh and dwelt among us, full of grace and truth" (John 1:14)—"full of grace and truth." The first thing in the Christian faith is grace—an act—an act of outgoing, forgiving, redeeming grace. Grace is first, for the first thing in God is love, and grace is love in action; it is the Word of love become flesh. If grace is "unmerited favor," here, it is Love favoring us when we are not favorable, loving us when we are not lovable, accepting us when we are not acceptable, redeeming us when by all the rules of the book we are not redeemable. Grace is love applied, the Word of love become flesh. That is the distinctive thing in the Christian faith.

The Word Became Flesh
(Week 3, Wednesday)

And We Have Beheld His Glory
Luke 9:28-32

We are studying "And the Word became flesh and dwelt among us, full of grace and truth; we have beheld his glory, glory as of the only Son from the Father" (John 1:14). We have considered that grace was first and truth was second. For the first thing in God is "God is love" (1 John 4:8), and hence the outflowing of that love is grace. If the first thing in God were "God is truth," then the outflowing of that truth would be a statement on how to live life. But that would be the word become word. God as truth would mean religion as philosophy, but God as love means religion as redemption, God acting in love to save us.

The Word Became Flesh
(Week 3, Saturday)

The Real Christian, the Most Universalized Person
Ephesians 5:20-21

For the real Christian is the most universalized person on earth. Loving Christ, a Christian loves everybody, for Christians love everybody in Christ. When it was said of the early Christians: "Behold how those Christians love one another," it was only partly true. They did not only love one another, they also loved their enemies, and they loved the unlovely. When we lose Love, we will lose love. And the more you know Love, the more you will know love. Without the Word become flesh you will soon have nothing but the Word become word.

The Word Became Flesh
(Week 4, Tuesday)

What Do I Want to Know about God?
Philippians 2:5-10

And Jesus reveals the central thing in God's character: Love! "Who is in the bosom of the Father" (John 1:18). Jesus is not in the arm of the Father—God's omnipotence, or in the mind of the Father—God's omniscience. Jesus is close to the Father's heart—the revelation of God's Love. So Jesus came, stripping himself of everything as he came— omnipotence, omniscience, omnipresence—everything except love. "He emptied himself" (Phil 2:7), emptied himself of everything except love: his only protection, his only weapon, his only method. And Jesus showed that love is the only omniscience, the only omnipotence.

The Word Became Flesh
(Week 5, Sunday)

The Highest Value—Love
1 Corinthians 13:1-3

We come now to discuss something that goes to the root of the question as to whether the Christian Way is written within us. The highest thing in the Christian faith is undoubtedly love. Is love the deepest thing in us? Is it written into the necessities of our life? In the deepest necessities? So much so that we can say, "No love, no life"?

Is love the highest thing in the Christian way, its primary value emphasis? It was a great moment in the moral and spiritual history of humankind when a lawyer stood up and asked Jesus which was the greatest commandment in the Law. There were over three thousand six hundred commandments to choose from. Would he pick the wrong one, or a marginal one? If he should choose the wrong one, then the humanity following his emphasis would go wrong with him. But if he chose the right one, humanity would go right with him. The ages held its breath, for it was a breathless moment. The oral and spiritual fate of humanity trembled in the balance. He went unerringly to the highest: "You shall love." He picked out love as the highest value. And he added to the value of that highest value when he defined the supreme and subordinate objects of that love. He replied: "Love the Lord your God with all your heart, with all your soul, with all your mind, and with all your strength....The second is this: 'Love your neighbor as yourself.' There is no other commandment greater than these" (Mark 12:29-31 NEB).

First, love to God. It is not an occasional, marginal love, but, as we have noted, a love that includes the total being. Love God with all your heart—the affectional nature, with all your soul—the volitional nature, with all your mind—the intellectual nature; the total person is to love God totally. And Mark adds, "with all your strength"—the strength of the emotion, the strength of the will, the strength of the mind. And the second is: Love other persons as you love yourself. That is the highest of values: Love to God and love to other persons.

The Word Became Flesh
(Week 11, Monday)

Is Science Coming Out to the Supremacy of Love?
1 Corinthians 13:8-13

We have seen that love is the supreme value in the Christian faith, consistently so. So if we work from Revelation down, we come to love as the supreme thing in God and humans. That is the verdict of Revelation. What is the verdict as we work up the other way, from the facts up and out to conclusions? Is some other value turning out to be the supreme value as we apply the scientific method of experimentation leading to verified knowledge? Or is scientific investigation leading to the same conclusion that love is the supreme value in human nature?

In one of my books, *Christian Maturity*, I took the position that the human personality is as mature as it is mature in love, and no more. One may be mature in culture and knowledge and in ability, but if one is immature in love, that person is an immature personality. And the psychologists are increasingly agreeing.

The Word Became Flesh
(Week 11, Wednesday)

What Is the Nature of Life?
1 John 4:20-21

Jesus said, "I give you a new commandment: love one another; as I have loved you, so you are to love one another." (John 13:34 NEB). The phrase that makes the difference is, "as I have loved you." This is the Word of love become flesh. It gives a criterion of what love is; it is to love as Christ loved. That puts content into the word love. Science can call it "cooperation" or "mutual support," but that leaves love thin and undefined. For "cooperation" and "mutual support" may mean cooperation and mutual support in any enterprise supposed to bring benefits upon each other: good, bad, indifferent. But "as I have loved you" gives a standard, sets by example. So no human exhortation to love is sufficient unless it is seen what we mean by love in the divine exhibition. The Word made flesh must illuminate the Word become word. Science is earthbound by earth meanings without the divine revelation of heavenly meanings.

The Word Became Flesh
(Week 12, Sunday)

Eros and Agape Contrasted
John 13:34-35

Eros is acquisitive desire and longing. Agape is sacrificial giving. Eros is an upward movement. Agape comes down. Eros is our way to God. Agape is God's way to us. Eros is our effort; it assumes that salvation is our own work. Agape is God's grace; salvation is the work of divine love. Eros is egocentric love, a form of self-assertion, even if it is of the highest, noblest kind. Agape is unselfish love; it seeks not its own, it gives itself away. Eros seeks to gain its life, a divine immortalized life. Agape lives the life of God, therefore dares to lose it. Eros is the will to get and possess, which depends on want and need. Agape is freedom in giving, which depends on wealth and plenty. Eros is primarily human love; God is the object of eros. Even when it is attributed to God, eros is patterned on human love. Agape is primarily God's love; God is agape. Even when it is attributed to humans, agape is patterned on divine love. Eros is determined by the quality, the beauty, the worth of its object; it is not spontaneous, but evoked, motivated. Agape is sovereign in relation to its object and is directed to both the evil and the good; it is spontaneous, overflowing, unmotivated. Eros recognizes value in its object and loves it. Agape loves and creates value in its object.

The Word Became Flesh
(Week 13, Tuesday)

Why Did God Create Us Free?
Genesis 1:26-27

We continue our meditations on the cross as the revelation of the heart of reality. I have often wondered why God dared to create us and to create us free. It was a risky business for God and the creatures created. To make us free would mean that God would have to be limited. God would have to step back and allow that free will to operate. God could not coerce it, if so the will would not be free. And the will would have to be free in both directions; it must be free to choose evil as well as good or it would not be free. To be able to choose in one direction only is not freedom. But suppose that will should go wrong; it would break its own heart and the heart of God too. For God would have to live alongside that straying, rebellious will as love. And it is the nature of love to insinuate itself into the sins and sorrows of the loved one and make them its own. If love stays out of the sins and sorrows of the loved one, it is no longer love. But if it gets in, it bleeds. All love has the doom of bleeding upon it as long as there is sin in the loved one.

God, the all-knowing, must have known this. Then why did God care? Well, why do parents create children? It is a risky business on their part to bring into the world children who might go astray and break their own hearts and the hearts of the parents. Then why do parents create? Simply because it is the nature of love to create objects of love upon which it can lavish love and be loved in return. Love by its very nature is bound to create. But the parents say, consciously or subconsciously, "If anything falls on that child, it will fall on us. Its joys will be our joys, its sorrows our sorrows, its sins our sins." Was it different in God, our Parent? Not if God were love. God saw the risk and took it on one condition, that anything that falls on us would fall on God also. God would bear our sin and sorrow in God's own body.

The Word Became Flesh
(Week 14, Tuesday)

Love with Love Unlimited
Matthew 5:43-48

Jesus breaks down another division—the division of dividing love—loving your neighbor and hating your enemy. And also the loving of those who love you and hating those who hate you. It must be love unlimited. He reminded his followers that that is the way God loves; God makes the sun to rise on the evil and the good and sends rain on the just and unjust. God loves with love unlimited; and if you love that way only, "so can you be children of your heavenly Father" (Matt 5:45 NEB).

This going down to the bedrock of undivided and undiscriminating love hits at the central division in human personality, loving only those who return love. This discriminating love is not even love, for it has a worm of self-interest eating at its heart. So it is self-defeating. You have to love with love unlimited or you don't love. For limited love is unlimited selfishness. One who loves only those who love in return really does not love the other persons; all one loves is what comes back from the other person, which is in essence, self-love, not love but selfishness.

And this kind of love Jesus expounds is not an imposition upon life from a high-sounding sage or potentate seated on a dictating throne of the universe; it is the actual revelation of God's character and conduct. That is what God is and does. And this kind of love in God and persons is the only kind that will save the world.

The Word Became Flesh
(Week 22, Tuesday)

The Divine Illustration
Mark 1:16-20

Jesus did not prove how pain and sorrow in the universe could be compatible with the love of God—he took on himself at the cross everything that spoke against the love of God, and through that pain and tragedy and sin showed the very love of God.

The Word Became Flesh
(Week 51, Tuesday)

PRAYER

Establish the Prayer Habit
Psalm 5:3; Luke 11:1-13; Acts 3:1; Ephesians 6:18; Colossians 4:2

The first discipline must be to establish the prayer habit.... Fix the habit, even if you have to get up earlier to do it....

Don't fool yourself into saying that you don't need the particular time and place, that you will find God all the time and everywhere. If you are to find God all the time, you must find God some time; and if you are to find God everywhere, you will have to find God somewhere. That sometime and somewhere will be the special prayer time and the special prayer place. Fix them. And, as you do, you put your feet upon the road that leads to victory.

Victorious Living
(Week 9, Wednesday)

We Pause to Consider Prayer
Psalm 37:4, 5; Proverbs 3:6; Matthew 18, 19, 20; John 15:7, 16

Let us get rid of certain notions about prayer. Prayer is not a lightning rod to save us from the bolts of God's wrath. Many think it is; if they don't pray, something will happen to them.... Prayerlessness means slow rot, not sudden calamity.

Again, prayer is not bending God to our wills; it is the bringing of our wills to God's. When we throw out a boat hook and catch hold of the shore, do we pull the shore to ourselves? Rather we pull ourselves to the shore. Prayer does not pull God to us, it pulls us to God. It aligns our wills with God's will, so that God can do things through us that could not otherwise be done.

An almighty Will works through our weak wills, and we can do things all out of proportion to our ability. Prayer is, therefore, not overcoming God's reluctance; it is laying hold of God's highest willingness. Those who pray link up with the willingness....

In real prayer, our will coincides with God's. That is what we mean when we pray "in Jesus' name." That is, we pray the kind of prayer Jesus would pray. But when we pray "out of God's will," we are "forging Jesus' name to a prayer."

Victorious Living
(Week 35, Thursday)

111

We Further Consider Prayer
2 Samuel 3:25; Psalm 109:4; Luke 21:36; Romans 12:12

In prayer, I seldom ask for things; more and more I ask God for God, for the assurance that my will and God's are not at cross-purposes, that we are agreed on all major and minor matters. I know, then, if this is so, I shall get all the things I need....If I get God in loving communion, then the prayer is answered and is effective. Things are a side issue....

Prayer is the power to get through difficulties, to be at your best, to become effective....For God, the Eternal God, works with us and in us. Prayer, then, "is the kind of a burden sails are to a ship and wings to a bird." Then pray, my brothers and sisters, pray, if you want to live victoriously.

Victorious Living
(Week 35, Friday)

Making the Prayer Hour Effective
Psalms 4:4; 24:3-5; Isaiah 64:4; 1 Timothy 4:15

First of all, have the prayer hour. Sacredly keep it. Build the habits of your life around that prayer hour. Make things fit into it, not it into things. People who, neglecting the fixed hour of prayer, say they can pray all the time, will probably end in praying none of the time....

In the beginning of the prayer hour, be silent. Let your mind relax and let it roam across your life to see whether it stops at anything wrong. If so, tell God you will right it. Let the first moment be a sincere moral search. If nothing is shown to be wrong, then, "Beloved, if our hearts do not condemn us, we have confidence before God" (1 John 3:21). We are ready for bold praying.

Then bathe your thought in God's Word. It will wash the dust from your eyes. Then you will see, have insight. You will get right attitudes through the Word, so you will pray right prayers. You are pulling your thought up alongside of God's thought, your purposes up to God's purposes.

Take a pen or pencil with you and write down what comes to you as you pore over the Word. That pen is the sign of your faith that something will come. And it will....."Prayer is a time exposure of the soul to God." Expose your inmost being to God's Word.

Take obedience with you into that hour, for you will know as much of God, and only as much of God, as you are willing to put into practice! For God will answer many of your prayers—through you.

Victorious Living
(Week 35, Saturday)

Grow through Obstacles By Prayer

Genesis 32:24-29; Luke 18:1; Acts 12:5; 1 Corinthians 16:9

Here was an obstacle—the madness of his opponents that drove them to counsel what they would do to Jesus. They felt they had the final say. Over against that, Jesus matched prayer. They counseled together as to what they should do to him, and he counseled as to what the Lord should do through him. Prayer made it possible that he should not be a victim of circumstances. He met his circumstances from above.

What will my circumstances do to me today? Rather, what shall I do today through my circumstances by prayer? Again, here are my limitations, and they conspire to cramp me, to keep me from being effectivee....

What shall my enemies do with me? Rather, what shall I do with my enemies through prayer? I shall have power to forgive them, I meet them from above....

You grow by the meeting of an obstacle, not merely through the obstacle, but through prayer induced by that very obstacle.

Victorious Living
(Week 46, Sunday)

The Seventh Step

Mark 1:35-36; Acts 10:9; Ephesians 6:18; 1 Thessalonians 5:17

Many feel that they can live in a state of prayer, without stated times for prayer. This is a mistake.

Jesus felt the need of three simple habits: (a) he stood up to read, "as his custom was" (Luke 4:16); (b) he went out into the mountain to pray, "as was his custom" (Luke 22:39); (c) he taught them again, "as he was wont" (Mark 10:1 KJV). These three simple habits: reading and meditating upon the Word of God; exposing oneself to God at the prayer hour; and teaching others—passing on what we have found—are as basic in the spiritual life as two plus two equal four are in mathematics. If Jesus couldn't get along without them, how do we hope to do so?

> In the pure strong hour of the morning, when the soul of the day is at its best, best, lean upon the windowsill of the Lord and look into his face, and get orders for the day. Then go out into the world with a sense of a hand upon your shoulder and not a chip. (Source Unknown)

Start the day right, and you will end it right.

Abundant Living
(Week 4, Saturday)

113

Prayer Is Surrender
Psalm 143:10; Matthew 26:42; 2 Corinthians 12:7-10

But the idea of surrender cuts across the usual idea of prayer as a method of obtaining from God your wishes. That idea is self-assertion. This is self-surrender.

Then is prayer passive submission? A denial of the will to live? Is it the will to die? Far from it. Prayer is a will to die on the level of a defeated, empty, ineffective, short-circuited life, and a will to live on the level of a victorious, full, effective, and cosmic-connected life. It is self-renunciation in order to find self-realization. Your petty self is renounced in order that your potential self might be realized. Prayer is the wire surrendering to the dynamo, the flower surrendering to the sun, the child surrendering to education, the patient surrendering to the surgeon, the part surrendering to the whole— prayer is life surrendering to Life.

Abundant Living
(Week 33, Sunday)

Prayer: The Greatest Single Power
Psalms 27:14; 30:2; Luke 11:1; James 5:16

The art of prayer must be learned, for reservoirs of power are at our disposal if we can learn this art. "If we learn it"—that is the rub. People expect results without any practice of the art.

Abundant Living
(Week 33, Wednesday)

Further Steps in Prayer
Psalms 46:1-2, 10; 55:22; 62:5

Still the mind. Just as the moon cannot reflect well on a restless sea, so God cannot get to an unquiet mind. "Be still, and know" (Ps 46:10); be unstill, and you do not know; God cannot get to you. In the stillness, the prayer itself may be corrected. For God not only answers prayer, but also corrects prayer and makes it more answerable. One night, I bowed my head in silent prayer before a sermon and whispered to God, "O God, help me." Very quickly came back the reply: "I will do something better; I will use you."

Abundant Living
(Week 33, Friday)

The Final Steps of Prayer
Psalms 40:1; 121:7-8; 1 Peter 5:10; 1 John 3:16-18

Prayer is the working out of what God works in.

Remember that no is answer, as well as yes.... God often holds off to deepen our characters, so that we won't be spiritual crybabies if we don't get everything at once....

Prayer is... the opening of a channel from your emptiness to God's fullness.

Abundant Living
(Week 33, Saturday)

114

A Sense of Mission and Submission
Isaiah 6:1-9; John 20:21; Acts 8:29

Whenever I stand up to preach, I ask the audience to bow their heads in prayer; and I invariably remind God of my verse, a verse given to me years ago at the very beginning of my ministry: "Ye have not chosen me, but I have chosen you, and ordained you, that ye should go and bring forth fruit, and that your fruit should remain: that whatsoever ye shall ask of the Father in my name, he may give it you" (John 15:16 KJV).

Repeating this verse gives me the sense of being sent, of having the backing of the Eternal, and of speaking in a Name not my own. But it does another thing: It lays on me the sense of obligation to surrender to and be obedient to the working out of this plan. It gives life a sense of mission and submission.

Abundant Living
(Week 36, Friday)

"Cultivate the Quiet Time"
Psalms 25:12; 27:4; 119:147

Cultivate the Quiet Time—preferably in the morning. We have talked about Christianizing your relationships; we come now to the central relationship, your relationship with God. When that relationship is intact, then every other relationship is toned up. If that relationship gets loose, then every other relationship goes loose with it. For the Christian, there is one responsibility and only one responsibility:—to keep in union with God. When that union with God is intact, everything flows from it. I know of no one thing that creates union with God more surely and constantly than the regular practice of the Quiet Time. If I have a Quiet Time, I have a quiet heart; but if the Quiet Time goes, the quiet heart goes with it. I can take it or leave it, but that is one of life's inexorables.

Close your eyes, drop into the silence of the heart, and then listen to God tell you how much time you can spend in the Quiet Time. Take the figure that fixes itself in your mind with a sense of approval, and start it. Pray by the clock. If it starts being mechanical, it will soon become medicinal; it will heal you at the heart.

The Way
(Week 12, Thursday)

Don't Fight Your Fears, Surrender Them
John 6:20-21; 12:15

Learn the art of prayer, for fears dissolve in an atmosphere of prayer.

The Way
(Week 14, Thursday)

The Way Is the Way of Prayer
Luke 11:9-13

Prayer is cooperation with God. In prayer you align your desires, your will, your life to God. You and God become agreed on life desires, life purposes, life plans, and you work them out together. That is prayer. Prayer, then, is not trying to get God to do our will. It is the getting of our will into line with God's will. But the will is not a separate portion of us; the will is the self in action. So prayer aligns the whole self to the whole Self of God.

The Way
(Week 29, Sunday)

To Rise Up as One Imperishable
Matthew 14:23; 17:20; Luke 9:29

[Prayer is Reality.] I know that when I pray, I'm better; when I don't, I'm worse. I touch life with a perishable touch when I touch it without prayer; but when I do pray, then I touch life with an imperishable touch. If you don't have a quiet time in the morning, you'll probably have an unquiet time at night.

The Way
(Week 30, Wednesday)

Prayer Is Receptivity
Luke 11:9-10; John 15:4, 16

Prayer is Receptivity. To put the first two together: Prayer is Receptivity to Reality. God the infinite Reality, is pervading us and invading us. The pathway over which God comes to the center of our being and purposes is receptivity.... Receptivity is the surrendering of all fears, all doubts, all inhibitions, especially all self; for the ego, even in God's presence, asserts itself, wants to be God. It must be surrendered.

The Way
(Week 30, Thursday)

Prayer Is Response
Acts 3:2-4; 14:8-10

Prayer is Response. If prayer were only receptivity it would leave us leaning too much to the passive side. It will leave us in an attitude of taking without undertaking. The taking of God must produce undertaking for God....

Prayer is creative. When our lesser life touches Life it becomes alive, alive to the fingertips....

Prayer is a form of energy, for those who pray do not waste energy in fussy activity—a running around in circles, getting nowhere fast. The poised, prayerful heart is sure of its directions, is sure of its resources, and moves from task to task with calm confidence. The prayerless are hurried, flurried, worried. They wear themselves out with frictions....

116

O God, wake us up to Jesus. Give us his passion for prayer and his passion for people. May our needs drive us to you and the needs of others drive us to them. For we have discovered a working force. Amen.

The Way
(Week 30, Friday)

Prayer Is Renewal
Romans 12:2; Ephesians 3:14-19

Prayer is Renewal. Like a watch, life has a tendency to run down. It needs rewinding. Prayer rewinds the springs of life.... Prayer brings resources....

It is so easy to get lost in the world. I come to the prayer hour to find myself and my directions again. Prayer is the period of circling, like the homing pigeon, circling to gain a homeward direction. To prayer we come, turning round and round on ourselves. From prayer we go with the homeward direction in the heart. The wings no longer hesitate for the heart is sure....

Prayer is a lift-up with no let-down, for it is no mere shot-in-the-arm, a stimulant. It is a renewal, a renewal of resources. For in prayer you have a life transfusion. You are God-infused.

The Way
(Week 30, Saturday)

Steps toward a Real Prayer Life
1 Timothy 2:1-2; 8; James 5:13-16

Fall in love with God, and you'll know what to say [in prayer]. "Religion is a long falling in love with God." But love needs to be cultivated. It is not always "love at first sight." Love often comes through insight, insight gained over a long period of contact [with God].

The Way
(Week 31, Thursday)

Quiet Prayer Unbinds Us
Luke 11:1-4

The fact is no dramatic experience can take the place of quiet prayer. If it is not followed by quiet prayer, then the experience will fade out and be inoperative. No experience is proof against prayerlessness.... Nothing can kill our experience of God so decisively as prayerlessness. Nothing can unbind you and let you go so wonderfully as a daily time spent in prayer....

I find I'm better or worse as I pray more or less. "Little prayer, little victory; much prayer, much victory; no prayer, no victory."

For in prayer you align yourself to the purposes and power of God, and God is able to do things through you that God couldn't otherwise do. For this is an open universe, where some things are left open, contingent upon our doing them. If we do not do them, they will never be done. So God has left certain things open to prayer, things that will

117

never be done except as we pray. It is, not a closed universe, but one open to the praying heart.

I sat one day in meditation and the question came: "If God would offer to give you one thing—and only one thing—what would you ask?" After a moment's thought, I replied: "Give me a prayerful heart." I have thought about it a good deal since then, and I've come to the conclusion that I could ask nothing better. For if I have the prayerful heart, all else follows.

The Way to Power and Poise
(Week 47, Tuesday)

The Sovereign Cure for Worry
Luke 11:5-8

Religious faith cannot be sustained without prayer. So prayer is at the heart of religious faith. As Mahatma Gandhi said, "Without prayer I would have been a lunatic long ago." If the years have left no scars on me, except radiant scars, it is that prayer has been my refuge and my strength.

The Way to Power and Poise
(Week 47, Wednesday)

Prayer Cancels Loneliness
Psalm 69:14, 17, 20

Someone has said, "Prayer cancels loneliness." It does, for it brings you into fellowship with God, and in fellowship with God there can be no loneliness. But prayer just for yourself will not cancel loneliness. It may aggravate it if you are thinking only of yourself. But if you bring the needs and sorrows of others into your prayer hours, then that cancels loneliness.

How to Be a Transformed Person
(Week 27, Thursday)

To Make the Quiet Time Effective
Isaiah 64:1, 4

If you are to pray always, there must be a specific time for the cultivation of such a spirit of continuous prayer. You cannot pray everywhere unless you pray somewhere. You cannot maintain the spirit of prayer unless you take off specific time or times for prayer. It will fade out. So take these steps:

1. Decide on the amount of time you can give to the Quiet Time, preferably in the morning. The morning is the best; it tunes your instrument [you] for the day.

2. Having fixed the time, stick to it. Pray by the clock, whether or not you feel like it.

3. Take your Bible and read a portion slowly. Let it soak in. If some verse strikes you, let your mind circle around it in meditation. It will render up new meanings to you. Write them in a notebook or on the margin of your Bible.

4. After the reading, let go and relax and say to God, "Lord, have you anything to say to me?" Begin to listen. Become guidable.

5. Then you say to God what you have to say. Prayer is dialogue, not a monologue.

6. Thank God for the answer. God always answers yes or no. No is an answer as well as Yes, sometimes a better answer. The answer sometimes may be in you—you are better for having prayed—you are the answer. In the Quiet Time, you become the focal point of transmission for transformation.

How to Be a Transformed Person
(Week 40, Wednesday)

I Just Want to Look at You
Luke 9:28-29

The Quiet Time is a period of just gazing at the face of Christ. Prayer is a time exposure to God. If no prayers are made or answered, nevertheless it is worthwhile for you become like that at which you gaze. You are made one degree more Christlike by your Christ-gaze. A little fellow came into his father's study, and the father asked him what he wanted, and the boy replied: "I don't want anything. I just want to look at you." So the boy sat and gazed into his beloved father's face and in the process became more like him. We often say "Prayer changes things"; it does, but more important, prayer changes the pray-er into the image of the face he or she gazes on.

How to Be a Transformed Person
(Week 50, Wednesday)

Doesn't Know How to Mourn
1 John 5:13-15

[My friend "Mary" wrote:] "Prayer always works in reverse with me. It should make me quiet and restful, but it always makes me feel that I have been injected with a tremendous dose of vitality, and I feel like going out and doing something about everything."

Growing Spiritually
(Week 31, Thursday)

Growth in Prayer
Matthew 6:5-6

We come now to an important area of growth, growth in prayer. This perhaps is the most important. I find I am better or worse as I pray more or less. Prayer tones up the whole of life. I can never be better in life than I am faithful in prayer. If prayer lags, life sags. If we know how to pray, we know how to live; if not, then we exist, we don't live....

Many think of themselves as reservoirs with a certain fixed capacity. If we are people of prayer, we are not reservoirs, but channels. We are attached to infinite resources and therefore have boundless possibilities.

Growing Spiritually
(Week 42, Sunday)

119

My Heart Is a Prayer Vigil
Matthew 7:7-8

The person of prayer in touch with the very magnetism of Christ becomes magnetized and magnetizes others in turn. But break the connection, and that person is very ordinary steel without attraction. Prayer is the connection; break that, and you break all.

And yet many go through life prayerless, except for a crisis when they get into trouble. Then they pray. And they wonder why God doesn't immediately pull them out, making God a cosmic grandfather! If you don't pray in the regular, you have no right to call on God in the irregular.... [When we don't pray regularly,] we run out of resources, get irritable, and say and do things concerning which we have to repent and apologize. If we had taken time for prayer, we could have saved time, the time we take in undoing the messes we get into....

Prayer deepens and heightens life.

Growing Spiritually
(Week 42, Monday)

Prayer Is Cooperation with God
Matthew 9:28-29

Prayer is cooperation with God. It is the purest exercise of the faculties God has given us, an exercise that links these faculties with the Maker to work out the intentions God had in mind in their creation. Prayer is aligning ourselves with the purposes of God. Prayer isn't bending God to our wills, but our bending of our wills to God's will. If prayer is the purest exercise of our faculties, it is also the most natural. For when we cooperate with God in prayer, then we are working out God's intention inherent in the very structure of our beings. We do what we are made to do, made to do by our very make-up. Prayer, then, makes us natural by our very contact with the Supernatural. We work out the purposes God has worked into us. Prayer, then, is the fulfillment of our very beings. In prayer we become supernaturally natural....

Prayer aligns us with God and therefore with ourselves....Prayer makes us stop fighting and makes us cooperate. Then infinite power works through our finiteness; an infinite mind thinks through our finite minds, and infinite love loves through our finite love.

Growing Spiritually
(Week 42, Tuesday)

By Small Accomplishing Great
Luke 11:1-4

Prayer means we are striking the same notes that God is striking. We thus become a part of a universal harmony, the music of the spheres. Our little notes are caught up and universalized. Prayer put us in tune with the infinite.

Growing Spiritually
(Week 42, Wednesday)

120

Prayer Is Communion
Hebrews 4:16; James 5:16

Prayer is a means, but as often it is an end in itself....

I have often said that the phrase I most often repeat to the Lord is this one: "Lord, you've got me." That phrase is still basically there and is repeated again and again, but there is another one that is in ascendancy, being repeated oftener: "Lord, I love you, I love you, I love you." It has become a refrain.

Growing Spiritually
(Week 43, Monday)

A Peg on Which to Hang My Gratitude
Psalm 37:4-5

When we have prayer as communion, we can fill in the hours and moments with quiet peace. I've learned the habit through long practice of dropping into the heart in prayer whenever I'm compelled to wait for an elevator, a friend, or an engagement. I head off the possible resentment and impatience by forestalling it with prayer. I occupy the conflict moment with a communion moment. The destructive is pushed out, and the constructive comes in....

And that communion, often wordless, more often turns to thanksgiving. Yesterday, I thanked the Lord for a peg on which to hang my coat. And then I said to myself, "I'm always hunting for pegs on which to hang my gratitude, and I find so many." I find myself thanking God for everything; for everything furthers you deeper into God if you will let it. As someone has said, "Never face a trouble without first thanking God for it." And then the trouble is no longer a mere trouble, it is an opportunity for victory through the trouble. Paul puts it this way, "Rejoice at all times" (1 Thess 5:15 Moffat). And the secret of rejoicing at all times is the next, "Never give up prayer" (v. 17). And the outcome is, "Thank God for everything" (v.18). If you are in a constant state of prayer, you can "rejoice at all times" and "thank God for everything." Your heart is a fountain of thankful rejoicing.

Growing Spiritually
(Week 43, Tuesday)

Thou Art the Breeze; Blow On
John 14:13-14

In order to grow in prayer set a framework of devotional life. Set aside a certain amount of time for prayer each day. Pray by the clock. If you say, "I'll pray everywhere at all times, but at no specific time," my prediction will be that you'll probably end by praying nowhere at any time. You'll not be able to sustain the "everywhere" except by a "somewhere," nor "all times" except by a "specific time."

Take your Bible into your prayer time....The Word of God will let you look into the face of Jesus as the first thing you see in beginning your prayer time. Then become silent before him and let him speak. Repeat the Chinese hymn: "I am the grass, Thou art the Breeze; blow on." Then pour out your unfinished business into his lap and ask for guidance. And believe the guidance will be given.

Growing Spiritually
(Week 43, Friday)

I've Always Had Tasks I Couldn't Do
Ephesians 3:20-21

People have asked me what is the secret of my life. I have invariably replied, "If there is any secret, it is in these two things: I have kept my prayer life intact, and I've always had tasks I couldn't do."

I knew I couldn't do them; they were too big for my inadequacies. So I've offered my inadequacies to God by surrender and have taken God's Adequacy by receptivity. It is so simple and effective.

Mastery
(Week 24, Friday)

The Mastery of Prayer
Luke 11:1-13

We come now to consider…the mastery of prayer. The mastery of the art of prayer is life's most important mastery. It can be summed up in one sentence: If we know and practice the art of prayer, we know and practice the art of living; if we don't know that art, then we don't know the art of living. To pray is to penetrate, to penetrate through this physical encasement into the spiritual world of light and power and to live within this physical encasement by that spiritual light and power. We live in two worlds at once: the physical world is interpenetrated by the spiritual and lifted to a new level of life. We can live literally by resources not our own; we can live by Another.

But while prayer is life's most wonderful resource, it can be twisted and turned into all sorts of things. First, into a formula. A minister's wife expounded at length on the beauty of the prayer book they used and then added, "Do you really think that God answers prayer?" She thought of prayer as a formula but not as a fact. Does God answer prayer? The answer is that, just as God has made an open universe contingent upon our action—so that things won't be done unless we do them—so God has left certain things open to prayer—things that won't be done unless we pray.

This is a universe of law and order, yet it is an open universe; things can happen within this universe if we decide to do them. The spiritual universe is also one of law and order and an open universe, open to cooperation with God for new things to happen. These are things that God wants to happen, but God can't let them without our cooperation. Prayer is cooperation with God, cooperating in carrying out unfinished creative purposes. God wants us to help finish an unfinished universe. So in prayer, we do not have to overcome God's reluctance; we only have to cooperate with God's highest willingness. Anything that ought to happen can happen to the one who prays. That person has linked with divine purposes and has, therefore, divine power at his or her disposal for human living. The person of prayer is the person of power.

Mastery
(Week 42, Sunday)

122

They Did the Most Incredible Things
Luke 9:28-31

Laws govern prayer as laws govern the universe. What are they? The people in the Acts evidently were guided by them, for they did an incredible thing. It was not telling lame men to walk and dead people to arise; it was infinitely more incredible. It was nothing less than accomplishing in a short space of thirty years something that philosophers and lawgivers and moralists had attempted for ages with little success. They lifted humanity onto a new plane of living and introduced into society the basic changes upon which humanity has lived ever since. They did the most difficult thing that has ever been done. And they did it with incredible ease, without strain and without drain; for they didn't do it; they let God do it through them. They did it through prayer.

Then we turn to the exciting adventure of seeing just how they used prayer and just how they did not use it. For this didn't just happen. It happened because they put themselves in line with God's purposes.

The Acts of the Apostles gives an account of the use of prayer that is the cleanest, the sanest, the wisest, and the most powerful ever seen on our planet—yes, ever....

First of all, they had seen prayer in Jesus. Jesus had cleansed prayer for them. After he cleansed it, he used it and used it mightily. In three great crises he prayed. First, at his baptism, and as a result the Spirit descended upon him "like a dove." Prayer brought the Holy Spirit. Second, he prayed at the transfiguration, and as a result he stood transfigured. Prayer made him luminous, showed what the material can be. Then third, he prayed when he was accomplishing the end for which he came, the atonement for sin. When he prayed, "Father, forgive them" (Luke 23:34 CEB), God could forgive because Jesus was dying for them that they might be forgiven. He answered his own prayer by making it possible for God to forgive.

Mastery
(Week 42, Monday)

Prayer for One Thing: the Holy Spirit
Luke 24: 45-49

Prayer in the Book of Acts was not primarily for things—for success, for healing, for power—prayer was a person wanting a Person. Prayer was wanting that Person so much that they were willing to surrender everything, including themselves especially, if only that Person would come in and take over. The Holy Spirit did, and how! "They were all filled with the Holy Spirit" (Acts 2:4 CEB). The hands of God were untied; God could do anything, everything, for people who didn't want anything except for God to come in and take over.

What a corrective to a great deal of modern praying, which makes prayer into a success cult, a healing cult, an ego-expanding cult! All this is making ourselves the center; we're using God. Prayer is prostituted. People try to capture the holy to serve them. Here God is the center. Humanity is surrendered to God. That is the right relationship. Anything can now happen.

Mastery
(Week 42, Tuesday)

123

Not for Safety but for Boldness
Philippians 1:12-14

As time goes on, I find myself praying less and less for things and more and more for God. For if I have God, I have everything—yes, everything—I need and more.

"And now, Lord, look upon their threats, and grant to thy servants to speak thy word with all boldness" (4:29). Here again prayer, was not for their needs but for the needs of others; they prayed for boldness to witness to others. God was first, others were second, and they were third. Prayer breaks the tyranny of self-preoccupation, absorbs you with God, and makes you interested in others. It is freeing. And it is inherent.

Mastery
(Week 42, Thursday)

Conclusions Regarding Prayer
Philippians 1:3-5, 9-11

In the Acts of the Apostles, prayer had been redeemed. From being a self-concerned act of getting benefits for oneself, it became the agent of a glorious redemption. Everywhere prayer was love in action through God. People were reaching out through God to touch others redemptively. In the process, prayer itself was redeemed. It was turned out instead of in; except in one instance, when they prayed for the Holy Spirit for themselves. Then we can pray all out for ourselves. For if Spirit comes, he takes over the self. Prayer then is not for us but for One to control and guide and use the self.

Then is there no place in prayer for our own personal needs? Is that ruled out? No, they are provided for, but indirectly.

Mastery
(Week 43, Sunday)

The Power of the Lord Was with Him to Heal
James 4:3-6

But prayer, which is often advocated today as a means of curing oneself of one's own ills, can be wholly wrong. It can add to one's self-preoccupation, using prayer for one's own purposes. Prayer has therapeutic, or healing, value only if it loosens you from self-preoccupation and gets you interested in something beyond yourself.

When Jesus spent all night in prayer to the Lord, the next morning the "power of the Lord was with him to heal" (Luke 5:17 RSV).

The all-night prayer meant the all-morning power and power to heal in two directions. It kept Jesus whole and made others whole. Our needs are automatically guaranteed if we let prayer carry us beyond ourselves. The self is lost in others and found in itself.

Mastery
(Week 43, Monday)

Maturity in the Life of Prayer
Luke 18:1; 11:1

One of the things the Spirit within helps us to find is maturity in the prayer life: "Likewise the Spirit helps us in our weakness; for we do not know how to pray as we ought, but the Spirit himself intercedes for us with sighs too deep for words. And he who searches the hearts of men knows what is the mind of the Spirit, because the Spirit intercedes for the saints according to the will of God" (Rom 8:26-27). Here we find Paul putting his finger on the central point of our "weakness," weakness in prayer life. And because we are weak in our prayer life, we are weak in maturity. If the prayer life is immature the whole life is immature. For prayer is the central resource for maturity in any person's life. And there is no exception. If we are weak in prayer, we are weak—full stop. If we are strong in prayer, we are strong—full stop.

As I travel through the world and get in contact with men and women of all races, I find that the greatest source of weakness in character and influence is to be found in the prayer life. Most of the casualties in the spiritual life are found at the place of a weakened prayer life. When the prayer life is toned up, the whole of the rest of the life is toned up with it. Prayer is pivotal. I find I am better or worse as I pray more or less. If prayer fades, power fades....In prayer our weakness is linked to Almightiness, our ignorance linked to Infinite Wisdom, our finite self to the Infinite Self.

Christian Maturity
(Week 44, Sunday)

Prayer Is Self-Surrender
Matthew 26:38-39

[In 1 John 5:14-15,] "anything" and "whatever" are qualified by "if we ask ... according to his will." That phrase is all-important, for without it prayer can become illusion. I can ask anything, and if I only have faith enough I will get it. My faith is the qualifying factor. That has caused an enormous amount of confusion and disillusionment. It has turned prayer into magic, the magic wand is faith. Wave that wand of faith over situations, and miracles happen! When we believe that faith is the only condition, we have missed the point. "According to his will" is the basic condition. Exercise faith within that condition and anything can and does happen.

But that condition defines prayer. Prayer is self-surrender. Not merely the surrender to the will of God of the thing for which we are praying, but deeper still; it means the surrender of the person who is praying to the will of God. And not a surrender of the person in reference to the particular thing at issue; it means a permanent surrender as a life attitude. When that is done, we are free to ask "anything" and God pledges "whatever" we ask! A freedom in prayer comes as a result of this losing of one's life into the will of God.

Christian Maturity
(Week 44, Monday)

Everything Seems Ordinary, Except...
Acts 4:13-14

Prayer is surrender and, consequently, receptivity. The unsurrendered person cannot receive. She withholds the inmost self and hence blocks the receptivity. He does not give; hence he cannot receive. When Jesus touched the dumb man who could not speak, he did not touch his tongue first, he touched his ears first (Mark 7:32-35)....When the receptivity became normal the activity became normal. Prayer as self-surrender clears the way for receptivity and hence for an amazing activity. The first law of life is receptivity; the second law of life is activity. Prayer is both.

Christian Maturity
(Week 44, Tuesday)

The Pull Has Gone
Acts 3:5-8

We know prayer does something for the pray-er: aligns us to the will of God, brings everything into focus, and adds a plus to all we do and says and are. But does prayer really influence things outside the individual?

We know that telepathy is a fact. One mind can influence another mind, and the distance doesn't seem to matter. If one person can influence another person across distances—can throw a thought into the other's mind, give the will a gentle push, and change the emotions—then why couldn't God and us, working together, influence persons and situations for good? For instance, at one of our Ashrams, a woman said that for twenty years she had been praying for her husband to become a Christian, but no response. We went into the chapel together and knelt and prayed for him to become a Christian. When she got home a week later, this was the first thing he said to her: "While you have been away I've decided to become a Christian. I'm joining the church next Sunday." Coincidence? Perhaps, but perhaps not!

Christian Maturity
(Week 44, Thursday)

What Is Mortal Sin?
Mark 3:22-24

We are invited to pray for our brothers and sisters, and "God will give him life for those whose sin is not mortal" (1 John 5:16). This invites us to intercessory prayer for others, and God has promised to give "life" to the one prayed for. This is a wide-open invitation and gives us infinite possibilities in influencing others. This is the highest kind of prayer, for it is the most unselfish. You are praying not for this thing, that thing, or the other thing for a particular person; you are praying for "life" for that person. And you can always pray with faith for "life" for people, since that is what Jesus came to give: "I came that they may have life, and have it abundantly" (John 10:10). So to pray for "life" for people is to pray in line with the purpose of his coming.

We are mature to the degree that we are mature in prayer, and we are mature in prayer to the degree that our prayer becomes intercessory prayer, and our intercessory prayer is mature to the degree that it asks for "life" for the one prayed for. When we stand before God, like the high priest, with the name of our brother or sister written on our heart, then we are really praying.

Christian Maturity
(Week 44, Saturday)

Conversion Is Conversion to Receptivity
Galatians 3:11-14

Prayer is receptivity. Its attitude is this: "Speak, LORD, for thy servant hears" (1 Sam 3:9). Many think of prayer as: "Listen, Lord, for thy servant speaks." This attitude is like that of the reporter who sees the president, with ten minutes for the interview. The reporter talks glibly for nine minutes and then says: "Mr. President, if you have anything to say to me, please say it." We do that with God. Our first attitude should be to listen, then request.

Christian Maturity
(Week 46, Saturday)

Surrender in General, Obey in Particular

We now come to the crux of our verse: "If you abide in me, and my words abide in you, ask whatever you will, and it shall be done for you" (John 15:7). The crux is in the if. The if covers two conditions—"abide in me, and my words abide in you." If you surrender to Christ in general—"abide in me," and if you obey Christ in particular—"my words abide in you," then the door is open to Christ's everything; ask whatever you will and it shall be done for you. This is the most limiting and yet the most unlimited conception of prayer ever propounded: limited to two conditions and limited to no conditions. He binds us and then frees us, frees us to ask anything! If you fulfill the first two conditions, then you will ask only what he would approve and will receive only what he knows is good for you—the best for you.

Does God answer all prayers? Some say yes, but the answer is no! God cannot, by the very divine nature, answer prayers of those who do not abide in God and in whom God's words do not abide. They would pray apart from the Spirit; and whatever is apart from the Holy Spirit is apart from our good, for whatever is good in God is good for us. God's will is our wealth.

Here prayer is put on its highest level; every prayer prayed in the spirit of Jesus is answered. That cleanses prayer and consummates prayer. "Love God and do what you like," could be amended: "Love Jesus Christ and ask what you like," for you will ask the things he likes.

This cleanses prayer from all self-reference; "the answers are within you," for they are not; they are in Christ. It cleanses prayer from "much speaking," for you are not answered for your persistence, but by meeting these two conditions.

In Christ
(Week 17, Thursday)

Rooted and Built Up in Him

You do not find the new life in Christ through discipline, but you cannot keep it without it. The daily quiet time spent in reading the Bible and prayer, the reading of the best books, the sharing with others—all these are a part of the process of being developed. We trust as if the whole thing depended on God, but we work as if the whole thing depended on us.

In Christ
(Week 40, Monday)

Speeches by Way of Prayers
Luke 18:9-14

Jesus…gave the Lord's Prayer, which is prayer reduced to its simplest and profoundest form; all adjectives squeezed out, where the words and reality coincide and are one. The self-regarding emphasis is precluded by the first word, "Our." So the prayer is self-purifying by its very nature.

And to remind his disciples of the very necessity of making the prayer an embodiment of attitudes toward others, Jesus turned back and said, "But if you don't forgive others, neither will your Father forgive your sins" (Matt 6:15 CEB). Prayer is the word of request become flesh, or it is mere words. So real prayer to God is a revelation of our attitudes toward others.

The Word Became Flesh
(Week 22, Friday)

Jesus Christ Means to Me First of All Redemption
1 Corinthians 1:30-31

A Hindu said to a friend of mine, "I believe in prayer, but it is a very deep belief on the part of us Hindus that prayer cannot do anything about the past; the past must be paid for now or in a coming reincarnation." But the prayer of repentance and surrender to Jesus Christ did something about the past; it was gone, wiped out as though it belonged to another person, now dead, a new one alive in that person's place.

The Word Became Flesh
(Week 52, Monday)

WITNESS

Growth in Quality of Life
Acts 20:28; 1 Timothy 4:16; 6:11; Hebrews 12:1

In Mark 13:9 (RSV), Jesus says to his disciples: "Take heed to yourselves." Why? So that you might escape coming calamity? No. "Take heed to yourselves" so you will be prepared to bear testimony." Be spiritually fit, he says, so that you may not be taken unawares when called on to give your witness before high and low. For that hour depends not on your circumstances but on you. Therefore, let everything go that will not help you in that hour. Grow in quality of spiritual fitness.

Victorious Living
(Week 46, Monday)

The Universal Witness to This Way
Romans 8:14-16; 14:17; Galatians 5:22-23; Hebrews 12:1-2

Universal witness to a universal fact is one of the most solemn and reassuring things in life. This Way is verified on a world scale; it works to the degree that people work it. On the contrary, life lived against this Way breaks down, becomes snarled up, is self-frustrated, won't work. If all this be so, then you may add, very quietly, "I too find it works."

Abundant Living
(Week 47, Wednesday)

Witnessing before Faithless Friendships
Psalm 41:9; Matthew 10:34-36; John 13:21-30

Again, you must witness before faithless friendships: your Judas. Often those who dip their hands in the same dish will betray you. When money or position or self-interest beckons, these friends fall away. It is not easy to keep from being embittered toward those who were once comrades in a cause and are now indifferent, or on the other side.

What shall we do? We can still do what Christ did in Dostoyevsky's story: Christ came to preach in a town in Spain. The Grand Inquisitor arrested him, and said: "Why did you come back? You left everything to us, the church—go back." Christ made no answer, but came and kissed his ninety-year-old, faded lips and went away (Based on Ivan's story of the Grand Inquisitor in Fyodor Dostoyevsky, *The Brothers Karamazov*, book 5, chap. 5).

Abundant Living
(Week 52, Tuesday)

Concerning Class and Race Relations
Acts 10:34-35; 17:26; Colossians 3:10-11

Christianizing our relationships: . . .
Become a witness to the new life. Nothing is yours that is not shared. . . . The simplest and most effective thing you can give away is just the thing you have received. Share it.

The Way
(Week 12, Wednesday)

It Must Work or Be Worthless
1 Corinthians 4:20; Acts 6:8-1

[For some,] Christianity is not bad; it is just dull. And that is bad, for the gospel is good news, the greatest good news that ever fell upon human ears. We make it into something that is as mechanical as a Buddhist prayer wheel. Hence our people do not have enough conviction to share it. Our faith is noncontagious.

The Way to Power and Poise
(Week 17, Saturday)

A Life Set to Obey
Hebrews 11:8-10

In your obedience obey the law of sharing. Now that you have launched out by faith and have become possessed of the Spirit, share the Spirit with others. Humbly and simply share whenever the Spirit prompts you to share with those in similar need. The Holy Spirit is like electricity; the Spirit will not come in where he cannot get out. "Freely ye have received, freely give" (Matt 10:8 KJV).

The Way to Power and Poise
(Week 26, Friday)

He Knows the Shepherd
Ephesians 3:14-16

A man with no legal help was assigned two lawyers by the judge, good lawyers. He shook his head and said, "Judge, is there any way I can swap two good lawyers for one good witness?" The disciples [after Pentecost] were no longer lawyers arguing the case for Jesus, they were witnesses who witnessed to the mighty power of Jesus in their lives to save, and to save now. It was all living and fresh and firsthand and vital. Their spiritual lives were no longer in quotes; they were no longer in quotation marks, but in "creation" marks.

How to Be a Transformed Person
(Week 35, Saturday)

The Past Can Be Used
Psalm 40:1

There are no skeletons in the Christian's closet, for they have all come out and are clothed in flesh and blood and walk as witnesses of the saving power of Christ.

Growing Spiritually
(Week 3, Tuesday)

The Life of Jesus May Come Out
Luke 11:9-13

Recently I was put on a diet, and the nurse, when she handed me the diet sheet, said, "Don't read it now. You won't like it." To my surprise I found it fun to try to live according to it in the midst of evangelistic campaigns. And I found myself saying, "I don't mind, Lord, if you feed me charcoal, just so the fire of witnessing to you is kept burning in my heart."

Lord, give me as little or as much as I need, but keep the fire burning within so I can witness effectively for you. Amen.

Growing Spiritually
(Week 42, Friday)

My Business Is Witnessing
Acts 13:2-4, 47

Yesterday, I...[asked each member of a group of] Japanese pastors and laymen...to tell his profession or business. One old man of eighty-two, with a very radiant and intelligent face, said: "My business is witnessing for Christ." And it was! And an interesting story lay behind it all. He had been the town roughneck, a seller of fish. He came to a church, and as he lifted up a long pole, said: "You kill the devil in me, or I'll kill you and the devil in you too." (It was the day in which the Christians were supposed to be possessed of devils.) That night he was soundly converted; the devil was killed in him. And now he and a lady of sixty-four are prayer partners and go out together to win people [to Christ]. And they do! That town roughneck is an honored, respected citizen of the city.

Growing Spiritually
(Week 46, Monday)

Mine Has Left Me with Answers
2 Corinthians 1:20-22

You don't have to be a saint to be a witness. For you're not witnessing to your self or to your attainments—you're witnessing to Christ. And don't argue with people; witness. A man who was very argumentative tried to argue with "Mary." She said nothing. When he was through, he said, "Aren't you going to answer me?" "No," said she, "for I was just thinking what a wonderful person God is going to get when he really gets you." He was disarmed! Another, a liberal, put up all his objections and questions; and "Mary" quietly answered at the close: "Your way has left you with questions; mine has left me with answers." Give that answer through witnessing!

Mastery
(Week 38, Saturday)

The Mastery of Trying to Change Others First
1 Peter 4:17-19

The disciples didn't fall into the snare of beginning with others; they began with themselves. They didn't start out trying to change the world; they began to change themselves. If they had begun by attempting to change the world, they would have been meddlers; but they began with themselves and became messengers.

Waiting for ten days to settle their own spiritual problems first was one of the wisest moves in history. Those ten days changed the people who were to change the world and made them witnesses instead of moralists. They told what had happened to them, and those who heard them wanted what they saw and heard.

Mastery
(Week 49, Thursday)

What Is Your Name
Genesis 32:22-30

Nothing reaches the heart that does not come from the heart. To preach and to witness out of the overflow are the only effective preaching and witnessing. Anything less than this reaches the head but not the heart.

Mastery
(Week 49, Saturday)

No Longer Religious Busybodies
John 15:16, 26-27

For ten days [the disciples] waited to have themselves changed, and for twenty centuries we have felt the impact of that change. They were no longer religious busybodies meddling in other people's problems; they were radiant witnesses to a mighty solution, a solution that had begun within and was now working out to others. They weren't meddling moralists; they were messengers, and their message was a witness. That struck the world as new. The word of the kingdom had become fact.

Mastery
(Week 52, Monday)

Contrasts of Eros and Agape
John 15:9-10

Eros never produces witnesses. It produces the exhorting, struggling, tense type of religion. But the note of witness is absent. It cannot witness, since to witness would be a witness to its own attainments or lack of them. Agape, however, can witness, for it is witnessing to the grace of Another. It is laying its tribute of gratitude at the feet of Another. It is Other-conscious, and hence its witness has the note of the Other in it.

Christian Maturity
(Week 21, Monday)

Two Cokes and a Decision
Psalm 40:1-3

In Korea, one would have expected the tides of war to leave the church in ruins. Instead, the Korean church doubled its membership during the war, from five hundred thousand to one million. Why? Because when the members were scattered they witnessed, set up little groups, for evangelism is an integral part of their Christianity. Before people are baptized they have to show someone they have been won to Christ, as a sign that they are real Christians. That is mature immaturity.

Christian Maturity
(Week 45, Thursday)

Not in Until They Get Out

New converts make the best evangelists. They cannot preach, so they do what they can do, witness. Witnessing is more effective than preaching in winning others. Witnessing comes from the heart; preaching may come from the head. That which is to reach the heart must come from the heart.

In Christ
(Week 23, Sunday)

Jesus Has Got into Your Blood
2 Corinthians 4:4-6

We linger on the preaching which is essentially witnessing. That which is to reach the heart must come from the heart. Deep must speak to deep.

A student came to me one day in India and said, "Sir, tell me how to find God." I took the Bible and began to go through it, pointing out the passages that pointed the way to find God. In the midst of it he leaned over, closed the book in my hand, and said, "Now, sir, you tell me how you found God." It was a real challenge, so I told him how I found God, or rather how God had found me and my response. At the close he said, "Thank you, that's what I want." Of course, we cannot close the Bible, for from its pages is revealed Jesus who is the Way—the Way to the Father. But unless the truth in the Bible becomes truth in the blood, it is bloodless truth, anemic and ineffective.

The Word Became Flesh
(Week 19, Friday)

I Adjure You by the Jesus Whom Paul Preaches
Galatians 2:6-9

[The] "this-ness" of Christianity sets the pattern of the proclamation of the Christian gospel by its very nature (see Acts 3:32-33). If the experience was the Word become flesh, the expression would also be the Word become flesh; it would be a witness, as Jesus said it would be: "But you shall receive power when the Holy Spirit has come upon you; and you shall be my witnesses" (Acts 1:8). "My witnesses"—not "my lawyers" to argue my case—but "my witnesses" to tell what has happened to you, of what you've "seen and heard." This was one of the secrets of its power. If "all great literature is autobiography" (Jorge Luis Borges, 1899–1986), so all great preaching is witnessing.

The Word Became Flesh
(Week 29, Wednesday)

Things We Have Seen and Heard
1 Timothy 1:4-6

"We are witnesses... and so is the Holy Spirit" (Acts 5:32): we have seen it with our eyes and we have known it in our hearts by the Holy Spirit who is within. We witness and the Holy Spirit witnesses to the same thing, the human and Divine blending in the witness. This fulfilled the promise of Jesus: "But when the Counselor comes, whom I shall send to you from the Father... he will bear witness to me; and you also are witnesses" (John 15:26-27). Here was the double witness: "He will bear witness to me; and you also are witnesses." It was a double witness, and yet one and the same witness, the witness of the Word become flesh.

The Word Became Flesh
(Week 29, Thursday)

Take Heed to Your Reactions
Luke 15:25-30

"But take heed to yourselves; for they will deliver you up to councils; and you will be beaten in synagogues; and you will stand before governors and kings for my sake, to bear testimony before them" (Mark 13:9). Here the emphasis is upon yourselves, upon yourselves at the moment of deep, unmerited injustice and suffering. Be sure that through this injustice you bear witness! This is an important word, for it clarifies the whole attitude toward unmerited suffering. It was the passage upon which my whole attitude toward unmerited suffering turned. I saw you could not merely bear it, you could use it. Every injustice was opportunity, every wrong an open door, an opportunity and an open door to witness. Not to preach at others about their wrongs but to witness by your rightness of demeanor and your deeds that the Word has become flesh in you. Don't bear evil, use it!

The Word Became Flesh
(Week 30, Friday)

The Place of Authority: At the Junction Where the Historical Becomes the Experimental and Is Corroborated By the Collective
Hebrews 12:1-3

So the Christian faith does not rest on the historical alone, nor the experimental alone, nor the collective alone. Each one alone would be weak. But all coming together and witnessing to the same thing brings the highest certainty that the human being can know. It is a threefold cord that cannot be broken; all other authority compared to this is weak.

The Word Became Flesh
(Week 33, Thursday)

3
THEOLOGY

If I were to put my finger on the most important verse in Scripture, I would unhesitatingly put my finger on this one: "And the Word became flesh." The whole passage reads this way:

> And the Word became flesh and dwelt among us, full of grace and truth; we have beheld his glory, glory as of the only Son from the Father....And from his fullness have we all received, grace upon grace. For the law was given through Moses; grace and truth came through Jesus Christ. No one has ever seen God; the only Son, who is in the bosom of the Father, he has made him known. (John 1:14-18)

This verse—"the Word became flesh"—is the great divide. In all other religions, it is Word became word—a philosophy, a moralism, a system, a technique; but for all time and all people everywhere, "the Word became flesh"—the Idea became Fact.

The Word Became Flesh
(Introduction, p. 9)

GOD

How Can I Find God?
Acts 17:23-28

In our quest for God let us look at a few preliminary things. Hold in mind that the purpose of your very being, the very end of your creation is to find and live in God. As the eye is fashioned for light, so you are fashioned for God.

Victorious Living
(Week 4, Sunday)

The Risk God Took
Matthew 25:34-40; 2 Corinthians 5:2

Was it not risky for God to create us with the awful power of choice and with the possibility that we might go astray and break our hearts and God's? Yes, very risky indeed. God might have made us without the power of choice, or with the power to choose only the good. But this would not be choice, for you must be able to choose in two directions, not one, for choice to be real.... There was no other way to create personalities except to give them freedom. Risky? Yes.

But parents take that same risk when they bring a child into the world. That child may go astray and crush their lives and its own. But parents assume that awful risk. Why? Because they are determined that whatever happens they will do their best for the child; they will enter into his or her very life, until the child's problems become their own, the child's troubles theirs, the child's growth and happiness theirs. This will mean a cross! Of course. But parenthood accepts that cross because it cannot to otherwise. So with God. Our creation meant that God would enter into our very lives. Our troubles are God's troubles, our sins God's sins, our joy God's joy. So creation, then, means a cross for God? Inevitably. But God took it. Love could not do otherwise.

Victorious Living
(Week 4, Monday)

God Fading Out
Genesis 27:35-36; 31:53 (Moffatt); 32:24-30

How has God faded out of the mind of this age? Well, the age, like thoughtless children, believed that the "toyland" of material wealth was a sufficient world; then God faded out, smothered by preoccupations....

Our forebears had firsthand experience of God through the evangelical revival of the nineteenth century. The next generation clung to the church for their fathers' sake, but God was only the "Awe"—the afterglow of a fading faith. The third generation is reaping the result of a fading faith, which is producing decaying morals and a decaying civilization. Our loss of God is working out in moral decay. We are going to pieces morally, for we have gone to pieces religiously. We have lost God and have thus lost the basis of morals. Jacob met God on Jabbok's banks in his midnight wrestle and emerged a new man....

Unless we, like Jacob, find a moral renewal in finding God, we are done for.

Abundant Living
(Week 1, Tuesday)

136

Our Freedom Complicates God's Game
John 4:34; 1 Corinthians 16:13; Galatians 2:21

In this freedom of ours lays God's problem and possibility. Our freedom is a problem to God. Someone has put it this way: "Here is a chessboard, and all the figures on the board, instead of being made of wood, are flesh and blood with wills of their own. The game for God would be simple if the figures would go where God desires them to go. But suppose, when God makes a move in the game against evil, the figures balk and refuse to move, and instead move on their own, to other positions, without reference to the Player-God. That would complicate the game and mess it up badly." That has happened, and that is God's problem.

But our freedom is also God's possibility. Suppose those figures should learn that failure and mix-ups come through moves on their own and refusal to cooperate with the Player, and should thus be chastened into choosing cooperation with the Player. Then, suppose God and humanity should play the game in cooperation—and win! How much finer that would be than to win against evil with only wooden pawns to play with!

You and I can cooperate with God, can align our wills with God's will, can make God's wisdom our own, and in the end can make the victory a joint victory. What a possibility for God and us! I would rather be a discontented man than a contented worm, for that discontent would drive me to God's feet. "Blessed are the homesick, for they will come home," says a German proverb.

Abundant Living
(Week 3, Wednesday)

How God Reveals God
Psalm 19:1-6; Hebrews 1:10-12; 2:6-9

The highest thing in our moral universe is moral character. If God can be found anywhere, it ought to be here. The highest illustration of moral character ever seen on our planet is Christ. If God can be found anywhere, it ought to be in the highest thing in our moral universe—the character of Christ. How could God show us the divine character except through perfect moral character?

The character of God matters. For what God is like we must be like; God's character determines ours. Just what is God like in character? I look up through nature and I come to the conclusion that God is law. I am grateful for that, but I want something beyond law. I am not a subject asking for a law; I am a child asking for a Parent. Nature cannot tell me of my Parent, not clearly. Nor could the perfect revelation come through prophet or teacher, for the revelation going through them becomes limited, sometimes distorted, because of the human medium. Nor could the revelation come perfectly through a book, for literature cannot rise higher than life; the life that surrounds the literature puts content into the literature. So the book would be pulled to the level of our highest experience. The only complete way of revelation is through a Life, a Character who would show us what God's character is like. That Character is Christ—the human life of God, that part of God we have been able to see. The Bible, then, is not the revelation of God; it is the inspired record of the revelation. The revelation is seen in the face of

137

Jesus Christ. Is God then Christlike? He is! I can say nothing higher. I can be content with nothing less.

Abundant Living
(Week 3, Thursday)

Be Silent to God
Isaiah 30:20-21; Jeremiah 1:4-10; Acts 15:28; 16:6-10

Many of us talk fast in the presence of God, afraid that if we keep quiet God will say something unpleasant to us. We must learn to listen, to live in the passive voice. A pastor arose in one of our Ashrams and said, "God is showing me that I must shift the emphasis of my life from talking to taking." He was learning receptivity.

One translator interprets the command, "Be still, and know that I am God," this way: "Be silent to God and he will mold you." Be silent to God and God will make and mold you to become the instrument of divine purposes. An almighty "Will," will reinforce your weak will, but only when that weak will is aligned to the purposes of that almighty Will. An all-wise Mind will brood over your mind, awakening it, stimulating it, and making it creative. An all-embracing Love will quicken your love into world-sensitivity until "He hath set the world into [your] heart" (Eccl 3:11 KJV).

God has three things in mind in reference to us: purpose, plan, and a person. God has a purpose to make you the best that you can be. God has a plan that embodies that purpose. God has a plan for every life. The next step is for you to be the person for carrying out that purpose and that plan. In the silence you listen for the unfolding of that purpose and that plan. You literally become the plan and purpose of God, an embodied thought of God, the word made flesh.

Abundant Living
(Week 37, Sunday)

The Berry in the Mouth
Isaiah 37:3-7; 41:10, 13; 42:16

"Christians, when he gets to the end of a rope, tie a knot and hang on." For they know that very extremity is God's opportunity.

Abundant Living
(Week 41, Monday)

The Center of the Christian Gospel: Reconciliation
Matthew 5:23-24; Romans 5:10-11; 2 Corinthians 13:11; Hebrews 12:14;
James 3:13-18

If I were to pick out the one verse that most nearly expresses the Christian gospel, it would be this: "God was reconciling the world to himself through Christ, by not counting people's sins against them. He has trusted us with this message of reconciliation" (2 Cor 5:19 CEB). God was in the positive business of an outgoing love that reconciled humanity to God when humanity did not want to be reconciled. We do what God does; God trusts us with the work of reconciling.

Abundant Living
(Week 48, Friday)

My Will and God's Will—Alien?
Psalm 119:37, 103, 130

The Christian way is the way that conforms to nature, real nature. Anything else is doomed.

We must have hold of this until it becomes a basic axiom: My will and God's will are not alien. When I find God's will, I find my very own. The idea that God's will always lies along the line of the disagreeable is false. The will of God is always our highest interest. It could not be otherwise and God be God. I am fulfilled when I make God my center. I am frustrated when I make myself the center. I am destined to be a Christian.

The Way
(Week 5, Thursday)

Islam Means Submission
Psalm 4:5-8

If everything that happens is the will of God, then what kind of a God is God? God's character is gone.

It is true that God, in making us free agents, is indirectly responsible for what we do with that free agency. God assumes that responsibility and discharges it at a cross, at a Cross where everything that falls on humanity as a result of the misuse of free agency falls on God. The world's sorrow and sin is "forced through the channels of a single heart" (Frederick Myers, "St. Paul," 1867), he bears it and redeems us through it.

But to tell a stricken mother that the taking of her babe, or the loss of a loved one in an automobile accident, is the will of God is to charge God with murder. The time is here when we should be ashamed to have children die, for we know that some law has been broken: by remote parents through heredity, or by the immediate parents through ignorance or carelessness, or by the wrong organization of society producing impossible living conditions, or through the wrong choices of the child. The death is the result of one or more of these wills, but it is not the will of God. God wills health, not sickness; life, not death.

The Way to Power and Poise
(Week 2, Tuesday)

From Imposition, to Imitation, to Indwelling
Acts 2:29-33

God the Father is God for us; God the Son is God with us; God the Spirit is God in us. I cannot be satisfied with only for, or with, or in God the Father is the Creator; God the Son is the Redeemer; God the Spirit is the Creator-Redeemer within.

[A good definition of the Trinity:] The Father's love, the divine intention; the Son's approach, the divine invasion; the Spirit's coming, the divine indwelling. God dwelt in a holy temple, then in a holy Person; now God dwells in us who want to be holy. God in the Old Testament is Light; God in Jesus is Life; God in us is Power. Each time God comes closer, until finally God comes to the ultimate place—within. Authority is never

139

authority until it is within. But when the authority is within, and when that authority is the Holy Spirit, then it must be spelled Authority.

The Way to Power and Poise
(Week 5, Wednesday)

Everything You Say and Do Is Heightened
John 14:20-21, 23

When we live in union with God, then we take on the significance of the One with whom we are united. To be conscious that, when you work, God works; when you think, God thinks; when you go ahead, you are not alone—that is the cure for inferiorities, for hesitation, for weak personality. "In him who strengthens me, I am able for anything (Phil 4:13 Moffatt)."

The Way to Power and Poise
(Week 18, Wednesday)

I Am Unable to Stand Myself a Minute Longer
Matthew 6:22-24

For almost all our problems are rooted in an unsurrendered self. Get yourself onto the hands of God, and your problems will be off your hands.

The Way to Power and Poise
(Week 31, Sunday)

Psychiatry without God, Questionable
Romans 6:20-23

Anything that leaves you centered in yourself or centered in something less than God—whether it is religion, psychiatry, or just plain secularism—is leaving you off-center, for you are not God.

How to Be a Transformed Person
(Week 6, Sunday)

Why Didn't He Come Himself?
John 10:15, 17-18

When I was speaking in India to a group about God loving the world, that God gave his Son to die for us, a village woman spoke up and said: "What kind of a father was he to send his son; why didn't he come himself?" It was a good question, and penetrating. Yes, why didn't God come himself?

"I love Jesus but I hate God, for God wanted to destroy the world, and Jesus wouldn't let him," said a little girl. If Jesus is a third person, standing between us and God, she is right. But Jesus is a mediator only in the sense that he mediates God to us. For when we take hold of Christ, we take hold of the very self of God. For, "In Christ God was reconciling the world to himself" (2 Cor 5:19). I cannot tell where Jesus ends and God begins in my experience. They melt into one. When I deepen the

Christ-consciousness, I deepen God-consciousness. They do not rival or push each other out. They are one.

How to Be a Transformed Person
(Week 18, Wednesday)

The Three Ends of the Atonement
Romans 1:1-6

We cannot go on to the way to grow until we settle the question. To whom do I belong, to myself or to God? You are not primarily called to do, or to be; you are called to belong: "called to belong to Jesus Christ" (Rom 1:6 Moffatt).

Growing Spiritually
(Week 3, Monday)

God Digs around Us
Hebrews 12:7-11

If, in our barrenness of soul, we feel proddings of conscience and unhappiness and upsetness of spirit, then that means God is digging around us. God's diggings are not just to give a "dig" as punishment, but they are constructive diggings to make us fruitful.

Just as physical pain is nature putting up a red flag and saying, "There is something wrong here; attend to it," so spiritual pain is that same red flag going up. It is God saying, "There is danger of death here. Attend to it." God's prods are all redemptive, never just punitive.

Growing Spiritually
(Week 4, Thursday)

God's Laws Are God's Preventive Grace
2 Chronicles 6:12-14

Disease is not the will of God; and God never sends disease. This must be clarified a bit. Indirectly God does. For God has made a universe of moral and material law. These laws are God's preventive grace saying, "Keep off. Danger." If we break these laws, we don't just break the laws; we break ourselves upon the laws. We get hurt—physically, spiritually, morally. We get the consequences in ourselves.

If we work with the moral universe, we get results; the moral universe will back us, sustain us, and further us. We will get results. But if we go against the moral universe, we will be up against it, frustrated and hurt. We will get consequences. Some people go through life getting results; others get consequences. But we get one or the other. And those results or consequences are passed on to others, for we are all bound up in a bundle of life together for good or ill. We have the power to hurt or to help one another, and that through succeeding generations. Just as individuals enjoys assets they are not entitled to as individuals, so they are called on to suffer liabilities that they do not individually merit."

So God, having made the laws, is remotely responsible for our suffering if we break those laws through the misuse of freedom. God is responsible for making us free and hence is responsible, remotely, if we misuse our freedom and suffer. God accepts that responsibility and discharges it at a cross. There God takes on everything that would and does fall on us and suffers with us and for us. There, the world's sin and sorrow "were forced through the channels of a single heart" (Frederick Myers, "St. Paul," 1867). There God provided an open door of release from all that hurts and hinders us in any realm of life.

Growing Spiritually
(Week 33, Monday)

Why Not Go Direct to God?
John 14:6-9

But someone asks: Why Jesus? Why not go to God direct? Why a mediator at all? The answer is that no one goes to God direct. God has to be mediated to us. If you try to go to God direct, you go through the category of your conceptions of God. Those conceptions of God mediate God to you. But they are not God; they are your conceptions about God....

Apart from Jesus we know little about God. Jesus is God disclosing the divine self to us in understandable terms, human terms. Jesus is not our view of God but God's view of Godself. God is the divine self-disclosure. Jesus is not therefore a third person, standing between us and God. He is God come to you; and when you take hold of Jesus, you take hold of the very self of God. So Jesus is a mediator only in the sense that he mediates God to you.

Mastery
(Week 5, Saturday)

At the Sight of This...I Am Down
1 Corinthians 1:20-24

So the eternal quest is not our search for God but God's search for us. God's quest and ours meet at the foot of the cross, where God finds us and we find God. The eternal quest ends, ends in finding and being found.

Mastery
(Week 6, Tuesday)

God and Life Will Our Maturity
Ephesians 4:14-16

And what kind of parent would God be if God did not disturb us toward maturity? No earthly parent could be content to have a child who refused to grow up. The parent's joy is in development, in growth, in going on toward maturity. God cannot be otherwise and still be God, our Parent. So the disturbances we feel in our immaturities are not signs of God's anger, but a manifestation of God's love. God loves us too much to let us settle down in halfwayness.

Christian Maturity
(Week 1, Monday)

God Comes to Us
Matthew 1:21-23

The very first step in maturity, is to be reconciled with God, our Parent. As long as the feeling of inner estrangement from God is eating at the center of our being, we will never be mature.

And at this place there are just two types of religion: the one type tries to meet God in reconciliation and realization at the top rung of a long ladder; the other meets God at the lowest rung. In the one we go to God, climbing up by our good deeds, by our prayers, by mortifying of ourselves, by gaining merit, by obedience to rites and ceremonies, and by faithfulness to law and duty; we can earn our maturity and our realization of God. Every way, except the Christian way, belongs to that category. It is humanity's search up for God.

The Christian way is quite different. We do not climb to and meet God at the top rung; God comes down the ladder to us and meets us on the lowest rung; God receives us as sinners. "I came not to call the righteous, but sinners" (Matt 9:13). That is new and that is revolutionary.

Christian Maturity
(Week 4, Thursday)

God Is Light on Four Things
Romans 1:19-20

When you see God in the face of Jesus, then "God is light," light on everything. When you lose God, you lose everything, and when you find God, you find everything.

God is light on these four things: (1) creation, (2) character, (3) conversion, (4) consummation. God is light on creation. God is light on the purpose of creation. Since God is love, it is the nature of love to create. For love wants beings with whom it can share love. Parents create because they want children upon whom they can lavish their love and from whom they can receive love in return. God, the Heavenly Parent, is love, and therefore wants children upon whom to lavish love and receive love in return.

God is light on character. In Jesus we see the character of God. God couldn't do an un-Christlike thing and still be God. So Jesus is the key to the character of God and people. In Christ we see what God is like and what we can be like. He sets the pattern of character for God and people. You can transfer to God every single quality of character in Jesus without lowering your idea of God. Lower your idea of God? You heighten it! For if God isn't like Jesus, God isn't good. You ask me my definition of goodness. I do not add virtue to virtue; I point to Jesus. He is goodness. If God isn't like Jesus I'm not interested in God. If he is, then he can have my heart without qualification or reservation. Having seen the character of God in Jesus, I now know here I must head in.

God is light on conversion. If God is light on character, when I look at my character and see God's character in Jesus, then I know my character has to be changed. But how? In Jesus I see the door, the only door, through conversion. He said, "Except ye be converted ... ye shall not enter into the kingdom of heaven" (Matt 18:3 KJV). There are just two classes of people: the converted and the unconverted, a division that really

143

divides and the only division that really divides. And through Jesus, God provides all the resources for conversion, a total conversion of the total person.

Christian Maturity
(Week 7, Wednesday)

God Is Light on Consummation
Revelation 22:1-4

We come now to the next thing upon which God is light, upon the consummation. The world process is not moving with aimless feet. There is a goal for all created things and that goal has been revealed. It is nothing less than the coming of the kingdom of God on earth. The earth and everything in it have a destiny and that destiny is to be the scene of the kingdom of God. That gives meaning and dignity to everything and makes every act in every human being significant; it is for or against the New Order.

Without the light that God sheds upon the consummation, life is a dull, drab thing moving with leaden feet toward extinction. With it, we see the meaning of the statement of Paul: "For the creation waits with eager longing for the revealing of the sons of God; for the creation was subjected to futility, not of its own will but by the will of him who subjected it in hope; because the creation itself will be set free from its bondage to decay and obtain the glorious liberty of the children of God" (Rom 8:19-21).

Christian Maturity
(Week 7, Thursday)

Inseparably One with God?
Psalm 8:4-6

[What about] those who find all the answers within themselves, asserting their own inseparable oneness with God.... The character of God is lost in this viewpoint, for if we are inseparably one with God, then what we do, God does. You cannot say you are metaphysically one and not morally one. You are one, in everything! But any of us who know ourselves—and others—know that when we act, we act and not God. For the outcome of that acting is the sum total of our moral mess. If all this mess we are in is the result of God's acting, then what kind of God is that? God's character and face are blackened. We have tried to make ourselves God, and we have lost God in the process if God is just ourselves writ large. But in the end, our moral nature revolts against such a projection of ourselves. We simply cannot worship the God we project. That God is too much like us.

Christian Maturity
(Week 13, Thursday)

The Climax

As long as we are in Christ Jesus God is glorified. You do not have to step out of Jesus and concentrate on God to glorify God. Stay in Jesus Christ and you glorify God; Jesus is God glorified because Jesus is God self-giving.

In Christ
(Week 33, Friday)

In Him All Things Were Created

Jesus is "the image of the invisible God" (Col 1:15); he takes the place of idols for us. Idols misrepresent God; Jesus represents God. Jesus is the express image of God's person; God is a Christlike God.

In Christ
(Week 38, Saturday)

Jesus Puts a Face on God
John 1:15-18

The psalmist asks: "He who planted the ear, does he not hear? / He who formed the eye, does he not see?" (Ps 94:9). And we may add: "He that made the human personality, shall he not be personal?" He can't be less than personal, for personality is the highest category of being we know. And when I say, "God is personal," I don't mean God is corporeal, an enlarged Person seated in the heavens. In personality, there are at least four things: intelligence, feeling, will, self-consciousness. So when we say that God is personal, we believe God thinks, feels, wills, has self-consciousness. God may be more than that but cannot be less.

The Word Became Flesh
(Week 2, Saturday)

JESUS

The Realism of Jesus—a Rejected Stone
Matthew 7:28, 29; 11:4-6; Mark 1:27; John 6:63

Of all the strange anomalies in history the strangest is this: the Man who was the greatest realist in history has been turned into the greatest idealist. Jesus' realism was so astonishing, so different that people did not know what to do with it. They had to act on it or reject it. But they couldn't bring themselves to do either, so they found a way by which they would both—hold Jesus and hold the older order of life—they made him into an ideal. That ideal would be practiced someday, but not now. They thus satisfied their sense of being loyal to the high while practicing the low. Christ was crucified on the cross of being irrelevant now.

So we adopted Christianity as an "idealism," lifted up high above life, inoperative except here and there in small things. Because we could hold high ideals, we thought we were thereby spiritual. But "all idealism is a concealed materialism," for it makes a divorce between body and spirit, and refers religion to the spirit, while other ways of life control the material. Hence idealism becomes materialism, for the latter is acted on.

Jesus was astonishingly realistic. So realistic, that we thought it idealism. When he said we must love our neighbor as ourselves, that is not idealism; it is realism, and we are discovering that it is the only realism possible, for nothing else will work. Unless you give an equal and fair chance to everybody, you will have none for yourself. Selfishness is suicide, collective and individual.

When Jesus said we must lose ourselves to find ourselves, this is not idealism, it is realism. It is obeying a fundamental law of life. Nothing else will finally work. The demand that religion be realistic is upon us. The world is perishing for the need of just this. So the realism of Jesus, rejected by the builders, is made the head of the corner.

Victorious Living
(Week 50, Saturday)

A Good Anger
Psalms 95:10; 97:10; Proverbs 8:3; Mark 3:5; Ephesians 4:30

Jesus was an example of controlled anger. When he was about to heal the man with the withered arm, he saw the hard faces of religious men who opposed the act because it was being done on the sabbath. He "looked "around at them with anger, deeply grieved at their unyielding hearts" (Mark 3:5 CEB). Here his anger was not personal pique, a wounded egotism; it was grief at the hardness of men's hearts that could block the healing of a poor unfortunate man. His anger drove him to oppose these men on behalf of the underprivileged. It was a righteous anger.

Abundant Living
(Week 8, Monday)

Final Steps for Overcoming Resentments
Matthew 11:25-26; Luke 6:37; 17:3-4; Ephesians 4:32

When Jesus announced his program at Nazareth, he read from Isaiah, until he came to the words, "the day of vengeance of our God" (see Isa 61:1-2; Luke 4:18-19). Then he closed the book. You do the same. Leave vengeance to God; use only redemptive good will.

Abundant Living
(Week 9, Saturday)

Can We Manipulate Life?
Psalms 25:12; 32:8; Matthew 5:5

For in Jesus I see the uncovering of the nature of the Divine. And my heart almost skips a beat when the thought forms: I wouldn't, if I could, have God otherwise than what I see in Christ. If I were to sit down to try to think out the kind of God I would like to see in the universe, for the life of me, I couldn't think of anything higher than that God should be like Christ.

The Way
(Week 1, Wednesday)

Is the Way Written in Us?
Romans 1:19-20; 2:14-15; Hebrews 10:16

If Jesus is a moralist imposing a moral code on humanity, then of course we can question that code and his authority. But suppose Jesus is the revealer of the nature of reality, then that makes him different. He is not only revealing the nature of God; he is revealing the nature of life. Life then works in his way and only in his way. Then the Christian Way becomes, not a side issue, but the central issue of life—the one issue of life.

The Way
(Week 1, Friday)

Life-Denying and Life-Affirming
Romans 9:33; 1 Corinthians 3:21-22

Jesus revealed God from within the process of life. He ate and drank and lived in homes; he used parables taken from life and nature; he lifted up the laws underlying life; showed God in the regularities, the natural. Not that he stopped with the natural. He showed God in the extranatural, the supernatural. But it was all supernaturally natural. He revealed Life within life. There is a kinship between the natural and the supernatural. Life was of one piece.

The Way
(Week 6, Thursday)

Listening to His Master's Voice
Romans 8:19-22

Just as the Rosetta stone furnished the clue to the hieroglyphics and made it possible to decipher ancient lore, so Jesus is the Rosetta stone that gives us the clue to the language of creation, to that hidden purpose running through all things. "He is God breaking through" into intelligibility, into redemption. He is God's "open secret."

The Way
(Week 7, Tuesday)

Is the Kingdom Our Good?
Acts 19:8-9; Colossians 1:13

But, strangely, Jesus did not begin with himself as the center of loyalty. He said, "Seek ye first the kingdom of God...; and all these things shall be added unto you" (Matt 6:33 KJV). He made the kingdom the center of loyalty.

The Way
(Week 9, Monday)

The Order and the Person
Acts 8:12; 28:23, 31

Jesus began with the kingdom of God. He went out "preaching the gospel of the kingdom" (Matt 4:23 RSV). But before he was through, he began to preach the gospel of himself: "I am the way, the truth, and the life" (John 14:6). "Come to me,...and I will give you rest" (Matt 11:28). He made "for the sake of the kingdom of God'" (Luke 18:29) and "for my sake" synonymous. He made himself and the kingdom synonymous. The Person and the Order were one.

The Way
(Week 10, Sunday)

Gathering Up Lessons Learned
Acts 5:3-5; 26:14

Jesus is the Door, not only to salvation; he is the Door to everything. Everything opens when you come in his Way.

The Way
(Week 26, Sunday)

The Open Secret
Luke 8:9-10 (Moffat); Ephesians 3:2-6

Jesus is the key to the meaning of the universe. Follow the clues he gives and you get the answers every time. But the answers are hidden answers; they are an "open secret." The secret is a spirit, the spirit of self-surrendered humility. Everything in the kingdom is open to those who surrender to and obey the kingdom. We are in the process of discovering that kingdom hidden in the nature of reality. The kingdom is there, the ground plan of our being.

The Way
(Week 26, Friday)

Grace Did Much More Abound
Romans 5:1-11

Jesus did not come to show us the Way, but to show himself as the Way. "He did not come to preach the gospel, but that there might be a gospel to be preached."

The Way
(Week 28, Sunday)

The Best Man That Ever Lived Believed
John 10:27-29; 12:24-25

Jesus was so right in everything. There isn't a thing he uttered that is not valid for today. There isn't an attitude he took that isn't the highest attitude now. There isn't an act of his that is not now a universal norm. He touched life in all its phases, and everywhere he touched it he rang true—more, he rang Truth.

The Way
(Week 43, Wednesday)

The Marks of Those on the Way
Galatians 6:17; 1 Timothy 6:11-16

Any word or person getting into touch with Jesus is heightened, for Jesus turns all our common nouns into proper nouns. The word *love* gets into contact with him, and you have to spell it *Love*; it's different now. Jesus turns the nobodies into the somebodies and the insignificant into the significant.

The Way
(Week 44, Sunday)

A Disrupted Interior and a Lusterless Face
Matthew 11:2-11

Take the actions of Jesus. They were wonderful, but his reactions were even more wonderful. About half of the New Testament is taken up with a description of his actions, and the other half with his reactions. And his reactions reveal him even more than his actions. His reactions were just as redemptive as his actions.

The Way to Power and Poise
(Week 40, Sunday)

That I May Not Be Shaken
1 Corinthians 15:56-58

"But God raised him up, having loosed the pangs of death, because it was not possible for him to be held by it" (Acts 2:24). The resurrection of Jesus was not based on the sovereign act of God raising Jesus, an act imposed on reality, it was based on the nature of reality: "because it was not possible for him to be held by it." It was impossible for a man like Jesus, who held death in his grasp, to be held by death. The nature of things would be reversed if Jesus should be held captive by death. So the resurrection was not based on an extraneous act of God; it came from the intrinsic fact: he had to rise, being what he was.

The Way to Power and Poise
(Week 45, Monday)

Called to Do the Impossible
Isaiah 6:7

"Now there was a disciple at Damascus named Ananias. The Lord said to him in a vision, 'Ananias.' And he said, 'Here I am, Lord'" (Acts 9:10 RSV). He put himself at God's disposal in a crisis....

One morning at the Sat Tal Ashram, as we sat on the prayer knoll, the Inner Voice said, "If you'll say one thing in every situation, "Here I am, Lord," then I'll take care of the rest. You need worry about nothing." I replied, "I close the bargain." Life was simplified. I had only to do one thing: put myself at God's disposal and God would take care of the rest.

How to Be a Transformed Person
(Week 14, Thursday)

The Word Is Nigh to You
Romans 10: 6-10

A little boy, child of missionaries, was in school in the United State at Christmas time. The principal said to him, "Son, what would you rather have most of all for Christmas?" The boy looked at the picture of his father framed on his desk and remembered acutely the absence of the father in a far-off land, and then quietly said, "I want my father to step out of that frame." The little boy voiced the cry of humanity: We want God our Father to step out of the frame of the universe, out of this impersonal relationship and meet us personally. Jesus is God stepping out of the frame of the universe: God simplified and God personalized, God become intimate and tender and redemptive.

How to Be a Transformed Person
(Week 2, Saturday)

The Divine Yes
Mark 9:21-23

"The divine 'yes' has at last sounded in him, for in him is the 'yes' that affirms all the promises of God" (2 Cor 1:19-20 Moffatt). In Jesus, the divine yes has at last sounded. People were not able to say a full-throated and a full-hearted yes to life until they saw it incarnate in Jesus. Up to that time it had to be yes and no. But when we saw the full meaning of life in Jesus, then at this place we can say yes with no inhibitions or hesitations. Here I am not saying yes at random—a yes for the sake of saying yes—which ends in mushy sentimentality; I'm saying yes in Christ, for in him life is good, creative, and open ended.

Here you can say yes with the stops out. Think, affirm, say, and accept the yes of Jesus, and life itself will become a yes. For you are affirming something that the universe affirms. You are echoing the creative Word of God; the Word that created the worlds, sustains them, and that redeems into affirmation all who affirm life with him. In saying his yes, you align yourself with the creative purposes of God, and all of them work in you and through you.

How to Be a Transformed Person
(Week 20, Tuesday)

The Nobodies Become the Somebodies
Acts 3:14-16

I love Jesus because, for one thing, he shed a shaft of light upon the disinherited peoples of the earth. "You come and walk through the compound of my humble cottage, and it will be purified of all its impurities and inferiorities," said a sweeper, the lowest of the low, to me after he had become a Christian by baptism. I knew his faith was misplaced; I couldn't do that. But I knew Jesus could do and did just that. He walks through our minds and spirits and homes, and lo, life is purified of its impurities and inferiorities....The nobodies become the somebodies; the ordinary become the extraordinary; life begins to live. Dead harps feel the sweep of a hand, and sleeping music is awakened.

Growing Spiritually
(Week 15, Saturday)

Jesus, the Perfect but Unfolding Revelation
Matthew 5:17; Romans 10:3-4; Galatians. 6:14

Life convictions that I hold are...that the revelation of God to humanity is progressive, appearing in varying degrees among all races, and culminating in the final

151

and perfect revelation in Jesus Christ. God apparently intends to redeem the race of humankind, for wherever the mind of humanity is open and receptive, God has revealed the divine self in varying degrees. God has not left himself without witness in any nation (see Acts 14:16-17)....

In Jesus Christ we see what God is like and what people can be like. He is the revelation of both God and people. And he is the final revelation. "Beyond that which is found in Jesus of Nazareth the human race will never progress," said Coleridge [no published source found]. And the years and the centuries say a resounding "Amen."

But if Jesus is final, he is also unfolding. New meanings are constantly breaking out from him and will continue to do so. He is on the other side of our century, beckoning us into the new day. Surprises and new, scintillating meanings break out of his person. Such infinity of revelation could come only from the infinite.

Growing Spiritually
(Week 51, Tuesday)

The Christian Way Works
John 3:35-36, 5:22-24

[Another conviction is] that Jesus Christ will have the last word in human events. It sounds like an incredible thing to say, but events all point to one thing, namely, that the man who walked our dusty roads is now on the throne of the universe and will have the last word in human affairs. This sounds absurd. And yet human affairs are working out just that way. Everything that embodies his will survives, and everything that goes against that will perishes. Jesus is the rock upon which we build or upon which we go to pieces. And there are no exceptions. He is the Alpha—the Christ of the beginning—and the Omega—the Christ of the final word.

Growing Spiritually
(Week 51, Saturday)

We Shall Be Like Him
Colossians 1:9-12

I saw a number of ropes going out from big trees in the forests of Japan to the little trees around. It meant that the big trees were pulling the little trees around them, which were inclined to crookedness, into straightness.

Jesus is the big tree, planted in eternity. I am bound to him by cords of love, and he is pulling me into straightness and will do so both now and forever. I'm out for eternal growth.

Growing Spiritually
(Week 52, Saturday)

The Master
Philippians 2:9-11

The Christian way is centered in...a Master. Jesus Christ was the most masterful Person this planet has ever seen. He walked into time and quietly divided it into before and after—BC and AD. He walked into the realm of thought and altered all our conceptions about God and life and destiny. He walked into our moral conceptions and codes, and now we are good or bad according to whether we embody his spirit or not. He walked into our sundered relations with God and healed them by his cross. He walked into the chaos of human relationships and projected a kingdom that is destined to gather all our chaos into cosmos, to be the goal and end of human history. He walked into our moral weakness and sin and imparted to the defeated and collapsed a moral and spiritual mastery which made them go out and impart to humanity such a stimulus that a movement was begun, which is destined to change the world. The Master mastered people into masterfulness.

Mastery
(Week 1, Sunday)

I Am Not Religious: I'm His
1 Timothy 3:16

Religion, which is to help you to Christ, often stands between you and Christ; you can't see the person for the paraphernalia.

The fact is that Jesus never used the word religion, nor did the early disciples use it. *Religion* means literally "binding back"—a binding back to God. It is humanity's attempts to bind ourselves back to God by various expedients. But the Gospel was not a series of expedients to bind us back to God; it was the good news of God's coming to man in incarnation, in redemption. Jesus didn't come to set a religion against other religions—a little better, a little bit more moral. He came to set the good news over against human need, whether that need be found in this religion, that religion, or no religion. Religion is our search upward; the gospel is God's reach downward. There are many religions; there is but one gospel.

Mastery
(Week 5, Wednesday)

The Earliest Creed: Jesus Is Lord
Philippians 2:9-11

How did it happen that this phrase [Jesus is Lord!] arose out of a fiercely monotheistic people whose central confession was: "Hear, O Israel: the LORD our God is one LORD" (Deut 6:4)? The people who had repeated, "The LORD our God is one LORD," now found themselves repeating, "Jesus is Lord." Was Jesus doing something that only God could do?

Was his touch upon nature and upon human nature the very touch of God? His impact upon nature and human living was so tremendous that they found their unwilling lips making the most momentous confession that ever fell from human lips anywhere at any time. It was life's central revelation. And the revelation was this: "This Man, who walked our dusty roads, slept upon our hillsides, was crucified on one of our trees, and was laid in one of our rock tombs, was at the right hand of final authority—was Lord and would have the final say in human affairs." That confession was breathtaking.

Mastery
(Week 25, Tuesday)

153

We Are Drifting into Humanism
John 17:1-3

Where groups have taken Jesus as teacher and example but not as Lord, there the key to God slips through their fingers. For them, Jesus as teacher and example takes his place among the other moralists and philosophers who point to truth. But they are not the truth. Jesus never pointed to truth; he pointed to himself and said: "I am the Truth." he never pointed to the Way as a signpost; he simply said: "I am the Way." He did not philosophize about life; he said: "I am the Life." And the amazing thing is that when we follow him, it works. He becomes the Way, the Truth, the Life. His ways become the Way. His truths become the Truth. His life becomes the Life. In him we see God. And apart from him, God is vague and uncertain.

Mastery
(Week 25, Thursday)

Turning the World Upside Down
Acts 17: 5-8

[The apostle Paul] not only positively changed people; he did something more—he "turned the world upside down." In his positive presentation of Jesus, a revolution in thought and act and attitude was taking place....

The revolution was accomplished by seed thoughts.... So Paul dropped seed thoughts into ancient structures, and they crumbled.

1. The Jesus that Paul preached reversed the method of revelation. Hitherto it was a verbal revelation—a book, a voice. Now it was a vital revelation—a Life, a Person.

2. Jesus reversed the method of salvation. Hitherto people were doing something for God; while in Jesus, God was doing something for people. Salvation was a gift.

3. Jesus reversed the method of inheriting the earth. Hitherto people tried to inherit it by conquest, by force; and here Jesus was teaching them to inherit it by meekness, by receptivity. The earth belongs to those who know how to inherit the earth by meekly learning its secrets and obeying its laws.

Mastery
(Week 26, Wednesday)

The Majors Reveals
Revelation 21:5-7

We are looking at the ways the world was turned upside down with the impact of the Jesus whom Paul preached.

Jesus reversed the method of greatness. Before Jesus, those who were greatly served were great; and the greater the number of servants, the greater the person. But Jesus reversed that by making those great who greatly served others. That opened greatness to all—not the getters but the givers were great. Jesus himself was an illustration of this....

Jesus reversed the method of being defiled. Before he came, you were defiled by "unclean" foods and by touching "unclean" persons and things. But Jesus said "It's not what goes into the the mouth that contaminates a person in God's sight. It's what comes

154

out" (Matt 15:11 CEB). That which goes to the person is physical, but that which comes out of a person—evil thoughts, evil words, evil acts—comes from the heart and defiles the person. Here he turned purity from the ceremonial to the moral, the greatest moral turn upward that has ever been made in human history and the most effective and decisive.

Mastery
(Week 26, Thursday)

The Mastery of the Secondhand
Romans 8:1-2

If Jesus is to be power, then it must not be by a repeating of his name at secondhand—the Jesus who is real to somebody else—he must be real to you....As "Mary" says: "They preach Jesus, but don't preach Jesus available." Jesus is never available if you are preaching a secondhand Jesus.

Mastery
(Week 34, Thursday)

Nobody but Me and Jesus
John 16:31-33

The God revealed in Jesus was personalized. He was not mere vague force; he was a Person with whom you could talk and have him talk to you in unmistakable terms. I can testify; I know Jesus better than I know any other person in the world. And he knows me better than anyone else in the world knows me, and he still loves me.

Mastery
(Week 50, Monday)

Jesus Is God Incarnate
Philipians 2:5-11

Everything hinged on Jesus as incarnate, not Jesus as inspiration, not Jesus as moral teacher, not Jesus as philosopher. But Jesus as incarnate God, that was the issue! And that might well be the issue, for if Jesus is incarnate God, then everything pales into insignificance beside the importance of the fact.

Christian Maturity
(Week 1, Saturday)

God-Salvation or Self-Salvation?
Ephesians 2:7-8

The starting point of the Christian faith is Jesus. As I said in another book: You cannot say God until you have first said Jesus, for Jesus puts content into God. You cannot say Christ until you have first said Jesus, for Jesus puts content into Christ. You cannot say the Holy Spirit until you have first said Jesus, for Jesus puts content into the Holy Spirit. You cannot say the kingdom of God until you first say Jesus, for Jesus puts content into the kingdom of God.

Christian Maturity
(Week 1, Thursday)

Getting Our Starting Point Straight
Revelation 1:17-18

You will be tempted in your quest for maturity to do what the Gnostics did, bypass Jesus and turn to something that seems more intellectual, more modern, more in keeping with the times, more intellectually fashionable. And you will end where the Gnostics ended, in oblivion. Gnosticism has died; Jesus lives on. All the intellectual descendants of Gnosticism will also end in futility and oblivion. Everything not centered in Jesus is off center.

Christian Maturity
(Week 3, Sunday)

Introduction

If you are in Christ, you are in life; if you are out of Christ you are out of life. If that proposition be true, then it cuts down through all veneer, all the make-believe in life.

In Christ
(p. ix)

Attached to Exhaustible Emphases

When your faith and loyalty and love are fastened on Jesus Christ centrally and fundamentally, they are fastened upon the inexhaustible. He never grows stale, trite, or empty of growing meaning. In him you find an eternal unfoldment. The more you see the more you see there is to be seen. In him there is a surprise around every corner. The Holy Spirit unfolds the unfolding revelation, taking care of the things of Christ and showing them to us. It keeps one running to keep up with unfolding truth. The absolute in him is always beckoning to our relativisms. We are under the law of an eternal change—a change "into his likeness from one degree of glory to another" (2 Cor 3:18).

In Christ
(Week 22, Monday)

In Christ Distinctions Obliterated

The next passage is rich beyond words: "There [in Christ] is neither Jew nor Greek [race distinction], there is neither slave nor free [social and economic distinction], there is neither male nor female [gender distinction], for you are all one in Christ Jesus" (Gal 3:28). Another pair of distinctions are added in Colossians 3:11: "Here there cannot be Greek and Jew, circumcised and uncircumcised, barbarian, Scythian, slave, free man, but Christ is all, and in all." "Circumcised and uncircumcised" [outer religious distinction], "barbarian or Scythian" [cultural distinction]: in Christ there "cannot be" race, social and economic, gender, outer religious signs or cultural distinction....All things that divide us are gone. A new society has arisen, where a person is a person—a person for whom Christ died.

In Christ
(Week 29, Tuesday)

156

To Walk in the Same Way

The one thing that brings assurance that we are in [Christ] is that we "walk in the same way in which he walked" (1 John 2:6). To walk as he walked is to live as he lived. Can we live as he lived? In the same circumstances? No. On the same principles? Yes. We can apply his principles to our circumstances.

1. He met life as a man, calling on no power for his own moral battle, [which is] not at your disposal or mine. He expected God to give him power to meet whatever came and to use it for higher purposes. He expected no favored treatment and got none. We can apply that principle: Meet life as it comes and make something out of it.

2. He kept up his disciplines of reading the word of God and praying. "As his custom was...he stood up to read" (Luke 4:16). "He went out to the mountain to pray" (Luke 6:12), "as was his custom" (Luke 22:39). We can apply that principle: Have a disciplined life of reading the Word and praying

3. He gave out what he found. "And again, as his custom was, he taught them" (Mark 10:1). We can apply this principle: Share with others what you have found from God.

4. He gave out love and only love to everybody, to enemies as well as friends. We can apply that principle: Love everybody, even enemies.

5. He made a full surrender to God: "not my will, but thine, be done" (Luke 22:42). We can apply that principle: A full surrender of the will.

6. "He set his face [steadfastly] to go to Jerusalem" (Luke 9:51). Applied: Face everything, even the hardest, with God.

In Christ
(Week 47, Sunday)

Why "the Word"
John 1:1-3

Why was Jesus here called "the Word" (in John 1:1)? Well, one's words are the expression of the hidden thought.... Only as the hidden thought is put into a word is the thought communicated.

Here is the hidden God, like the hidden thought, and we cannot know what God is like unless God communicates through a word. If one says, "I can know God in my heart intuitively and immediately, without the mediation of a word," then the answer is, "But your 'heart' then becomes the medium of communication, and knowing the heart as one does—with its sin and crosscurrents and cross-conceptions—we know it is a very unsafe medium for the revelation of God." God must be revealed.

The Word Became Flesh
(Week 1, Sunday)

The Word Is the Child of the Thought
John 1:4-5

Jesus is God available. Jesus is not a third person standing between you and God. When you take hold of Jesus, you take hold of God. Jesus is a mediator only in the sense

157

that he mediates God to you. When you know Jesus, you know God. Just as the thought and the word are one, so Jesus could say, "I and the Father are one" (John 10:30).

The Word Became Flesh
(Week 1, Monday)

The Silence of Eternity Has Been Broken
1 Corinthians 2:9-10

If you are to see God face to face you must see God in the face of Jesus Christ. For Jesus is God approachable, God available, God simplified, and God lovable. The Word has become flesh.

The Word Became Flesh
(Week 1, Saturday)

A Person to Be Followed
John 21:18-19

A great many people think Jesus was a moralist imposing a moral code upon humanity; a code for which humanity is badly made. It is an impossible code, which humanity, being what it is, cannot fulfill. But Jesus was not a moralist in that sense at all. He was a revealer of the nature of reality. First, of God; he said if you want to know what God is like look at me. "He who has seen me has seen the Father" (John 14:9). We see the Father in the face of the Son....

Second, Jesus was a revealer of the laws that underlie the universe. He seldom used the imperative, almost never the subjunctive, almost entirely the indicative. "This is," he said, "and you must come to terms with it, or get hurt." When Jesus finished the Sermon on the Mount "the crowds were astonished at his teaching, for he taught them as one who had authority, and not as their scribes" (Matt 7:28-29). The scribes quoted authorities, secondhand teaching; Jesus spoke with authority, firsthand teaching. The term "with authority" could be translated "according to the nature of things." Jesus revealed the nature of things. He was a revealer of the nature of reality.

The Word Became Flesh
(Week 3, Thursday)

Jesus Was the Message
1 Corinthians 2:1-5

You see God in the face of Jesus Christ, the Son, or you do not see God. You may see your imagination of God, but you do not see God. That is what Jesus meant when he said: "I am the way, and the truth, and the life; no one comes to the Father, but by me" (John 14:6).

The Word Became Flesh
(Week 4, Saturday)

"I Am the Way, and the Truth": Right Order?
John 14:5-7

It is no mere chance that the order, "I am the way, and the truth, and the life" (John 14:6), is as it is; the Way first. Jesus had to be the Way before he was the Truth and the

Life. If "the truth" had been put first, that would mean that we would have been sent on a quest for verbal truth; Christianity would have become a philosophical system or a theological system.

No, Jesus is the Way before he is the Truth. For truth has to be put under life to see if it is truth.

The Word Became Flesh
(Week 5, Wednesday)

Sermon on the Mount Unrealistic?
John 7:14-17

The Sermon on the Mount is beyond most of us, but it is not thereby idealism. What we are trying to live is an inverted realism—a realism that is a bad idealism, which won't work—it lands us in a mess. Nothing sustains it except our own unrealistic wills. The universe doesn't sustain it, hence to live some way other than the Sermon on the Mount turns out badly, turns out to be the kind of mess we are now in, individually and collectively.

But the Sermon on the Mount is realism. First of all, it is a portrait of Jesus himself. He put into words the principles and attitudes he was acting upon. This Sermon is not preaching but revelation, a revelation of the inner life and character of Jesus. It is the Word become flesh in relationships. Jesus is here not imposing an impossible code on human nature, a code for which humanity is badly made. He is lifting up principles underlying the universe. When he finished speaking, "the crowds were astonished at his teaching, for he taught them as one who had authority, and not as their scribes" (Matt 7:29). The phrase as "one who had authority" could be translated "according to the nature of things." He lifted up out of reality the principles that were according to "the nature of things." The people who heard Jesus felt the "authority" of what he was saying. It hit them with an inner thud. Impossible idealism doesn't do that. It arouses you emotionally, but it doesn't come with authority.

The Word Became Flesh
(Week 21, Sunday)

No Difference ... If Jesus Never Lived
1 Corinthians 15:13-19

We are looking at those who bypass the Incarnation as the antichrist. Why does the non-Christian prefer that we preach principles and not the Person? It is simple; the Person demands decision and commitment: Follow me. The principles demand study and weighing, but no life commitment. Principles demand no more than mental assent; but Jesus, the Person, demands us as persons—the total person—not mental assent, but life decision and dedication. The difference is profound. Another Hindu said to me, "We are all interested in the universal Christ." And when I asked him, "Not in the incarnate Jesus?" he replied, "No, we are only interested in the universal Christ." The reason was obvious: Into the universal Christ—the Christ not rooted in history—they could put any content, even a Hindu content. But you cannot put any content you want into Jesus, the

159

Incarnate, for he has put his own content, the content of his life and teaching lived out in history. He is in history, though now universal, and demands that we follow him in history and in our own day-by-day lives.

The Word Became Flesh
(Week 32, Monday)

The Concrete Christ
Luke 11:27-28

[Jesus] is the Concrete Christ.

Jesus, the mystic, was amazingly concrete and practical. Into an atmosphere filled with speculation and wordy disputation, where people were drunk with the wine of their own wordiness, he brought the refreshing sense of practical reality. Jesus taught, but he did not speculate. He never used such words as perhaps, maybe, I think so. Even his words had a concrete feeling about them. They fell upon the soul with the authority of certainty. They were self-verifying.

He did not discourse on the sacredness of motherhood; he suckled as a babe at his mother's breast, and that scene has forever consecrated motherhood.

He did not argue that life was a growth and character was an attainment. He "increased in wisdom and in stature, and in favor with God and man" (Luke 2:52).

He did not speculate on why temptation should be in the world; he met it, and after forty days' struggle in the wilderness he conquered, and "returned in the power of the Spirit into Galilee" (Luke 4:14).

He did not discourse on the dignity of labor; he worked at a carpenter's bench, and this makes the toil of the hands honorable.

The Word Became Flesh
(Week 51, Sunday)

He Did Not Discuss Immortality; He Raised the Dead
Luke 10:29-37

As Jesus came among us, he did not try to prove the existence of God; he brought God. He lived in God, and people looking upon his face could not find it within themselves to doubt God.

Jesus did not argue, as Socrates, the immortality of the soul; he raised the dead.

Jesus did not speculate on how God was a Trinity; he said, "If it is by the Spirit of God that I cast out demons then the kingdom of God has come upon you" (Matt 12:28). Here the Trinity—"I," "Spirit of God," "God"—was not something to be speculated about, but was a working force for redemption, the casting out of demons and the bringing in of the kingdom.

Jesus did not teach in a didactic way about the worth of children; he put his hands upon them and, setting one in their midst, tersely said, "To such belongs the kingdom of heaven" (Matt 19:14), and he raised them from the dead.

He did not argue that God answers prayer; he prayed, sometimes all night and in the morning "the power of the Lord was with him to heal" (Luke 5:17).

He did not paint in glowing colors the beauties of friendship and the need for human

160

sympathy; he wept at the grave of his friend Lazarus.

He did not discuss the question of the worth of personality as we do today; he loved and saved persons.

The Word Became Flesh
(Week 51, Monday)

The Divine Illustration
Mark 1:16-20

Jesus did not discourse on the equal worth of personality; he went to the poor and outcast and ate with them.

He did not argue the worth of womanhood and the necessity of giving women equal rights; he treated them with infinite respect, gave to them his most sublime teaching, as to the woman at the well, and when he rose from the dead he appeared first to a woman.

He did not teach in the schoolroom manner the necessity of humility; he girded himself with a towel and washed his disciples' feet.

He did not prove how pain and sorrow in the universe could be compatible with the love of God; he took on himself at the cross everything that spoke against the love of God, and through that pain and tragedy and sin showed the very love of God.

He did not discourse on how the weakest human material can be transformed and made to contribute to the welfare of the world; he called to him a set of weak people, as the Galilean fishermen, transformed them, and sent them out to begin the mightiest movement for uplift and redemption the world has ever seen.

He wrote no books, only once are we told that he wrote and that was in the sand; but he wrote upon the hearts and consciences of people about him and it has become the world's most precious writing.

He did not point to a utopia, far off and unrealizable; he announced that the kingdom of heaven is within us and is "at hand" and can be realized here and now.

We do not find Jesus arguing that the spiritual life should conquer matter; he walked on the water.

The Word Became Flesh
(Week 51, Tuesday)

161

He Loved.
Mark 6:35-42

[Jesus] did not discourse on the beauty of love; he loved.

He greatly felt the pressing necessity of the physical needs of the people around him, but he did not merely speak on their behalf; he fed the five thousand people with five loaves and two fishes.

He did not speak only on behalf of the Gentiles; he went across the lake and fed the four thousand, made up largely of Gentiles, and ate with them as a kind of corporate Communion....

He did not argue the possibility of sinlessness; he presented himself and said, "Which of you convicts me of sin?" (John 8:46).

The Word Became Flesh
(Week 51, Wednesday)

Jesus Christ Means to Me, First of All, Redemption
1 Corinthians 1:30-31

The first thing Christ means to me is redemption. I met him first at an altar of prayer. I came there with nothing to offer except my moral and spiritual bankruptcy. To my astonishment he took me, forgave me, reconciled me to God, to myself, to others, to nature, to life, and sent my happy soul singing its way down the years.

The Word Became Flesh
(Week 52, Monday)

Resources and Guidance
2 Corinthians 1:20, 22

The second thing Jesus means to me is resources. I ran for about a year after my conversion under cloudless skies, and then I ran into stormy weather. But the storms were within—deep within—from the fact of an unredeemed subconscious. My conscious mind was converted in conversion, but apparently my subconscious was not. So a crisis ensued. In that crisis I surrendered all I knew—the conscious, and all I didn't know—the subconscious. And then something happened. When I arose from my knees, a quiet but profound joy possessed me. I knew the Holy Spirit had moved into the subconscious and had cleansed it, coordinated it with the conscious. So now conscious and subconscious were under one control, the control of the Holy Spirit....

The third thing [Jesus] means to me is guidance. My life had become, not a self- or circumstance-guided life, but a God-guided life. In all the great crises, and in the smaller crises—and more, in the daily round—I have felt a hand not my own on the helm. Not automatically, I can still insist on my way, can take the helm myself, and pay the penalty. But God never leaves me and takes over again, with my penitent consent, when I'm about to go on the rocks. And I've found it profoundly true, in the words of a group, "Where God guides, God provides."

The Word Became Flesh
(Week 52, Tuesday)

162

Adequacy: The Power to Make Everything Contribute
Philippians 1:12-14

The fourth thing that Jesus Christ means to me is adequacy, the power to use everything that comes. I do not ask for special treatment, to be God's spoiled child (though sometimes I wonder if I'm not) but to be able to take what comes—good, bad, and indifferent—and make something out of it....But I was a long time learning that secret. After a period of fumbling it came as a revelation through the Scriptures; when you are delivered up before courts and magistrates "this will be a time for you to bear testimony" (Luke 21:13). The injustice that brought you before courts can be used for a testimony. The injustice becomes opportunity. In Jesus everything is opportunity. So I do not ask for special treatment, or for exemptions, I ask for adequacy to use what happens and make something out of it. Everything—literally everything—furthers those who follow Christ.

The Word Became Flesh
(Week 52, Wednesday)

Jesus Christ Means Education
John 6:33-37

The fifth thing Jesus means to me is education. I've always felt uneducated. I have nothing but a college degree, and from a small college at that. I have some honorary degrees but I've felt uneducated when in company with the really educated. When MAs and PhDs get their degrees by dissertations on "The Theology of E. Stanley Jones," my reaction is, "Have I a theology?" What theology I have is a byproduct of evangelism among the intellectuals of India and other parts of the world. An author of twenty-three books? It all seems a mistake, for I never intended to be an author. I simply write when I see a need and the urge is upon me. Then somehow I must be educated. The secret is in Jesus. He is the Awakener, Awakener of the total person, including the mind. Since I've never felt educated, I've made life and people educate me, a lifelong process. My mind has become a magnet, so I pull from every person, every situation, some information, and some truth to further me. And as I am compelled, or impelled to give, so I am compelled to get in order to give.

The Word Became Flesh
(Week 52, Thursday)

My Code Is a Character
John 7:37-39

The sixth thing Jesus means to me is health. I don't make that first, but as a byproduct of all I've said before, health emerges. In a health crisis a few years ago, Jesus said to me: "In me you are well and whole." It was important, for it meant that if I stepped out of him into resentments, fear, self-preoccupation, and guilt, I was not well, and I was not whole. I can only be "well" as long as I am "whole," and I am "whole" only as long as I remain in Jesus.

The seventh thing Jesus means to me is that my code is a character, that character is Jesus Christ himself. You can outgrow a code, but you never outgrow a character if that character is a divine character. The more you see the more there is to be seen. He is an unfolding revelation, forever with you and forever beyond you. There is a surprise around every corner, life is popping with novelty, never a dull moment.

The Word Became Flesh
(Week 52, Friday)

In Jesus I Have Everything
John 1:29-34

The eighth thing Jesus Christ means to me is the kingdom of God, God's total answer to our total need. Without this fact of the kingdom our faith would be a personal allegiance to a person; it would lack total meaning, individual and corporate. But with Jesus and the kingdom one—he is the kingdom—then "all authority" is in him both "in heaven and on earth." I belong to the sum total of reality and the sum total of reality belongs to me.

Ninth, Jesus Christ means eternal life to me. I don't need to wait until the hereafter; I have it now in him. I am sure of heaven, for I'm sure of Jesus. To be in him is to be in heaven wherever you are. So whether I live or die, so-called, is a matter of comparative indifference.

Tenth, Jesus Christ means to me a divine-human fellowship in the church....The church has been the mother of my spirit; at her altars I found Christ. When I found Christ, I found the church. But I do not belong to the church, though I'm a member of it; I belong to Christ; the church belongs to me, a gift of grace. It's the most precious fellowship the world holds.

Eleventh, Jesus Christ means to me self-surrender. Not a self-surrender once and for all—it is that—but a continuous, moment-by-moment surrender of my self and my problems as they arise. I say to him, "I am yours and this problem is yours; tell me what to do about it." One morning as I got out of bed, I said to myself, "Stanley, how are you?" And I found myself replying, "Well, I am his." That settled everything. So when I have Jesus Christ—the Word become flesh—I have everything. For he has me, has me with the consent of all my being as "I commend my Savior to you" (Charles Wesley, "Thy Faithfulness, Lord, Each Moment We Find," 1741).

The Word Became Flesh
(Week 52, Saturday)

MIRACLES

Overcoming the World of the Spectacular
John 7:2-8

Jesus was fiercely tempted at the place of being spectacular. He had the power, could it not be used to impress people? Of course it would all be in the furtherance of the kingdom, and would it not therefore be right? But he turned down very decisively this temptation. He overcame the world of the spectacular. He would win by worth and service alone. Everything else was of the devil. He was right. Had he advertised himself, we should have forgotten him. His reticence was more vocal than his self-display would have been. He did not go to the pinnacle of the temple, but we put him on the throne of the universe for this very reason. He refused a miracle before Herod, and we denounce the asking and remember the refusal.

Victorious Living
(Week 18, Thursday)

Do Not Dress Up Negativism as a Friend
John 6:66-68; Galatians 5:1; 2 Timothy 1:7

No startling miracle of deliverance will happen unless we cooperate. The miracle of deliverance will work as we work, but only as we work. Don't sit helplessly and expect either God or humanity to perform a miracle on you. But both God and humanity can perform a miracle through you if you cooperate.

Abundant Living
(Week 15, Wednesday)

God Guides through Mental Processes
Mark 12:29-30; Luke 12:57; 2 Timothy 2:7

Just as God uses guidance enough to show us God is there, but not too much to weaken initiative, so God works miracles, but sparingly. God's self-revelation is not a magical but a moral revelation. Just enough miracle to fortify the moral.

The Way
(Week 41, Thursday)

In Everything God Works for Good
2 Corinthians 6:3-10

Affirmation for the Day: I shall not look for miracles today; I shall be one, a miracle of grace.

The Way to Power and Poise
(Week 23, Monday)

Many Religions—One Gospel
Romans 8:3-4

We must now look at the most stupendous thing this planet has seen: God being transformed into our image that we may be transformed into God's image. The Incarnation is the miracle of miracles. Grant that central miracle, and all other miracles in the New Testament become credible in the light of this central miracle.

How to Be a Transformed Person
(Week 2 Thursday)

The Nobodies Become Somebodies
Ephesians 4:22-24

Wherever the impact of the New Testament is made on life today the same miracles of changed lives appear.

How to Be a Transformed Person
(Week 12, Sunday)

He Turned Beer into Furniture
1 Corinthians 1:17-18

A skeptic was heckling the Christians. "Do you believe that Jesus turned water into wine?" he asked. "Well, I don't know," said one man, "but this I do know, that in my home he turned beer into furniture." The miracle of changed lives is taking place today in the degree that it is being tried. "Whosoever" (see John 3:16 KJV) works wheresoever and by whomsoever, whenever it is really tried.

How to Be a Transformed Person
(Week 18, Thursday)

Growth in the Fruits of the Spirit
1 Corinthians 1:20-23

Paul says there are nine [fruits of the Spirit]: "Love, joy, peace, good temper, kindliness, generosity, fidelity, gentleness, self-control" (Gal 5:22 Moffatt).

These nine qualities of life are the natural outcome of the Spirit within. Now note that every one of these is a moral quality and not a magical power. To be filled with the Spirit is often looked on as making one a seven-day wonder—healing the sick, stopping tornadoes, changing the weather—signs and wonders. The Spirit-filled person becomes a dispenser of miracles. Now miracles do happen in the Christian impact; the sick are healed, and unexpected things do happen, but nowhere as a central emphasis. They are byproducts of something deeper. When you emphasize the byproduct and underemphasize the product, you will lose both the byproduct and the product. The product is life characterized by nine qualities, all of them moral, not one of them magical. The emphasis therefore is thrown—and rightly thrown—on the moral and spiritual instead of the magical and wonder-working. This is sound. This keeps the

Christian impact redemptive, functioning as moral and spiritual changes in character instead of miracles in nature.

Growing Spiritually
(Week 18, Sunday)

On Dividing What God Has Joined
Acts 6:1-6

One comment on speaking in tongues. My conviction is the Pentecost type of tongues—the power to speak effectively in other languages without an interpreter—has disappeared; but the Corinth type of tongues—needing an interpreter—appears here and there. They are not the same. Many come to India hoping to reproduce the miracle at Pentecost and speak in the languages of India without an interpreter or learning the language. It hasn't happened. The wreckage of those hopes is strewn across India. You learn the language or use an interpreter, or you don't get your message across.

This special miracle at Pentecost, for this special purpose, served that purpose and disappeared. For God performs miracles, but just enough, not too many. Too many would make us lazy. Too few would make us hazy.

Mastery
(Week 12, Tuesday)

The Unity of the Spirit
Ephesians 3:1-6

We have seen the…unities that came into being with the coming of the Holy Spirit. They are an amazing list: unity with God, with themselves as persons, among the inner circle—the twelve—unity of all believers, with enemies, and in material relationships. To these must be added some unities we have seen previously: unity of the secular and the sacred, of all classes, all races, all ages—old and young—both genders in a spiritual equality, the ministry and the laity. Everybody and everything were brought into a living unity, called the "unity of the Spirit."

Mastery
(Week 18, Thursday)

By the Grace of God I Am What I Am
1 Peter 1:22-23

The eyes of the disciples and of the people were on Jesus as the source of the miracle. They weren't seven-day wonders, dispensing miracles because of their divinity or their perfection; they pointed to Jesus.

Mastery
(Week 28, Saturday)

167

The Eternal God Becomes Like Us
Colossians 1:15-17

This is the central miracle: the Eternal God became like us that we may become like the Eternal God.

Christian Maturity
(Week 2, Sunday)

The Water I Give...Shall Become a Spring

["The water I shall give him will become...a spring of water welling up to eternal life" (John 4:14).] This is a miracle of giving! To give to people and not weaken them or make them dependent is difficult. Here what Christ gives from above becomes a spring from beneath. He gives and produces initiative in the recipient. That is not only grace, it is also a revelation of the intention of grace; it is to produce creative personalities.

In Christ
(Week 15, Thursday)

He Hath Visited and Redeemed
Luke 1:67-68; 76-79

Jesus called on no power not at our disposal for his own moral battle. He performed no miracle to extricate himself from any difficulty. If Jesus had power, he had power to restrain power, holding it only for the meeting of human need in others. He never performed a miracle just to show power or to confound an enemy. Jesus lived a normal life, so normal that it became the norm. He dwelt among us as one of us.

The Word Became Flesh
(Week 3, Monday)

168

RELIGION

In Which Religion Is Defined for Us
John 1:14; 1 John 1:1-4

Yesterday we said that religion resulted from the double movement of our aspirations and God's inspirations. His life impinges upon ours at every point. The result? Something disturbs [us]; we aspire, we pray, we revolt against what we are.

The meeting place of this upward movement and this downward movement is Christ. He is humanity ascending and God descending—the Son of man, the Son of God. Since he is the meeting place of the two sides of religion, he becomes its definition. To the one hundred and fifty definitions we add one more: Christ. This is not a spelled-out definition, but a lived-out definition. Some things cannot be said, they have to be shown. So it has been shown us what constitutes religion: Christ's spirit of life. His relationships with God and people, his purity, his love, his mastery over the environments of people and things, his care for the sinful and the underprivileged, his redemptive purposes for us and for society, his overleaping sympathy that wiped out all race and class and bound us into a community, his final willingness to take all our pain, all our defeat, all our sin into his own heart and die for us, and his offer to us of a new way and program of life—the kingdom of God on earth—all this, and his sheer victory of spirit amid it all, constitutes religion.

Victorious Living
(Week 2, Tuesday)

Why I Should Give My Allegiance to the Church
Acts 20:28; Ephesians 3:14-15; 5:23-32; Colossians 1:17-18

There is no such thing as solitary religion. If it is solitary, it is not religion, for Jesus expressed religion as love to God and love to people. There can be no love to people unless life is lived out in relationships. "To be is to be in relationship." The Christian's life can be lived only in the give-and-take of corporate relationships.

Abundant Living
(Week 45, Thursday)

Can We Be Too Christian?
Matthew 19:16-22

A prominent member of the church showed in these words that he thought the Christian way is alien to life, that you might have too much of it: "You can have too much of religion. You must live a balanced life and make religion one of the interests of life." Of course you can have too much of religion that is off center, not centered in Christ; but if the Christian way is the Way, then it is not one of the interests of life, it is Life controlling all life.

The Way
(Week 6, Sunday)

169

The Christian Way Is Sense
James 3:13-18

A doctor flung himself in a chair in front of me and eagerly asked, "Is religion natural?" His acceptance or rejection of it depended upon the answer. I could answer, "If you mean by religion, Christ—for he is my definition of religion—then the answer is an unqualified yes." Moreover it can be added, everything that doesn't fit into his spirit is unnatural.

The Way
(Week 6, Saturday)

A Religion of the Spirit
2 Corinthians 3:15-18

The Christian faith is a religion of the Spirit....

But it is a religion of the Spirit conditioned by the content that Jesus puts within it by his life and teaching. If Jesus reveals the nature of the Father, he also reveals the nature of the Spirit. For people have odd ideas of the nature of the Spirit and the Spirit's possession. If God is a Christlike God, then the Spirit is a Christlike Spirit.

The Way to Power and Poise
(Week 5, Thursday)

The Word Become Flesh
John 1:14-18

There are many religions; there is but one gospel. So the gospel does not stand alongside other religions and philosophies; it confronts all religions, all philosophies, all life, with the good news.

The Way to Power and Poise
(Week 9, Monday)

All Places Sacred
John 4:21-24

When the Holy Spirit came upon that group in a home [at Pentecost], it lifted God's availability out of the hands of priests, places, and the paraphernalia of organized religion. These things and persons may be useful in helping us to find God, but not one of them is necessary. God's hands are not tied by anyone's cords of validity and sanctions. Wherever the human heart meets the inner conditions, there God is available. This is the most freeing thing that ever happened in religion. God will use any person, any building, any rite or ceremony, that looks beyond itself and is the instrument of the divine; but God is not confined to anything, except two avenues: God comes through Christ and God comes to a person, whoever and wherever that person may be, provided that person lifts up a surrendered, trusting heart to God through Christ.

The Way to Power and Poise
(Week 13, Sunday)

Intellectual, Spiritual, and Moral
Romans 16:25-27

Religion, in order to be effective, must have intellectual penetration, spiritual insight, and moral power. The first two without the last are moonshine. The last without the first two is a wild-fire. The combination is light and power.

The Way to Power and Poise
(Week 17, Friday)

Life Is Reduced to Simplicity
Titus 3:3-6

The idea that religion is imposed and unnatural is perhaps the chief hindrance to its wholehearted acceptance. A little boy sampling a new and delicious Thanksgiving pudding said, "I know this must be bad for me, for it is so good." But the good is good for us, and the bad is bad for us. We are made by the Spirit for the Spirit; and therefore when we receive the Spirit, we find ourselves.

The Way to Power and Poise
(Week 18, Friday)

Is There Any Divine Initiative?
Hebrews 1:1-3

The religious urge is found in [the] life urge. It is the life urge turned qualitative. It is the cry for life turned into the cry for better life. And the moment we say better, we have standards; and the moment we have standards, we have religion. As long as people want to live fully and better, we will be religious. The forms of religion may come and go, but the spirit of religion is deathless from age to age. For it is the cry for life turned qualitative.

How to Be a Transformed Person
(Week 2, Wednesday)

"Tenigue" (*Tension* and *Fatigue*)
2 Corinthians 11:23-28

At an altar of prayer, two men knelt beside a penitent and whispered opposite advice. One said, "Hold on," and the other said, "Let go." These two bits of advice depict two types of religion. One says, "Grit your teeth, fight, whip your will, hold on." The other says: "Surrender your will, accept the Gift of God, let go and let God." They issue in two types of persons: one strained, the other confident.

Growing Spiritually
(Week 7, Thursday)

I Am Not Religious: I'm His

1 Timothy 3:16

Religion, which is to help you to Christ, often stands between you and Christ; you can't see the person for the paraphernalia.

The fact is that Jesus never used the word religion, nor did the early disciples use it. *Religion* means literally "binding back"—a binding back to God. It is humanity's attempts to bind ourselves back to God by various expedients. But the gospel was not a series of expedients to bind us back to God; it was the good news of God's coming to us in incarnation, in redemption. Jesus didn't come to set a religion against other religions—a little better, a little bit more moral. He came to set the good news over against human need, whether that need be found in this religion, that religion, or no religion. Religion is our search upward; the gospel is God's reach downward. There are many religions; there is but one gospel.

What terms did Jesus use if he didn't use the term religion? He used the "kingdom of God," the "Way," and both were embodied in himself: "I am the way." All these terms are inward pushes toward the person Jesus and through him to God.

Mastery
(Week 5, Wednesday)

The Mastery of Sacred Places

1 Peter 2:9-10

The Holy Spirit came upon them when they were in the most common place—a place where we all live—a home. Under that apparently insignificant fact lays a deep significance. It was an amazing emancipation for religion. For up to this time religion had been associated with sacred places, sacred vestments, and sacred persons. Now the center of gravity in religion shifted from places to persons, from vestments to vitality, from services to service. It was a most important shift. It saved religion from sterility and saved humanity to vitality. Religion was put where it belongs—in the human heart.

Mastery
(Week 9, Sunday)

The Way, Which They Call a Sect

Matthew 5:17-20

Many Christians, and practically all non-Christians, make the Way into a sect by making it a religion....But Jesus never used the word religion, nor did he conceive of himself setting one religion alongside other religions. He came to set the gospel over against all human need, whether in this religion, that religion, or no religion. He came to set the Way over against ways.

Mastery
(Week 29, Wednesday)

The Mastery of the Secondhand
Romans 8:1-12

Secondhand religion is always overpowered by firsthand evil. The comparative impotence of the church is caused by the secondhand nature of its religion. Its religion is in creeds, in rituals, in books, in services, in prayers; but it is not a fountain of firsthand living experience of Jesus.

Mastery
(Week 34, Thursday)

Religion: Humanity's Search for God
Acts 17:22-28

All religions are humanity's attempt to climb to God; Jesus is God's descent to humanity. All religions are our's search for God; Jesus is God's search for us. Therefore there are many religions, but there is but one gospel. So Jesus did not bring a religion to set alongside of other religions—one a little better, more moral, more spiritual. He came to set the gospel over against human need, whether that need be in this religion, that religion, or in no religion.

Christian Maturity
(Week 1, Friday)

The Eternal God Becomes Like Us
Colossians 1:15-17

Religion? [Jesus] never mentioned the word, but if you were to ask my definition of religion, I would point to him: he is religion.

Christian Maturity
(Week 2, Sunday)

Right Is Right, Everywhere and Eternally
James 3:10-12

This linking of religion and morality is important, for both religion and morality. There can be no real religion without morality, and there can be no real morality without religion. Both are rooted in the ultimate fact of the universe—God.

Christian Maturity
(Week 9, Wednesday)

Go Directly to Jesus

In the world of Paul, the mystery religions, particularly Gnosticism, had built up between people and God a hierarchy of angels and principal power as intermediaries. You could not get to God except through them. They were beneficent, but were blocks on the climb to God; you had to go through them. Paul sweeps away these intermediaries when he says, "There is one mediator between God and men, the man Christ Jesus" (1 Tim 2:5).

In Christ
(Week 9, Monday)

Principles Instead of a Person?
2 Corinthians 3:4-6

[Here] is the difference between philosophy and real religion: one is cold, calculating, and uncommitted; the other is warm, uncalculating, and committed with a life committal.

The Word Became Flesh
(Week 2, Wednesday)

THE CHURCH

Thronging or Touching?
Matthew 7:21; Mark 5:24-34

As Jesus was going along, the multitudes thronged him. A woman in deep need came timidly through the crowd and touched his garment. "Who touched me?" asked Jesus as he felt the power go forth. "The multitudes throng you, so why do you ask, 'Who touched me?'" said his disciples. "But somebody touched me," said Jesus (see Mark 5:24-32).

There is a difference between thronging Jesus and touching Jesus. Those who throng Jesus get little; those who touch Jesus get everything....

Sunday after Sunday the multitudes go to church and listen. Their thoughts throng Jesus. But how many of the thronging multitudes really touch him—set up a connection with him, and live by him? How many touch him so that they go away not merely better, but well?

Victorious Living
(Week 6, Thursday)

The Corporate Fellowship
Psalm 133:1; Acts 2:43-47; Hebrews 10:45

The spiritual life cannot be lived in isolation. Life is intensely personal; it is also intensely corporate, and you cannot separate them. If you should wipe out the church today, you would have to put something like it in its place tomorrow. For there must be a corporate expression of the spiritual life as well as an individual expression.

The idea that it is your duty to support the church seems to be to be all wrong. The church is not founded upon a duty imposed on you from without. It is founded on the facts of life. Your very inner nature demands it. American evangelist, D. L. Moody, in answer to a man who said he did not need the church, quietly pulled a coal from the hearth and separated it, and together they watched it die. It was a legitimate answer....

I know the stupidities and the inanities and the irrelevancies and the formalities of the church. Yes, I know them all. But nevertheless, the church is the mother of my spirit, and we love our mothers in spite of weakness and wrinkles. My word, then, to you is that, as you begin this new life you begin it as a member of the church family.

Victorious Living
(Week 10, Sunday)

The Cloud over Our Churches
Romans 12:2; Colossians 2:8, 20; 1 John 2:15-17

No one has to argue that there is a cloud over the church life of Christendom. Our vague uneasiness has grown into a fear that all is not well. Why? Again, divided loyalty, inner division.

The divided loyalty is this: In each nation, instead of keeping the gospel of Christ in a framework of universal reference, we have more and more identified it with national

175

cultures. The conquest of the gospel of Christ by local national cultures is going on apace, and this process means the slow de-Christianization of our churches. On the "Antioch Chalice," which is claimed by some to be the original Holy Grail, the figure of Christ is seen sitting above the Roman eagle. That was the position Christ occupied in those early centuries.—he was first and the nation was second.

Today the nation is using the national culture for its own ends, and because the church has become so domesticated, so identified with that national culture, it is using the church too for its nationalistic ends....

We are divided between Christ and national culture. Which is supreme?

Victorious Living
(Week 31, Wednesday)

The Cloud over Our Churches
Romans 15:5-6; 1 Corinthians 1:9-13; 12:13; Ephesians 4:3

But the division within Christendom is not merely between allegiance to the national culture and the allegiance to Christ; there is division between the churches themselves. The household of Christ is divided against itself. And as a result of our church family divisions a cloud has come over us, and under that cloud we are fearful, and for good reason, for a divided church has little moral authority in a divided world. We must adjust our differences or abdicate our moral leadership....

We have so exhausted our resources in putting up ecclesiastical walls between ourselves and others, and in keeping them in repair, that we have little left to use in helping redeem a world. If the time and intelligence and soul-force we have expended in proving that we were right as against our brothers and sisters had been expended in united action against the problems that now confront the world, they would not now be so far from solution. And we would be leading the procession of events instead of being led by them.

These divisions have brought a cloud over our religious life—dark, rainless clouds, clouds that presage storms of revolt, clouds that produce fear. God is today speaking out of that cloud, and God's voice is as of old: "This is my Son; hear him." And what does the Son say: "Lord, I will that they may be one" (see John 17:20-21). When we become one, the clouds will lift. But not until then.

Victorious Living
(Week 31, Thursday)

The Kingdom and the Church
Matthew 16:18; Ephesians 4:11-16; 5:25-27

The kingdom of the church must bend the knee to the kingdom of God. Just as we want our state, our race, our class to be dominant, so we want our church to be dominant. The church can be our religious self writ large; but it is still the self. It can be the group self asserting itself toward supremacy, albeit covered up with religious trappings. If the kingdom of God comes in, we, as a church, would like to bring it in, since the fact that we brought it in would leave us dominant....

The kingdom of the church must surrender itself to the kingdom God. The church is not an end in itself; it is a means to the end:—the kingdom of God. If the church is an end in itself, it will lose itself. The church, like the individual, must lose itself in the kingdom of God to find itself again.

Abundant Living
(Week 32, Friday)

Why I Should Give My Allegiance to the Church
Acts 20:28; Ephesians 3:14-15; 5:23-32; Colossians 1:17-18

In order to give full inner consent to allegiance to the church, perhaps you can take these steps:

(1) There is no such thing as solitary religion. If it is solitary, it is not religion, for Jesus expressed religion as love to God and love to people. There can be no love to people unless life is lived out in relationships. "To be is to be in relationship." The Christian's life can be lived only in the give-and-take of corporate relationships.

(2) The Christian church is founded on a necessity in human nature....Those who try to cultivate their spiritual lives alone, apart from the church, are attempting to live a vertical spiritual life, without the horizontal—they are attempting the impossible. Human nature is against it.

(3) The church, in a sense, is an extension of the life of the Incarnation. I say "in a sense," for there was only once when "the Word became flesh"; but the church attempts, in varying degrees, to reincarnate that Word in corporate relationships. It is the only group in human society living, not for its own purposes, but for the purpose of manifesting in time an Eternal Purpose.

(4) With all its faults, the church is the best serving institution on earth. It has many critics but no rivals in the work of human redemption. It has filled the world with schools, hospitals, orphan and blind asylums, and churches. There isn't a spot on earth where, if is free to do so, it hasn't done so. Christians are people who care.

Abundant Living
(Week 45, Thursday)

The Church: The One Unbroken Fellowship
Acts 2:46-47; 7:37-38; 16:5; 1 Corinthians 16:19-20; Ephesians 1:17-23

(5) The church, with all its faults, contains the best human life in the world. Its character is higher and finer and more dependable....

(6) The church is the one unbroken fellowship around the world. All other ties have snapped; the tie between Christians remains unbroken....The church...is holding an unbroken fellowship. The Christians are therefore the bridge across all chasms.

(7) The church is the one institution that delivers you from the present century and gives you a sense of solidarity with all the centuries. When you are in the church, you are not a prisoner of your date—you have a sense of belonging to the ages.

(8) The church, at its truest, breaks down all class and race barriers, and makes humankind feel it is one.

Abundant Living
(Week 45, Friday)

The Church: The Mother of Movements
Acts 14:22-23; 1 Corinthians 1:2; Hebrews 2:11-12

(9) The church has been and is the mother of movements. It is a creative society. It gave birth to the arts, to education, to reform, to missionary movements, to democracy. It may be said that democracy is a child of the Christian faith....If the root of democracy decays, the fruit will die.

(10) The denomination is not the church. The church is bigger than the denomination....The denominations are parts of a continuous river—the church. The church is bigger than the denominations. To think that we have roped off the grace of God and confined it within our denominations is as absurd as to say that the areas roped off for swimmers on the 'beaches are the ocean.

(11) As the denomination is not the church, so the church is not the kingdom. The church contains the best life of the kingdom, but is not synonymous with the kingdom. It is a means to the ends of the kingdom, and not an end in itself. It must lose its life for kingdom ends and then it will find itself.

(12) The primary function of the church is the worship of God. Here we get in living contact with God, the Eternal, in order to meet Time, the fleeting.

Abundant Living
(Week 45, Saturday)

One Greater Than the Church
Ephesians 4:11-16

One greater than the church is here. The church is a fellowship of believers, a fellowship around Christ, not around themselves. He, and not they, is the center. When they become the center, the light has turned to darkness. And how great is that darkness!

John said to Jesus: "'Master, we saw a man casting out demons in your name, but we stopped him because he is not a follower of ours.' Jesus said to him, "'Do not stop him; he who is not against you is for you'" (Luke 9:49-50 Moffatt). John tried to make "in your name" and "a follower of ours" synonymous. We still do that. We make our group the issue. Jesus showed the difference, saying, in essence, "He who is not against you is for you. For 'you' are not the issue; but as for me, I am the issue. He who is not with me is against me. Here you must take sides: if you are not for me, you are against me." One greater than the church is here. The church behind Christ is the greatest serving institution on earth; in front of Christ it is an idol. If it becomes an end in itself, it loses itself. If it loses itself in Christ and his kingdom, it finds itself again.

The Way
(Week 8, Saturday)

Thy Kingdom Come
Matthew 6:25-33

Is it any wonder that the church has had nothing but problems through the ages? When it drew up its creeds—the Apostles', the Athanasian, the Nicene—it mentioned the kingdom of God once in all three of them, and then only marginally, beyond the borders of this life, a heavenly kingdom. No wonder the church has stumbled from problem to problem when its supreme value was lost or only marginally held. The church will never get straightened out until it puts the kingdom where Jesus put it in [The Lord's Prayer]—the first consideration and the first allegiance.

The Way
(Week 29, Thursday)

What Produced the New Testament Church?
1 Corinthians 15:35-49

The New Testament Church...arose immediately after the death and resurrection of Jesus. It didn't emerge after long years, giving time for myths to grow up, upon which the movement could live precariously. It arose at once. At one moment the disciples were timid believers "behind closed doors because they were afraid" (John 20:19 CEB), clinging pathetically to a blasted hope, a hope that had been blasted by Christ's death. The next moment they were irresistible apostles, out from behind closed doors facing the Sanhedrin and crowds from all over that ancient world, and proclaiming with joy— an amazing, irrepressible joy—that Jesus had arisen and that he was Lord and Savior. They did it with such power and assurance that the multitudes who had witnessed his death saw in these men his resurrection. [This fact makes me believe in the resurrection!]

What could have produced that church? A dead Christ? It would have been an effect all out of harmony with the cause....The news was signaled from a hill called Calvary, "Jesus defeated...," and the mists came over for three days—the saddest days of human history. Then on Easter morning, the mists cleared, and the world got the full message, "Jesus defeated death." And the world has never been the same since. Nor has death been the same since. "O death, where is thy sting? O grave, where is thy victory?" (1 Cor 15:55 KJV). Earth's blackest day and earth's brightest day are only three days apart. But those three days divide the ages. On one side, doubt and despair; on the other, hope and happiness.

The Way
(Week 43, Friday)

The Making of a Christian Church
Acts 4:32-37; 1 Thessalonians 3:3-4

The roots of our Western Christianity are in Antioch, not Jerusalem, for it was out of Antioch that Paul went to spread the gospel to Europe, and hence to us.

Three things went into the making of this church:

(1) People who suffered for their faith founded it. "Those who had been scattered by the trouble which arose over Stephen, made their way as far as...Antioch" (Acts 11:19 Moffatt). The marks of the cross were upon the founding of the church. The cross was in it; hence the lift of the resurrection was in and through it. If our faith costs nothing, it contributes nothing.

(2) An international mind went into the making of the church. The Jews preached the gospel only to Jews; but the Cypriotes and Cyrenians, bringing to the gospel a wider

outlook, an international mind, preached to the Greeks as well. "The strong hand of the Lord was with them" (Acts 11:21 Moffatt), as it is always with those who think and love in large terms. This bringing of an international mind to the situation was important, for God guides within the framework of our thinking, and it was from the framework of that thinking that Paul was sent to Europe and to us.

(3) The third element going into the making of the church was Barnabas, the most Christianized of the group at Jerusalem. He was the kind of man who could rejoice in the work of another; when he "saw the grace of God he rejoiced" (Acts 11:23 Moffatt). The test and sign of a real Christian is to rejoice in someone else's work. He was interested in the kingdom, not in his part in that kingdom.

The Way
(Week 45, Monday)

A Corporate Sense
Romans 12:3-10

We must now look at the marks of a Christian church.

(1) There was a strong corporate sense. Paul and Barnabas were "guests of the church" for a whole year, guests of the church, not of individuals. As the people "were worshipping the Lord and fasting, the Holy Spirit said, 'Come! Set me apart Barnabas and Saul for the work'" (Acts 13:2 Moffatt). They were so one that the Holy Spirit could speak to the whole church and guide it. They were not a group of worshiping individuals but a corporate body,—"an organism of the Holy Spirit." The thing that won that ancient world to Christ was not only the message but this new society, an undecaying society in the midst of a decaying society, a society that loved and loved widely and without barriers in the midst of a society that knew only how to hate or love in grooves. The society had faith, hope, and courage in the midst of a society that had lost its nerve and its hope church. . . .

The church of today must regain that sense of corporateness, of being a society that has meaning for all life, that when men belong to it they belong to something that has present and ultimate meanings.

The Way
(Week 45, Tuesday)

The Worth of a Person as a Person
Philippians 2:1-11

(2) There was the sense of the worth of a person as a person—class was abolished. In the naming of those who constituted the prophets and teachers of Antioch, Barnabas was named first and Saul last; they were not headlined at the top. In the midst of the list is "Manaen, a foster brother of Herod" (Acts 13:1 Moffatt). To catch the brother of a king was big. We would have displayed it. They tucked Manaen in the center with a man from North Africa and a Cyrenian above him. Evidently all class distinction was wiped out, and a person was a person,—"someone for whom Christ died" (Rom 14:15 CEB). It was a vast leveling process. A new worth and dignity came into every

human being as a child of God and therefore equal to everyone else. A classless society emerged.

Had this spirit been maintained, it would have captured the earth....

The early church would have choked on [notions of class]. The later church swallowed it, and became class-filled and Christ-empty. Something universal died, and the ugly spirit of class was born. The Christian faith began to be a class faith. Unless we regain the original spirit of a classless society, [something else will replace the church]. This is no idle threat.... If the church does not stand for people, the people will not stand for the church. The church must have a passion for souls, but must also have a passion for people—soul, mind, and body. For it is possible to love people's souls and be unconcerned about what happens to their bodies, their minds, their dwellings, their environment.

The Way
(Week 45, Wednesday)

All Race and Class Barriers Removed
2 Corinthians 8:13-15; Galatians 3:28; Colossians 3:11

(3) The church had wiped out race and color lines. In the account of the prophets and teachers at Antioch there is mention of "Symeon (called Niger)" (Acts 13:1 Moffatt), literally "the Black." That was the place of the black person in the early church. They were not just tolerated, on the edge, or patronized. They were at the center, having an honored place among "prophets and teachers," and Symeon's hands were laid on Paul and Barnabas as they went forth to preach the gospel to white Europeans. Ordained by a black man! When we depart from that, we depart from the original gospel. No amount of orthodoxy can atone for a lack of this orthopraxy. To treat a person on the basis of color is to introduce into the Christian body a foreign substance, a foreign substance that will fester and poison the whole body. This foreign substance is now festering, and no amount of plasters of rationalization can cure this festering sore. It can be cured by an attitude of equality of opportunity for all, apart from race and birth and color.

(4) The church had a sense of economic solidarity. The account says that when a famine befell the church at Jerusalem, the disciples of Antioch "put aside money, as each of them was able to afford it, for a contribution to be sent to the brothers in Judaea" (Acts 11:29 Moffatt). The Christians drew no line between the spiritual and the economic. Life was one.

The Way
(Week 45, Thursday)

Holding Together Conservative and Radical
Romans 12:9-16

(5) The church held together in a living fellowship the conservative and the radical. "In the local church at Antioch there were prophets and teachers" (Acts 13:1 Moffatt). The teacher is usually the conservative, conserving the values of the past. On the one hand, the conservative has a real function in human society. The good of the past must

be brought into the structure of the present; we live by yesterday, as well as by today and tomorrow. A present cut off from yesterday becomes a cut-flower civilization, without roots. The conservative conserves.

On the other hand, the prophet is the one who believes that the values of the past should be applied to the present and the future in ever-widening areas of application, the radical. Strangely enough, the word "radical" comes from a word meaning "the root." A real radical has the root of the past within, but demands that the root bear fruit now in the total life. Radicals demand that implications become applications.

The church held radical and conservative together in unbroken fellowship, each cross-fertilizing the other. They were both held together in a living tension. That tension produced a growing point. The church that does not hold both conservative and radical in a living tension will have no growing point; it will become sterile. "An arid liberalism and an acrid conservatism" are both alike sterile. Together they could be fruitful.

The church must not allow these two groups to split and sink a cleavage down through the life of the church. We need a radical conservatism and a conservative radicalism. Jesus was both: "I am not come to destroy, but to fulfil" (Matt 5:17 KJV)—that is conservatism. "Ye have heard that it was said by them of old time ... but I say unto you" (v. 27)—that is radicalism. The past married to the future brings forth the living present. But conservatism married to nothing but itself, or radicalism married to nothing but itself, brings forth nothing, nothing but controversy or conjecture. Married, they bring forth progress. The conservative has something, the fundamentals of the gospel; the radical has something, the demand that those fundamentals be applied now.

The Way
(Week 45, Friday)

Holding Together Strong People
1 Corinthians 3:1-9

(6) The church held together in an unbroken fellowship strong people who differed. Paul and Barnabas parted "in irritation" (Acts 15:39 Moffatt) over the question of taking John Mark because he had deserted them at Pamphylia. Here was a good chance for two denominations. One would be the Barnabasites, those who believed the church should be redemptive; Mark should be redeemed and given another chance. The other would be the Paulites, those who believed the church should be kept clean; Mark should be cleansed away. Both very good ideas for a new denomination! ... But the church at Antioch held them in unbroken fellowship. As they parted, they were "commended by the brothers to the grace of the Lord" (Acts 15:40 Moffatt). I am sure they commended them to the grace of the Lord with a twinkle in their eyes: "Brothers, you both need it!" They parted, but they both came back to Antioch, their spiritual home, held together in spite of difference.

(7) The church was redemptive. As the church received Mark and Barnabas into their fellowship in spite of Mark's lapse, they made him over again by the loyalty of Barnabas and the healing fellowship of the church. Paul sat down in later years and dictated to his amanuensis: "Pick up Mark and bring him along with you, for he is useful in helping

182

me" (2 Tim 4:11 Moffatt). I can see the amanuensis glance up with a quizzical smile; Paul thinks for a moment and says, "Yes, I mean just that. Barnabas was right. He was a better Christian than I was. He was always taking people no one else would take; he took me when nobody believed in me. Grand Christian, Barnabas." And a tear trickles down his cheek. The church was redemptive.

(8) The church was creative. As they fasted and prayed, the Holy Spirit said, "Set apart Barnabas and Saul for the work to which I have called them" (Acts 13:2 RSV). The whole history of Western civilization was in that hour, for out of that hour went two men who gave the gospel to Europe, and to us. When the church listens to the Holy Spirit, it becomes creative. New movements are born.

The Way
(Week 45, Saturday)

They Can Take It
Matthew 12:46-50

We turn this week to see the power of the corporate life to loose us and to let us go. The fellowship of a group is one of the most freeing things known, provided it is the right kind of fellowship.

The church is designed to provide that fellowship. It is the corporate expression of the Christian life. No corporate life; no Christian life. The idea that you can be a solitary Christian without corporate relation with the church has been proved false by the facts. I have watched it across the years. Those who try this soon have Christianity fade out of them, and then they fade out of the picture. Strong, outgoing, contagious character is nourished within the church, even with all its faults.

The Way to Power and Poise
(Week 48, Sunday)

The Only Redeeming Agency
Ephesians 5:25-27

We now come to the last portion of the definition: "Conversion is the penitent, receptive response to the saving divine initiative in Christ, resulting in a change, gradual or sudden, by which one passes from the kingdom of self to the kingdom of God and becomes a part of a living fellowship, the church." Note the last portion: "And becomes part of a living fellowship, the church."

Suppose one tries to take the conversion without the fellowship, of church. Will it work? Across the years I have found that where the fellowship of the church fades out, conversion and its fruits fade out. ...

A. J. Muste, after leaving the church for Marxian communism, came back to it. "I return to the church," he said, "because these years have taught me that the church of the redeemed is the only redeeming agency" (quoted in Federal Council Bulletin, 1937).

How to Be a Transformed Person
(Week 8, Friday)

The Society of the Forgiven and the Forgiving
Ephesians 2:19

The church has many critics but no rivals in the work of human redemption. There isn't a spot on earth—from the frozen north to tropical islands of the seas—where they have allowed us to go that we haven't gone with schools, hospitals, orphan asylums, leper asylums, the gospel—everything to lift the soul, the mind, the body of the people. No other institution has done anything like it. . . .

I said to myself, "I've been hard on the church, but with all its faults, it holds the best of humanity within itself. So I'm for it." . . .

The church is made up of Christians-in-the-making. The church should be the society of the forgiven and forgiving.

How to Be a Transformed Person
(Week 8, Saturday)

A Group that Cares, Shares, and Dares
Matthew 22:15-16

A good description of a church . . . is that a church is a group that cares, shares, and dares. But first it cares. Friedrich von Hügel's definition of "a Christian is one who cares" [no published source found] is a profound one. And the more Christianized, the wider and deeper the caring. The real Christian cares for everybody, even for enemies.

Growing Spiritually
(Week 44, Thursday)

From Preparation, to Promise, to Performance
Ephesians 5:24-27

In the opening chapters of Acts the church is not mentioned either by Jesus or by the disciples, for it was not yet born. Even by the descent of the Holy Spirit at Pentecost the church was not born.

So when we say that Pentecost was the birthday of the church, this is only partly true. Forces were loosed that produced the church through producing the Fellowship, the *koinonia*. The *koinonia* became the soul of the church. Out of it the church grew. It was the organism out of which grew the organization. And where there is no fellowship, no *koinonia*, there is no church.

Mastery
(Week 3, Sunday)

Intellectually Mature, Emotionally Immature
1 Corinthians 2:10-12

The church today is in large measure halfway between Easter and Pentecost and is behind closed doors in fear. The grandest good news that ever broke upon human ears had broken freshly upon them: Jesus was alive, yet that didn't free them; they were still locked behind closed doors.

Mastery
(Week 4, Saturday)

184

Called in Now and Then
2 Corinthians 3:16-18

We have seen that the difference between modern church life and [that presented in] the Acts is in the place the Holy Spirit occupies. In Acts, the Spirit was in control of life, and in modern church life the attempt is made to control the Holy Spirit in the interests of success. The Spirit is called in only to help out. We are at the center, and the Spirit is to help us. So he silently stays away—on those terms. We frustrate the grace of God and remain frustrated. Then we question whether Christianity will work. The truth is we are not working it.

The position of the church in regard to the Holy Spirit is like that of a man who courts a girl, admires her, enjoys her fellowship, but stops there and doesn't invite her to be his wife, to come into his home and take charge of it, to live out life with him. All else is preliminary to this; if it doesn't happen, there is a halfwayness, a frustration. The church has companionship with the Holy Spirit, seeks the Spirit's counsel, adores the Spirit—does everything but ask God's Spirit in to take over the within, including the subconscious.

Mastery
(Week 13, Saturday)

The *Koinonia*
Ephesians 4:1-6

Many think it was the church that was born at Pentecost. There is no evidence from the Scriptures that this was so. The writer of the Acts seems to be at a loss to say just what it was the converts were coming into, "The Lord added daily to thecommunity those who were being saved" (Acts 2:47 CEB). "Many who heard the word became believers, and their number grew to about five thousand" (4:4 CEB). . . . The word church is not used in the Acts until the eighth chapter: "And on that day a great persecution arose against the church in Jerusalem" (v. 1). This *koinonia*, or fellowship, was antecedent to the church and formed the soul of the church. The description of the fellowship is found in Acts 2:42: "The believers devoted themselves to the apostles' teaching, to the community [*koinonia*], to their shared meals, and to their prayers."

Mastery
(Week 18, Friday)

The Relation of the *Koinonia* to the Church
Ephesians 5:25-27

The fellowship, or *koinonia*, was antecedent to and formed the soul of the church. Out of it the church grew. . . .

This brings an important truth to light: Where there is the fellowship, the *koinonia*, there is the church. But where the fellowship is absent, there we have an organization but no organism. We have a body but no soul—we have a corpse.

Where the Holy Spirit is, there is the fellowship—the fellowship of the Spirit—and where there is the fellowship, there is the church. In other words, where the Holy Spirit is, there is the church; and conversely, where the Holy Spirit is not, there is not the church.

Mastery
(Week 18, Saturday)

The Relationship of the Kingdom and the Church
Ephesians 2:17-22

Out of this *koinonia*, the fellowship, came the ecclesia, the church.

But there was something beyond and above both the fellowship and the church, and that was the kingdom. The kingdom was best seen in the church as it, in turn, embodied the fellowship, but it was not to be identified with the kingdom. The kingdom is the absolute; the fellowship and the church are relatives. They are related to something higher than themselves—the kingdom. The kingdom is not related to something higher; it is the absolute order confronting all relatives with an offer of grace and demanding complete surrender and obedience. "Seek [first God's] kingdom, and these things shall be yours as well" (Luke 12:31 RSV). The kingdom is first; all else, including the fellowship and the church, is to be related to it. If they become first, they become idolatry; for where a relative order becomes an absolute order, there is idolatry. The fellowship and the church are not ends but means to the ends of the kingdom.

You cannot go out and say, "Repent, for the church is at hand." It would sound absurd. But it doesn't sound absurd when you say, "Repent, for the kingdom of heaven is at hand." For we feel that here we are confronted with the Absolute to which all life must be related or perish. The church contains the best life of the kingdom but cannot be identified with the kingdom. "Christ is the head of the church, that is the savior of the body" (Eph 5:23 CEB). Christ saves the church but not the kingdom. The kingdom is salvation; it offers salvation to all, including the church. The church must lose its life in the kingdom and then it finds itself again. But if it saves its life—makes itself the end—then it loses itself. The fellowship within it dies; and when that dies, the church is dead. The kingdom is universal, for all worlds; the church is particular, for this world.

Mastery
(Week 19, Monday)

Our Spiritual Roots Are in Antioch
Acts 13:1-3

The roots of our spiritual lives are in Antioch, not in Jerusalem. The missionary journeys Paul and Barnabas took were begun in and continued to be centered in Antioch. Those journeys took them into Europe and laid the foundation of the Christian faith there, and from there we got it. Antioch is the mother of our spirits. We can well be proud of our spiritual heritage, for the marks of Christ were truly on this church. We must see ourselves in the light of it. As someone has said, "It is the depravity of institutions and movements that, given in the beginning to express life, they often end in throttling that very life, so they need recurrent criticism, constant readjustment, and a perpetual bringing back to original purposes and spirit." This is particularly true of the

Christian movement and more particularly of the Christian church. We must see what the pattern of the New Testament church really is before we can make our churches into its image.

Mastery
(Week 19, Wednesday)

The Center of Gravity in the Pew
Acts 6:8-10

We come now to look at the church at Antioch as having within it the marks of the New Testament church.

We must note first of all what went into the makings of that church. It was founded by the lay group that was scattered through the persecution that arose over the martyrdom of Stephen. . . . The founding of the church by a lay group is important. It put Christianity just where it ought to be—not in the profession but in the person. . . . No movement is strong unless it is a lay movement. If the church is organized around the minister, it is a weak church. The center of gravity must be not in the pulpit but in the pew. The minister must be the guide, the stimulator, the spiritualizer, of an essentially lay movement. Every Christian must be the bearer of the good news.

The Antioch church was a lay church.

Mastery
(Week 19, Thursday)

The Mark of the Cross upon the Church
1 Corinthians 2:1-2

The second thing that went into the founding of that church was the fact that it was founded by people who suffered for their faith. . . . The church at Antioch had the marks of the cross upon it—people who suffered for their faith founded it. If our faith is costing us nothing, it will be worth nothing. "As soon as we cease to bleed, we cease to bless" (John Henry Jowett, *A Passion for Souls* [New York: Fleming H. Revell Co., 1905], 30). . . . The blood of the martyrs became the seed of the church.

The third thing that went into founding this church was an international mind. . . . Jews who came down from Jerusalem spoke the gospel to the Jews only, but the group from Cyprus and Cyrene spoke also to the Greeks. . . .

This bringing of the international mind into the making of the church at Antioch was important; for when God wanted to get the church to send out Paul and Barnabas on their missions to the Gentiles, God found an international mind ready to be guided.

Mastery
(Week 19, Friday)

Barnabas, a Great Man Because a Good Man
Acts 4:36-37

We note the fourth thing that went into the founding of the church at Antioch. It was Barnabas. "When the church in Jerusalem heard about this, and they sent Barnabas

187

to Antioch. When he arrived and saw evidence of God's grace, he was overjoyed and encouraged everyone to remain fully committed to the Lord. Barnabas responded in this way because he was a good man, whom the Holy Spirit had endowed with exceptional faith" (Acts 11:22-24 CEB).

The church at Jerusalem did here what they did in Samaria, they sent down representatives to regularize what they could not produce. The lay group produced the spiritual movements, and the apostles attempted to regularize them. They were trying to keep up. Be that as it may, they could not have sent a better man than Barnabas, a man who was always taking hold of people whom no one else would take and making them over again. He took Paul when the disciples at Jerusalem were afraid of him, and introduced him. He took John Mark when Paul refused to have anything to do with him, and made him over again so that Paul was later glad to have him back.

When Barnabas "saw evidence of God's grace"—saw it incarnate in a group—he rejoiced. He was big enough to rejoice in the work of another. Some of us are not. And when he saw the type of Christianity produced here, he conceived the idea of exposing the young man Saul to this type of Christianity. "Barnabas went to Tarsus in search of Saul. When he found him, he brought him to Antioch" (Acts 11:25-26 CEB). This simple statement was one of the most important things in history. For exposing Paul to the type of Christianity in Antioch determined the type of Christianity we would get in the West through his missionary work in funding the faith among us. . . . This Christianity was the closest approximation to the Christianity of Christ that had emerged. It was a stroke of spiritual genius on the part of Barnabas to expose Paul to Antioch. We must remain forever grateful to him.

Mastery
(Week 19, Saturday)

The Strong Corporate Sense of the Church
Romans 12:4-8

We have seen the things that went into the making of the church at Antioch. We must now turn to the authentic marks of Christ as seen in that church.

First, the church had a strong corporate sense. They were not a group of individuals coming together periodically to worship, then returning home. They were an organism, not merely an organization. The *koinonia*, the fellowship, was at the basis of this church. How do we know? Two things let us see into its heart. The account says of Paul and Barnabas, "For a whole year they [were guests of] the church" (Acts 11:26 RSV). They were not the guests of a rich individual in the church, but the guests of the whole church.

The next thing that lets us understand the corporate sense of the church was the fact that when they fasted and prayed, the Holy Spirit could speak to the whole church and say, "Appoint Barnabas and Saul to the work I have called them to undertake" (Acts 13:2 CEB). They listened and obeyed as a corporate entity. They were so attuned to one another and to God that they heard corporately and acted corporately. . . .

The faith spread partly by its message and partly by the fact that the ancient society was decaying; a feeling of spiritual insecurity was pervading it. This new society in the church was an un-decaying society in the midst of a decaying society. So people pressed into it for spiritual security. Here they found love across all race and class lines; here they found a people who cared—for everybody.... When they joined this society, they inwardly felt: This is it. I've found ultimate reality in human relations.

Mastery
(Week 20, Sunday)

The Material an Expression of the Spiritual
1 Corinthians 15:46-49

We come now to the second mark: this strong corporate sense was not confined to the spiritual; it included the material.....

The apostles at Jerusalem separated the spiritual from the material, said they would give themselves to the spiritual and turn over the material to others....The material is part of life; and if you put it out the door, it will come back by the window....The "spiritual" apostles were dependent on the "material" laity. So the church at Antioch was in line with Jesus, who taught, healed, and fed people as a part of the coming of the kingdom. This was Jesus succession instead of apostolic succession....

And they sent "everyone... according to each person's abundance." Note "according to each person's abundance"; a sound basis for giving, the only basis for real giving. And note "everyone"; they were all in with all they had. They *really* went to church!

The test of the reality of the spiritual is whether it functions in material terms. If it doesn't, it is unreal.

Mastery
(Week 20, Monday)

A New Race Made Up of All Races
Colossians 3:10-11

We have been noting the characteristic marks of the New Testament church as seen in the church at Antioch. We now come to the next mark: the church was without race and class—a raceless and classless society....

This church was a church beyond race. A new race was emerging, made up of all races. We can see how far we've come from that original church when I remind you that in Jaffna, Ceylon, in the early days, there was a mission church with two pulpits: a higher pulpit from which the white man preached and a lower pulpit from which the Ceylonese preached, and there was no interchange....A *burgher* (mixed blood) wanted to enter the ministry; but since he was not "white," he would have had to speak from the lower pulpit. He refused to accept this position, gave up the idea of the ministry, and became attorney general for all Ceylon.

Now there is one pulpit in that church, from which I have spoken. But the picture of the two pulpits is a symbol of the divided gospel we have been preaching on race. In the early church there was no division on the line of race—a person was a person, one for whom Christ died. They had the kingdom of God, and we have had the kingdom of Race.

A religion that is identified with the superiority or the supremacy of one race is a backward eddy in the stream of history where people of all races and all colors flow toward oneness in community.

Mastery
(Week 20, Tuesday)

Blending the Conservative and the Radical
Matthew 5:17-20

Another mark—the church held together in a living blend the radical and the conservative. The account says, "The church at Antioch included prophets [radicals] and teachers [conservatives]" (Acts 13:1 CEB).

[Both prophets and teachers] have a function in human society. All progress is made between the tension of the two.... But between the pull back of the conservative and the pull ahead of the radical we make progress in a middle direction.

The church should hold within its ample bosom and cherish and appreciate both. ...Life is bigger than conservatism and bigger than radicalism, but it includes both and goes beyond each.

The tragedy in American church life is that we have allowed a split to run straight through the denominations on this issue. We are fast dividing up into two camps: the conservative and the liberal. We are becoming two camps instead of one fellowship of the Spirit. Each needs the other. Each must spiritually cross-fertilize the other. For each is weak without the other. The strong person is the conservative-radical and the radical-conservative.

Mastery
(Week 20, Thursday)

Holding Together Strong Men Who Differ
1 Corinthians 3:3-9

We continue to look at the incarnation of the kingdom of God as seen in the church at Antioch. The next thing we note about that church is it held together strong people who differed on principles and persons—Paul and Barnabas.

An issue arose over taking Mark with them on the second missionary journey. He had turned back from Pamphylia. Why? Was he weak-kneed, homesick—the usual explanations? There is another: "John [Mark] was with them as their assistant" (Acts 13:5 CEB). Or as the King James Version puts it: "to their minister," to minister to or serve them. Mark might have been, not an equal partner but a glorified servant—at best an assistant instead of associate minister. They put him in a subordinate place; then Paul complains he left them. The relationship was basically wrong in the new society, a remnant of the old. John Mark pulled out and came back the equal associate of Barnabas.

We often complain of people being unhappy and unadjusted in situations we have made for them, unjust situations. The fault is not in the persons but in the basic injustice of the situation we have created.

Paul argued they should keep the movement clean; they had to purge John [Mark], who turned back. Barnabas argued they should keep the movement redemptive; they didn't break a man because he made one blunder. Both ideas were good: one that the movement must be pure, the other that the movement must be redemptive. They parted over these principles—"in irritation," says Moffatt (15:39)—Paul taking Silas and Barnabas taking John Mark. But in the midst of that unhappy situation is this bright spot, "being commended by the brethren to the grace of the Lord" (Acts 15:40). The punctuation would imply both groups were commended to the grace of the Lord, as if to say, "You both need the grace of the Lord!" The church held both groups within its loving bosom. When they returned, they both returned to Antioch—the home of their souls. The church held together in its love and interest strong men who differed widely; it was the reconciling place of the strong. The church should do that today!

Mastery
(Week 20, Friday)

A Fellowship of the Spiritually Contagious
2 Timothy 4:1, 5

We now come to another mark of Christ upon the church at Antioch—it was redemptive. A spiritual contagion was inherent in early Christianity. "The Lord's power was with them, and a large number came to believe and turned to the Lord....A considerable number of people were added to the Lord... teaching large numbers of people" (Acts 11:21, 24, 26 CEB). Evangelism was something, not imposed on the church, but exposed out of the very heart of the situation. It was endemic.

The evangelism was so potent that it evangelized the evangelists, including Paul....If the Christian fellowship of Antioch had not burned up [his] Hebrew bonds, [Paul] would probably never have been the missionary and evangelist to all races. He may have been born a Jew but was reborn a brother of all.

I love to feel, though it is not said, that Antioch had a living part in the remaking of Mark. It did indirectly through Barnabas, who was influenced by the Antioch church. Certainly Mark emerged a new man, so much so that Paul, after years apart, wrote, "Take Mark, and bring him with thee: for he is profitable to me for the ministry" (2 Tim 4:11 KJV). I like to think this version is correct; he was profitable "for the ministry." He started out ministering to Paul and Barnabas—they used him—but here he is profitable for the ministry of Christ. The angle and the attitude had changed, and Mark gladly came to Paul.

The church at Antioch redeemed everything it touched. For at its heart was the Spirit of Jesus, and he is redemption. The church today must be just that: a society of the being redeemed and a society of the redeeming. It should be the fulfillment of the question of the Korean woman, who knocked on the church door and asked, "Is this the place where they mend broken hearts?" It should mend broken hearts, broken homes, and broken people.

Mastery
(Week 20, Saturday)

The Mastery of the Secondhand
Romans 8:1-2

Secondhand religion is always overpowered by firsthand evil. The comparative impotence of the church is caused by the secondhand nature of its religion. Its religion is in creeds, in rituals, in books, in services, in prayers; but it is not a fountain of firsthand living experience of Jesus.

Mastery
(Week 34, Thursday)

There Is No Dilemma
Acts 18:14-17

We come now to a modern answer to the dilemma "What shall we do?" The modern answer says, "Go to church." This answer is good; but if it stops there, it is not good enough. It may result in a spiritual stalemate, a secondhandedness in religion, with the feeling that there is something missing. It leaves one walking in a fog of dimness and uncertainty....

In the Acts, going to church was not the means of salvation; it was the result of salvation. They just couldn't stay away, for Christ was there! To stay away was to miss him.

Mastery
(Week 39, Wednesday)

They Might Be with Him
Mark 3:13-15

Being "with him" (Mark 3:14) while he was here on earth deepened into the *koinonia* after Jesus left the disciples. This *koinonia*—literally, "fellowship"—emerged from Pentecost, the coming of the Holy Spirit. The church was not born at Pentecost; the church came later.... The *koinonia* was the organism out of which the church became the organization. What the soul is to the body, so the *koinonia* is to the church. Without the *koinonia* the church is soulless. But a body without a soul is a corpse. Without this inner fellowship, the *koinonia*, the church is a mere body of doctrine and worship; it is dead. The church is mature as an institution to the degree it can and does produce the *koinonia*!

Christian Maturity
(Monday, Week 11)

Three Cardinal Urges
Acts 2:46-47

If churches or individual Christians lose their power to convert, they have lost the right to be called Christian. If we cease to be evangelistic, we will soon cease to be evangelical, for it is a law of the mind that that which is not expressed dies....

If we fail to win others to Christ and to the church, there will be no Church in the future. When we of the church today die, the church dies with us, unless the church of tomorrow has been won in the meantime. If you, as a member of the church, fail to win someone else, you have a part in the death of the church. If others fail with you there will be no Christian church one hundred years from now. Every year your church loses many from its membership through unconcern, change of address, or death. If you do not win at least that many new Christians, your church is dying....

If you think you can live as a Christian in a private world of your own, you are an idiot. For that is what the word *idiot* literally means, one who lives in a private world. There are no private worlds in Christianity.

Christian Maturity
(Week 45, Monday)

One Body in Christ

Everybody who belongs to Christ belongs to everybody who belongs to Christ. One may betray that relationship, but you cannot deny it, for it is inherent. The inspired record puts it: "so we...are one body in Christ" (Rom 12:5). Not "ought to be," or "are called to be," or "must recognize ourselves as such," but "are one body in Christ." You are in that body, and you can't get out of that body without getting out of Christ. As long as you stay in Christ you are in one body.

That doesn't mean that we are all to be in one church—my church or your church— to be in the "one body." The text says: "so we, though many, are one body in Christ" (Rom 12:5). It provides for the "many" and the "one." The New Testament knows of many churches, but knows of *one* church. The many churches were branches of the one church. They were the local expression of the one universal church. The modern idea of many churches—separate, sovereign, independent—is unknown in the New Testament. It is utterly foreign to the New Testament. Paul cried out when separate denominationalism put up its head: "Is Christ divided" (1 Cor 1:13)? If you are in Christ, you are in one body.

In Christ
(Week 11, Tuesday)

The Marks of a Christian Church
Romans 12:6-8

We have many modern discussions on the nature of the church.... We see [the church first] at Antioch: "And in Antioch the disciples were for the first time called Christians" (Acts 11:26).

In those days they gave names according to characteristics.... So at Antioch a name was given that fitted the group. The characteristics of Christ were in this group, so they are called "Christ-ians." The group formed a Christian church; the words "Christian church" become flesh. We must examine its marks.

First, it was essentially a lay church. It was founded by laypersons, and laypersons constituted and carried on the church. That made it true to the essential nature of Christianity as a lay movement.... This church was founded by a lay group, scattered

193

under the persecution which arose over Stephen, a layman. That fixed the New Testament church as a lay church. Jesus and the disciples were laymen, no hands having been laid on them in ordination, and the Seven, the lay group, became the center of spiritual contagion. Paul, a layman, became the spearhead of this lay movement. The Christian movement continued a lay movement until the third century when it was changed into a clerical movement and the laymen were pushed to the margin.

The Word Became Flesh
(Week 35, Sunday)

Next Great Spiritual Awakening Will Come through the Laity
Acts 17:24-27

The word *laos* in Greek, from which the word *laity* comes, means literally, "the chosen people of God"; the laity were "the chosen people of God," not only by language derivation but by divine appointment and intention. And this conception and practice held there until the Council of Nicea, when the church authorities made it into a church of bishops and clergy, and laypeople were relegated to the margin....This was perhaps the greatest tragedy that ever struck the church. Revival will come only when the New Testament emphasis on the laity is rediscovered. The next great spiritual awakening will come through the laity. The clergy will be the guides and spiritualizers of an essentially lay movement.

Second, the New Testament church had the marks of the cross upon it. It was established by a lay group that had suffered for its faith....Their faith had cost them something, so it was worth something. If the lay group is to be the center again of the Christian movement, it will again cost them something to be Christian. Then and then only will it be worth something.

Third, the church at Antioch was founded by people who made it interracial. The Jewish laymen from Jerusalem preached only to the Jews, but laymen from Cyrene and Cyprus, with larger racial contacts and sympathies, preached the Word among the Greeks. So the church was made up of Jews and Greeks. And blacks. "Now in the church at Antioch there were prophets and teachers, Barnabas, Simeon who was called Niger"—literally "the black." Simeon was not on the margins, just tolerated; he was a "prophet" or "teacher" and laid his hands on Barnabas and Paul. So Barnabas and Paul were commissioned or ordained by a black man to preach the gospel to white Europe (Acts 13:1).

The Word Became Flesh
(Week 35, Monday)

The Marks of Barnabas and Paul Were upon This New Testament Church
Acts 9:19-22; 26-28

Fourth, this New Testament church had the marks of Barnabas upon it. Those in church at Jerusalem were wise in sending a layman like Barnabas. Had one of the apostles been sent, it would have interrupted the lay character of the Antioch church. This choice fitted in. For Barnabas was one of the most beautiful characters in the New Testament. He was a man, a Levite, from Cyprus, who sold a field and laid the proceeds at the apostles' feet....

He encouraged everybody. He took Paul when the authorities at Jerusalem were afraid of him and presented him as real. And he took John Mark when Paul refused to take him. He was big-souled. "When he came and saw the grace of God, he was glad" (Acts 11:23); he could rejoice in the work of others.... The spirit of Barnabas went into the making of this New Testament church.

Fifth, the spirit of Paul went into the church and the spirit of this church went into Paul. When Barnabas saw this type of Christianity, he said to himself, "This is the kind of Christianity that young man Saul needs. I must expose him to it." So he went off to Tarsus, sought out Saul, and brought him to Antioch. One of the best things Barnabas ever did. The church and Paul cross-fertilized each other and both were enriched.

The Word Became Flesh
(Week 35, Tuesday)

A Church That Cared
Acts 15:7-11

Sixth, the church at Antioch was a church that cared. Friedrich von Hügel has defined a Christian as "one who cares" [no published source found]. Well, the Antioch church was Christian, for it cared, cared that the believers in Judea were in need of economic help. "And the disciples determined, every one according to his ability, to send relief to the brethren who lived in Judea" (Acts 11:29). That caring was a pattern for the church of the ages....

Seventh, their spirituality functioned in material terms and also in social terms. In the church at Antioch there was Simeon, a black man, and also "Manean, a member of the court of Herod the tetrarch" (Acts 13:1). Not only were racial distinctions transcended but social distinctions. Manean was from high society, and Simeon was probably from a much lower class. But here race and class distinctions were canceled; a person was a person for whom Christ died. The Christian faith is class-blind and race-blind.

The Word Became Flesh
(Week 35, Wednesday)

The Conservative and the Radical
Luke 5:35-39

Eighth, the church at Antioch held within itself the conservative and the radical. The account says: "Now in the church at Antioch there were prophets and teachers" (Acts 13:1). The "teachers" are usually the conservative element in society, passing on the lessons and values of the past to the next generation. The "prophets" are usually the radicals, wanting to apply those lessons and values to wider and wider areas of life. There is usually a tension in every group and society between these two, the conservatives pulling back and the radicals pulling ahead.

But these two are necessary for any progressive society; we need to conserve values, and we need to apply values to larger and larger areas of life....

Jesus was a living blend of conservative and radical. He said: "Think not that I have come to abolish the law and the prophets; I have come not to abolish them but to fulfill

195

them" (Matt 5:17). And then he presented the kingdom of God, which demanded total change. He was conservative and radical. The church must be the same.

The Word Became Flesh
(Week 35, Thursday)

Collective Guidance
Luke 3:1-3

Ninth, the church was sufficiently united so the group as a group could receive collective guidance. "While they were worshiping the Lord and fasting, the Holy Spirit said, 'Set apart for me Barnabas and Saul for the work to which I have called them.'" (Acts 13:2). Here was a group so attuned to God and so attuned to each other that the Holy Spirit could give them a united guidance. We would have thrown it open to debate, then have taken a vote, and the majority would have ruled. This would have left a disgruntled minority. But their method of guidance was different, they desired to come a common mind—and did—under the guidance of the Holy Spirit. "It has seemed good to the Holy Spirit and to us" (Acts 15:28); that was the classic phrase that characterized the early church....

The [Antiochian] church, unlike the modern church, did not insist on their label being put on the sending [of missionaries]. They did not say, "Missionaries, sent out by the Antioch Church, through the Holy Spirit." We would have had our denominational labels, prominently displayed. There is no limit to the good you can do provided you do not seek credit for it. That church asked for no credit and forgot themselves into immortality.

The Word Became Flesh
(Week 35, Friday)

Held Together in Spite of Difference
1 Corinthians 12:12-26

Tenth, this church held together good people who honestly differed, held them in spite of difference. Paul and Barnabas had a contention—a contention over taking John Mark on another journey when he deserted them on the first journey....

The account says: "And there arose a sharp contention, so that they separated from each other; Barnabas took Mark with him and sailed away to Cyprus, but Paul chose Silas and departed, being commended by the brethren to the grace of the Lord" (Acts 15:39-40). That "being commended by the brethren by the grace of the Lord" is a part of one sentence and could refer to both Barnabas and Mark and Paul and Silas. In other words they held together brethren in difference. They commended both to the grace of the Lord—and they both needed it!

These ten marks of a Christian church showed that the church at Antioch was the Word become flesh in a group. No wonder they were first called *Christians* at Antioch. This group was an organism of the Holy Spirit. Without these ten marks the church is an organization of humans—the Word become word. Hence powerless.

The Word Became Flesh
(Week 35, Saturday)

John 3:16 and 1 John 3:16
2 Corinthians 9:9-12

In the early church there were two breakings of bread: one, the bread of the Communion, and the other, the bread of the love feast. The first symbolized our sharing his broken body; the second symbolized the sharing of our bread with our brothers and sisters, Communion with God and communion with people. The last dropped out of church practice, the first remained. It was easier to accept what God did than to accept what we must do.

The Word Became Flesh
(Week 44, Tuesday)

The Kingdom and the Church
Ephesians 5:25-27

[While at an altar of a church, I found Jesus Christ,] but you are not saved by the church. If the church is the subject of redemption, how then can it dispense it? "Christ is the head of the church, his body, and is himself its Savior" (Eph 5:23). If the church needs saving, how can it give salvation? If the church takes you by the hand and takes you beyond itself to the feet of the Savior, it is wonderful. But if it stops you at itself and makes itself the issue, it is not wonderful, it is idolatry. The kingdom is the absolute, the church is the relative. The kingdom commands, the church obeys. The church loses its life in the life of the kingdom and finds itself again.

The Word Became Flesh
(Week 46, Sunday)

"O Jesus, If It Weren't for You I'd Not Be a Christian Five Minutes"
Colossians 1:11-14

A very sensitive and dedicated Christian, after a deep disappointment in some of her trusted colleagues, threw herself on her bed and cried, "O Jesus, if it weren't for you I'd not be a Christian five minutes." He held her steady through that letdown. I believe in the church because I believe in Jesus. He is redeeming it, and redeeming it the hard way. And that church will stand before him without spot or wrinkle.

But to talk about the church now as though it were the body of Christ is unrealistic. Today it is the crucified body of Christ, crucified on the cross of its own unfaithfulness. And we must suffer, as Paul did, to help make up a share of Christ's sufferings for this crucified body. We must feel faithless in its faithlessness, feel a sense of shame in its shameless betrayal, be crucified in its self-imposed crucifixion, and be humiliated in its pride.

The Word Became Flesh
(Week 46, Friday)

197

THE GOSPEL

The Cross Becomes Inevitable
Matthew 10:28; Luke 14:26; Acts 20:22; Galatians 6:14

The effect of the gospel is to deepen and widen one's sympathies. This means that your sympathies have been so widened that life will touch you on a wider front. So the process of your Christianization is the deepening of your capacity to suffering. Each new friendship you form, each new convert you win, each new injustice in the social order you come in contact with, each new sin in others to which you expose yourself, each new task you take on yourself, will become a possible suffering point. Through the gospel there is a sensitizing of the soul and a universalizing of the sympathies of that sensitized soul. The cross thus becomes inevitable.

Victorious Living
(Week 43, Wednesday)

"For They Were Afraid Of"
John 19:38-44; 20:19-23

How crippled, how unsatisfactory, how far short of human need would our Christianity have remained, if the Gospel had stopped at the pre-Pentecost stage! And yet that is where most of our Christianity has stopped.

Abundant Living
(Week 22, Friday)

Adjusting Our Vocabulary to Fact
Luke 4:22; Acts 6:10; James 3:1-13

We must reclothe the eternal truths of the Gospel in the language that each age can understand. But even that will not do, if the reclothing is just adopting the words of a new age. The words must have content, reality in them, or they will say nothing.

Abundant Living
(Week 43, Sunday)

An Open Universe
Mark 11:23-24; 2 Timothy 1:12-14

Our gospel is not primarily *resolution*—a whipping up of the will. It is primarily *faith*—a surrender of our will to the will of God. Linked with Almighty Resources, you can now add resolution, for the resolution now is not an anxious fretting—trying in one's own strength and power—but a restful, confident resolution to take infinite resources.

The Way
(Week 36, Friday)

The Steps in the Preparation
John 1:29-34

Here are the two characteristic things in the Christian gospel: clearing the way between humanity and God by the atonement; clearing the way between humanity and itself by the indwelling. One is *atonement*; the other is *attunement*. We need to get right with God and to get right with ourselves, to be at one with God and at one with ourselves. The Christian gospel makes it possible to live with God and to live with ourselves, therefore with others. If you won't live with God, you can't live with yourself, and hence you can't live with others. The gospel makes you live, in every direction and in ever portion of your being.

The Way to Power and Poise
(Week 6, Sunday)

Many Religions—One Gospel
Romans 8:3-4

Religions are humanity's search for God, the gospel is God's search for humanity. There are many religions; there is but one gospel.

How to Be a Transformed Person
(Week 2, Thursday)

Unable to Adapt Themselves
Luke 9:12-17

We have a total gospel for the total need of a total humanity, and we must totally apply it if we are to survive.

Growing Spiritually
(Week 28, Monday)

Guilts Upset the Body
Jeremiah 33:6; Malachi 4:2

The most blessed fact of the Christian gospel is the offer of divine forgiveness. This is the most healing fact that can steal into the depths of personality. It pervades one as a sense of release and well-being.

Growing Spiritually
(Week 34, Thursday)

The Gospel Is God's Search for Humanity
John 1:9-13

The gospel doesn't begin with God, it begins with Jesus.

The gospel then begins with the incarnation. All religions are humanity's search for God; the gospel is God's search for humanity; therefore there are many religions, but one gospel. All religions are the Word become word; the gospel is the Word become flesh. Therefore all religions are philosophies; the gospel is a fact. Philosophies may be good views; the gospel is good news. The gospel is not primarily a philosophy—it is a fact. The philosophy grows out of the Fact. The Fact of Jesus is our starting point and is our gospel.

It is the gospel of Jesus before it is the gospel of God or the gospel of the kingdom. The gospel lies in his person—he didn't come to bring the good news—he was the good news. This gospel is not spelled out, therefore verbal; it is lived out, therefore vital. Jesus didn't come to bring the forgiveness of God—he was the forgiveness of God. There is no other way to God, for Jesus is the Way from God. He is God coming to us. Therefore there can be no other way.

Mastery
(Week 1, Thursday)

God a Half-God Ruling over a Half-Realm
Matthew 13:37-41

Jesus started out "preaching the gospel of the kingdom of God" (Mark 1:14 KJV), the only thing he ever called his gospel. And he sent out his disciples to preach the gospel of the kingdom of God. Then he seemed to change his emphasis and began to preach himself. "I am the way.... No one comes to the Father except through me" (John 14:6 CEB). Which was his message—the Order or the Person? Or did they coalesce and become one? They became one; he used interchangeably "for my sake" and "for the kingdom's sake." He was the kingdom personalized; the Order came to embodiment in him. The Absolute Order and the Absolute Person came together and were one. That meant religion was personal in that it had personal relations with a Person; it was also social in that it had relations with an Order embodied in that Person. It was not now personal and now social; it was both by its very nature. So I do not want a personal gospel or a social gospel; I want one gospel that redeems the total life, individual and social. That is as it should be, for God is not a half-god ruling over a half-realm. God is the God of all life. God's kingdom is a total kingdom.

Mastery
(Week 29, Monday)

Expectation of Perfection, an Illusion
James 3:1-2

The blood of Jesus Christ is the life of Jesus Christ, laid down sacrificially for us; that life cleanses us from all sin. And so at the heart of our gospel is a continuous cleansing element. This makes possible a fellowship, for within the fellowship is this redemptive principle and power at work, cleansing away the impediments to fellowship as they arise.

Christian Maturity
(Week 11, Saturday)

Taste of Love in Fruits of Spirit
Ephesians 5:1-2

In the gospel, love is not something put in and then canceled out by other emphases. It is the whole motif.

Christian Maturity
(Week 17, Saturday)

Depleting and Defeating
Galatians 2:16

John the Baptist represented the gospel of a demand: "You can't do this; you must do that." And Jesus said: "He who is least in the kingdom of heaven is greater than [John the Baptist]" (Matt 11:11). Why? Because the kingdom of God did not present the gospel of a demand, but the gospel of an offer. We are to "receive" the kingdom, not whip up ourselves into it. Those who are in the kingdom of an offer, though they be the very least, are greater than those who are in the kingdom of a demand. For those who are under a demand end in depletion; those who are under an offer end in repletion and fullness. They are replete with all it takes to live, for they are attached to infinite resources. They live by the grace and power of Another.

Christian Maturity
(Week 32, Wednesday)

I Got Her In

We pause to look at our passage again: "For I became your father in Christ Jesus through the gospel" (1 Cor 4:15). Note the phrase: "through the gospel." If we preach a philosophy (ideas about life), or a moralism (principles and practices upon which life can be lived), or religious practices (techniques of religious life), we do not become a "father in Christ Jesus"; we do not beget spiritual children. It is only "through the gospel" that we become creative....

The gospel is the redemptively creative activity of God. And Jesus himself is that gospel.

In Christ
(Week 22, Friday)

Introduction

This verse, "And the Word became flesh" (John 1:14), sets the gospel off in a class by itself. And yet while it is in a class by itself, a sui generis, nevertheless it relates it to everything: God, life, the material everything. For it is planted in life: spiritual, material, and social. But planted in life, it is different, apart, and unique.

The Word Became Flesh
(pp. 11–12)

The Nazareth Manifesto
Matthew 13:12-17

We come now to a key passage, which reveals the whole Christian gospel as the Word become flesh. Not only in the initial incarnation in human flesh, but as a continuing incarnation, as a method and attitude in everything connected with that gospel; it was all an application of the principle of the Word become flesh, the principle become practice. As Jesus stood up to read in the synagogue at Nazareth, he announced his program and purpose: "The Spirit of the Lord is upon me, because he has anointed me to preach good news to the poor [the economically disinherited]. He has sent me to proclaim release to the captives [the socially and politically disinherited] and recovering of sight to the blind [the physically disinherited], to set at liberty those who are oppressed [the morally and spiritually disinherited], to proclaim the acceptable year of the Lord [a fresh world beginning—the corporately disinherited]" (Luke 4:18-19). He closed the book and began to say to them: "Today this Scripture has been fulfilled in your hearing" (4:21); today this word of Scripture becomes flesh, in me. And it did!

In his own person, Jesus embodied this fivefold redemptive impact upon life and started movements, which then and now are leading to the emancipation of the poor from economic bondage, the downtrodden masses from social and political captivity, the physically disabled from their disabilities, the morally and spiritually bruised from their guilts, the world from total bondages in the total life. The program became the Person and the Person became the program; they were one. The text became clothed in flesh and blood. No wonder "they were surprised that words of such grace should fall from his lips" (Luke 4:22 NEB). It was the grace of embodied fact, the grace of being and doing.

The Word Became Flesh
(Week 19, Monday)

THE HOLY SPIRIT

A Personal Word [about the Holy Spirit]
Acts 4:20; Luke 1:2; Acts 1:8

I was a Christian for a year or more when one day I looked at the library shelf and was struck with the title of a book, *The Christian's Secret of a Happy Life* (Hannah Whitall Smith, 1885).

As I read it, my heart was set on fire to find this life of freedom and fullness. I reached page 42 when the Inner Voice said very distinctly, "Now is the time to find." I pleaded that I did not know what I wanted, that when I finished it [the book], I would seek. But the Inner Voice was imperious, "Now is the time to seek."

I tried to read on, but the words seemed blurred. I was up against a divine insistence, so closed the book, dropped on my knees, and asked, "What shall I do?" The Voice replied, "Will you give me your all—your very all?"

After a moment's hesitation I replied, "I will."

"Then take my all, you are cleansed," the Voice said with a strange, inviting firmness.

"I believe it," I said and arose from my knees. I walked around the room affirming it over and over, and pushing my hands away from me as if to push away my doubt. This I did for ten minutes, when suddenly I was filled with a strange refining fire that seemed to course through every portion of my being in cleansing waves. It was all very quiet and I had hold of myself, and yet the divine waves could be felt from the inmost center of my being to my fingertips. My whole being was being fused into one, and through the whole there was a sense of sacredness and awe and the most exquisite joy.

Very emotional? So be it! But I knew then, and know now, that I was not being merely emotionally stirred, but the very sources of my life were being cleansed and were taken possession of by Life itself. My will was just as much involved as my emotion. The fact is the whole of life was on a permanently higher level.

Victorious Living
(Week 16, Saturday)

The Power That Gives Release
John 4:14; Acts 1:8; 2 Corinthians 3:17-18

"Where the Spirit of the Lord is there is freedom" (2 Cor 3:17), freedom from cramping bandages and inhibitions and paralyzing sins.

But this age has lost grip upon the Holy Spirit. We have taught this age to follow Jesus as an example, and it has produced a pale, colorless Christianity. For the gospel does not ask you to follow Jesus as an example; it offers you the resources of the Holy Spirit in the inner life and then you follow Jesus because of an impulsion. This kind of Christianity becomes colorful and red-blooded. It has resources, therefore power.

A modern translation of the Gospels spells the "holy spirit" thus, without capitals. That is symbolic of what has happened to this age. It has turned the Holy Spirit into a "holy spirit," a vague, impersonal influence, to our impoverishment. That is not the Holy

Spirit of the Acts of the Apostles. There the Holy Spirit was no mere vague, impersonal influence; There the Holy Spirit was God meeting them inwardly, reinforcing, cleansing, fusing the soul forces into a loving unity, and setting them ablaze with God.

When the disciples got hold of that secret [the Holy Spirit] at Pentecost, they were immediately and decisively freed from cramping inhibitions and spiritual bondages and became flaming evangels of the Good News. We need to rediscover the actual resources of the Holy Spirit; or else, we remain in bondage.

Victorious Living
(Week 38, Friday)

The Holy Spirit Works in the Subconscious
John 14:25; 15:25; 16:7-14

Here is where the Christian Church is weakest. It believes in and teaches the Holy Spirit—partly. The disciples were at this stage when Jesus said to them: "He [the Holy Spirit] remains with you and will be within you" (John 14:17 Moffatt). The Holy Spirit was with them, but not within them. The same is true today. Most Christians know the Holy Spirit is with them, disturbing them by momentary touches, flashes of nearness, illuminations and insights, saving here and saving there. But all this is "with," and not "within." The Spirit goads us rather than guides us, illuminates rather than invigorates, prods us into activity rather than penetrates all activities—it is from without in, instead of from within out. This sense of outsideness will persist in religion until we enter into what the disciples entered into at Pentecost. There they passed over from the "with" stage to the "within" stage. Their religion was no longer a prodding, but a penetration; no longer a restriction, but a release.

Abundant Living
(Week 22, Thursday)

Steps in Receiving the Holy Spirit
John 14:16-17, 26; 16:7, 13; Acts 1:8

Believe it is in the divine intention for you to receive the Holy Spirit. Fix it in your mind that the gift of the Spirit is not an exceptional gift for exceptional people who are in exceptional work, but a gift that is the birthright of every Christian. "Jesus said this concerning the Spirit. Those who believed in him would soon receive the Spirit" (John 7:39 CEB). Note: "would soon receive"—receiving was in the divine intention and program for them. For whom? "Those who believed in him." Here then is no exception. You, the ordinary Christian, are to receive the Holy Spirit, for you are counted among those who believe in him. "You will receive the gift of the Holy Spirit. This promise is for you, your children, and for all who are far away" (Acts 2:38-39 CEB). You belong to those "far away." You are in the stream of the divine intention.

Abundant Living
(Week 23, Monday)

Concerning the Holy Spirit
John 14:15-17; 15:26-27

The Holy Spirit means the human-divine togetherness. In the Incarnation, God came part way; in the Indwelling God comes the full way, comes into the citadel of our spirits. And God comes, not as a transient visitor, but "to abide with your forever" (John 14:16 KJV).

The Way
(Week 39, Monday)

"It Is All Empty Inside"
Acts 1:8; 2:17-18, 33

In our faith, in our unity, and in our virtues the Holy Spirit is central. But the Holy Spirit is not central in our present-day Christianity. The emphasis upon the Holy Spirit has been pushed from the mainstream of Christianity into the cults. There the teaching has been thrown out of balance, often identified with rampant emotionalism. And yet the almost entire absence of emphasis on the Spirit has impoverished the mainstream of Christianity. It often degenerates into a humanistic striving to be good.

The Way
(Week 39, Wednesday)

A Holy Spirit-Less Christianity
Acts 19:1-7

A Holy Spirit-less Christianity lacks contagion. It hasn't that plus that carries over from a contained faith to a contagious faith. Our Christianity can be contained—contained with us as a comfort, a refuge, a belief, a hope, an inspiration. Good, but not good enough. Nothing is ours that is not shared; nothing is ours that cannot be carried over and duplicated in other lives. Nothing really lives that isn't life giving.

The Way
(Week 39, Saturday)

On Possessing the Spirit
Luke 24:49; Acts 2:37-39

The church has in large measure tried to bypass Pentecost and go after its problems without the "tarrying." Consequently, it is exhausting itself against the problems of the day. Had the disciples tried to bypass Pentecost, we would have never heard of them again. They would have exhausted themselves against the problems of that day....

But the question is asked: Doesn't every Christian possess the Holy Spirit? And the answer is yes. But the difference is probably this: In the new birth, you have the Holy Spirit; in the fullness, the Holy Spirit has you.

The Way
(Week 40, Sunday)

To Be Spirit-Possessed Is to Be Self-Possessed
Philippians 2:1-5

When surrendered to the Spirit we become inwardly harmonized and hence outwardly effective.

The Way
(Week 40, Wednesday)

Steps to Receive the Holy Spirit
John 7:37-39; Galatians 3:2

Say to yourself: God has come a long way in approaching me. God has come through an incarnation, an atoning death, a resurrection, down to the door of my heart. Having come so far, I know God will come the full way; God will come within me. The Holy Spirit is God coming within me....

As I search the Scriptures, I note that the Holy Spirit is given on four conditions: (1) I must ask—"How much more will the heavenly Father give the Holy Spirit to those who ask him" (Luke 11:13)? (2) I must accept the Holy Spirit by an act of appropriating faith—"By faith we might receive the promised Spirit" (Gal 3:14 Moffatt). (3) But I cannot accept the gift of the Holy Spirit without paying the price of that gift, the gift of myself. If God gives Godself, then I must give myself. (4) I must obey God—"The holy Spirit which God has given to those who obey him" (Acts 5:32 Moffatt). I must therefore ask, accept, give, and obey. I am now committing myself with all my being to do those four things.

The Way
(Thursday, Week 40)

The Last Steps—Self-Giving and Obedience
Acts 4:29-33; 5:32

We come now to the two remaining steps in the receiving [and retaining] of the Holy Spirit: self-giving and obedience. [The first two steps are asking and receiving by faith.]

Perhaps we should have put the step of self-giving before the act of receiving by faith. It belongs before. You cannot accept the gift of the Holy Spirit without involving the prior gift of yourself. And yet it belongs after acceptance too. For it is a once-for-all giving, and yet it is a continous giving. It is like being married; there is a completed act when each gives the self to the other in marriage, and yet marriage is a continous process of mutual self-giving. It is crisis and continuity.

But, you ask, how shall I know I have given myself? Silenece the heart before God and see if anything arises to the surface unsurrendered. If nothing arises, then you must take it for granted that there is nothing left behind. To be sure that everything is covered, tell God you surrender all you know and all you don't know. If anything unsurrendered is shown to you in the future, then that belongs to God too.

And now the continous obedience. God is in control. God uses you as the instrument of God's purposes, provided you cooperate. We retain the Holy Spirit as long as God retains control. When we take over, God quietly steps out—not completely out—but

God shuts off the sense of divine presence and power until we decide to give over the reins again. "To these facts we bear witness, with the Holy Spirit which God has given to those who *obey* him" (Acts 5:32 Moffatt, emphasis added). The "obey" is present and continous.

The Way
(Saturday, Week 40)

The Holy Spirit Is God Where It Counts: Within
Luke 3:16, 17

The Holy Spirit has been lost in large measure from modern Christianity. We are presenting a Holy-Spiritless Christianity, a demand without a dynamic. A prominent Christian leader said that he did not hear a sermon on the Holy Spirit until he was forty-five, and he had attended church all his life. A note has dropped out....Pentecost [had] been skirted.

The Way to Power and Poise
(Week 5, Sunday)

For They Were Afraid
John 20:19-23

The Holy Spirit is the missing note in much of present-day Christianity. This was not true in early Christianity. The Holy Spirit was the dynamic by which is was propelled. You couldn't tell where the early apostles ended and the Holy Spirit began. The translators have been puzzled as to whether to use a small *s* or a capital *S* in place after place, for it could be either or both. The human spirit and the divine Spirit had joined forces and seem to be coterminous. And yet the human was not swamped in the divine. It was heightened and released by the divine indwelling....

Suppose there had been no Holy Spirit? Just what kind of Christianity would have faced the world? It would have been the four Gospels without the Upper Room and the coming of the Spirit. Let us glance at the way the Gospels end: Mark ends at chapter 16, verse 8: "For they were afraid." The rest has been added by later writers, so the scholars tell us. Suppose the gospel had ended on that note: "for they were afraid." And that isn't a supposition, for this is what we find in John's Gospel: "The doors being shut where the disciples were, for fear of the Jews" (20:19). Although the resurrection had taken place, yet they were bound by inward fears, and the closed doors were the outer expression of their tied-up condition. Their emotions were stirred by the news of the resurrection of Jesus, but those emotions were not changed from fear to all-conquering faith. No mere event outside of us, however great, can take the place of an indwelling of God, the Holy Spirit within us. Only an Indwelling can rid us of indwelling fears. The church today is largely at the same place, behind closed doors for fear.

The Way to Power and Poise
(Week 5, Monday)

The Content of Divine Power: Important
Philippians 2:1-5

The nature of the Spirit is determined by what we see in Jesus. The fact is that the Holy Spirit and the Spirit of Jesus are used interchangeably: "Having been forbidden by the Holy Spirit...; the Spirit of Jesus did not allow them" (Acts 16:6, 7). The Holy Spirit seemed to the disciples to be the Spirit of Jesus within them; they were one.

The Way to Power and Poise
(Week 5, Friday)

The Word Become Dynamic
Ephesians 3:14-20

When the Holy Spirit comes within us, then anything becomes possible. For the same power that worked in Jesus works in us. The Holy Spirit takes over our natural powers, cleanses and heightens them, and makes them go beyond themselves. There is a "plus" added to life. Ordinary people do extraordinary things, all out of proportion to their powers. They are a surprise to themselves and to others.

The Way to Power and Poise
(Week 9, Saturday)

The Promise of the Father
Luke 24:44-49

But what did [Jesus] pick out as of the greatest importance, the last thing of which he would speak? Both Luke's Gospel and the Acts of the Apostles are agreed on this: he urged them to stay in the city until they were "clothed with power" (Luke 24:49), and "you shall receive power when the Holy Spirit has come upon you" (Acts 1:8). In both cases, it was described as the last thing he said: "Then...he parted from them" (Luke 24:50-51); "and when he had said this,...he was lifted up" (Acts 1:9).

Jesus knew if they missed this, they had missed the whole point of redemption. For the Holy Spirit is redemption, continuing redemption within us. Apart from the Holy Spirit, the redemption is outside of us—in history in the historical Jesus—but the historical becomes the experiential in the Holy Spirit. The redemption would not be complete unless it became experience. So the last words of Jesus were: "You believe it, now experience it! Lo, I am with you always, in you always in the Holy Spirit. Tarry till the Spirit comes within."

The Way to Power and Poise
(Week 10, Sunday)

Tired of Working on the City of God
2 Corinthians 1:20-22

The bane of the spiritual life is its impermanence. So many are sighing over lost ecstacies, lost touch with God, lost victory. It is largely because they are living, not "the life of the Spirit," but the life of following an ideal with their own resources, stirred by emotion through a sermon or plagued by a demand laid upon them. So they grow tired and give up. A Chinese scholar was working on a translation of Augustine's *City of God* and sent the following message to the mission board: "I'd like another assignment. I'm tired of working on the *City of God*." A lot of people are tired because they are working on the City of God, instead of the City of God working in them. The Holy Spirit is the City of God working in us. We don't work at the City of God; we let the City of God work in us, take possession of us. The Holy Spirit is the guarantee of the City of God. Not that we cannot fall, but the chances minimized, for by the sealing the guarantee can be applied. Spiritual permanence sets in. The wobble is taken out of us. I have watched it across the years: Where people come to India through romance, or through duty, or through wanting to serve, they often fall by the wayside, get tired, and give up. Only where there is a surrender to, and a possession of, the Holy Spirit do people have that "stickability" that makes them, not only endure to the end, but enjoy to the end. The Holy Spirit guarantees to keep us in repair, guarantees enough gas for the journey, guarantees the course we take, and guarantees arrival.

The Way to Power and Poise
(Week 21, Saturday)

The Holy Spirit Is Power, Where It Counts
Ephesians 3:14-21

Religion without the Holy Spirit is also inadequate. It imposes a set of rules and regulations but doesn't give power to perform. The Holy Spirit, however, when consented and surrendered to, moves in to be the spring of action and motive. This divine reinforcement within makes the ideal real, the impossible possible. The Holy Spirit is power, where it counts.

The Way to Power and Poise
(Week 17, Thursday)

The Best Gift for the Asking!
Jude 24-25

The Holy Spirit supplies that lack so often found in psychiatry, the lack of an intimate divine aid.... With the Holy Spirit within and in control, we can relax—relax at the center—for we know we are now being held by power not our own, and held from within. The Holy Spirit is the center and secret of our relaxation. We are not sitting on a lid; there is no need to, for the subconscious and the conscious are both under a common control, the control of the Holy Spirit. Released at the center, then we are released at the margins. Life is all of a piece, and it is happy and contagious.

The Way to Power and Poise
(Week 47, Monday)

You Can Love Yourself
Romans 8:3-4

"The Spirit of life in Christ Jesus" (Rom 8:2) is the equivalent of the Holy Spirit. The Holy Spirit "fathoms everything, even the depths of God" (1 Cor 2:10 Moffatt). And we may add: and the depths of humanity.

For the Holy Spirit, when we surrender to the Spirit's control all we know—the conscious—and all we don't know—the subconscious—then the Holy Spirit does nothing less than move in to take over, cleanse, control, and coordinate the whole of the inner life, conscious and subconscious. And more: the Holy Spirit fills our inner life with the unutterable sense of divine presence, so that the exquisite joy of that presence makes irrelevant and absurd and conflicting lesser joys. It is the expulsive power of a divine affection. Everything is caught up in the love of God; and the power of the lesser loves is not broken but fulfilled in a higher love....

This is more than sublimation; it is total self-expression. You are expressing yourself in the way and in the sphere for which you are made—God—and now you are truly natural. You are truly natural because possessed by the Supernatural. Everything then becomes a a dancing joy, a play spell.

No wonder, when the early Christians received the Holy Spirit, onlookers thought them to be drunk. They were, intoxicated with God and with their own consequent freedom. Such a sweeping answer to all their fears, inner conflicts, inhibitions, and guilt was enough to make them appear intoxicated, with joy.

How to Be a Transformed Person
(Week 21, Friday)

He Knows the Shepherd
Ephesians 3:14-16

We come now to see what is at the basis of the dullness in Christian lives. It is the absence of the Holy Spirit. The Holy Spirit is the Spirit of Creation, and where the Spirit abides within, there creation continues.

Up to the coming of the Holy Spirit at Pentecost the disciples were copyists; they were copying Jesus with more or less spotty performance. But when the Holy Spirit moved into them, they were not copyists but creators. They were no longer cold, dead moons lighted by reflected light; they were suns burning with fire and light within them.

They were no longer merely disciples—learners; they were apostles—ones sent. Timid believers had become irresistible apostles....These disciples were no longer lawyers arguing the case for Jesus, they were witnesses who witnessed to the mighty power of Jesus in their lives to save, and to save now. It was all living and fresh and firsthand and vital. Their spiritual lives were no longer in quotes; they were no longer in quotation marks, but in "creation" marks....

When the Holy Spirit moves within us in response to surrender and accepting faith, then you know Jesus, not by hearsay, but by heartsay. You know him intimately, vitally, and savingly. An inner dullness gives place to an inner dancing. Everything within you is under the law of creation. You are no longer tense and tired, but relaxed and refreshed. You have learned the secret of drawing upon your inner resources, the Holy Spirit.

How to Be a Transformed Person
(Week 35, Saturday)

The Holy Spirit, Birthright of Believers
John 7:35-38

[Another conviction is that] the Holy Spirit is the birthright of believers. I am persuaded that the Holy Spirit is the applied point of redemption. The Spirit brings redemption where it counts, namely, down among the basic springs of life. Psychologists tell us that the subconscious mind really determines the conscious. If this is true, then it is of the first importance to human living that something very redemptive control the subconscious. This need is supplied by the Holy Spirit. If we turn over to the Spirit all we know—the conscious mind, and all we don't know—the subconscious mind, then the Holy Spirit takes over the control of the driving urges, and cleanses and redirects them and dedicates them to the purposes of the kingdom of God.

This takes the precariousness out of the spiritual life, for the depths—the deepest depths—are held by the divine. Therefore fears and anxieties drop away.

The Holy Spirit is possessed by all who truly believe in and follow Christ, but when there is complete surrender to him, we not only possess the Spirit; the Spirit possesses us. That change is important, very important. You do not work so much as you let the Spirit work through you.

Growing Spiritually
(Week 51, Friday)

The Applied Edge of Redemption
2 Corinthians 1:21-22

For the Holy Spirit is the applied edge of redemption. The Spirit is redemption where it counts, namely, down amid the driving urges on the inside of us. If the Holy Spirit can move in and cleanse and control and consecrate these driving urges, then salvation has come and has come where it counts, namely, within.

Mastery
(Week 2, Saturday)

Nothing Is Ours Until It Gets Within
Ephesians 3:14-19

As a Christian movement we have stopped short of the one thing that would make all God's preparation and promises into performances in and through us. That one thing is the Holy Spirit. We have stopped short of receiving the Holy Spirit and therefore everything. For it is in and through the Holy Spirit that God gives us everything now. Luke tells us that Jesus "had given commandment through the Holy Spirit to the apostles" (Acts 1:2). He was from that time on commanding and working through the Holy Spirit. If we don't receive the Spirit, we are cutting ourselves off from Christ and

God.... [We now have] a religion of the Spirit. If you do not receive the Spirit, you automatically shut yourself off from all God promised and Jesus procured for us. He said all manner of sin and blasphemy shall be forgiven, but not blasphemy against the Holy Spirit. Why? Because the Holy Spirit is the "finger of God" casting out the evil spirits within us, then filling us with his presence and power. But if we reject God's outstretched hand by refusal to cooperate or by positive blasphemies as God offers us grace, then God can give us nothing. We have tied the process of redemption in knots, just where it would be operative.

Mastery
(Week 3, Monday)

The Great Simplification
Romans 10:6-13

There was one mediator—and only one mediator—between God and humanity, and that was Jesus. It was he who gave the Holy Spirit: "This Jesus, God raised up. We are all witnesses to that fact. He was exalted to God's right side and received from the Father the promised Holy Spirit. He poured out this Spirit, and you are seeing and hearing the results of his having done so" (Acts 2:32-33 CEB). That forever fixed the source from which we receive the Spirit; we receive the Spirit from Jesus and him alone, or we do not receive the Spirit. This gift comes from a nail-pierced hand or not at all....

Jesus was the Way. Humanity couldn't get to God, so God came to humanity—came in Jesus. This coming of the Holy Spirit was like a cleansing wind from heaven, cleansing the fetid atmosphere of religion from a thousand controversies and claims. Everything was simplified. The vast complications of law and ritual and rite and creed were all swept away before the vast simplification.

Mastery
(Week 5, Tuesday)

Not Vague Power, but a Vital Person
John 14:25-26

The Holy Spirit is not an *it*. "He will guide you in all truth" (John 16:13 CEB); the Holy Spirit is a he. And not a vague depersonalized person; he is a person with a very definite personalized content. And the content is the content of Jesus.

Mastery
(Week 5, Thursday)

The Creative Spirit
Ephesians 3:7-9

Wherever the Holy Spirit is, there is creation; for the Holy Spirit is the Spirit of Creation. Wherever the Holy Spirit is not, there are stagnation and death. It is a simple test, but a decisive one.

Mastery
(Week 21, Sunday)

212

Steps in Finding the Holy Spirit
Ephesians 1:11-14

The Holy Spirit is primarily a believer's gift. When the disciples received the Holy Spirit, they were believers. The account says, "Jesus said this concerning the Sprit. Those who believed in him were to soon receive" (John 7:39 CEB). Note "those who believed in him would soon receive," a believer's gift. When we came to the Christ, in the first coming we wanted forgiveness, reconciliation. We knew little or nothing about asking for the Holy Spirit. But now that we are children of God and are sure of our standing in God, we want to enter our birthright, which is nothing less than the Holy Spirit. In the new birth we received a measure of the Spirit; now we want more, we want to receive the fullness of the Spirit. We want to possess the Spirit; or better, we want to be possessed by the Spirit. We want more of what we have.

Mastery
(Week 51, Sunday)

The Gifts of the Spirit
Romans 12:3-8

There are many gifts but one Spirit, and Paul urges that we seek the highest gifts: love and prophesying (which is not foretelling but forthtelling the good news). The Holy Spirit is the gift for all, but divides the gifts according to the Spirit's will, for the collective good. To pick out one of these gifts and say, if we do not have this gift, we do not have the Holy Spirit, is to cut across this passage. Paul urges that we "earnestly desire" (v. 31) the two highest gifts: love and prophesying, the power to witness effectively. They are the safest and most needed gifts.

Mastery
(Week 51, Thursday)

Spring of the Emotions in the Subconscious
John 7:38-39

We were meditating yesterday on the impossibility of becoming mature through the daily repeating of verses of Scripture, through slogans and outward observances. Such methods may help, but we remain immature unless and until we get into vital contact with the Spirit of Truth, the Holy Spirit within....

If we surrender to the Holy Spirit all we know—the conscious, and all we don't know—the subconscious, the Spirit will enter into the subconscious and cleanse and control and coordinate the driving urges and consecrate them to kingdom ends. Then the conscious mind and the subconscious mind will not be at cross-purposes, but under a single control.... Mind and emotion and will are no longer pulling in different directions; held by the charioteer, the Holy Spirit, they are driven toward the goal of maturity.

Christian Maturity
(Week 42, Friday)

Psychotherapy Does Not Create Saints
1 Corinthians 1:22-24

Prior to the coming of the Holy Spirit on the day of Pentecost, the disciples were very immature disciples of a very mature Master. But when the Holy Spirit entered into them, took them over and made them over, they suddenly became mature in their reactions and their relationships. They loved enemies, walked out of councils with joy when beaten, went into prisons with no more jolt than when one passes from one room to another. They embraced death singing and praying for their tormentors. How could such advanced maturity come out of such immaturity, and how could it come out suddenly? The only answer: the Holy Spirit was within them!

Christian Maturity
(Week 42, Saturday)

The School of the Spirit
Titus 2:11-14

We emphasized the fact that Jesus had said that the Spirit of Truth, the Holy Spirit, would set up within a private school of the Spirit where he would "teach" us "all things" (John 14:26) and "guide" us "into all the truth" (John 16:13). And [1 John 2:27] adds: "the anointing whichyou received from him abides in you, and...teaches you about everything."

There are three things here: (1) the Spirit of Truth will teach us all things—the intellectual conception; (2) the Spirit will guide us into all truth—the emotional acceptance; (3) the anointing of the Holy Spirit teaches us about everything—the volitional dedication. The stages are important: first, the concept must be grasped by the mind—"teach you all things"; second, the concept must be emotionally accepted and made our own—"will guide you into all the truth."...The Holy Spirit teaches and guides you into possession of truth, or better, the truth takes possession of you. Third, the anointing teaches you about everything—the anointing, which involves dedication to, means that we learn the truth by being dedicated to the truth. In other words, we learn the truth by doing the truth. This is the modern emphasis of "learning by doing." So here is a school of the Spirit in which the mind grasps, the emotion accepts, the will acts upon. The total person is informed of, transformed by, and dedicated to—truth....

This school of the Spirit set up within the depths of our personality trains the mind to grasp truth, the emotion to accept truth, and the will to act upon truth, thus making the total person truth, hence mature. This means that we are under the intimate, twenty-four-hour-a-day tutelage of the most mature fact of the universe, the Holy Spirit. If we respond, our maturity is guaranteed.

Christian Maturity
(Week 43, Tuesday)

Attached to Exhaustible Emphases

When your faith and loyalty and love are fastened on Jesus Christ centrally and fundamentally, they are fastened upon the inexhaustible. He never grows stale, trite,

214

or empty of growing meaning. In him you find an eternal unfolding. The more you see the more you see there is to be seen. In him there is a surprise around every corner. The Holy Spirit unfolds the unfolding revelation, taking of the things of Christ and showing them to us. The absolute in Christ is always beckoning to our relativisms. We are under the law of an eternal change, a change "into his likeness from one degree of glory to another" (2 Cor 3:18).

In Christ
(Week 22, Monday)

How Do We Receive the Spirit

Many are puzzled as to how the Holy Spirit is received. Someone has said, "The biggest question in theology is this: How do we receive the Holy Spirit?" Paul is clear. "Let me ask you only this: Did you receive the Spirit by works of the law, or by hearing with faith?...Does he who supplies the Spirit to you and works miracles among you do so by works of the law or by hearing with faith?" (Gal 3:2, 5).

Salvation and the gift of the Spirit are both by the hearing of faith, by receptivity, or faith-filled receptivity. There are some still among us who believe that you can get the Holy Spirit by stepping into a long line of apostolic succession and having a bishop's hand laid on you. If you have faith that, only because you are in this line of succession you will thereby receive the Holy Spirit, the certainty is that you won't receive the Spirit. You are trying to receive the Holy Spirit by a mechanical contrivance—by a so-called unbroken line of laid-on hands—and that is trying to receive the Spirit by the works of the law. That Jesus should commit his most precious gift, the gift of the Holy Spirit, to that mechanical contrivance is unthinkable. The open heart, surrender, receptivity upward, and not an [unsecured] line backward, is the way to receive the Holy Spirit.

In Christ
(Week 28, Wednesday)

The Word Continues to Be Flesh
Acts 2:32-33

I am persuaded that the Word become flesh is not only an event in the time of Jesus; it is a continuing principle, a fact that is inherent in the Christian faith. And this is seen and realized in the coming of the Holy Spirit. The coming of the Holy Spirit was the Word become flesh in receptive and obedient believers. The Word became flesh, not only in "the body of Christ"—the church—but in the bodies of believers as individuals and persons.

The Word Became Flesh
(Week 26, Sunday)

The Holy Spirit Is the Successor of Jesus
Acts 2:38-39

Jesus provided for no successor except the Holy Spirit. By the very nature of things, the successor of Jesus had to be a divine successor....

"Nevertheless I tell you the truth: it is to your advantage that I go away, for if I do not go away, the Counselor will not come to you; but if I go, I will send him to you.... When the Spirit of truth comes, he will guide you into all the truth; for he will not speak on his own authority, but whatever he hears he will speak, and he will declare to you the things that are to come. He will glorify me, for he will take what is mine and declare it to you" (John 16:7, 13-14). The Holy Spirit was to continue the work of Jesus, to be his successor.... The Spirit's revelation will not be different, but simply more of the same....

The Holy Spirit is the applied edge of redemption.

The Word Became Flesh
(Week 26, Monday)

The "This-ness" of the Gospel
1 John 4:13, 17

[At Pentecost,] the Holy Spirit did exactly what Jesus said the Spirit would do, guided them into all truth. For ten days—the ten days that shook and shaped the world—the apostles were guided to surrender this, that, and the other until they came to themselves and they surrendered that last barrier. And the Holy Spirit, the Spirit of Truth, flooded them as if the Spirit had been pent up for ages. This was the moment. God was to rule persons from within, by their consent, according to a pattern fixed in Jesus and according to a power supplied by the Holy Spirit.

The Word Became Flesh
(Week 29, Monday)

I Am Never Tired in My Work
2 Timothy 4:1-5

The Holy Spirit within makes actual what Jesus made possible. The Spirit is the applied edge of redemption—redemption to body, mind, and spirit—to the total person. Without the Holy Spirit you are the victim of your circumstances; with the Holy Spirit within you are on top of your circumstances.

The Word Became Flesh
(Week 31, Monday)

THE KINGDOM OF GOD

The Central Emphasis in the Definition
Matthew 4:23; Luke 17:20-21; 21:27-28

In another book I said the kingdom of God is a new order founded on the Fatherly love of God—redemption, justice, and brotherhood, standing at the door of the lower order founded on greed, selfishness, exploitation, unbrotherliness. This higher order breaks into, cleanses, renews, and redeems the lower order, within both the individual will and the collective will.

This is true, but not the full truth. It is an offer from without. It is "at our door." And yet it is within us—"The kingdom of God is within you" (Luke 17:21 Weymouth). This kingdom has been "prepared for you from the foundation of the world" (Matt 25:34). Did Jesus mean that this kingdom has been built within the very foundations of the world and within the very structure of our own mental and moral makeup? Yes, I believe he meant just that.... But it does mean that the kingdom is written, not merely in sacred books, but in the very structure and make-up of the universe and of ourselves and of society. When we study the laws deeply embedded in the universe, in our own mental and moral and physical being, the laws that constitute true sociological living, we discover the laws of the kingdom.

Victorious Living
(Week 2, Wedneday)

The Kingdom Written Within
Jeremiah 31:33; Romans 2:14-16; 2 Corinthians 3:1-8

What does the psychologist mean by saying, "To be frank and honest in all relations, but especially in relations with oneself, is the first law of mental hygiene"? Doesn't that mean that the universe and you and I are built for truth, that the universe won't back a lie, that all lies sooner or later break themselves upon the facts of things? Since the kingdom stands for absolute truth, and our own mental makeup demands the same thing, then are not the laws of the kingdom written within us?

Victorious Living
(Week 2, Thursday)

The Kingdom and Life
John 11:25, 14:6, 1:4, 17:8, 20:31

Life will not work in any way except God's way. When we find the kingdom, we find ourselves....

The kingdom is "within us," but it is also "at our doors." Something from without is prepared to invade us, to change us, to complete us. When that happens, we too shall have to spell life with a capital "L." For every fiber of our being will know that this is Life....

The kingdom, then, is life-plus....The kingdom is the Ought-to-be standing over against the Is—challenging it, judging it, changing it, and offering it Life itself.

Victorious Living
(Week 2, Friday)

The Half-Truth of the Coming of the Kingdom as Only Sudden
Matthew 11:23, 24:42-51, 25:1, 13

Modern liberalism has insisted that the coming of the kingdom will be by gradual changes. It has drawn its inspiration from two sources: modern democracy and certain teachings in the New Testament that teach gradualism. Modern democracy has committed itself to a faith in democratic process of change according to constitutions. This means by vote instead of by sudden, catastrophic revolution. Liberalism has felt that the processes of the kingdom would be the same.

In this they have been supported by passages in the New Testament: the leaven that leavens the whole lump, the kingdom like the growth of the corn—first the blade, then the ear, then the full corn in the ear. These passages seemed to fit in with the spirit of democratic, evolutionary change.

But with the recent decay of faith in democratic government, much of this faith of liberalism in gradualism has decayed with it....

[Democracy] should hold to its principle of gradualism. For that lets the responsibility rest where it should rest, namely, on us, to bring in the kingdom by individual and collective endeavors cooperating with the redemptive God....For gradualism is in the New Testament as a living part of the outlook of the Gospel. It is ineradicable.

But it is only a half-truth. We should remember that. There is another side.

Victorious Living
(Week 25, Thursday)

The Half-Truth of the Coming of the Kingdom as Only Sudden
Matthew 13:31, 33; Mark 4:26-28; Luke 17: 20- 21

Modern fundamentalism in many cases has rejected the principle of gradualism and has said that in the Second Coming of Christ the kingdom will in fact be set up. This coming will be sudden and catastrophic.

In this, they have been supported by passages in the New Testament that teach his coming as a thief in the night, by the nobleman who went into a far country to receive a kingdom and to return to set it up, and so on. That the New Testament does teach this sudden and catastrophic phase of the coming of the kingdom there is no doubt whatever.

But it is a fact that the holding of this phase alone has produced a mentality that has withdrawn interest from social change by gradual processes, has made those who hold it discount those changes and has made them look for a worsening of things in order to reach a final, sudden triumph at the coming of Christ. This has been a moral and social drain.

Christian thought has moved from the catastrophic to the gradual and back again: thesis producing antithesis. It is now time for us to come to the synthesis. And the synthesis is this: there is in the pages of the New Testament both the teaching of gradualism and the teaching of the apocalyptic. Both are there and are integral to the account. They cannot be explained away. And in the interest of the kingdom, they must not be explained away, for we need both phases of the kingdom. Each is a half-truth that needs the other to complete it. We need to understand that the task is ours and must be assumed as such, and we must also see that it is God's and that God will complete it, perhaps even when we least expect it.

Victorious Living
(Week 25, Friday)

The Synthesis
Matthew 25:14-30

To accept this synthesis of gradualism and apocalyptic [regarding the coming of the kingdom of God] would leave us just were we should be as Christians: within the stream of human history and yet above it, within the world process to suffer and bleed and thus remake it and yet above the process as its judges through Christ who is to be its final Judge.

Victorious Living
(Week 25, Saturday)

The Kingdom of God—Another Rejected Stone
Matthew 6:33, 21, 43, 44; Luke 4:43; Acts 1:3

When we study the records, we find that the message of Jesus was the kingdom of God. When we study "church history" (significant phrase, for the history of the Christian centuries is "church history" rather than "kingdom history"), we find that the message was the church. Why this supplanting of the kingdom of God by the church? Jesus intended that the church should be subordinated to and a servant of the kingdom. But we have reversed that....

The kingdom is more Christian in its conception than the church, for it obeys the fundamental Christian law of losing oneself and finding it again. Hence the kingdom has gone further than the church.

If you doubt this, ask yourself: Is the church a sufficient founding upon which to build a new world society? To ask it is to answer it. It was tried during the Middle Ages and failed. But ask: Is the kingdom of God a sufficient basis for a new society? The answer is, that it is the only foundation.

This stone that the builders, both secular and sacred, rejected, has now become the head of the corner. [The kingdom of God] is emerging as the only solid foundation for human society....We have hid this kingdom light under the bushel of ecclesiasticism. We must now put it on top of the bushel as a candlestick. If we do, we save both. The church can be revived only as it becomes,'no longer an end in itself, but the servant of the kingdom, which is far larger than the church. For the world's need cries out for the kingdom.

Victorious Living
(Week 50, Wednesday)

The Laws of the Kingdom Are Self-Acting
Proverbs 28:16; 29:6; Hebrews 1:9, 11, 13

This fact of the kingdom of God within us is so important that it must be pursued. These laws, which are written in us, are self-acting. The action and the result are one. The result is not something imposed by God from without. It is something inherent. Sin and its punishment are one and the same thing. Sin literally is "missing the mark," the thing for which we are inwardly made; and to miss the mark is, by that very act, to sin against oneself.

Abundant Living
(Week 2, Friday)

The Kingdom Belongs to You!
Matthew 5:1-10; Luke 18:16-17

Remember that you do not merely belong to the kingdom of God; the kingdom of God belongs to you. Here is a fact that you must lay hold of, for in grasping it you turn the whole tide from defeat to victory. Possess this, and it will possess you.

Abundant Living
(Week 16, Friday)

The Homeland of the Soul—the Kingdom of God
Micah 6:8; Luke 17:20-21; Romans 8:9-11

When Jesus said, "The kingdom of God is within you" (Luke 17:21 KJV), he voiced one of the most important things ever uttered. The seeds of a new humanity are in that statement. It has seldom been taken seriously by orthodox Christianity; only the cults have taken it up and have used it. It must now be reclaimed and used. It must be put back into the stream of orthodox Christianity and become potent there. For this great truth is potent. I know the fear that has kept that verse from becoming current coin. If the kingdom of God is within us, in everybody, even the unchanged (for this verse was spoken to Pharisees who were unconverted), then the necessity of a new birth is gone. A merely optimistic view of human nature takes the place of the tragic view of human nature as sinful and in need of redemption; therefore salvation comes by insight, instead of by repentance and surrender and faith. I appreciate that fear, but do not share it.

Abundant Living
(Week 28, Monday)

The Kingdom of God and Business
Matthew 22:36-40; 25:34

The kingdom of God is within you! Psychology, education, and even business are stumbling upon the laws of the kingdom in their search for a workable way to live. I say "stumbling upon," for that expresses the chance discoveries that are being made. Someday our prejudices will drop away, as all other ways become manifestly unworkable, and we shall methodically and with abandon give ourselves to the discovery of the laws of the kingdom. Then in a decade, humanity will leap further forward in progressive abundant living than it is now doing in a century.

Abundant Living
(Week 29, Monday)

God Rules in Terms of Christ
John 1:1-5; 10:38; 14:7-11

The kingdom of God is at your doors! The Divine Invasion is near! The nature of that Divine Invasion is seen in Christ. He is the Personal Approach from the unseen. In him, the nature of reality is uncovered. In him, we see into the nature of God and also into the nature of God's reign. God redeems in terms of Christ. God also rules in terms of Christ. Christ is the revelation of God and also the revelation of the kingdom of God. He identifies with God and also with the kingdom of God.

Abundant Living
(Week 30, Monday)

Get the Spiritual Straight and the Material Will Be Guaranteed
2 Corinthians 8:14-15; Philippians 4:5-6, 11-13, 19

In seeking first the kingdom of God, Jesus says, the material basis of human life will be guaranteed to you. You will get what you need. "Your heavenly Father knows that you need them all [these things]" (Matt 6:32 KJV). Note that you will get according to your need, not according to your greed. You have a right to as much of the material as will make you mentally, spiritually, and physically fit for the purposes of the kingdom of God. You and I are constitutionally made in such a way that if we get less than we need or more than we need, we harm ourselves. Therefore, those who strive to get more than they need are working for their own harm.

Abundant Living
(Week 31, Thursday)

Is the Kingdom Our Good?
Acts 19:8-9; Colossians 1:13

That cosmic Home is the kingdom of God. Jesus said, "Seek God's Realm [kingdom] and his goodness, and all that will be yours over and above" (Matt 6:33 Moffatt). He makes the kingdom and goodness synonymous. His rule is our good—our physical, intellectual, emotional, spiritual, economic, social, political; and international good. God's rule is good for us, is our highest interest. Any other rule is bad for us. Self-rule equals self-ruin. God-rule equals good rule. The kingdom is our cosmic Homeland— our total Security.

The Way
(Week 9, Monday)

An Unshakable Kingdom
1 Timothy 6:13-16; 1 Peter 5:10-11

No wonder the writer of Hebrews says, "Let us be grateful for receiving a kingdom that cannot be shaken" (Heb 12:28). I am grateful with every fiber of my being that we have an unshakable kingdom. For the kingdoms of this world and the rotten civilizations they have built up are going down in blood and ruin. They are shakable. Paul speaks of "the dethroned Powers who rule this world" (1 Cor 2:6 Moffatt). These Powers still rule, though they are dethroned. Life has passed judgment on them, but they still rule on under the law of decay.

The Way
(Week 9, Wednesday)

The Kingdom of God Is Totalitarian
1 Corinthians 15:24-28

We have seen that the kingdom is the worldview of the Christian. It can be summed up in these words: "May your kingdom come and may your will be done on earth as it is done in heaven." There are three things here: (1) The kingdom is. It is a kingdom that is in operation, and its operation produces heaven. Where it is not in operation, that is hell.

(2) The kingdom that is, nevertheless, comes on earth as earth is willing to accept it and submit to it.

(3) The kingdom comes in a total way. The coming of the kingdom means the doing of the will of God on earth as it is done in heaven. How is the will of God done in heaven? In the individual will? Yes. In the collective will? Yes. In the total social arrangements in heaven? Yes. Then may the kingdom come in this total way on earth as it is in a total way in heaven.

The kingdom of God is a completely totalitarian order demanding a total obedience in the total life. It was presented to the individual will; it was presented to the collective will: "The kingdom of God will be taken away from you and given to a nation producing the fruits of it" (Matt 21:43 RSV). "But," cries my reader, "we are getting rid of one totalitarianism, and you are introducing us to another, even more thoroughgoing and absolute." True. But there is this profound difference: When you obey the kingdom of God, you find perfect freedom. When you obey other totalitarianisms, you find perfect bondage, for they are not the way you are made to live. When you obey the kingdom of God, you find perfect self-fulfillment.

The Way
(Week 9, Thursday)

The Kingdom Invades and Pervades
Romans 11:36; Colossians 1:26-29

I find ten laws written into our beings, and as we study them, they turn out to be the very laws of the kingdom of God.

(1) The universe is a universe of moral consequence. (2) The morally and spiritually fit survive. (3) The Christian way is written in the structure of the universe. (4) Humility

222

and obedience are the secret of knowledge and power. (5) An organism expends as much as it receives and no more; therefore receptivity is the first law of life. (6) The second law of life is that you must lose your life to find it again.

(7) Greatness comes through service. (8) Love is the fundamental law of human relationships. (9) Life is an eternal growth. (10) All life is lifted by self-sacrifice, by a cross. Wipe, then, the gospel of Jesus from the pages of the New Testament and you will find intimations of it in yourself....

The kingdom of God both invades you and pervades you. It invades you from without and pervades you from within. It descends and it ascends. We are made for it; therefore its coming is like a home-coming, a naturalizing, a finding of one's self.

The Way
(Week 9, Saturday)

The Open Secret
Luke 8:9-10 (Moffatt); Ephesians 3:2-6

Jesus is the key to the meaning of the universe. Follow the clues he gives and you get the answers every time. But the answers are hidden answers; they are an "open secret." The secret is a spirit, the spirit of self-surrendered humility. Everything in the kingdom is open to those who surrender to and obey the kingdom. We are in the process of discovering that kingdom hidden in the nature of reality. The kingdom is there, the ground plan of our being.

The Way
(Week 26, Friday)

The Holy Spirit Brings Unity
John 16:7-15

The Way is the way of the Indwelling. God's laws are written within us, "'The kingdom of God is within you" (Luke 17:21 KJV). This is without our consent. But the Indwelling is with our consent. In the Indwelling our personality is preserved, purified, permeated, and perfected.

The Way
(Week 39, Tuesday)

The Kingdom Has the Final Word
Matthew 15:13; 1 Corinthians 15:24-25; Revelation 1:17-18

The starting point for the Christian is the kingdom of God. From this, we work down to all life. But this has to be clarified. The starting point is the kingdom of God embodied in Christ—the Order embodied in a Person. Christ + the kingdom = the Way. Everything not conforming to the kingdom is destined to perish....

O God, my Lord, I see that your kingdom is my good, and my kingdom is my bad. Help me, then, to give myself to your kingdom with all my heart and with all my influence. For if this is true, then nothing else matters. But it is true. I know it. Amen.

The Way
(Week 49, Monday)

223

How the Kingdom Comes
Matthew 13:31-33; Luke 17:20-21; 1 Thessalonians 1:5, 8

A good many earnest and sincere Christians feel that the kingdom of God cannot be an issue now, since it will not come till Jesus comes. "No kingdom without the King," is the slogan. "He will come to set up his kingdom on earth, but until then we can do little or nothing to bring in a better order on earth. The best we can do is to rescue individuals, for the earth is going to smash, getting worse until he comes."

But as we look closely at the teaching of Jesus, we find the kingdom comes in three ways. First, by gradualism. "First the stalk, then the head, then the full head of grain" (Mark 4:28 CEB). The kingdom of God "is like a grain of mustard seed...; it grows up and becomes the greatest of all shurbs" (vv. 31-32). The kingdom of God "is like leaven... till it was all leavened" (Luke 13:21). These and other passages teach that the kingdom will come by permeation, by gradualism.

Other passages teach that the kingdom of God will come suddenly, by apocalypticism, with the return of Christ. Some people extract the gradualistic passages, others the apocalyptic. That disrupts the account, for both are there, and we need both. The gradualistic gives me my task, and the apocalyptic gives me my hope. So I shall trust as if the whole thing depends on God and work as if the whole thing depends on me. As this passage puts it, "The hidden issues of the future are with the Eternal our God, but the unfolded issues of the day are with us" (Deut 29:29 Moffatt). I shall therefore deal with the unfolded issues and leave the hidden issues to God. "It is not for you to know the times or the seasons" (Acts 1:7). Our task is clear: We can be the agents of the coming of that kingdom now.

The Way
(Week 49, Tuesday)

A Measureless Coming
John 3:31-36

Just as you have to have brains to enter the kingdom of knowledge, an aesthetic nature to enter the kingdom of beauty, an emotional nature to enter the kingdom of love, so you have to have a spiritual birth to enter into a spiritual world—the kingdom of God.

The Way to Power and Poise
(Week 6, Tuesday)

I'm In
Acts 15:8-11

Nobody is ever farther than three steps from the kingdom of God: (a) self-surrender, which includes sin-surrender; (b) acceptance of the gift of God, the gift of salvation; (c) obedience, obedience to the unfolding will of God. Anybody, anywhere, any time, can take these three steps and be "in." It works with an almost mathematical precision.

How to Be a Transformed Person
(Week 7, Saturday)

The Real Apostolic Succession
Matthew 4:23; Mark 1:1

We are studying Philip as the type of the humble, surrendered people through whom the Spirit of God breaks old molds and begins creative movements.

Philip was the first of the early disciples to put together the two things Jesus indissolubly put together: Jesus and the kingdom of God. "But when they believed Philip as he preached good news about the kingdom of God and the name of Jesus Christ" (Acts 8:12). None of the apostolic hierarchy seems to have grasped this, but Paul did (see Acts 28:23, 31). And this was vastly important. In Jesus, two important things came together: the Order—the kingdom of God; and the Person—Jesus Christ. The absolute Person and the absolute Order coincided, making our relationships with him both personal and social. The whole of life, individual and social, was to come under a single sway, the will of God. This was a completely totalitarian order, demanding a total obedience in the total life. But when it is totally obeyed, it brings total freedom.

How to Be a Transformed Person
(Week 42, Thursday)

That Imponderable Something
Luke 13:18-21; 19:12

The kingdom of God is God's total answer to humanity's total need. The totalitarianisms took over where we abdicated, saying to us, "We will leave you the inner mystical personal experience of the kingdom of God now, and the collective experience hereafter in heaven; we will take over the rest and control it." And yet they can't, simply can't. They are always running up against something imponderable, something that always breaks them. What is it?

It is nothing less than the kingdom of God that is written into the nature of things....

That kingdom has been "prepared for you from the foundation of the world" (Matt 25:34); it is built into the structure of the world as the laws of its being. If we live according to the kingdom, we live ("the Kingdom of God" and "Life" are used synonymously in Mark 9:45, 47 Moffatt). If we live against it, we perish....

The kingdom of God is not something imposed on humanity; its laws are not imposed, but exposed from the nature of things. Here is a kingdom whose decrees are the very decrees of our necessities, the complement of us. When we find them, we find ourselves; when we break them, we break ourselves. What an advantage that is! A kingdom that has its seat in our nerves, our blood, our tissues, our organs, our relationships—how ultimate and inescapable it is!

How to Be a Transformed Person
(Week 49, Monday)

The Kingdom Written into Us
Acts 9:2, 19:23, 22:22

The kingdom of God is written not only into the Bible, but into the nature of reality and into us. The kingdom is the revelation of what heaven's order is and what earth's order ought to be. It is the way we are to live individually and collectively and is therefore the Way....

The "kingdom of God" and "life" and the "way" are the same [see Acts 19:8-9; Mark 9:43, 47, Moffatt]. But these terms are also used of Jesus: "I am the way...the life" (John 14:6). Then Jesus and the kingdom are one. The absolute Order—the kingdom, and the absolute Person—Jesus Christ, are the same. God redeems through Christ, and God reigns through Christ.

Growing Spiritually
(Week 51, Wednesday)

The Kingdom of God Is God's Total Answer
Matthew 6:33; Acts 16:25-34

The kingdom of God is God's total answer to humanity's total need.

The rise of modern totalitarianisms is a symptom of humanity's felt need for something to totally command us, to bring life into integration under a single control and direct it toward a single end. Without this, life is at loose ends. Hence in religion, the [totalitarian church]; in political life, the totalitarian state....These are symptoms of an inner disease, the lack of total meaning felt by modern humanity. These half answers let people down. When you totally obey them, you find total bondage.

But has God no total answer to humanity's total need? God, who put order in the lowest cell, has God left unplanned the most important portion of life on our planet: the total life of humanity? No! The total answer to humanity's total need is the kingdom of God. When you totally obey it, you find total freedom.

Growing Spiritually
(Week 51, Thursday)

The Gospel Is God's Search for Man
John 1:9-13

You cannot say the *kingdom of God* until you have first said Jesus, for Jesus puts content into the kingdom of God.

Mastery
(Week 1, Thursday)

The Kingdom Primarily a Youth Movement
Luke 9:59-62

The kingdom is the most radical conception ever presented to the mind of humanity and the greatest challenger ever confronting our creative longings. When given to that, both youth and old age cannot help coming together in a common endeavor for change.

Mastery
(Week 9, Friday)

226

A Person for Whom Christ Died
Revelation 14:6, 22:2

The kingdom of God is a classless society; there is only one class, the class of the children of God. That simple fact dooms all distinctions set up to segregate person from person.

Mastery
(Week 10, Wednesday)

Everything Anchored to Jesus
Hebrews 2:7-9

The kingdom of God is anchored to Jesus. He fixes in his own person the character of the kingdom. The kingdom is the spirit of Jesus universalized.

Mastery
(Week 25, Wednesday)

The Two Emphases: The Person and the Order
John 1:14-19

The kingdom of God is the all-embracing conception that gives cosmic and total meaning to life and redemption. In the Acts the kingdom and Jesus are the two emphases: one the Order and the other the Person. Note: "After they came to believe Philip, who preached good news about the God's kingdom and the name of Jesus Christ, both men and women were baptized" (Acts 8:12 CEB). Note the good news was not just Jesus, the Person, nor the kingdom, the Order—it was both. Paul had these two emphases also, "From morning until evening, he explained and testified concerning God's kingdom and tried to convince them about Jesus" (28:23 CEB). And again: "Paul lived in his own rented quarters for two full years and welcomed everyone who came to see him. Unhindered and with complete confidence, he continued to preach God's kingdom and to teach about the Lord Jesus Christ" (28:30-31 CEB).

Mastery
(Week 29, Sunday)

A Kingdom That Cannot Be Shaken
Matthew 7:24-29

The kingdom of God gathers up all the loose ends of life and weaves them into total meaning. It is the Cosmic Loom upon which all the little things and big are woven into fabric, into meaning....

"A kingdom that cannot be shaken" (Heb 12:28)....I've seen people building up kingdoms that I knew were shakable: the kingdom of money, the kingdom of position and pride, the kingdom of honor and glory, the kingdom of pleasure, the kingdom of learning, the kingdom of physical love. I knew in my heart of hearts they were shakable, for I'd seen them shake and fall before my very eyes.

Mastery
(Week 52, Friday)

Became Life in Him
John 10:9-10

This earth of ours is to be the scene of the coming of the kingdom of God: "Thy kingdom come on earth" (Matt 6:10). Events are not moving with goalless feet. They are moving toward God's kingdom, or they destroy themselves.

Christian Maturity
(Week 8, Saturday)

The Center Is Self, the Margin Is Disorder

Everything that is transferred from the kingdom of self to the kingdom of God has life in it—eternal life. It has security in it—eternal security. Everything transferred from the kingdom of God to the kingdom of self has death in it—eternal death.

In Christ
(Week 2, Wednesday)

The Material World Has a Meaning and Destiny
Romans 8:19-21

When Jesus announced the new order, the kingdom of God, he said that we were to pray that the kingdom may come on earth, and come on earth as it is in heaven. The earth was not be deserted and destroyed, but to be delivered and dedicated, the scene of the kingdom of God. The earth, therefore, has a goal and a destiny, and its goal is to added back to heaven from which it fell. "I saw a new heaven and a new earth" (Rev 21:1); heaven and earth were to be wedded and both were to be new. That puts faith and hope and optimism at the heart of our dealing with this material world. It has a future.

The Word Became Flesh
(Week 6, Sunday)

Science Teaches Surrender to the Will of God
Matthew 6:22-23

The kingdom of God is the ultimate order, the ultimate authority, the ultimate good. All this is open to those humble enough, surrendered enough, to receive it. That leaves you centered on another, on Jesus, on the kingdom of God; and when you seek first the kingdom, all these things, including yourself, are added to you.

The Word Became Flesh
(Week 21, Wednesday)

The Kindom: Not Talk but Power
2 Corinthians 13:3-4

Nothing could be more to the point than this verse: "For the kingdom of God does not consist in talk but in power" (1 Cor 4:20). This plants the Christian gospel in the Word become flesh and not in the Word become word.

And yet the whole of the Christian setup is around the kingdom of God consisting in talk. Our "services" are sermons, with a padding of hymns and prayers; they are "talk," lip services instead of life services. We don't go out of these "services" asking, "What do I do next?" but commenting, "It was a good sermon. I enjoyed it." You are supposed to react in comment and not in commitment.

But the kingdom of God is "in power": power to change lives, power to remake character, power to start movements, power to lift horizons and nerve people to live, power to turn inner and outer defeat into victory, power to break chains and make people free, power to enable people to do what they cannot do—power!

The Word Became Flesh
(Week 31, Friday)

The Incarnation and the Kingdom
Matthew 4:17, 23

We come now to one of the most important aspects of the application of the Word become flesh, its application to the kingdom of God. For if this incarnation is God's incarnation then it must have total meaning for the total life. The Christian conception of the Incarnation is unique in that the Incarnation is not only to be in a person, but in an order, the kingdom of God. Jesus made himself and the kingdom of God synonymous. He used interchangeably "for my sake" and "the kingdom's sake." He was the kingdom. One's relationship to Jesus determines one's relationship to the kingdom. Not only was absolute love embodied in Jesus, but absolute authority. God was not only redeeming in Jesus, God was ruling in Jesus. The Incarnation is redemptive rule. The kingdom came with Jesus. The kingdom is Jesus, and Jesus is the kingdom. The kingdom is the Christlike spirit universalized. So the Incarnation is not only in a personal body, but also in a cosmic body. To have relations with Jesus is to have relationship with an Order. Religion is at once individual and social.

The Word Became Flesh
(Week 45, Sunday)

We Wanted Something That Would Bring Life into Total Meaning
Luke 9:1-2

An English bishop said, "Stanley Jones seems to be obsessed with the kingdom of God." My reply was, "Would God that I were. It would be a magnificent obsession." For Jesus was obsessed with it. He used the phrase or its equivalent one hundred times. And, depend upon it, anything he used that often is important, the ages being witness, for he was never misled by a subordinate issue, never got on the marginal, the unworthwhile. And Jesus made the kingdom central.

The Word Became Flesh
(Week 45, Monday)

The Kingdom of Heaven Has Been Forcing Its Way Forward
Revelation 11:15-17

This passage is luminous: "Ever since the coming of John the Baptist the kingdom of Heaven has been subjected to violence and violent men are seizing it" (Matt 11:12 NEB). A footnote gives an alternate translation: "The kingdom of Heaven has been forcing its way forward" by its own inherent truth and reality. But people of force try to use force to further it and to violate the inner nature of the kingdom ends.

When in Russia in 1934, I was shaken to see them building up a civilization without God. I needed reassurance. This verse spoke to my condition during my Quiet Time in Moscow: "Therefore let us be grateful for receiving a kingdom that cannot be shaken" (Heb 12:28). Was the kingdom of God the one unshakable kingdom? Everything within me answered yes, and continues to answer yes, with increasing emphasis. I went to my Bible the next morning, and this verse arose authoritative: "Jesus Christ is the same yesterday and today and forever" (Heb 13:8). Is Jesus Christ the unchanging person, the same yesterday, today, and forever? Everything within me answered yes, and does so increasingly. I came out of Russia with an unshakable kingdom and an unchanging person, the Absolute Order and the Absolute Person. They were two then. Now they have become one; I see that the Absolute Order—the kingdom of God—is embodied in the Absolute Person—the Son of God. They are one. The Word of final authority has become flesh in Jesus Christ. In him is not only Absolute Goodness, but Absolute Authority. God not only redeems in Jesus; God rules in Jesus. Jesus is Lord!

The Word Became Flesh
(Week 45, Saturday)

The Divine Illustration
Mark 1:16-20

[Jesus] did not point to a utopia, far off and unrealizable; he announced that the kingdom of heaven is within us and is "at hand" and can be realized here and now.

The Word Became Flesh
(Week 51, Tuesday)

In Jesus I Have Everything
John 1:29-34

[Another] thing Jesus Christ means to me is the kingdom of God, God's total answer to our total need. Without this fact of the kingdom, our faith would be a personal allegiance to a Person; it would lack total meaning, individual and corporate. But with Jesus and the kingdom one—he is the kingdom—then "all authority" is in him both "in heaven and on earth." I belong to the sum total of reality, and the sum total of reality belongs to me.

The Word Became Flesh
(Week 52, Saturday)

THE WORD BECAME FLESH

The Cleansing of the Kingdom
Luke 17:20-21; Acts 1:3-8

Since I have seen the Word become "flesh" I can no longer be afraid of "flesh," the material, for it has within it the possibility of expressing the Divine. Jesus cleansed the material. I never really saw the material until I saw him. Then my world was new. And an amazingly worthwhile world is the scene of the coming kingdom.

Victorious Living
(Week 17, Friday)

Religion Needs a Cosmic Guarantee
Revelation 21:1-5

Is the Way a principle or a Person?

It is both! Jesus put them together in this statement, "I am the way" (John 14:6). Here the Word became flesh, the Path became a Person.

The Way
(Week 7, Monday)

Christ Written in the Texture of Things
John 1:1-5, 10

We cannot give ourselves to something that is time-bound, and therefore to be time-destroyed. It must be eternal. And then that "eternal greatness" must be "incarnate in the passage of temporal fact" (Alfred North Whitehead, *Adventures of Ideas* [New York: Macmillan, 1933], 33). It must meet us where we are, walk our dusty ways with us, redeem us, not by proxy but by proximity; the Word must become flesh. What other faith can fulfill the demand except that of Jesus?

But there is a further consideration. This Word that becomes flesh must be not only a revelation of God; it must have a kinship to the flesh, must be the interpretation not only of God but of life.

The Way
(Week 7, Saturday)

The Barrier down beween Flesh and Spirit
1 Corinthians 6:12-13

The Holy Spirit broke down the barrier between flesh and spirit. "I will pour out my Spirit upon all flesh" (Acts 2:17). Here "Spirit" was to come upon "flesh." It is true that "flesh" is often used as "people," but the very fact that "flesh" was used instead of "people" was significant and fits in with the genius of the gospel. For that gospel is founded on "the Word made flesh," the incarnation.

If the Word had become printer's ink, it would have become a code. If the Word had

231

become idea, it would have been a philosophy. But the Word became flesh and therefore became a gospel, the good news.

The Way to Power and Poise
(Week 14, Sunday)

Faith through Fingertips
John 20:19-20

The Christian faith is founded on an incarnation, the Word became flesh. So the flesh now becomes Word, and one can find faith in and through the material.

How to Be a Transformed Person
(Week 15, Sunday)

The Transformation of the Material
Luke 12:13-15

Affirmation for the Day: Since the center of my faith is in the Word become flesh, now my flesh and my material possessions must become word.

How to Be a Transformed Person
(Week 41, Sunday)

The Word of Christianity Become Flesh
1 John 1:1-4

The very center of the Christian faith is the Incarnation, in which the Divine Word becomes flesh; the idea becomes fact. All other faiths are the word become word, the idea projected as an idea. In Jesus, the idea walked. It spoke in human life and manifested in human relationships. It transformed religion from idealism to realism.

Growing Spiritually
(Week 30, Sunday)

The Word Become Flesh
John 1:1-4

Jesus: the Word become flesh of "everything Jesus did and taught from the beginning" (Acts 1:1 CEB). Our starting point is Jesus. But someone objects and says, "The gospel begins with God." No, for until Jesus came, there were views about God and there was news about God, but no good news. Apart from Jesus we know little about God, and what little we know is not good news. The conception of the character of God apart from Jesus is questionable. In Jesus our question marks about God turn into exclamation points. In the face of Jesus we know what God is like and what we must be like if we are to be good. If God is other than Jesus, God is not good; if like Jesus, God is good. That is an astounding thing to say; yet when I say it, I hear the ages give a resounding Amen. And it reverberates through all things.

Mastery
(Week 1, Wednesday)

Introduction

If you ask my definition of maturity, I give you not a verbal but a vital definition: Jesus! He is Incarnate Maturity, the Word of Maturity become flesh.

Christian Maturity
(p. xii)

God Salvation or Self-Salvation?
Ephesians 2:7-8

John has no hesitancy in pointing straight to the heart of the matter: the center of faith is a Person and that Person is Jesus: "That which was from the beginning, which we have heard, which we have seen with our eyes, which we have looked upon and touched with our hands, concerning the word of life—the life was made manifest" (1 John 1:1-2). Here, over against human speculations about God, John points to God's authentic self-revelation: Jesus, the Word become flesh.

Christian Maturity
(Week 1, Thursday)

Religions: Our Search for God
Acts 17:22-28

In Jesus the Word became flesh; in Gnosticism the word became idea. We must broaden and even universalize that statement by saying: In Jesus the Word became flesh; in all other systems of religion and philosophy the Word became word. Jesus is good news; all else is good views.

Christian Maturity
(Week 1, Friday)

The Eternal Purpose

In Jesus, purpose became performance, the idea became fact, and the Word became flesh. In all other religions, it is the word become word—a philosophy or a moralism. In Jesus, and in Jesus alone, the Word became flesh.

In Christ
(Week 33, Tuesday)

God through Philosophy and Moralism
Job 23:1-2, 8

There have been two great attempts to find God apart from the Word became flesh. They are the attempts of philosophy and the attempts of moralism. The attempt of philosophy has been seen in the great philosophical nations: Greece, India, and China. The great philosophical systems were all three completed just before the time of the coming of Jesus. They took humans as high as they could go by philosophical reasoning. Beyond these systems, the human race will not progress in philosophical thought. The human brain strained itself to the utmost, and having reached its apex, went progressively bankrupt as an adequate method of finding God.

The Word Became Flesh
(Week 2, Sunday)

The Material World Has a Meaning and Destiny
Romans 8:18-20

We turn now to another phase of "The Word became flesh" (John 1:14). We have been emphasizing "the Word," but what about the "flesh"? The flesh stands for the organized material, the material organized for the use of the person. It, therefore, stands for the whole material universe. This means that the Divine assumes a material body, not as a temporary garment put on and off at will. The word "dwelt among us" could be translated "tabernacled among us," a permanent dwelling.

This means that the material is going to be used for the purpose of the redemption of not only the spiritual being called human, but the whole person, body included; and the whole material universe is going to be redeemed. The material is just as much the subject of redemption as the spiritual.

This plants the faith of Jesus squarely in the midst of human relationships; nothing is alien to it except sin and evil. Anything that concerns life concerns the faith of Jesus, for he is Life and, therefore, includes everything comprehended under the term Life. The fact is that the Christian faith is the most materialistic of religions, the only one that really takes the material seriously. It starts out by saying that when God created the material universe, God "saw that it was good"; the material was God-made and God-approved.

The Word Became Flesh
(Week 6, Sunday)

Through the Ages One Word
Ephesians 4:4-6

We have been studying how the main facts of the Christian faith—the incarnation, the creation of the world through Christ, the *preparita evangelica* in the body, the redemption through the cross, and the resurrection of Jesus—all are founded in and illustrated as the Word became flesh. We must now turn to see if the New Testament Scriptures in general support this thesis. Are these outstanding facts standing above, unsupported by the rest of the New Testament? Or is the whole of the New Testament a whole? And is there one message running through the whole, the message of the Word became flesh? One modern commentator says, "After the one statement in John about the Word becoming flesh, the rest of the New Testament dismisses it, so we can dismiss it." Can we? If you dismiss it, do you dismiss the very genius of the Christian faith and turn that faith into a philosophy or moralism—people's search for God—instead of a redemptive invasion of us—God's search for us? If so, then the Christian faith takes its place as one of the religions of the world, a philosophy of good views, but with no good news.

The Word Became Flesh
(Week 17, Wednesday)

The Word Continues to Be Flesh
Acts 2:32-33

I am persuaded that the Word became flesh is not only an event in the time of Jesus; it is a continuing principle, a fact that is inherent in the Christian faith. And this is seen and realized in the coming of the Holy Spirit. The coming of the Holy Spirit was the Word become flesh in receptive and obedient believers. Here the historical passed into the experiential. The Word became flesh, not only in "the body of Christ"—the church—but in the bodies of believers as individuals and persons. There was a collective manifestation of the Word become flesh in the new community and an individual manifestation in the new person.

The Word Became Flesh
(Week 26, Sunday)

Conversion? I Haven't the Slightest Idea What It Means
John 3:9-12

Abandonment of the Word became flesh in favor of the Word become word, and its results, are seen in this: A professor of religious education in a Methodist theological college said to a friend of mine, "What do you mean by conversion? I haven't the slightest idea of what it means." He was brought up in a theological climate where Christianity was a system of thought to be learned. The knowing would heal you of your moral and spiritual ailments. It is salvation by knowledge, a lineal descendant of Gnosticism or the "Knowers." If you know about it that saves you. That is proving its sterility in the realm of religion and in the realm of psychology and psychiatry.

In the realm of religion it is producing uncertain believers. "Here you found him?" "I hope so." "Do you know him?" "Maybe." "Have you assurance?" "No, I'm afraid not." This making Jesus Teacher and Lord is putting the Methodist and other churches back in the days of Wesley before his conversion. There Wesley was depending on knowledge and discipline. It left him empty. But when he passed from knowledge and discipline to surrender and faith and acceptance—made Jesus Lord—then he became teacher, and how! Wesley's whole being became illuminated: mind, body, spirit. Jesus was converted from Teacher and Lord to Lord and Teacher. And the conversion was profound. And Wesley had a message, a message that set the world on fire. Religious education, as in the person of this professor, knows little or nothing of conversion. For it doesn't believe in it or depend on it; it depends on information, not transformation. So it produces moonlight, not sunlight, information about secondhand moonlight, not sunlight firsthand: "This is eternal life, that they know thee the only true God" (John 17:3); not know about thee, but "know thee" as Lord and hence Teacher. Religious education doesn't produce people of passion, people with a message.

The Word Became Flesh
(Week 37, Thursday)

4
CHALLENGES

My central faith in eternal life is found in Jesus. The best man who ever lived went down through death and came back, and the first thing he said was, "Fear not"—there is nothing here to fear. He who was so right in everything else, the ages being witness, is he wrong here? He who never let us down in one single area of life, will he let us down in this central area? I believe it is impossible.

The Christian faith is the only faith that lights up that dark area of life—death. And it lights it up not with word, but with a Word made flesh. Jesus went through it, and the word of resurrection became flesh in him. Anyone who lives in him is as deathless as he is deathless.

Jesus lays his mind upon ours, and I believe in his beliefs, and he believed in and demonstrated immortality. Jesus said, "Because I live, you shall live also." His living guarantees our living. He didn't stay dead, I too shall not stay dead!

How to Be a Transformed Person [1951]
(Week 44, Wednesday)

DEATH

The Most Solemn Pause of All: Death
Job 19:29; Philippians 1:21-25; 2 Timothy 4:6-8

[The most] awful solemn pause of all is death. Our work is stopped, our plans are broken off, our ties with others are snapped, the pitcher is broken at the well—just when it was going to draw water for someone. This is the most devastating pause of all. But is it? It may be the pause that will turn out to be only life's sweetest, gladdest music in the making.

It was so with Alice Means, one of the rarest missionaries we have ever had in India. What an amazing life she was living: building, teaching, making leaders! And then cancer struck her. She thought she might get to America before she died, but was stopped in Bombay by the doctors, knowing she would never reach America. This is the letter she wrote me from the Bombay hospital, after knowing she would be denied even the privilege of going to her homeland to die:

> How thankful I am for all these years of perfect, abounding health! What a happy life I have had! Let me tell you of the experience of these last two months. With a host of others I am working along in a great field, digging, sowing, weeding, watering, never noticing I had reached the edge, until I heard, "Alice, that's enough, come over here and sit down a bit." I looked up and there stood Jesus smiling at me. I went over and sat down on the grass by him, and he said—"You have been busy working and have not had time for all those intimacies that go with a great friendships, such as I want with you. Come along and let us walk together here." He put his arm through mine and we walked along an avenue all covered with grass and flowers, and the birds were singing. Oh, it is beautiful! As I look down toward the river it is a little misty. But I know he will see me through that. Even now I am forever with my Lord. His peace within me is wonderful. Nothing can separate us now. It is heaven. That's all. The doctors and the nurses cannot understand how I can calmly discuss my condition and outlook.

Who can say that this pause of death to her was not music in the making? And vaster.

Victorious Living
(Week 35, Tuesday)

Making All Things Work Together for Good
Romans 8:28-39; Philippians 1:12-14

Christianity gives a set of the soul, so that when trouble and frustration and disaster strike one, the Christian goes up, with soul wings set in that direction. The same disaster strikes another, and, with soul attitudes tilted earthward, the person writhes in anguish in the dust. Death strikes a home, and in it leaves bitterness and frustration; in another, calm and quiet victory and greater usefulness.

Abundant Living
(Week 41, Wednesday)

The Way Makes a Difference in Death
Philippians 3:20-21; 2 Thessalonians 1:4-6

A friend of mine, a layperson, was asked to conduct a funeral, so he went to the New Testament to see how Jesus conducted funerals. He discovered "that Jesus didn't conduct funerals—he conducted resurrections." Jesus never conducts funerals of anything. He conducts resurrections of everything! For everything in his hands lives!

The Way
(Week 35, Wednesday)

"I Can Take It—Can You?"
Psalm 42:1-7

The Brazilians have a saying: "God can write straight even on a crooked line." The lines of your life may be crooked, not make sense, but God can write straight, can bring good out of crooked events. The outer events of Jesus' life were crooked, but God wrote redemption on them.

The Way
(Week 35, Friday)

A Ladder to Serenity
Philippians 20:29; Acts 2:17

A woman said in one of our Ashrams, "I am about to jell into the kind of a person I don't want to be." Many of us are about to "jell," to become fixed as the kind of person we would not like to be. How can we remain flexible and growing, even through old age? Here is how to reach an old age with power and poise:

Surrender into the hands of God your fear of old age and death. This is basic. For if you hold to an inner fear of old age and death, then all attempts at victory are whistling in the dark to keep up courage. It will be putting make-up on faded cheeks.

Go aside and on bended knee say to God, "You have promised to deliver all those who, through fear of death, were subject to lifelong bondage; now I will be in fear of old age and in bondage unless you take out this fear. That you may take it out I surrender it, surrender it once and for all. It is gone, gone forever. I thank you." And believe that God takes it away.

The Way to Power and Poise
(Week 39, Wednesday)

Building Your Nest Too Low?
Philippians 4:11-13

We pursue the thought of being thankful that we can be thankful for the worst that can happen. An outstanding philosopher, giving his philosophy of life, ended his volume by saying: "Goodbye, dear reader, I'm going out in the garden and play with my children." That was the center of his life, the simple joys of human relations. My inner comment was: But suppose your children should be taken away by death? Then? You have built your nest too low; the floods may reach it and sweep it away. Your philosophy of life is vulnerable. In order not to be vulnerable you must be able to be thankful for the loss of that relationship, because you have a relationship that cannot be touched by any human happening.

The Way to Power and Poise
(Week 44, Monday)

Nothing Is Solved That Is Evaded
Matthew 8:26; 2 Corinthians 7:5

Perhaps the underlying fear is the fear of death. Many go through life with the undertone of a fear of death. Life is spoiled by forebodings about the tomorrow that may hold death within it. Or many just put it out of mind, refusing to think about it....But death is not evaded by evasions. As someone has said, "The refusal to confront death might almost be called the 'twentieth-century evasion,' for it is the distinctive mark of the modern mind." Nothing is solved that is evaded. It simply comes back as hidden complexes within, an undertone of fear that puts a discord at the center of life. Fears we try to evade come back to pervade.

How to Be a Transformed Person
(Week 23, Saturday)

Look Fear Straight in the Face
Isaiah 43:1-2

Death is one of the least of the calamities that can happen to the Christian. By surrender of the self, the Christian has already died. What can death now do to? The Christian has already died!

How to Be a Transformed Person
(Week 24, Tuesday)

On Transforming Death
Revelation 21:3-4

We must now look a little longer at the central cause of our gloom: death. For unless we conquer the fear of death—the central fear—we are subject to an unrelieved gloom. The concern regarding death throws a shadow across all our hopes and achievements—across us—unless we see light there.

But suppose there no light there? If the worst came to the worst and there is no future life, is all lost? No, if I come to the end of this life and look out and see nothing but a vast blank, a vast oblivion, I shall look the universe in the face and say: "Well, I thought better of you. I thought this thing that I have in Christ had the feel of the eternal upon it, but now I see it didn't. Well, I don't repent that I was a Christian. It was a better way to live. I've had a brief experience of heaven, though denied an eternal one. I shout my victory in the face of oblivion." That's not rhetoric. I mean that.

Arthur John Gossip, in a vivid passage, depicts Jesus leaving the world, and after being gone some time, he returns weeping bitterly: "Oh," he says, "it's all a mistake. I misled you. I told you there was a heavenly Father back of things, but I've explored the entire universe and there is no heavenly Father. It's all blank. I'm sorry, I'm sorry I misled you" [no published source found]. What would we say if we heard that announcement fall upon our incredulous ears? Well, after the first shock was over, I'd turn to Jesus and say, "With You, I'm sorry too. But I've still got you. Your way of life has worked. I'm glad I followed it. It's been wonderful to live in company with you. I do not repent or regret; I am full of gratitude. If there is nothing after death, it does fill me with awe and gratitude that I had such a wonderful companion on my way to oblivion."

Will such a thing happen? If so, then everything we know about the universe would be reversed. The conservation of values would be obliterated. The highest value is character, and if that value is obliterated by death, the universe adds up to nonsense.

How to Be a Transformed Person
(Week 44, Tuesday)

The Death Fear
Proverbs 1:24-27

Many go through life with the single aim to avert death. And yet how completely futile the attempt is! It is bound to fail. "As certain as death and taxes" is pretty certain.

There are three reasons for this attempt to avert death. (1) We are afraid of the unknown. (2) We have not lived our lives the way they should have been lived, so we hesitate to go where "We shall know as we are known" (see 1 Cor 13:12). (3) We are afraid that death is equivalent to extinction. The urge to live is strong within us. Some of these are contradictory, but then life is often a contradiction....

Many go through life spoiling it because of a fear of death. It overshadows all they do. This verse expresses it: "And release from thraldom [bondage] those who lay under a life-long fear of death" (Heb 2:15 Moffatt). Look at the terror in those words: "thraldom...lay under... life-long fear of death."

Is this necessary? Are we bound to be tossed from one horn of the dilemma to the other, namely, between the life fear and the death fear? Can there be a release from both fears?

It is to the glorious possibility of freedom from both fears that we now turn. The word "release" in the above sentence points the way to an open door.

Growing Spiritually
(Week 5, Saturday)

Impervious to Praise or Blame
2 Corinthians 5:12-15

Jesus reacted constructively to what happened to him. He took the worst thing that could happen to him, namely, his death, and turned it into the best thing that could happen to the world, namely, its redemption. We must learn the secret of reacting constructively.

Growing Spiritually
(Week 12, Friday)

Plus Ultra
1 Corinthians 15:51-58

But set death in the center of the Christian conception of life with an eternity of growth stretching beyond, and death really has no sting.

There was a sign at Gibralter with the words "Ne Plus Ultra" ("Nothing Beyond") on it. That was before the new world was discovered. Then when it was discovered, they had to change it by rubbing out "Ne" to "Plus Ultra" (Everything Beyond). Before Jesus rose from the tomb, over the portals of death was written, "Nothing Beyond"; after he arose, it had to be written "Everything Beyond." For in Jesus death is not even an interruption; it is a larger beginning.

Growing Spiritually
(Week 52, Wednesday)

Any Prods to Perfection There?
Revelation 21:22-26

We are now being compelled to look for an eternal growth. Everything sensible points in that direction.

I believe that we begin in heaven where we leave off here. This means that rewards in heaven are not arbitrarily given for faithful service to God. The reward is in the quality of being we take with us. We will start in heaven with the capacity for the enjoyment of God than we have developed here. The greater the capacity we take with us, the greater the enjoyment of God, hence the greater the reward. Each will be enjoying God with the capacity we bring with us. Hence there can be no jealousy of another's greater reward. We won't even know others have a greater reward; only God and they will know that. Hence there can be no asking for bonuses or jostling for rewards.

There will be no first seats or peanut galleries; everyone will take from the Infinite what God's capacity for taking will allow. Everyone's cup will be full, but some cups will be larger. They made them so through the years.

Will heaven provide incentives to growth? In a perfect environment where is the stimulus?...Are there any prods to perfection [in heaven]? I do not know. Perhaps the prods are within us. We are made for perfection, and that inward prod will be eternally with us.

But the greatest prod will be the sight of God. When we see God with the veils off ourselves and off God, we will be so overwhelmed with longing to be like God that we will need no prods; this pull will be sufficient. Love will love us into its likeness.

Growing Spiritually
(Week 52, Friday)

We Shall Be Like Him
Colossians 1:9-12

Will there be tasks in heaven? If not, how could we grow? In almost all the Japanese schoolyards there is a statue of a boy with a load of wood on his back, walking along, reading an open book. Is that boy the eternal pilgrim? We will never cease to be like that boy. In our hands there will eternally be the Book of Life, and on our backs will be the eternal burdens to bear. Will there be no kindergartens in heaven where we will be able to teach the beginners in the Way? And no postgraduate courses for us to take? And are there no other worlds to be evangelized? Give me twenty-four hours of rest in heaven, and I'll ask for an assignment to one of those worlds! The call of the beyond is upon me now. And then?

Will we ever grow and grow until we become God? I think not, and I hope not. In Psalm 8:5, we read: "Yet thou hast made him little less than divine" (Moffatt). That "little less" is important. We are finite and God is the Infinite. The finite will infinitely approach the Infinite, but we will never become the Infinite. In that growth of the finite in the image of the Infinite will be our eternal happiness.

But I don't want to be God. I just want to love God. And I couldn't love God if I were God. To love God is enough for time and eternity. I want nothing else. I don't want to be lost in the Ocean of Being. I want to be myself, a redeemed self, which will produce humility; and yet I want to look at my Savior, which will produce the incentive for growth. For when I see him, I see what I am and what I can be in him.

I saw a number of ropes going out from big trees in the forests of Japan to the little trees around. It meant that the big trees were pulling the little trees around them, which were inclined to crookedness, into straightness.

Jesus is the Big Tree, planted in eternity. I am bound to him by cords of love, and he is pulling me into straightness and will do so both now and forever. I'm out for eternal growth.

Growing Spiritually
(Week 52, Saturday)

"Jesus Began" Almost Everything
Luke 4:16-21

The test of a person's life is this: Is the person dead when dead? Or does that person live on with greater power after death? Judged by that test, Jesus has really lived; for he was more powerful after his death than before. During his lifetime, through incessant teaching and preaching, he gathered at the highest estimate "five hundred brothers and sisters" (1 Cor 15:6 CEB); but after his death he drew, through people filled with himself, five thousand disciples in a single day.

Mastery
(Week 1, Tuesday)

243

Three Cardinal Urges
Acts 2:46-47

If we fail to win others to Christ and to the church, there will be no church in the future. When we of the church today die, the church dies with us, unless the church of tomorrow has been won in the meantime. If you, as a member of the church, fail to win someone else, you have a part in the death of the church. If others fail with you there will be no Christian church one hundred years from now. Every year your church loses many from its membership through unconcern, change of address, or death. If you do not win at least that many new Christians, your church is dying.

Christian Maturity
(Week 45, Monday)

Death Becomes Life

Spiritual death, which separates us from God, the source of our life, and which separate us from our highest selves and our greatest possibilities, is a calamity. But physical death to those who are in Christ is not a calamity but an opportunity. It is a part of redemption, the redemption of our bodies. It is a sowing, a sowing of a mortal body and reaping an immortal body; it is a sowing of a diseased, broken-down body and the reaping of disease-free, death-free, decay-free body. So death cannot separate; it can only integrate.

In Christ
(Week 8, Friday)

Peace...in Christ Jesus

There is the peace of Christ. It is a peace of adequacy, a peace of assurance that you are adequate for anything, for you can not only bear everything, but can use everything that comes your way—good, bad, or indifferent. This is the peace without illusions. It says pain, sorrow, sickness, and death are real. There is a reality within that faces this reality without and transforms it into character and achievement, hence peace!

In Christ
(Week 46, Wednesday)

Sadness: A Christian Virtue

The person who is in Christ is in a heavenly place come sickness, come health, come life, come death.

In Christ
(Week 32, Monday)

I Take a Bite, You Take a Bite
Luke 4:1-4

Jesus "taste[d] death for everyone" (Heb 2:9), but he also tasted life with everyone. He asks us to do nothing but what he himself does.

The Word Became Flesh
(Week 3, Tuesday)

Illustrations That Illustrate
John 14:5-7

Jesus did not merely tell us that death need have no terrors for us; he rose from the dead, and lo, now the tomb glows with light.

The Word Became Flesh
(Week 51, Friday)

EVIL

Evil Is Self-Destructive
Psalm 1:1-6; John 3:20; 1 Peter 3:9-13

Evil entangles every situation, for evil is against the nature of reality. Therefore, to try to straighten out a situation by an evil is only to entangle it the more. Therefore, evil is not only evil; it is stupid. Somebody has suggested that the word *evil* is the word *live* spelled backward. It is: evil is the will to live put into reverse; it is life turning against itself. "Human nature is allergic to evil. Evil is the way" human nature is not made to work. In evil, life desires to gain freedom, but gains only the freedom to destroy itself. It runs away from salvation! It revolts against life!

Abundant Living
(Week 27, Thursday)

Sin Has No Future
Psalm 1:3-6

All evil is a parasite upon the good. You have to throw enough good around evil to keep it going. When it is pure "Beast," it is pure blight. It has no future. It is not-the-way.

The Way
(Week 3, Tuesday)

Is the Christian Way the Natural Way?
Luke 15:17-24

If evil were the natural, how could you with justice be punished for living according to nature? That would be most unfair. But you are punished whenever you take sin into your life. The fact is that sin and its punishment are one and the same thing. By its very nature, sin is disruptive; that disruption is the punishment. You don't have to punish a cancer for being a cancer; cancer is its own punishment. You don't have to punish the eye for having sand in it; sand in it is punishment. The word *evil* is the word *live* spelled backwards. It is life attempting to live against itself.... It is an attempt to live against the nature of reality and get away with it. It is an attempt at the impossible. The result is inevitable—breakdown and frustration.

The Way
(Week 4, Wednesday)

The Only Sickness Is Homesickness
Psalm 139:7-12

Sin and evil are intrusions, aberrations, things for which we are not made. They are foreign bodies in the personality of humanity, and set up festering places exactly as a foreign body does in the physical.

The Way
(Week 5, Tuesday)

The Three Levels of Life
Matthew 5:43-48

Remember the three levels of life and decide which one you are going to live on. (a) The level of life where you return evil for good—the demonic level. (b) The level where you return evil for evil—the human, legal level. (c) The level where you return good for evil—the Christian level, the divine level.

You become born of the qualities you give out. If you give evil for good, then you become evil, you become the thing you give out. If you give evil for evil, you become a tit-for-tat person, legalistic, unlovely, and unloved. If you give out good for evil, then you are born of the good, you become good.

The Way
(Week 16, Monday)

You Can Use Suffering
Philippians 1:12-14; 2 Timothy 3:10-12

The Way recognizes that some diseases can be gotten rid of now, but some will have to await the final cure in the resurrection. The Way would abolish all evil of the body and mind, but there is a residue that must await the final cure. The mortal frame breaks down finally in a mortal world; we are not constructed to be eternally here.

But the Way offers this possibility for the residue that cannot now be remedied: You can use it. You can take it up into the purpose of your life and make it contribute to the rest of life. There is no pain, no suffering, no frustration, and no disappointment that cannot be cured or taken up and used for higher ends. In either case, you have a way out. You are relieved of it or enriched by it. You are not nonplussed; the Christian never is. Christians always have a way out. We are never stymied, for if we can't do this, we can do that, both equally good in the final result. The Way always has a way.

The Way
(Week 34, Monday)

Life Is Determined More by Reactions
Romans 8:35-39

Life is determined perhaps more by reactions than by actions. Life comes to you without your acting; it forces situations upon you without your asking or your acting. It is then that the reaction counts. You can react in self-pity and in frustration; or you can react with confidence and courage and make the evil thing make you better. Its origin may be evil, but by the time it gets through you its destination is good; you have turned evil into good.

The Way
(Week 34, Tuesday)

The Final Cure
1 Corinthians 15:36-44

God heals through the final cure—the resurrection. Some diseases must await the final cure in the resurrection. We live in a mortal world, a world where physical death is a fact. It is a beneficent fact, for if we didn't pass away and make room for the next generation, the earth would be so crowded that there wouldn't be any but "Standing Room Only." But we are on the way to a world of immortality where decay will not invade. Here it does invade, by the very nature of things. The body must break down sometime. Just as the soul must die to live, so the body must die to live.

The Way
(Week 38, Wednesday)

The Way Is the Way to Simplicity
Matthew 16:5-12

Evil is always complex, roundabout, tangled. Goodness is always a reduction of life to simplicity. Lies are roundabout, complicated. Truth is straightforward and uncomplicated. If you lie, you have to have a good memory; you have to remember each time what you have said. But if you speak the truth, then you don't have to remember what you have said; you simply tell the truth each time. All great discoveries are a reduction from complexity to simplicity.

The Way
(Week 42, Sunday)

Convincing Witness
Acts 14:1-3

Evil has met its match, has been defeated, and now we face no evil that hasn't the footprint of the Son of God on its neck.

The Way to Power and Poise
(Week 8, Tuesday)

Life Is Reduced to Simplicity
Titus 3:3-6

Under the Spirit's cleansing, all unnatural evil is taken out of us, and we are supernaturally natural. Life is reduced to simplicity. Evil is very complex; the good is simple. The universe is against one and backs the other.

The Way to Power and Poise
(Week 18, Friday)

Our Supreme Weakness: Prayerlessness
Ephesians 6:13-18

So we harness evil itself to our purposes and use it. That possibility gives us inner steadiness of heart. Of one prominent and dynamic minister it was said: "He always talks

248

as if he held four aces in his hand." Christians can face life with supreme confidence, knowing that we have resources to meet anything—literally, anything—for God works in everything—good, bad, and indifferent—and makes it work for good. Life may deal you a very bad hand, but you know that you can turn all evil into a good. You are in complete mastery.

The Way to Power and Poise
(Week 22, Saturday)

The Earth Came to Help
John 14:27-31

The idea that evil is strong is pure illusion. It talks big and blusters; it has to, for it knows that at the center it is weak. The superiority complex of evil is the inverse side of its inferiority complex; it asserts outwardly, for it sinks inwardly. But virtue doesn't have to assert anything loudly; it can wait for the revelation of the nature of reality. It therefore has a basic poise....

Every evil is swallowed up sooner or later. The universe is not built for lies, dishonesties, or selfishness. It is built for truth, honesty, and unselfishness. The earth swallows up evil; look at history, and believe! The earth sustains good; look at history, and believe!

The Way to Power and Poise
(Week 45, Sunday)

One of Those Half-Conversions
Genesis 27:41-45

If a person is critical of others, usually it is because that person is unconsciously critical of himself or herself. The people who are always complaining of others are simply externalizing their out-of-sortness with themselves. The pay-off of evil is that you have to live with an evil self.

How to Be a Transformed Person
(Week 11, Monday)

He Who Treads Softly Goes Far
Romans 12:19-21

How [are we] to overcome resentments and hate[?]...

Alan W. Watts says very pertinently: "Our attitude toward evil must be free from hatred....Satan rejoices when he succeeds in inspiring us with diabolical feelings to himself....A continual denunciation of evil and its agents merely encourages its growth in the world—a truth sufficiently revealed in the Gospels, but to which we remain persistently blind" (*Behold the Spirit* [New York: Vintage Books, 1972], 205; quoting Nicolas Berdyaev, *Freedom and the Spirit* [1935],182).

The only way to overcome evil is with good, hate by love, the world by a cross. It works. And nothing else will work.

How to Be a Transformed Person
(Week 27, Sunday)

249

Two Ways of Dealing with Evil
Galatians 5:22-24

There is an exquisite story in the Gospels that [in my opinion] got into the canon because they couldn't keep it out. It fits the mind of Christ.

The two methods of dealing with sin are seen in the account of the woman taken in adultery—stones and sympathy. The scribes and Pharisees felt that the way to deal with sin was moral and physical stoning: moral stones of disapproving aloofness and scorn, and physical stones where the case allowed. The evildoers would be corrected by criticism. Jesus took the opposite method. He dealt with evil by sympathy for the evildoer. But *sympathy* in the original sense (*sym* = "with" and *pathy* = "suffering"), a suffering with the evil doer. As he was hungry in the hunger of the hungry, so he felt sinful in the sinner. He projected himself into the inner life of the sinner and became so one with the person that he was one with the sin. That is what it means when it says that he bore "our sins in his body on the tree" (1 Pet 2:24).

This identification with the sin and shame of the sinner comes out in the account here when the religious leaders dragged the woman taken in adultery into the midst of the crowd and said, "Moses has commanded us in the Law to stone such creatures; but what do you say?" (John 8:5 Moffatt). They felt he would say something different. And he did! His eyes followed the eyes of the woman toward the dust. She was inwardly crumpled with shame, and he shared shame with her. The eyes of the rest were upon the woman in self-righteous disapproval. Jesus suffered with the woman, yet disapproved of her sin.

He began to write with his finger in the dust. What was he tracing? I think something like this: "God loves you." So out of the dust came the message of God's redeeming love. If we are in the dust, then in that very dust God writes redemption. God identifies with us at our lowest place of need. If you are in hell, then Christ is in hell with you— "He descended into hell" (Apostles' Creed)—and Christ is there to get you out. The fact is that Christ holds the keys to death and hell. He has unlocked both and walked out of both to freedom. The door is open!

How to Be a Transformed Person
(Week 34, Sunday)

Destroyed by No Mortal Blade
Luke 17:20-21

Evil has the seeds of its own destruction within it; for evil is an attempt to live against the nature of things, against eeality. Evil is not only bad, it is silly, for it is an attempt to live life in a way life is not made to work.

How to Be a Transformed Person
(Week 49, Tuesday)

He Opened His Armor!
Acts 5:1-5

It is the ten righteous people who spare Sodoms, ancient and modern. The people of fidelity are the ones who hold together the situation long enough for the people of infidelity to practice their infidelity within that situation. Take them out and make evil pure evil, and it will destroy itself. For all evil is a parasite upon the good.

Growing Spiritually
(Week 27, Wednesday)

Bitter to Digest
Romans 6:12-14, 23

[Evil] "will taste sweet as honey, but it will be bitter to digest" (Rev 10:9 Moffatt). Evil has an initially sweet taste; then it is bitter to digest. The system is not made for it, cannot assimilate it. To lie, to steal, to commit adultery, to get revenge on enemies, to criticize others: all these are sweet to the taste, but they are bitter to digest. The soul rejects them, for the soul and evil are allergic to each other.

Growing Spiritually
(Week 50, Saturday)

Evil a Parasite upon the Good
Hebrews 12:1-2

Goodness and love are stronger than evil and hate. Evil and hate seem strong, and they are, in the beginning. But they have nothing behind them, nothing except the force of the evildoer and the hater. The universe doesn't back them, sustain them, or further them. They are alone in a world of moral qualities. Therefore all evil and hate are doomed to self-destruction. For they have within them the seeds of their own destruction. A target practice by the military has an interesting method of disposal of shots that miss the target. If they don't hit the target, they explode of their own accord. That is what evil and hate do. Give them enough rope, and they will hang themselves. No situation can stay together with evil and hate at its center. There is no cement in sin. You have to throw enough good around evil, enough love around hate, to keep them going. All evil is a parasite upon good; all hate is a parasite upon love. Make evil pure evil, and it will destroy itself. Make hate pure hate, and it will destroy itself. Therefore goodness and love will wear down all evil and hate.

Mastery
(Week 26, Friday)

Evil a Parasite upon the Good
1 John 3:4-8

[In response to a statement of hopelessness], "The only way to keep evil going is to throw enough good around it to make it work. For evil is an attempt to live life against itself, and it cannot be done. So evil is not only bad, it is stupid." I challenge you to build a society on absolute dishonesty, no one would trust another; on absolute impurity, it would rot; on absolute selfishness, no one would think in terms of others; on absolute hate, it would be so divisive, so centrifugal, it would not hold together.

Then what conclusion must I come to? This: that every dishonest person is a parasite upon the honesty of some honest person whose honesty holds together that situation long enough for the person to be dishonest in it. Every impure person is a parasite upon the purity of some good person whose purity holds together that situation long enough for the person to be impure in it. Every selfish person is a parasite upon the unselfishness of some unselfish person whose unselfishness holds together that situation long enough for the person to be selfish in it. And every person of hate is a parasite upon the love of some loving person whose love holds together that situation long enough for the person to be hateful in it.

The universe is not built for the success of evil; evil sooner or later destroys itself.

The Word Became Flesh
(Week 8, Thursday)

Some Questions Jesus Raises in His Body
Luke 28:18-23

How far can evil go in a world of this kind? How far can force go? How far can lies and clever manipulation go? How far can you cover up the designs of evil in the cloak of good and religion? The answer is that evil can go a long, long way; it can put the Son of God, the Creator of creation, on a wooden cross, wood that he created. That's a long, long way. How far can force go? It can nail the Creator's hands upon the cross. And it can lift it up for all to see what force can do. How far can lies and clever manipulation go? It can twist the truth of him who was the Truth and make it into a falsehood and can thus crucify him on misquotations. How far can evil designs be wrapped in the cloak of religion and good? It can go a long way; it can make evil seem good. They crucified Jesus in the name of God, his Father. They made it appear that they were protecting the sacred name of God. "You have heard his blasphemy!" (Mark 14:64) they cried. Evil, force, lies, perverted religion can go a long way in a world of this kind.

They can do these things today and tomorrow, but the third day? No! For Jesus gathers all these questions in his body and answers them in his resurrected body and spirit the third day!

The Word Became Flesh
(Week 16, Friday)

Debate Ends and Dedication Begins
Matthew 28:2-4

Evil is self-defeating. The universe is not made for the triumph of evil. Force can go a long way; it can fill the earth with wars and devastation. But force is now shown to be bankrupt, shown on a world scale. God is saying to humanity, "You have used force through the ages to settle your disputes, now I'll let you see force." And God uncovered the heart of an atom. When we saw it we turned pale, for God also said, "But if you use it again, both sides will be ruined irretrievably." That is the utter bankruptcy of a method, the end of the Rake's progress: Use it again and everybody concerned is ruined. This took two thousand years of experimentation to prove itself. But Jesus exposed the impotence of force; when in the presence of the Resurrected One, "the guards trembled and became like dead men" (Matt 28:4). The custodians of force were helpless in the presence of this new power. People wouldn't take that embodied answer, so two thousand years of agony and pain have ensued, and the great fear is over our heads and in our hearts. God has two hands. We wouldn't take the answer from the hand of grace, so we have to take it from the hand of judgment.

The Word Became Flesh
(Week 16, Saturday)

HUMAN SUFFERING

Individuals and Their Circumstances
2 Kings 17:6-11; Proverbs 22:6

The possibility of using one's very adverse circumstances and sufferings for the furtherance of the spiritual life must not be dimmed....I still maintain that the use of suffering is the privilege of the ordinary Christian.

Victorious Living
(Week 24, Saturday)

Victory through Suffering
2 Corinthians 1:7; Philippians 1:29, 3:10; 2 Thessalonians 1:4-5

We come now to the question of pain and suffering....The question is, What shall we do with them, and what will they do with us?

First of all, we must note that pain has probably saved the race from physical extermination. Had there been no such thing as pain, we should probably not have survived as a race. For if we did not know that thrusting our fingers into fire would cause pain to us, we should probably let our fingers be withered by fire. If disease did not cause us pain, we should probably think little about it, and we should succumb to it, because unwarned by pain. Pain says, "There is something wrong;—attend to it."...Pain is God's preventive grace, built into the structure of our physical life, to keep us from committing individual and collective suicide.

Nevertheless, there is much needless pain; it is in the world far beyond its biological uses in survival. For we inflict it on ourselves and on others needlessly. Much of this pain is curable and should be cured by individual and collective action.

Suffering is a broader term. It may be caused by pain, but it has other and deeper causes. Suffering may be intensely mental and spiritual. Suffering too may be a part of God's preventive grace. It may be God's danger signal that something is wrong....

Our first step, then, is to look on pain and suffering not entirely as enemies—they may become our allies in gaining fuller life.

Victorious Living
(Week 33, Sunday)

Are Christians Exempt?
1 Peter 4:1; 12-16, 19

Pain and suffering are the common lot of all. We are environed by nature, by other human beings, by our own physical bodies and through these avenues pain and suffering come to us. The fact of our being Christians will not exempt us from their coming....

I grant you that real Christians are exempt from sufferings that come from within, from their own wrong moral choices. This does save them from an enormous amount of suffering that comes upon those who sin, and suffer as a consequence of those sins. But it does not save Christians from sufferings that come through nature, through other human beings, and through their physical bodies. Nor does it exempt them from the suffering that comes from the very fact that they are a new moral and spiritual creature, a departure from the world. That departure itself brings suffering.

Victorious Living
(Week 33, Monday)

What Attitudes Are We Taking?
Acts 5:41; Romans 8:12, 18; Colossians 1:24

We said yesterday that sufferings happen to us all,—the good included. But while the same things happen to all of us they do not have the same effect upon us all. The same thing happening to two different people may have an entirely different effect. It all depends upon inner attitudes. As someone has said, "What life does to us in the long run depends upon what life finds in us."...

There were three crosses that day on a Judean hill. The same event was happening to three people. But it had three different effects upon them. One thief complained and railed on Jesus for not saving himself and them; another saw this tragedy as a result of his sins, repented, and through it saw an open door into paradise; the third through that cross redeemed a race.... So the thing that matters is not what happens to you, but what you do with it after it does happen to you. Your cross can become the bitterest of unrelieved agonies, or it may become to you the most blessed of unlimited opportunities....

Suffering leaves some people writhing in helpless agony; others it leaves stronger and more capable of meeting more suffering, capable of meeting anything.

Victorious Living
(Week 33, Tuesday)

Do You Know What to Do?
Acts 8:3-8; 2 Corinthians 12:7-10

In *Christ and Human Suffering* [New York: Abingdon, 1933], I took the position that we were not to escape suffering, or merely to bear it, but to use it. We can take suffering up into the purpose of our lives and make it contribute to the ends for which we really live. The raw materials of human life, the things that come on us day by day can be woven into garments of character....

[Christians] know what to do [when suffering happens]. The Christian can say to herself or himself: "I cannot determine what happens to me, but I can determine what it shall do to me after it does happen. It shall make me a better person and more useful." That is victory.

Victorious Living
(Week 33, Wednesday)

255

The Pain God Is Allowed to Guide
2 Corinthians 4:8-12; 6:4-10

The pain from which we are suffering may have come from some evil source. The question is not where it came from, but where it is going! Where it goes is determined by whether we allow it to be guided to life or guided to death. And that is determined by whether we put God into the pain, and offer it to God as we offer everything else, and make it a part of God's redemptive purpose for us. The cross is an example of God-guided pain. It issued in salvation. So may our crosses issue in salvation, if God is allowed to guide the pain involved in them.

Victorious Living
(Week 33, Thursday)

Is Trouble God's Punishment?
Habakkuk 3:17-19; Luke 13:1-5; Hebrews 2:10

Many feel that when trouble comes, it is God's punishment for some sin. This attitude makes victory impossible.

We must admit that this is a world of moral consequence, and that sin does bring trouble. But Jesus repudiated the idea that calamity and sin are always connected....

As someone has said, "It is wonderful what God can do with a broken heart, if God can get all the pieces." Let God put your broken life together again, perhaps in a new glorious pattern. God had to break it to make it.

Victorious Living
(Week 34, Wednesday)

Life Strikes Away Our Crutches
John 16:7-8; Hebrews 12:8-12

We must pursue the thought that our troubles may not be God's punishment, but God's pruning....

There are many things in your life and mine upon which we lean heavily: family, relationships, money, and position. They may not be wrong, but they can become crutches that weaken our moral fiber. We depend on them too much. Then calamity strikes them away. At first we are stunned and crushed. Our crutches are gone; what is left? Why, our feet, our own backbones, and the grace of God! That is enough upon which to begin life anew.

Victorious Living
(Week 34, Thursday)

Life Looked at through a Cross
1 Corinthians 2:1, 12; Galatians 2:20; Colossians 1:20

No one can look into the face of [sudden] tragedy without raising ultimate questions about the universe: Is there meaning and purpose in the universe? If there is a God, does

God care? I have no answer—except as I look at life through the cross. There I see a God who comes into the very struggle and suffers all I suffer, and more....

The cross means...that God goes with us and lets everything that falls on us fall upon God's own heart. I can love a God like that....

The cross saves us from pessimism by using that pain and sorrow and tragedy for redemptive purposes. Through it all it shows the very love of God, seeking, redeeming, healing, saving. The cross is light—the only light.

Victorious Living
(Week 43, Friday)

Abundant Living "In Spite Of"
John 15:11; 16:33; Romans 8:35-39

Abundant living is sometimes "on account of," but perhaps more often, "in spite of." When circumstances are against us, we must be able to set the sails of our souls and use even adverse winds. The Christian faith does not offer exemption from sorrow and pain and frustration. It offers the power to, not merely bear, but use these adversities. The secret of using pain and suffering and frustration is, in many ways, life's greatest secret. When you have learned that, you are unbeatable and unbreakable....

The Christian "can take it," because he or she can take hold of adversity and use it. A teacher of slum children was drawing up a list of the qualities in Jesus that appealed to the youngsters. When the list was apparently completed, a grimy-handed newsboy put up his hand and said, "They hung him on a cross, and he could take it." The boy was right, but the reason Jesus could take it was not because of a stoic attitude. The reason goes deeper: he could take it because he could use it. He bore the cross for he could use the cross. You cannot bear the cross long; it will break your spirit unless you can take that cross and make it serve higher purposes. The stoic bears the cross; the Christian makes the cross bear fruit.

Abundant Living
(Week 40, Monday)

Working with a Wound in Your Side
Matthew 14:12-21; 16:21; 1 Peter 2:21-24

So important is this power to turn the worst into the best, that we must tarry another week with it. For if we learn this secret, we know how to live. If we don't learn it, then we fumble this business of living. It is simply impossible, in reference to suffering, always to explain why. You cannot unravel the mystery of suffering and give a logical answer. But, while you cannot explain the Why, you can learn the How—the How of victory over it and through it and around it. There is no logical answer, but there is a life answer; you can use suffering. It is much better to give a vital answer than a verbal one. Cease worrying over the Why and get to the How!

Abundant Living
(Week 41, Sunday)

The Berry in the Mouth
Isaiah 37:3-7; 41:10, 13; 42:16

"Christians, when they get to the end of a rope, tie a knot and hang on." For they knows that very extremity is God's opportunity. Someone has suggested that the "silence in heaven for about half an hour," spoken of in Revelation 8:1 (RSV), was God shifting the scenes for the next act. The silent, suffering spaces in your life may be God getting you ready for the next great act. Hold steady; the next act will come. In the meantime, take hold of your dull drab moments and make them give forth music. Speaking of a certain person, someone suggested: "Give him a laundry list, and he will set it to music."

Abundant Living
(Week 41, Monday)

The Five Steps out of the Dungeon
Acts 26:16-18; James 4:6-10; 1 John 1:5-7

Perhaps our world as a whole will have to find grace in the dungeon. As a world, we are suffering from self-inflicted pain and self-chosen bondages. We are in dungeons of our own making. Perhaps we shall find grace in our dungeons....

Christianity teaches that these [Crisis, Ordeal, Catharsis, Charisma, Resurrection] are the very steps through which the individual or society must go.

Abundant Living
(Week 49, Saturday)

Disciplined beyond Timidity
Joshua 1:5-9; Acts 4:13, 29; 5:41-42

When I was traveling in China in 1937, amid sections that were being bombed, this verse came to me again and again: "Whatever happens, be self-possessed, flinch from no suffering, do your work as an evangelist, and discharge all your duties as a minister" (2 Tim 4:5 Moffatt). Here in America, facing reconstruction [after WW II], I have to repeat it again and again.

Abundant Living
(Week 50, Saturday)

The Question of Unmerited Suffering
1 Peter 4:12-19

But what about disciplines we do not choose, things we are compelled to bear without our choices?...

This is one answer: take the way of refusing to recognize anything as evil. Meet suffering and pain and catastrophe with a barrage of mental affirmation of the good. This method has a very great truth in it. It is better than affirming evil as evil, suffering as suffering, and letting it go as that. You can get rid of a great deal of suffering and evil by simply affirming them away; "a great deal," but not all. And that residue that cannot

258

be affirmed away is the rock upon which many go to pieces, physically and spiritually. The Way must be able to answer every thing, including that residue.

The Way
(Week 34, Sunday)

You Can Use Suffering
Philippians 1:12-14; 2 Timothy 3:10-12

The Way offers this possibility for the residue that cannot now be remedied: You can use it. You can take it up into the purpose of your life and make it contribute to the rest of life. There is no pain, no suffering, no frustration, and no disappointment that cannot be cured or taken up and used for higher ends. In either case, you have a way out. You are relived of it or enriched by it. You are not nonplused; the Christian never is. Christians always have a way out. We are never stymied, for if we can't do this, we can do that, both equally good in the final results. The Way always has a way.

The Way
(Week 34, Monday)

Buddha Would Cut the Root of Desire
Psalm 1:4-6

Desire, fastened on things that let us down and cause frustration and suffering, must be replaced by desire fastened on things that do not let us down; [desire] must be fastened on God.

The Way to Power and Poise
(Week 2, Monday)

To the Tune of "Suffering"
1 Peter 1:6-9

We now turn to the transformation of suffering and tragedy. Many of us are not dull; we are alive, with pain. Some of that pain is mental and spiritual, and some physical; all of it spells pain. The title of Psalm 53 in Moffatt reads: "From the Choirmaster's collection. To the tune of 'Suffering.'" Many of us live our lives to "the tune of "Suffering"; that is the dominant note.

What is the Christian answer? It is not merely bearing it, submitting to it as the will of God, as in Islam; nor is it escaping it, as in the Old Testament answer. The Christian faith does not promise you exemption from suffering. How could it, when at the heart of that faith is a cross where the purest heart that ever beat writhed in an agony of unmerited suffering? Then what is the answer? It is found in that very cross where Jesus took the worst thing that happen to him, namely, his crucifixion, and made it into best thing that could happen to the world, namely, its redemption. When you can take the worst and turn it into the best, then you are safe. You can stand anything, because you can use everything.

How to Be a Transformed Person
(Week 36, Sunday)

The Kingdom's Is God's Total Answer
Matthew 6:33; Acts 16:25-34

The way to meet unmerited suffering and injustice is not to bear them, but to use them. When I saw that possibility years ago through this verse, "That will turn out an opportunity for you to bear witness" (Luke 21:13 Moffatt)—the unjust bringing you before judges and governors to be tried—an entirely new world opened before me. I had been trying to explain suffering, and now I saw that we are not to explain it, but to use it. Everything that happens to you—good, bad, or indifferent—can contribute to you if you know how to use it. Everything furthers those who follow Christ, provided they know how to set their sails. All winds blow you to your goal. It is the set of the soul that does it. When you know this secret, you are afraid of nothing, because you can use everything. That makes you march up to every human happening, with the possibility tucked away in your mind of plucking a blessing out of the heart of everything.

Growing Spiritually
(Week 51, Thursday)

The Mastery of Unmerited Suffering
Hebrews 12:6-11

Many modem interpretations teach that God will save followers from the sickness and calamities that fall on others. It is a sign of divine favor.

Of course it is true that the righteous are saved from many self-inflicted pains and illnesses and troubles that befall the unrighteous. The righteous know better how to live; they are not always barking their shins on the system of things. They know their way around better among the moral laws of the universe. But while this is true, nevertheless the righteous are not exempt from the ordinary sicknesses and accidents incident to human living in a mortal world. They get their share. And rightly so. Otherwise God would be bribing us into goodness, which would not be goodness....

How could a faith that has a cross at its center promise to exempt us from suffering when the center of that faith—Jesus—was not exempt?

Mastery
(Week 21, Thursday)

A Thing of Beauty Wrapped around Trouble
2 Corinthians 6:4-10

How [could] a faith with a cross at its heart...offer exemption from suffering when the purest heart that ever beat was not exempt? But Jesus, while not exempt, was not passive in suffering. He took hold of this injustice and made something of it—turned it into redemption. When one can take hold of the worst thing that can happen to one—the cross—and turn it into the best thing that can happen to the world—its redemption—that is mastery of the very highest type ever exhibited upon our planet.

This mastery of unjust suffering was not a lone and unique thing—a lone star in the firmament—Jesus passed this power of mastery over to his disciples and their spiritual children. It became a characteristic of the Christian movement and of the individual

Christian. They seemed to have the strange power to transform everything—good, bad, and indifferent—into something else, something better.

Mastery
(Week 21, Friday)

Joy **Is the Christian Word**
Philippians 1:25-26

Yesterday we said that there is something deeper than happiness, and that is joy. Happiness comes from happenings, but joy may be within in spite of happenings. *Happiness* is the world's word; *joy* is the Christian's word. The New Testament does not use the word or promise *happiness*; it uses the word *joy*. And for a reason.

Many people are expecting happiness from following the Christian faith; "God will arrange the things that happen to me so they will all add up to happiness." When the things that happen to them do not mean happiness, such people are dismayed and feel God has let them down. "Why should this happen to me?" They expect to be protected from happenings that make them unhappy. This is a false view and leads to a lot of disillusionment. For the Christian is not necessarily protected from things that make people unhappy. Was Jesus protected from happenings that make people unhappy? Was Paul? Their Christian faith got them into opposition, into persecution, into death. How could a faith that has a cross at its center promise exemption from happenings that ordinarily bring unhappiness? Then what is the answer? The Christian faith offers joy in the midst of happenings that make people without that faith unhappy. When the Christians don't find joy on account of happenings, we can always find joy in spite of them....

We must make our happiness not dependent upon happenings. We can make everything into something else; we can use everything.

Christian Maturity
(Week 37, Wednesday)

Granted to Suffer Is High Privilege!

"For it has been granted to you that for the sake of Christ you should not only believe in him but also suffer for his sake, engaged in the same conflict which you saw and now hear to be mine" (Phil 1:29-30)....The word *granted* is used, implying that it was a privilege, an honor, to suffer for his sake. Instead of...asking "Why should this happen to me?" we are told to look on suffering for Christ as our highest privilege and honor....When Moses and Elijah talked with Jesus on the Mount of Transfiguration, the account says: "who appeared in glory and spoke of his departure, which he was to accomplish at Jerusalem" (Luke 9:31). He was "to accomplish" his departure, his death at Jerusalem. Usually death is looked on as an acquiescence, submission to the inevitable. Here it was an accomplishment! Jesus accomplished more in the few hours on the cross that he did in all the rest of his lifetime. He opened his heart to the world's sin and sorrow and allowed it all to be forced through the channel, the single channel of his own broken heart. That broken heart was the healing of the world. It was granted to him to suffer, and that granted suffering became his chief glory.

261

Whether the suffering to be a pinprick or a stab, it is granted to us to take it and do what Jesus did with his departure: accomplish something through it.

In Christ
(Week 35, Friday)

To Be in Christ Is to Be in the *Koinonia*

Jesus, Lord, I do not ask to be exempt from suffering. I ask only power to use whatever comes: good, bad, or indifferent. In you I am able for anything. So I am safe, since I can use all. In your blessed name. Amen.

In Christ
(Week 41, Saturday)

The Incarnation Universalized
1 Corinthians 6:19-20

Christ is incarnate on a universal scale: every person's hunger is his hunger, every person's sickness his sickness, every person's bondage his bondage. To do it to them is to do it to him. To refuse to do it to them is to refuse to do it to him.

This broadens and deepens and universalizes the Incarnation. Jesus does not merely have a body that suffers as our bodies suffer; he is suffering in everyone's body, hungry in everyone's hunger, bound in everyone's imprisonment. To suffer in one body— his own—is one thing; to suffer in everyone's body is another, and different and breathtaking. It is beyond imagination.

But we could never have known this universal Incarnation if Jesus had not shown it in a particular Incarnation in a particular body. If it had been written in a book that God suffers in everyone's suffering, is hungry in everyone's hunger, we would have shrugged our shoulders in incredulity. But having seen it in the Word become flesh, we do not shrug our shoulders—we bend the knee. And we mention it in awe and adoration. It is beyond us, but it grips us and we say to ourselves: The God we see in Jesus would do just that.

The Word Became Flesh
(Week 6, Friday)

Take Heed to Your Reactions
Luke 15:25-30

"But take heed to yourselves; for they will deliver you up to councils; and you will be beaten in synagogues; and you will stand before governors and kings for my sake, to bear testimony before them" (Mark 13:9). Here the emphasis is upon *yourselves*, upon yourselves at the moment of deep, unmerited injustice and suffering; be sure that through this injustice you bear witness! This is an important word, for it clarifies the whole attitude toward unmerited suffering. It was the passage upon which my whole attitude toward unmerited suffering turned. I saw you could not merely bear it, you could use it. Every injustice was opportunity, every wrong an open door, an opportunity and an open door to witness. Not to preach at others about their wrongs but to witness by your rightness of demeanor and your deeds that the Word has become flesh in you. Don't bear evil, use it!

The Word Became Flesh
(Week 30, Friday)

Jesus the Concrete Word
John 9:1-5

When his disciples asked, "Who sinned, this man or his parents, that he was born blind?" (John 9:2), Jesus dismissed both hypotheses. He showed them how "the works of God might be made manifest" (v. 3), even through suffering and disability. Then Jesus proceeded to illustrate in his own life the price of using suffering, turning the worst into the best; he took the worst thing that could happen to him, namely his death, and turned it into the best thing that could happen to the world, namely its redemption.

The Word Became Flesh
Week 51, Saturday)

THE CROSS

The Cross in Action
Matthew 25:34-40; Romans 9:1-3; Galatians 4:19

Someone has said that he wanted to build a house with no windows and no doors, save the slits of a cross as the only opening, so that he could look out upon the world through a cross alone. Beautiful. But we must not only look out on life through a cross; we must touch life through a cross. Our very contacts must become vicarious.

We must deliberately take on ourselves what really doesn't belong to us, save as Christ makes us belong to everybody, and, therefore, everyone's sorrows belong to us.... Our love crimsons into sacrifice as it meets the world's sin. In a world of this kind, a crossless Christian is a Christless Christian.

Victorious Living
(Week 43, Thursday)

Life Looked at through a Cross
1 Corinthians 2:1, 12; Galatians 2:20; Colossians 1:20

The cross means...that God goes with us and lets everything that falls on us fall upon God's own heart. I can love a God like that....

The truth in pessimism is this: this is a world of pain and sorrow and tragedy. The cross saves us from pessimism by using that pain and sorrow and tragedy for redemptive purposes. Through it all it shows the very love of God seeking, redeeming, healing, saving. The cross is light—the only light.

Victorious Living
(Week 43, Friday)

The Four Who Bore Crosses
1 Peter 2:19-24; 1 Peter 3, 14, 17, 18; Mark 14, 41, 42

The third cross was laid upon the shoulders of Simon, the Cyrenian. They laid on him an undeserved cross: "They put the cross on his back and made him carry it behind Jesus" (Luke 23:26 CEB). Life does that with us: it lays hold on us and puts on our unwilling shoulders a cross. It changed the whole course of life for him and his family, for his two sons, Alexander and Rufus, became well-known Christians. Simon did not bear his cross, he used it. When Life lays its cross on us, we can make that cross throw us in company with Christ, and that contact will forever change us. "It is not suffering that ennobles, it is the way it is borne." Simon bore it well, and it made him.

Victorious Living
(Week 43, Saturday)

The Fear of Failure
Isaiah 5

A great many people go through life in bondage to success. They are in mortal dread of failure. Why should they be? Jesus cared little about success or failure. The story of Jesus is a story of apparent failure; rejected by his nation and crucified by the Romans, he ended on a cross. A faith that has a cross at its center cannot be a faith that worships success. I do not have to succeed; I have only to be true to the highest I know; success and failure are in the hands of God. On my way to India, I once said in England, "The romance of missions has gone for me. I know what I'm up against. If you should say to me that I go back to India to see nothing but frustration and failure and that I would see no more fruit whatever, I would reply, "That is an incident. I have the call of God to India, and to be true to that call is my one business; success and failure are not my business, to be true is." I made that statement one day in a meeting, and a minister came up and said: "All my life I've been in bondage to success; I've looked at everything from the success standpoint. You have released within me the greatest tension of my life. I have only to be true, thank God."

Abundant Living
(Week 12, Thursday)

One Greater Than the Church
Ephesians 4:11-16

One greater than the cross is here. We sometimes say we are saved by the cross. Rather, we are saved by the Christ who died for us upon the cross. The cross can become a matter of contention instead of conversion if detached from Christ. On the cross he took into his own heart all we have done and been and made it his own. If therefore I identify myself by surrender to and faith in Christ; identify myself, not with my past life and its sins, but with Christ, who thus died for me on the cross, I am saved. But I am saved by him, not by the cross. One greater than the cross is here.

The Way
(Week 8, Saturday)

Another Road with a Dead End—Criticism
Matthew 7:1-5

But the center of the Christian faith is not a judgment seat but a cross, a cross where people are not merely criticized but died for. The center is not a sideline criticism but an identification with humanity, which makes human sin its own, and in the process cries, "Father, forgive them; for they know not what they do" (Luke 23:34). Redemption is by suffering with and for and instead of, rather than by a sideline pointing out of sin by criticism. People are not converted by criticism. They are converted by a cross.

The Way
(Week 19, Sunday)

265

The Cross Inherent
Matthew 25:34-40

We have been taught that Christ died once and for all. He was "once offered." It was a finished fact in a certain point in history. We agree. Something did happen there at the cross that doesn't have to be done over again. But if the cross were suddenly imposed on history at a given point, something extraneous, then it would lack a cosmic validity. But if the cross is the scarlet thread that runs through the whole garment of existence, then it would have inescapable meanings. "The Lamb slain from the foundation of the world" (Rev 13:8 KJV) points to the cross as inherent.

The cross is the ground plan of the universe. If so, we would expect to see intimations of that ground plan everywhere. We do—some of them crude, all of them are unmistakably pointing to the cross.... The seed dies that the plant may live. The mountains are barren that the valleys may be rich. The white corpuscles circulate through the bloodstream watching for infection. When they find it, they absorb it if possible; but when they cannot, they fling themselves upon the intruder and die that the rest may live. The cross is in our blood.

The Way
(Week 28, Thursday)

Using Cyclones
Isaiah 51:7-8, 12; 54:17

"Well, what is God doing?" God is doing what God has always done: helping us to rescue a good out of a bad, to make a new world out of an old one. God did that at the cross. Jesus took the worst thing that could happen to him—his death—and made it into the best thing that could happen to the world—its redemption. God is doing that now, helping us to us make the worst serve the best.

The Way
(Week 35, Sunday)

The Making of a Christian Church
Acts 4:32-37; 1 Thessalonians 3:3-4

The marks of the cross were upon the founding of the church. The cross was in it; hence, the lift of the resurrection was in and through it. If our faith costs nothing, it contributes nothing.

The Way
(Week 45, Monday)

The Way Is the Way of Reconciliation
Ephesians 2:14-22

The one verse that sums up the Christian gospel better than any other, I believe, is this, "In Christ, God was reconciling the world to himself,... and entrusting to us the message of reconciliation" (2 Cor 5:19 RSV). God was reconciling people when they didn't want to be reconciled, and the price God paid to get to people in spite of their sins was the cross. And what God does we must do; we must reconcile people, even though it costs a cross.

The Way
(Week 46, Monday)

The Word Become Vicarious
Revelation 1:5; Acts 20:28

So the cross is not an afterthought of God; it is the scarlet thread running through the whole garment of creation.

The Way to Power and Poise
(Week 9, Wednesday)

In Everything God Works for Good
2 Corinthians 6:3-10

This verse tells us: "We know that in everything God works for good with those who love him" (Rom 8:28). Note, the thing itself may not be good; its source and its content may be evil, but God works in that evil to turn it for good. The very genius of the cross is that. The cross is evil, and yet God works in that evil and makes it redemptive. The cross is sin turned saving. With that at the heart of our gospel, we will expect to be saved, not from trouble and evil, but through them.

The Way to Power and Poise
(Week 23, Monday)

The Central Revolt
Luke 15:13-14

God gives us the awful power to ruin ourselves. On what condition? The condition is that God gets into the whole transaction, suffers in Godself the consequences of our wrong choices, makes them God's own and redeems us through that identification. The cross is the acute point of that identification where the continuous fact comes to light in history.

How to Be a Transformed Person
(Week 17, Monday)

I Got in Too
1 John 1:5-3

A pastor of a fashionable church was called one night by a little girl appearing at his door and saying, "My mother sent me to ask you to come and get her in." Wondering what she meant, he followed her into a slum section, up a flight of rickety stairs, into what was the room of a harlot dying of consumption. He sat alongside her bed and told her of Jesus, the great teacher, but she shook her head and said sadly, "That's not for the likes of me." Then tried Jesus as a doer of good, but again she shook her head and repeated the same words. He was at end of his tether when he reached back into the past and pulled out something he had discarded; he talked to her about Jesus dying on the cross to save sinners. She began to nod her head, "Yes, that's it. That's for the likes of me." Telling of it afterward, he said, "And we got her in," and then added slowly, "And I got in too." The cross met the need of both!

How to Be a Transformed Person
(Week 18, Friday)

Badly Placed for Wintering In
1 John 2:16-17

Many religious cults are fair-weather cults. It was said of the harbor named Fair Havens, on the island of Crete, that it was "badly placed for wintering in" (Acts 27:12 Moffatt). A good many are taking shelter in harbors named "Fair Havens," but they are "badly placed for wintering in"; they give no protection when the winter winds of sorrow, sickness, of death blow....

But there is one place of complete security in the universe: "Thus there is no doom now for those who are in Christ Jesus" (Rom 8:1 Moffatt)....

There is no doom in your inherent being. You will hold together whatever happens. "In him all things hold together" (Col 1:17)....

The saddest sight on our planet is a graveyard without a cross in it, and I see them every day in Japan. But the gladdest sight on our planet is a graveyard with a cross—and hence a resurrection! "There is no doom" to our relationships!

O Christ, You are my surety and my security. You guarantee against the decay and shock of death. It's all there, forevermore. I thank you. Amen.

How to Be a Transformed Person
(Week 52, Monday)

The Cross Breaks Us
1 Corinthians 2:1-5

The cross conquers the self without violating it. It frees the self from itself and then attaches that self-love to the One who hung on the cross. Deliverance has come.

Growing Spiritually
(Week 3, Friday)

Winning a Positive out of Every Negative
2 Corinthians 4:15-18

Find the positive in every negative situation....

Jesus did that. The Pharisees criticized him, complaining that he ate with publicans and sinners, implying that he was thereby like them in character. That was negative, very negative. Did Jesus meet a negative with a negative? No, instead he gave the three parables of the lost sheep, the lost coin, and the lost son—a positive presentation of the seeking love of God. He came out on the positive side of the negative situation.

He always did that. At the cross, Jesus won a positive out of a negative. The cross was sin, and he turned it into the redemption from sin; the cross was hate, and he turned it into a revelation of love; the cross was humanity at our worst, and Jesus through it showed God at God's redemptive best. This made Jesus the great Affirmation. "The divine 'yes' has at last sounded in him" (2 Cor 1:19 Moffatt).

Growing Spiritually
(Week 17, Monday)

Jesus, the Perfect but Unfolding Revelation
Matthew 5:17; Romans 10:3-4; Galatians 6:14

The deepest place of the revelation [of God in Jesus] is the cross. There God let us see the divine heart through the broken heart of Jesus. There was illustrated on a cosmic scale what takes place in a home where pure love meets sin in the loved one. At the junction of that love and that sin a cross of pain is set up. For it is the nature of love to insinuate itself into the sin and sorrow of the loved one and make them its own. All love has the doom of bleeding upon it as long as there is sin in the loved one. The cross is the meeting place where the pure love of God meets sin in the loved ones, in us. And there that pure love bore in its own body our sins on a tree. God being what God is and we being what we are, the cross was inevitable. It was inherent.

Growing Spiritually
(Week 51, Tuesday)

Love Bears and Shares
Romans 5:6-11

The cross is the place where God deals with this awful fact of sin. The cross is the price that God pays to get to us in spite of our sin. God being what God is and humanity being what it is, the cross became inevitable.

For wherever pure love meets sin in the loved one, at the junction of that love and that sin a cross of pain is set up. It is the nature of love to insinuate itself into the sorrows and sins of the loved one and make them its own. All love has the doom of bleeding upon it as long as there is sin in the loved one—inevitably so. If God is love, then when that love comes into contact with sin in the loved ones, a cross of pain will be set up at the junction of that love and that sin. But how would I know there is a cross upon the heart of God—God is a Spirit, and I am bounded by my flesh—how could I know there is the unseen cross on the heart of God? How would I know except God show me— show me by lifting up a cross in human history so that I can see through the outer cross the inner cross upon the heart of God? That has happened.

The cross lights up the nature of God as vicarious, suffering Love.

The outstretched arms of the cross are the arms of God stretched out to gather to God's heart all the sin and sorrow of the world to make it God's own....

The cross is God saying...: "I love you enough to bear your sins in my own body and make them my own." The cross is Love caring and sharing and bearing.

Mastery
(Week 2, Monday)

Evil a Parasite upon the Good
Hebrews 12:1-2

The preaching of Jesus created a revolution—turned the world upside down.

The cross was the revelation of the heart of God. That was new and almost unthinkable to that ancient world. Cicero said: "The very mention of the cross should be far removed not only from a Roman citizen's body but from his mind and his eyes and his ears" (as quoted in Phil Moore, *Straight to the Heart of Galatians to Colossians* [Oxford, UK: Monarch Books, 2014], 233; a footnote cites Cicero's legal defense of Gaius Rabirius in 63 BCE as the source for the quotation). Even to think about the cross would defile the proud Roman. But Jesus accepted the cross as his very own and through it showed the love of God. The cross was hate, and through it Jesus showed love. The cross was sin, and through it Jesus accomplished the healing of sin. The cross was humanity at its worst, and through it Jesus showed God at his redemptive best. To atone for sin through the action of sin is new. To show the best through the worst, that was new and revolutionary. The thought and the outlook of antiquity were reversed.

Mastery
(Week 26, Friday)

To Sit with Me on My Throne

Our God rules from a Cross. "And I, when I am lifted up from the earth, will draw all men to myself" (John 12:32). When he was weakest, he was strongest; when he was most helpless on a cross, he was most powerful—the magnet that draws all people to himself. The universe has at its head One who obeys his own laws, and especially the deepest—finding life by losing it.

In Christ
(Week 15, Tuesday)

Hope...in the Lord Jesus

Christians never know when we are beaten. We begin with defeat, the defeat of the cross. You cannot defeat defeat. It starts with defeat and turns that defeat into victory, the cross into an Easter morning. Christians are incorrigibly hopeful. When Christians cannot sing of what is, we sings of that which is to be. When that which is to be looks hopeless, we still sing on general principles! In spite of!

In Christ
(Week 36, Monday)

The Cross—Touchstone of Being in Christ

A steadying passage: "Therefore, my brethren, whom I love and long for, my joy and crown, stand firm thus in the Lord, my beloved" (Phil 4:1). Paul, after having talked of the upward call of God in Christ, here talked about holding steady, "stand firm thus in the Lord." He points to the cross as the place to hold steady: "For many, of whom I have often told you and now tell you even with tears, live as enemies of the cross of Christ" (Phil 3:18). Evidently there were those who claimed to be in Christ, but in Christ without the cross. Stand fast at the place of the cross, Paul pleads, even with tears.

Was Paul right? Is the cross the touchstone of being in Christ? Yes. Just as self-surrender is the touchstone on our part of being in Christ—no being in Christ without it—so the divine self-surrender in the cross is the touchstone of the real gospel from the side of God. God cannot save without a cross. The cross is the price God must pay to get to us in spite of our sin.

In Christ
(Week 37, Tuesday)

The Son Who Is Effulgence of God's Splendor
Hebrews 12:2-3

And Jesus "is the effulgence of God's splendor" (Heb 1:3 NEB). God's glory point is the Incarnation, where God took it all on. And the center of that glory point is the cross, where God felt the acutest pain of all—the pain of our sin. At the transfiguration, Jesus burst into light when he talked about "his departure, which he was to accomplish at Jerusalem" (Luke 9:31). But this was the word of the cross become word. But at the actual cross it was the Word become flesh. It actually happened. Therefore the actual cross is "the effulgence of God's splendor." God's bitterest shame was turned into the greatest glory. The God of the Scars has become the God of the Stars—all worlds.

The Word Became Flesh
(Week 49, Wednesday)

KARMA

Self-Salvation, or Salvation through the Cross?
Galatians 6:14-15

We come now to a question at the heart of our quest for maturity. It is raised in connection with this verse: "If any one does sin, we have an advocate with the Father, Jesus Christ the righteous; and he is the expiation for our sins, and not for ours only but also for the sins of the whole world" (1 John 2:1-2). This verse raises the question of the cross. What relationship has the cross to maturity? Does the cross weaken character with an offer of easy forgiveness, as some would say? Or is the cross the very center of maturity, and there is no real maturity without it? That is perhaps the most vital question that can be raised in religion. It divides the religious world in two groups: those who depend on salvation by their own efforts and attainments—a *self*-salvation, and those who depend for salvation on what has been done for them at a cross—a *God*-salvation. Really there are no other issues in religion, except marginal ones. This is it!

Christian Maturity
(Week 13, Sunday)

Karma and the Cross
Galatians 6:7-9

Karma says that there is no forgiveness; you reap what you sow, somewhere, somehow. The Hindu statement is: "Just as a calf will find its mother among a thousand cows, so your deeds will find you out among a thousand rebirths." An American who had become a Buddhist said, "My brother, who is a Roman Catholic priest, is praying for my soul, and the joke of it is that I have no soul. I'm just a coming together of past deeds, and when they are dissolved, I dissolve into Nirvana—*sunnyavadi*—or nothingness." And then he added, "I do not want a God offering to forgive my sins. I prefer to work them out myself." He implied that it was more mature to take the way of karma than the offer of redemption.

We must examine this matter carefully; a misstep here means a destiny misstep. The chair of one of my meetings in India, a Hindu member of the Legislative Assembly, said to an audience: "Twenty-six years ago when I was a student in a Christian college, I heard the speaker speak on a subject I've never forgotten. For weeks after that address, inside the classroom and outside, the student—and faculty—discussed that address. It was entitled 'Karma and the Cross.' He saw that the title brought to a head the religious choice of the whole of the East."

And this choice is at the basis of our religious life of the West. For this thought of self-salvation through positive thinking and affirmation is an atmosphere both inside and outside much of the church life of today. Now of course there is a truth underlying karma. This is a world of moral law. You *do* reap what you sow. Christianity affirms that and affirms it strongly: "Do not be deceived; God is not mocked, for whatever a man sows, that he will also reap" (Gal 6:7). If you work with the moral universe, you will get results; it will back you, sustain you, further you. But if you work against the moral universe, you get consequences; you'll be up against it, frustrated. Some people go through life getting results; others get consequences.

Christian Maturity
(Week 13, Monday)

His Religion Is Producing Tension
Romans 7:22-25

We have seen that there is a truth in karma, the law of sowing and reaping. There is also a truth in salvation and health through affirmation, through being positive, that is "self-salvation." Negative attitudes bring negative results. If you affirm disease—the negative of health—you'll probably have disease. Our lives, like the hands of a dyer, are colored by that with which we work. If the atmosphere of your mind is pessimistic, fearful, and negative, then your body, mind, and spirit will be affected by it. You, as a person, will become negative....

So this positive attitude toward life will give you a shot in the arm. But it is only a shot in the arm, for at its best it is self-salvation. And everything that leaves you preoccupied with yourself, even an exhortation to forget yourself, leaves you in the quagmire of self-centeredness, even if it be a religious self-centeredness. That is the fatal defect of both karma and self-salvation. They both leave you self-centered in their endeavor to improve, to release, and to realize yourself. You are still at the center of your world, hence off-center.

Christian Maturity
(Week 13, Tuesday)

Deeds without Desire for Reward
Matthew 6:1-5

We have seen that both karma and self-salvation suffer from a fatal defect; they leave you preoccupied with yourself. Karma tries to get out of the tangle of self-preoccupation by saying that you are to do good deeds without desire for reward—*nishphal karma*—karma without desire for fruit. This sounds wise and helpful, but actually it is self-defeating. For the very desire to have a desireless action is a desire for desireless action and leaves you struggling with yourself to be freed from yourself, hence more tied to yourself. It attempts to deliver you philosophically and leaves you concentrated on yourself in fact. The attempt to keep yourself from thinking of a certain thing brings that thing back into the focus of attention in the mind.... So the emphasis on "action without desire for fruit" results in a self-conscious desire to be freed from desire for fruit. The fruit of the whole thing is a self-centered piety.

The same thing can be said of the movements that claim you have the answers within you; just discover and develop your own divine potentialities, your own perfection. Here is a declaration of principles from a recent international gathering of such a movement: "We affirm the inseparable oneness of God and man, the realization of which come through spiritual intuition, the implications of which is that man can reproduce the

273

Divine perfection in his body, emotions, and in all his external affairs." Note that "God and man" are "inseparable," one; no matter what humanity is, has done, or will do, nothing will be able to break that oneness. It is not a moral and spiritual oneness; it is a oneness of essence, an inseparable oneness. If that means anything it is this: since God and you are one in essence, then you are one in action; what you do God does. Then what kind of God is God if God does what we do? God's character is gone.

Christian Maturity
(Week 13, Wednesday)

Inseparably One with God?
Psalm 8:4-6

[What about] those who find all the answers within themselves, asserting their own inseparable oneness with God....The character of God is lost in this viewpoint, for if we are inseparably one with God, then what we do, God does. You cannot say you are metaphysically one and not morally one....But any of us who know ourselves—and others—knows that we when we act, *we* act and *not* God....We have tried to make ourselves God, and we have lost God in the process if God is just ourselves writ large. But in the end, our moral nature revolts against such a projection of ourselves. We simply cannot worship the God we project. That God is too much like us.

But this emphasis doesn't lead you to worship God. You are not to worship God, but to discover and realize God in yourself; you are to discover yourself as God....It leaves you concentrated on yourself to discover and to develop your own essential divinity....

This gives you an initial shot in the arm, a lift, a sense of your worthwhileness....

But it has a fatal defect; it leaves you preoccupied with yourself. You are left with an endeavor to try by various slogans and practices to convince yourself that you are inseparably one with God. You are the center of your attention and that leaves you with a self-conscious piety, a piety that has to act a part, which must keep up its illusion of manifest divinity. That is playacting of a very serious kind.

Christian Maturity
(Week 13, Thursday)

Aham Brahm
1 Corinthians 3:18-23

We are considering the self-preoccupation that results when we endeavor to make ourselves inseparably one with God. I was visiting a swami in his Ashram in India. He was supposed to be a *jiwan-mukta*—one who has attained salvation while alive, one who has realized that he is God—*Aham Brahm* ("I am God"). But that has laid on him the burden of acting a part, the part of playing God. He showed himself at regular times so that his followers and devotees could take his *darsham*—literally, "take his presence." He sat in the meeting that I addressed in a be-pillowed kind of elongated chair, surrounded by flowers and burning incense. He arose...about ten minutes after I had begun, interrupted the address, garlanded [me] and the visitors, and returned to his reclining throne....And he received the adoration of his followers, who prostrated

274

themselves before him with folded hands. He was the center of attention for himself and others. You didn't think of God when you experienced him; you thought of the swami!...It was all self-salvation through self-realization by self-attention. And the nemesis was self-attention, and hence self-conscious attention. And it was all so self-defeating.

Into that circle came a Greek woman who had renounced, not the world, but herself, in complete self-surrender to Christ. This self-surrender released her from self-preoccupation and released her to give herself to others in pure, disinterested service. She was a trained masseuse and treated everybody regardless of condition or race or religion, even lepers. She is now treating lepers with her own hands, massaging their sores. She rubs the love of God into everybody, giving a massage and a message at the same time. The swami, seeing the prodigality of her love and service given in self-forgetful humility, said to his followers; "This is the kind of love and service I would like to see produced here." But it simply could not be.

Christian Maturity
(Week 13, Friday)

Know by Intuition or by Incarnation?
Romans 1:22-25

The principles of a movement bent on the realization of its devotees as having "an inseparable oneness with God," state that "the realization comes through spiritual intuition." You bypass the revelation of God in Jesus and look within to discover your own divinity...by "spiritual intuition." You are the means of the discovery of your own inseparable oneness with God. This is a modern version of Gnosticism. The Gnostics said they were the superior knowers...from the Greek gnosis, to know. You know directly by turning in on yourself; you know by intuition. You do not have to turn to Jesus as the self-disclosure of God in understandable terms. You turn to yourself as the means of your own self-disclosure as God.

This outlook and method may be baptized here and there with Christian terminology to make it palatable to Christians, but it is fundamentally unchristian. It urges that you see God through yourself by intuition and not through Jesus by interpretation. This is self-salvation through self-discovery. The Christian faith is God-salvation through self-surrender to Jesus Christ, who brings God to us. The self is surrendered, not discovered. The basis is changed from self to God. We are then God-centered persons, not self-centered persons. That leaves us on the right center—God.

The temptation of the Garden of Eden was correct: If you eat of this tree of knowledge, "you will be like God" (Gen 3:5). The temptation was to make themselves "as God" through special knowledge. Adam and Eve fell for it and lost paradise, and themselves. Jesus came to restore that paradise through knowledge of himself, by self-surrender. And the moment we do it, our paradise returns. We have lost our lives through self-surrender and have found them again through God-realization. We come through Jesus and find God and ourselves, and everything!

Christian Maturity
(Week 13, Saturday)

275

Drunk with the Wine of Wordiness
1 Corinthians 15:42-44

We are considering whether we are saved by the cross—the self-giving of God, or by intuition—the discovery of ourselves. The quotation given on Wednesday (see above) ended with these words: "the implications of which are that man can reproduce the Divine perfection in his body, emotions, and in all his external affairs."...It talks about God, but centers on people as the center of this perfection and the producers of it. Humanity is deified. God doesn't come down, as in the incarnation, but people go up through a spiritual intuition. And this perfection is thoroughgoing; it includes the "body," "emotions," and "all...external affairs."

This statement is drunk with the wine of its own wordiness. It is the Word become words, and words only. It never becomes flesh. For where do we see the perfection in the body? If the body were perfect it would be deathless. When I saw a French "Mother" who mediated between Arabindo Chose, the Hindu swami, and the outside world, she said to me: "He is trying something different. He is not only making his soul divine, he is making his body divine as well." But that "divine" body died like the rest of us....

We gain physical perfection, not by asserting the perfection of the body, but by realizing that in Jesus our bodies are made perfect through his resurrection when we are identified by surrender to him. His deathlessness becomes ours!

As to perfection of "emotions," you don't find it by asserting the perfection of the emotions, but by loving God "with all your heart"—the emotions—and in loving God we find our emotions come back to us perfected as we perfectly love God. As for "perfection in all our external affairs," that comes when the kingdom comes, and the kingdom comes when we "receive" it by surrender. We make an external paradise through the Holy Spirit within.

Christian Maturity
(Week 14, Sunday)

Humanity Tries to Restore Fellowship
Micah 6:6-7

We have been considering methods of self-salvation through self-assertions about the self. We now turn to the method of God-salvation through the divine self-sacrifice, the cross.

Humanity, in feeling the estrangement between ourselves and God, has taken various ways to get back into fellowship with God. First, we sacrificed to God to appease God by offering possessions—cattle, sheep, or goats—in sacrifice, sometimes the produce of toil: grain, fruit, or money. Second and higher, we offered to God in sacrifice our righteous deeds, moral endeavors, penances, and piety; in short, our worthiness. Third, and this is the method we have just been considering, we offers to God our wordy assertion of our oneness with God, the claim that there is nothing between God and humanity except our ignorance of our own divinity. This is people bridging the gulf between us and God, made by human sin, by saying there is no sin and hence there is no gulf. These attempts heal everything by self-asserting words about humanity's divine perfection.

But we cannot get to God, either by offering the sacrifice of the fruit of our work, or by the sacrifice of our works, or by the sacrifice of our words. We can't get to God by any of these ladders; God must come to us. The Word must become flesh. And that Divine Word must bear our sins in his own body on a tree. That has happened.

We mentioned the truth in the law of karma, the truth that we reap what we sow. This is a universe that is not indifferent to your virtue or your vice. It takes sides. You are free to choose, but you are not free to choose the results or the consequences of your choices. They are in hands not your own. And you do not break these laws written into the nature of things; you break yourself on them. And these laws are color-blind, race-blind, and religionblind. Break them and you get broken.

Christian Maturity
(Week 14, Monday)

The Truth in Karma
Luke 6:37-38

There is an important and an all-embracing truth in karma. We cannot expect to evade the results or the consequences of our moral sowing. Our chickens do come home to roost. Our deeds will boomerang upon us. The result or the consequences register themselves in us automatically. The payoff is in the person. You don't break these laws; you break yourself upon them. Sin and its punishment are one and the same thing. You don't have to punish the eye for having sand in it, the body for having a cancer in it. Nor do you have to punish a boy for taking a skunk in bed with him!...Sin...is trying to do something that simply cannot be done, an attempt to live life against reality.

But while there is a profound truth in karma, as usually interpreted, it is only a half-truth. For the usual interpretation is that the individual who does the sowing does all the reaping. According to the law of karma, it would be unjust for anyone except the sower to get any of the reaping. But the facts indicate otherwise. The father who sows a good life passes on the results of his karma to his family, to his community, to his country, and faintly to the world. Everybody reaps what he sows. However, those who sow a bad life pass on the consequences of that bad life to family, to country, and faintly, to the world. They wish that they alone could reap the consequences of their sowing and did not have to pass on to their children the shame of their deeds.

When Mahatma Gandhi sowed his life in sacrifice for the freedom of India, did he alone reap the results? No, the results of his karma were passed on to millions of people. They reaped freedom from this sowing. The fact that other people reap the results of our sowing opens the door to the vicarious. We can pass on to others through love the results of our sowing. This points us to the cross.

Christian Maturity
(Week 14, Tuesday)

WAR

Another Cause of Sin: War
Psalm 68:30; Isaiah 2:4; Matthew 26:52

Another phase of selfish competition is war. Selfish competition moves into international relationships and then war!

Even with the clouds of war in the sky and the world filled with increasing armaments, I am not hopeless about getting rid of war. Look where we have come from! In 2 Samuel 11:1, we read: "In the spring of the year, the time when kings go forth to battle,...David remained at Jerusalem." Kings went out to battle when the springtime came, exactly as a farmer goes to spring plowing, and as regularly. It was news when David stayed at home....

If the very center of life could be changed from competition to cooperation, then war would drop off like a dead leaf. But war is almost inevitable in a world based on competition.

Victorious Living
(Week 22, Wednesday)

My Attitude toward War
Exodus 20:13; Isaiah 9:6; John 18:36

During World War I, preached on these two texts: "Herod and his soldiers treated Jesus with contempt" (Luke 23:11 CEB) and "When the mob saw the commander and his soldiers, they stopped beating Paul" (Acts 21:32). Militarism treated Jesus with contempt, but then it does defend the weak and defenseless. That was my theme. Of course German militarism was treating Jesus with contempt; and we were on the defensive protecting the defenseless. How blinded I was! Every nation felt the same.

The distinction between the offensive and defensive war has for all practical purposes broken down. There is nothing left to do but to renounce all war. And that I do. And I'll tell you why. My chief reason is that war causes people to sin. People caught in the war spirit do things they would not dream of doing otherwise. It causes us to sin in the following ways:

1. It poisons the air with lies. The first casualty in war is Truth. You cannot fight your enemy unless you make the enemy out a devil. Lying propaganda attends to that.

2. It poisons the air with hate. If the first casualty is Truth, the second casualty is Love. Bitter, burning hate settles into the breasts of millions. The very air becomes poisonous with it. You cannot breathe without breathing it. Hellish hate.

3. It makes people sin economically. [At the time of World War I] a shot from a big gun cost $500, the equivalent of 20,000 loaves of bread.... War is economic sin—a sin against hunger.

4. It causes us to sin against persons. One estimate of the indirect and direct loss of life from World War I reached 40,000,000 lives, so that if these dead could march past us 10 abreast, it would take 184 days for them to pass. And they the flower of our race!

Victorious Living
(Week 22, May 31)

My Attitude toward War
Micah 4: 8; Mathew 5:21- 22; James 4:2

5. [War kills] the conscience....

6. It lays hold of the finest virtues and prostitutes them. It lays hold of patriotism, heroism, self-sacrifice, idealism, and turns them toward destruction....

7. It sins against the helpless. War protects? When? Where?...Protect the helpless? It produces them.

8. It stands against everything that Christ stands for. It sins against Christ. If war is right, Christ is wrong; and if Christ is right, war is wrong....

Christ and war are irreconcilables....If I must make my choice, I choose Jesus. Therefore I renounce war.

Victorious Living
(Week 22, Friday)

We Face the Question of War
Romans 14:4; 1 Peter 3:12-17

What shall be my attitude toward war? If we do not face that question and find abundant living through, and not around it, we shall have abundant living that is unreal. It would be easier not to face this question, for equally good people are on both sides of it; it would be easier and more deadly. Sometimes in our discussions, I have used the pronoun "I" in a representative capacity; but here I must use it in a strictly personal way, and tell you how far I have gone in my thinking and attitudes.

(1) I have determined that my attitude toward war shall not break my fellowship with those who differ from me. I believe in liberty of conscience so much that I must give the other person liberty of conscience to differ from me without inwardly de-Christianizing him or her, even in thought. The fellowship must not be broken.

(2) I am completely disillusioned about the war method. During the first world war, I preached on two texts: "Herod and his soldiers set Jesus at naught" (Luke 23:11 KJV)—militarism sets Jesus at naught. "But when they saw the soldiers, they stopped beating Paul" (Acts 21:32)—military power can be used to protect the innocent. This last text allowed me to approve of the war. Since then I have been completely disillusioned about the ability of the military method to accomplish what its advocates believe it can.

(3) The military method cannot and does not protect the innocent. It protects the guilty, who are behind the lines, and involves the innocent, both civilians and soldiers alike, in insensate, useless slaughter. To compare the military method to that of protecting your wife or daughter from a ravisher is a false analogy; for war exposes wife and daughter—in fact, all innocents—to ravishment: spiritual, mental, and physical.

Abundant Living
(Week 44, Thursday)

279

Is War a Surgical Operation?
Romans 12:17-21; Philippians 2:5; 1 Peter 3:8-12

War is a means out of harmony with the ends it hopes to accomplish. People everywhere acknowledge that the war method is wrong, but they hope to use it to accomplish good ends. This is a fond and futile hope, for "the means preexist in and determine the ends." You cannot dismiss the means before they have shaped the ends. They go straight into and determine the ends. Evil means produce evil ends. If good has ever come out of war, the reason was that other constructive influences have been introduced into the process and have produced constructive ends in spite of the war method.

To liken war to a surgical operation is a false analogy. A surgical operation posits an immaculately sterilized surgeon with immaculately sterilized instruments, or else it will do more harm than good. I know this from my own experience, for I was infected with tetanus when operated on for appendicitis. What nation as it goes to war can claim immaculate sterility for itself and its instruments? If it did, then the first germ that would infect the body of humanity would be hypocrisy. War cannot be carried on in an immaculately sterile manner—its weapons are lies, deceits, and hypocrisies. "The first casualty in war is truth"; the second is love, for it is absurd to say that you can go to war loving your enemies. If you loved your enemies you would be very poor soldier.

Abundant Living
(Week 44, Friday)

Using Cyclones
Isaiah 51:7-8, 12; 54:17

The war [World War II] has left a harvest of devastated homes, hearts, and hopes. "Why didn't God stop the war?" is the anguished cry. How could God do so without taking away our wills, depersonalizing us, making us things? The war was of our making. We produced the conditions out of which [totalitarism flourished]. The soldiers at the front were not dying for us; they were dying for our sins. The only good that will have come out of this war is what we rescue in making a new world for everybody.

The Way
(Week 35, Sunday)

Worshipping Gods Conquered in War
Isaiah 8:9-15

The method of war is incapable of producing the results expected of it. The means are out of harmony with the ends sought. For getting rid of evil by evil means you infect yourself with the very evil you try to get rid of.

The Way
(Week 47, Tuesday)

A PERSONAL WORD

Matthew 26:51-52; 2 Corinthians 10:3-5; Revelation 13:10

Then the period of disillusionment set in. I saw that the basis on which I could support war was flimsy and based on a fallacy: militarism protects the innocent and the weak. I saw that innocent and guilty alike were unprotected in war; it made no moral distinctions. Further, I saw that war did not protect the weak; it involved them and hit them especially. Whatever power militarism has had in the past to protect the innocent and the weak, it has lost all such power. More civilian casualties took place in this war from wounds, famine, and disease than military casualties. War protects no one anywhere. It does the opposite.

I saw that the whole thing was a vast waste of humanity and goods....Economic waste! I saw that war was a vast illusion, a vast waste. It built nothing. It blasted everything. It built nothing beneficial that we could not have built without a war.

Then I saw that not only did life not approve it, but also Life. When I worked from Christ down to this business of war, it seemed so utterly incompatible with everything I knew about him that it just didn't fit. So I repudiated it and determined I would give the balance of my days to finding a better way for myself and mankind.

The Way
(Week 47, Saturday)

World Government Means of Collective Security
Isaiah 2:1-4

We must help [foster] individual poise [composure] by taking away the nightmare of impending war from a defenseless humanity. As long as war is an imminent possibility, the poise of the individual is under a strain too great to bear. And when war comes, that poise cracks, except in very exceptional cases. War is our chief collective enemy, our chief collective sin. Our chief enemy is not [totalitarian ideologies]; it is war. Get rid of war, and these other problems can be solved. But how do we get rid of war? By world government....

That is lacking in world affairs. We have no government over us to which we can all be loyal. Hence every nation has to go around armed and fearful, and ready to fight it out at the drop of a hat. We must have a world government over us under which we will all be secure. It will not be any more impossible than it was to make the contending, suspicious thirteen colonies come together in a union. The entire plan of federal union was considered "utopian," "a visionary project," "an indigestible panacea." But they did it, and it worked.

The Way to Power and Poise
(Week 38, Thursday)

281

Freedom from War
Revelation 21:24-26

People don't want war. They hate it...—they want peace. But the political leaders of the nations don't seem to be able to get together. Here is a world hating war, afraid of war, and yet drifting into war. Are we in the hands of a cruel fate, or is there something wrong with us and our attitudes?...

We can become mature only by saying and meaning one word: *we*....If we said *we*, then we would be free, from war. The education of the human race is education in one word, and only one word, the word *we*. When we learn that one word, we shall be mature as a race.

How to Be a Transformed Person
(Week 38, Monday)

The Means to Transformation
Galatians 5:6; 1 John 4:7

So God, being love, uses love in the means to bring in the transformation, individual and collective. That rules out the method of war. For war is a means out of harmony with the ends it proposes. When it gets to those ends, the ends are spoiled by the very means. War therefore is the vast illusion, the illusion that you can get to right ends by wrong means. It simply can't be done. Twice in one generation we thought we were making a new world, through a world war. We succeeded, not in making a new world, but in making a new war. Like produced like. We cling to the illusion that though this has been true of war in the past, it will not be true of the next one. But each time we are let down. The only good that can possibly come out of war is something good rescued out of it in spite of war. And all these goods could have been had by other means. All human attempts at getting into a new world by wrong means have ended in dead ends. Only God's method will get us there. And that method is love. That method works to the degree it is tried. History has rendered one verdict, and that verdict is, that only that which is founded on love lasts; everything else perishes.

How to Be a Transformed Person
(Week 51, Sunday)

War Must Be Abolished
Micah 4:3-4

The conscience of humanity is slowly expanding to include war in its central repudiations. For we are being pushed into this position by the very weapons we use. If war comes again, it will be fought with atomic energy, and no one will win an atomic-energy war. Both sides will be ruined in perhaps twenty-four hours. No one will be victor. One side may crawl out as survivor, but no one as victor. God is almost certainly coercing our consciences into a repudiation of war. We have relied on force in human affairs, and now God has let us see into the heart of an atom. God points to it and says, "You have believed in force. There it is in an atom! But if you use it, both sides will be ruined. Now choose." And we are in the hour of fateful choice. Have we attained sufficient moral maturity to choose wisely?

Growing Spiritually
(Week 44, Wednesday)

The Christian Way Works
John 3:5-36; 5:22-24

Jesus, the man of love, stands up under every tempest and emerges stronger at the end. Love will wear down all hate. And because I believe in the power of love, I believe that war will be banished from the earth.

Growing Spiritually
(Week 51, Saturday)

We Cannot Kill a Man for Whom Christ Died
Isaiah 2:2-4

We have believed in force and leaned on it to settle our disputes, and now God has put us in a corner. With the discovery of atomic energy such force has been put into our hands that we are appalled. God is seemingly saying, "You put your faith in force; I'm going to let you see into the heart of an atom. You wanted force, and now I'm giving it to you. But—and this is the terrible point—if you use it again, you will destroy yourselves." That is the terrible dilemma; we got what we wanted—force—but if we use it, we annihilate ourselves. For no one can win an atomic-energy war. Both sides will be ruined, probably in twenty-four hours. Some may crawl out of the ruins as survivors but nobody as victor. So after a long bloody march through the warring centuries we're back again where the early Christians started. They started with the renunciation of war. We, too, have come out at the same place, the renunciation of war. They did it by their faith; we have to do it by our fate. But war must go, or we go.

Mastery
(Week 45, Monday)

Can Satan Cast out Satan?
1 Peter 3:8-9

We have been studying the immaturity of physical violence and force, and the maturity of soul force, the force of love.

Jesus put the matter thus: "Can Satan cast out Satan?" (Mark 3:23). Can you, by acting like the devil, get the devil out of people? War is an attempt to act like the devil and thus get the devil out of people. It won't work. You cannot get rid of darkness by going out and fighting it with your fist; bring in a light and the darkness is gone. You can overcome evil only with good, hate with love, the world with a cross.

War is the most immature method imaginable of settling international disputes. But, someone asks, are you going to let another nation walk over you? Listen to a parable: Two goats met on a one-plank bridge over a chasm. If one tried to push or butt the other off, both would go overboard. So the more sensible goat lay down on the plank and let the other walk over him to safety. Then he, too, got up and went on to safety. Did the goat that lay down and let the other walk over him debase himself? Apparently, for the moment. But he got up with an inner sense of superiority; he was able to live with himself. The other goat wasn't able to live with himself; he was a debate, trying to justify himself. We look on and choose the goat that lay down as the superior goat, superior in intelligence and in spirit. Soul force is maturity; mere physical force is immaturity. The war god Mars would have whispered to each of the goats: "Butt him off!" And both would have gone into the abyss. War is not only a brutal and costly way of settling disputes, it is stupid.

And now we have come to the end of Rake's progress. We have discovered atomic energy, the ultimate in physical force, and God is saying: "You wanted force; I let you discover it in the atom. But remember, if you use it again both sides will be ruined, inevitably. So choose." We got the force we were looking for and now we dare not use it.

Christian Maturity
(Week 29, Tuesday)

A New Man out of Both Parties

A very informative verse [on the topic of war is] "that he might create in himself one man in place of two, so making peace" (Eph 2:15). This verse arose out of the Scriptures during World War II and became my guiding star during the war, and has been since. How do we find peace? Paul lifts up out of reality a universal method of finding peace: Get each party to change and come to a third position, a "new man" out of both parties. There is no other way to peace, from the simplest relationship to the most complex.

In Christ
(Week 32, Friday)

What Jesus Christ Means to Me
Psalm 103:2-5

When the attack upon Pearl Harbor took place, I was in Urbana, Illinois, and was to speak that afternoon in a university convocation on "Peace."...Here I was on the way to speak on peace and peace was gone....I told that shocked audience that obviously I could not speak on peace, for peace was gone, but I would speak on "What Christ means to me." When that world of peace we had tried to build up had crashed, did anything remain? Yes, all the values, the real values, of my life were intact, for "Jesus Christ is the same yesterday and today and forever" (Heb 13:8). When things crashed, he remained.

The Word Became Flesh
(Week 52, Sunday)

WORRY AND FEAR

One Day at a Time
Matthew 6:25-34

Meet Today, today. Jesus showed very penetrating insight when he said: "So do not be troubled about tomorrow; tomorrow will take care of itself. The day's own trouble is quite enough for the day" (Matthew 6:34 Moffatt). He was not saying there were no troubles to be met. There are. Life is bound to bring trouble. It is made that way. But don't telescope the troubles of tomorrow and of the next day into today. Meet today, today; for if you put the troubles of next week into today by anticipation through worry, then you spoil today. You are meeting two sets of troubles at once: one set that is actually here, and the set that you bring in by worrying about tomorrow's troubles. You are therefore meeting your troubles twice: once before they come, and once when they are actually here. Such a telescoping of trouble is a double expenditure of energy and needless. Worry is the advance interest you pay on troubles that never come. Some of them do come, and you can meet and conquer them separately. But tomorrow's troubles plus today's can "break" you.

Abundant Living
(Week 11, Saturday)

Your Commission Free from Stain of Worry and Fear
Matthew 6:24-34; Philippians 4:4-7; 1 Peter 5:7

Keep your commission free from the stain of worry and fear. Worry is not merely weakness; it is wickedness. It is atheism. It says that God has abdicated, and that we have to hold the world together by our worrying. The opposite happens. Worriers wreck their world....

Worry, therefore, is sin—sin against God and ourselves....

Fears are usually homegrown. Babies will handle snakes without fear, if there are no signs of fear on the faces of those around. To impose fears on children is crime. Don't impose them on yourself or others. Live by cheer rather than by fear. Very few worries live long unless you give them careful nursing.

Abundant Living
(Week 51, Tuesday)

Cleanse Your Past
Luke 19:8-10

Make restitution where it is necessary or possible. I say make it where "necessary or possible" because sometimes it is not possible. There are things beyond your recall. Do not spend time in useless worrying over a past you cannot change. God forgives; let that suffice. God wipes it from the "book of remembrance." So must you.

The Way
(Week 12, Sunday)

Roads with Dead Ends
Matthew 14:29-31; 1 John 4:18

Fear has three things against it: (1) It is disease producing. (2) It is paralyzing to effort. (3) It is useless.

If these three things are true, then to conquer fear is one of the first conquests of life. Without that conquest, we limp through life....The first word of the gospel was the voice of the angel, "Fear not." The first word of Jesus after his resurrection was, "Have no fear!" (Matt 28:10 Moffatt). Between the first word and the last word, the constant endeavor of Jesus was to get people released from fear. We must learn his secret.

The Way
(Week 13, Sunday)

Many Diseases Rooted in Fears
Psalm 55:4-6; Luke 12:32

We know how fear and worry cause disease and how they hinder convalescence. Wounds would not heal, or heal slowly, if fear is at the center of life. Faith is healing and fear is hindering.

Release from fear is a physical necessity as well as a moral and spiritual necessity. It is a life necessity.

The Way
(Week 13, Monday)

Worry Is Sand in the Machinery
Psalm 31:10; Proverbs 15:13

Fear and worry often upset the natural functioning of the digestive tract....
Fear also upsets the mental processes....

O Christ, you have come to remove all fears; remove mine. For I know I cannot be at my best, your best, unless I am delivered, completely delivered, from fear. I would be whole. Amen.

The Way
(Week 13, Wednesday)

Don't Fight Your Fears; Surrender Them
John 6:20-21; 12:15

When worry comes to the door, don't give it the best seat and entertain it. Gently close the door and say: "I have surrendered you into the hands of God. You have no place or part with me anymore. I'm free from you."

O Christ, these fears of mine I've held within my heart, and now I'm turning them over to you. I cannot master them, but you can. From this time on, they are in your hands and off mine. Amen.

The Way
(Week 14, Thursday)

God and You Meet Life Together
Isaiah 30:15; 35:3-4

Identify yourself, not with your fear, but with Christ. By surrendering fears to Christ, you are no longer identified with them. You are identified with him. "In the world you have tribulation; but be of good cheer, I have overcome the world" (John 16:33). He has overcome your world of fear. You have become identified with him, and therefore you are identified with his victory.

The Way
(Week 14, Saturday)

How the Kingdom Comes
Matthew 13:31-33; Luke 17:20-21; 1 Thessalonians 1:5, 8

Yesterday we saw that the kingdom of God is to be sought first, last, and always. If you seek something else first, an inner restlessness will possess you; you will have a dull sense that you are not on the Way. Jesus said, "So do not seek food and drink and be worried" (Luke 12:29 Moffatt). Note that if you seek anything else first you do become "worried"; you know inherently that you've missed the Way.

The Way
(Week 49, Tuesday)

This Is All That Life Means
Matthew 6:27-30

Robert Louis Stevenson is widely quoted as writing: "Anyone can carry his burden, however hard, for one day. Anyone can live sweetly, patiently, lovingly, purely, till the sun goes down. And this is all that life means."

If you are fettered by the fears of tomorrow, then surrender tomorrow into the hands of God and do it now, and then go out to live happily and effectively today. And tomorrow will blossom with joy because you have lived—really lived—today.

The Way to Power and Poise
(Week 46, Friday)

Life by the Inch Is a Cinch
Matthew 6:25-29

It is good that God has so arranged that life comes to us in manageable portions, one day at a time. Suppose all the future were dumped into our laps at one time. We would be overwhelmed. But the wise God broke life up into portions so small that anyone can manage it if we take it as it is given, one day at a time. So shut off yesterday and do not admit tomorrow; deal with today, today. The worries of yesterday plus the worries of tomorrow piled into today break the stoutest spirit. But divide your worries and conquer them.

Life by the yard is hard.
Life by the inch is a cinch.

Growing Spiritually
(Week 7, Tuesday)

"Tenigue" (*Tension* and *Fatigue*)
2 Corinthians 11:23-28

Worry is like a rocking chair; it will give you something to do but won't get you anywhere.

Growing Spiritually
(Week 7, Thursday)

5
ENGAGING WITH OUR WORLD

What are some of the principles which we should embody if we are to live together well?

(1) We should recognize that life is corporate. Many do not recognize this. They still look on life as an individual thing. The consequence is that they are continually in trouble with other people. They want to turn whole situations to themselves, instead of relating themselves to the whole....They look at what they can get from the whole instead of what they can give to it....

After we recognize that we are corporate we must proceed (2) to fix our loyalty to the group in which we are in immediate contact. There are degrees of loyalty of course. There is the loyalty to oneself, one's family, one's group, one's nation, and the kingdom of God. Our final loyalty should be to the kingdom of God. Where loyalty to that conflicts with any of the lesser loyalties, then the lesser must give way and the kingdom must remain supreme and final....

(3) Loyalty to the group should mean that we will never criticize any member behind his or her back....Criticism should always be open and frank and always redemptive....You cannot have fellowship, if you know or suspect that secret criticism is taking place....[A] motto on our Ashram wall is this: "When about to criticize another, ask three questions: (1) Is it true? (2) Is it necessary? (3) Is it kind?" If it can pass these three tests, then the criticism should be given openly and frankly.

Religious people are in the business of endeavoring to be good; they are therefore tempted to point out the faults of others, so that by implication they themselves may appear better. It is a miserable business....

(4) We should not only be willing to criticize another for his or her good; we should also be willing to take it for ourselves. And rejoice in it. Many of us are willing to give it, but we hesitate or refuse to take it for ourselves. No one has earned the right to criticize another unless he or she welcomes the possibility of criticism by others....

(5) But we should be on our guard that we do not thus become petty, always seeking for something to correct in others. We should perhaps be more inclined to compliment and encourage than to correct. We need not be afraid that we will make people proud, for sincere souls are often more humbled by compliments that by criticism....

The emphasis should be on the search for the good, for people are made more by compliments than corrections.

Victorious Living
(Week 42, Sunday–Wednesday)

289

COMMUNITY

Principles of Corporate Living
Acts 2:41-47; 4:32

Many of our spiritual problems do not arise from ourselves; they arise from our relations with others. It is not an easy thing to adjust oneself to other people and their wills. Christianity should teach us that very thing, for Christianity is the science of living well with others according to Jesus Christ. Many of our attempts to live together with others are haphazard; they do not obey the underlying principles of corporate living, for there are principles or laws of corporate living as well defined as those that underlie nature. We must attempt to discover them and live by them. All of us have to live in relationship with others. Many try to do it without any underlying principles, and it ends in disaster with its resultant bitterness and strife.

Victorious Living
(Week 42, Sunday)

Plenty for All—Poverty for Many
Matthew 15:32-37; Luke 3:10-11

Cooperation is a higher principle [than competition] with a higher result. A management engineer puts it this way: "If a business insures the security of its employees by profit sharing, it automatically insures itself." That same principal of cooperation must be applied to community relationships. Cooperatives may not be the final answer, but they are a step on the road to the final answer, for they distribute wealth widely through cooperative effort.

The Way
(Week 51, Thursday)

Love's Burden Is Light
Deuteronomy 10:12; James 1:27

There is fun and freedom in loving, and the more widely and deeply you love, the more fun and the greater freedom you have.

Growing Spiritually
(Week 19, Saturday)

Growth in Freedom
John 8:31-36

We come this week to consider growth in freedom. Everyone wants freedom....

We all want freedom, but so few know how to get it. They seek it first, and if you seek freedom first, you'll miss it. We are made not primarily for freedom, but for obedience. Freedom is a byproduct of obedience. If you put freedom first, it will be the freedom to get tied up with yourself and others. Some try to get freedom by doing as they like;

others try to get freedom by doing as they ought. Only the latter find freedom. The first freedom turns to futility. The second freedom turns to fertility.

The first lie ever told was about this matter of freedom. Satan said to Adam and Eve, if you do as you like, "ye shall be as gods" (Gen 3:5 KJV). More people get hooked on that bait than on any other. Satan is a skillful player and lets you win the first few tricks in the game of freedom, and then he cleans you out.

But Satan isn't quite as clever as he seems. In reality he is a fool. For everything he brings on others comes on him. When he prepares a hell for others, he himself has to live in it. He seems to have a freedom to ruin, but it turns out to be a freedom to ruin only himself.

There is only one way to be free, and that is through obedience. But this must be qualified thus: obedience to the right thing. You can obey and end in bondage if you are obeying the wrong authority. The center of your obedience must be set straight....

So freedom comes only through obedience to the right thing.

Growing Spiritually
(Week 50 Sunday)

The Faultless Law of Freedom
Galatians 5:1, 13-14

Where is the "faultless" law of freedom? It is not really a law; it is a person. That person is Christ. It is a strange and incredible thing, but the more we belong to him, the more freedom we enjoy. And I mean "enjoy." It is freedom without a "catch" in it. You are not always waiting for the blow to fall. It is what Jesus meant when he said: "If the Son makes you free, you will be free indeed" (John 8:36).

Growing Spiritually
(Week 50, Tuesday)

ECONOMICS

Economic Inequality—A Cause of Sin
Matthew 19:22-26; James 2:1-4

In tracing back the various causes of sin we come across the fact that the unequal distribution of wealth causes a great deal of sin. This inequality works in several directions. First, it works harm to those who have more than their legitimate share. It often produces in them the feeling that they must in some way deserve all this, and that God must be very pleased with them, when the fact of the matter is that they may have been only clever enough to choose their parents!

Inequalities produce superiority complexes. We often think that because we have more we are worth more, which doesn't necessarily follow. It might make us decidedly worthless. Without it, we might give a great contribution to life; with it, we give only contributions. It also sets the stage for lack of ambition, parasitism, selfish hedonism, and wasted time in general.

Again, it creates the mentality that tries to justify this condition of inequality. Rationalization sets in and with it an unconscious hypocrisy....One of the severest indictments that can be drawn up against unequal distribution of wealth is that it sends cleavages through life everywhere and separates person from person. And the deepest need in the world at the present time is fellowship. The Christian must question everything that makes fellowship more difficult.

Victorious Living
(Week 23, Tuesday)

Causing Sin to the Underprivileged
Leviticus 19:13-15; Job 32:13-22

Unequal distribution of wealth causes hurt to those who have more than their share, but it also causes hurt to those who have less than their share. It tends to create in the one a superiority complex and in the other an inferiority complex. In an acquisitive society, where people are judged as to their "worth" by their wealth, not to have wealth brands one as inferior. This is a positive sin against personality.

Moreover, from the Christian standpoint, it loads the dice against inward peace and harmony....

Among the Zulus, there is the saying, "The full-belly child says to the empty-belly child, 'Be of good cheer.'" Our preaching of contentment and cheer to the poor, while leaving untouched the causes of their gloom and lack of contentment, adds insult to injury....No one today has any message to that gloom and misery unless he or she has an ax in hand to strike at the root of that misery.

Victorious Living
(Week 23, Wednesday)

Economic Insecurity
Isaiah 33:15-16; Ezekiel 3:5-6; 12:18-20; Philippians 4:19

In many ways, [economic insecurity] is the most prolific cause of sin in human society....If [business peeople in a competitive society] get more than they needs, somebody will have less than is needed.

And the wage earners? Their economic destiny is not in their own hands, nor in the hands of fellow laborers, but in the hands of the ones who own the capital. They, therefore, live in constant dread of joining the ragged ranks of the unemployed. That haunting fear is one of the most desperate things in human life at the present time, and it may disrupt society in an awful explosion. If it does not cause an explosion, it will drive people to sycophancy, subservience, and denial of their own personhood that will be just as disruptive of society as an explosion.

Thus economic insecurity causes the sin of fear. The employer is afraid to give better wages, be undercut by competitors, and go on the rocks; the laborers are afraid of losing their jobs.

Victorious Living
(Week 24, Wednesday)

What Is to Be Done about It?
Mathew 14:15-16; Luke 3:15; 1 John 3:17

Certain things in the social structure set the stage for sin, cause sin: selfish competition, the wage system under competition, war, race prejudice, economic inequality, the existence of classes, unemployment, subjection of one race by another, nationalism, wrong attitudes toward women, and economic insecurity....

If religion has no message at this point, if it undertakes to live victoriously without facing these issues, then the method used is one of evasion, and this violates two fundamental principles of victorious living, namely, mental honesty and courage to face the facts....

Obviously, the first thing to be done is to look at these things as causes of sin and therefore an evil in human society, something to be eradicated and not tolerated. At this point our greatest difficulty lies. Many think that these things are an ineradicable part of society's structure, accepted fatalistically. This defeatest mentality is our greatest problem. It must be broken. Just as the individual, in order to have personal victory over personal sins, must have the faith that it can be done, so we must gain attitude of faith that these social sins are a disease, and as such are no normal part of human living and can be eradicated. The health of the society demands it.

Victorious Living
(Week 24, Thursday)

Victory at the Place of Money
Mark 12:15; Acts 2:6; 4:36-37; 1 Corinthians 6:12; Philippians 4:11-12

Money must be individually surrendered. That is, we will say something like: "I know I need money in a world of this kind, but I don't need more than I need. I will draw a line at the place where my needs end, for at that place others people's needs begin, and to go beyond that line is to steal from them, and I cannot do that and be Christian. In prayer and counsel with others, I will find that line, and put the surplus at the disposal of other people's needs."

We master money by making it minister to our needs and to the needs of others. If money makes us more mentally, morally, physically, and spiritually fit for the purposes of the kingdom of God, it is legitimate and right, a servant of the kingdom.

Victorious Living
(Week 43, Monday)

Is the Way Impersonal?
1 Corinthians 13:1-3

Science, philosophy, education, economics, business, politics, sociology—all branches of human approach to life—are going to converge upon one thing: the discovery of the Way. The discovery of gold amid the dust of the earth is going to be tame alongside the discovery of the Way hidden at the basis of life. Someday scientists are going to put it all down on the table, and they are going to say, "This is not the way to live," and, "This is the way to live." As we look at it, our eyes will bulge with astonishment, and we shall exclaim, "But fellow humans, the way you say is not the way to live is the unchristian way, and the way you say is the way is the Christian way." They will reply, "We cannot say anything about that, for that is not our province; but this is not the way to live, and this is the way to live."

The Way
(Week 7, Sunday)

Plenty for All—Poverty for Many
Matthew 15:32-37; Luke 3:10-11

An economy where the privileged insist on being kept warm by those on the edges of privilege is a doomed economy. Privilege must be distributed to all or be taken away from all.

The Way
(Week 51, Thursday)

I Never Called Her Mine
Luke 12:33-34

Holding our possessions at God's disposal does something more than settle a money issue. It settles a life attitude. You are then under orders, with a sense of mission, a sense of direction and goal.

When you let go of your possessions and let God have them, then life takes on a sense of stewardship. You are handling something on behalf of another. That does something to the whole of life; puts sacredness into the secular, lifts the sordid into the sacred. Then the Word becomes flesh, and the flesh becomes Word. Money becomes a message. When the pastor of the Chicago Temple used to call the collection "an offering of minted personality," he was right. When given to God, it is just as sacred as the words that fall from dedicated lips in the pulpit. Both speak the same message, and equally.

How to Be a Transformed Person
(Week 41, Tuesday)

Making Money for God
Luke 12:22-24

Jesus, in sixteen out of the thirty-eight recorded parables, dealt with stewardship. This means that while he taught that "you cannot serve God and mammon" (Matt 6:24), nevertheless you can serve God with mammon.

This means that he may call some to go into business as definitely as he calls some to go into the ministry. There they may use their powers of organization to make money for God.

Someone asked Jane Addams [1860–1935, founder of Hull House] what was the secret of her life, and she replied, "I looked into the faces of ruffian children, and then I looked into the face of Christ, and I gave my life to bring them together" [no published source found] I can imagine a businessperson saying: "I looked into the faces of the poor of the world, and then I looked into the face of Christ, and I gave my life to business to help meet that need." Or if not the poor, then the other areas of need in the world, at home and abroad. And I can see the businessperson go to tasks with lightness of step, sureness of direction, and a sense of mission. That person is making money for God. A Service of Commission should be held for such men and women as they go forth in Christ's name. Then ledgers would be handled with the same sense of sacredness as sacred books in a pulpit.

How to Be a Transformed Person
(Week 41, Wednesday)

Streamline Your Life for Kingdom Purposes
Luke 12:25-28

We are studying the necessity of a sense of stewardship in life. David Livingstone (1813–1873) had it when he said these immortal words: "I will place no value on anything that I have or possess except in relation to the kingdom of Christ. If anything I have will advance that kingdom, it shall be given or kept, as by giving or keeping it I shall best promote the glory of him to whom I owe all my hopes both for time and eternity" (widely quoted). That first sentence should become the life motto of every Christian in the world. Each Christian should repeat it slowly to every day, "I will place no value on anything that I have or possess except in relation to the kingdom of Christ." If it furthers that kingdom, it has value, it can stay. If it is useless to that kingdom, is valueless, it must be made useful or go. Streamline your life for kingdom purposes.

How to Be a Transformed Person
(Week 41, Thursday)

Stewardship of Treasure, Time, and Talent
Luke 12:29-31

Stewardship may be of treasure, time, and talent. Everyone has some of each; some have more, some less.

How to Be a Transformed Person
(Week 41, Friday)

The Material Becomes the Meaningful
Revelation 1:4-6

The Christian faith accepts the material, and dedicates it. There are passages that seem to say the opposite: "You cannot serve God and mammon" (Luke 16:13). True. But it doesn't say, "You cannot serve God with mammon." If money is dedicated to God along with the soul, then this money is just as sacred as the soul. When Jesus said to the rich young ruler: "Go, sell what you possess;...and come, follow me" (Matt 19:21), what the young man lacked was not poverty, but following Jesus, and the riches stood in the way of that following. If he had followed Jesus with his riches in his hands, ready to give to human need as it arose, he could have followed Jesus.

The Word Became Flesh
(Week 6, Thursday)

FAITH AND SCIENCE

Science and Religion
John 7:17; Philippians 4:8; 1 Thessalonians 5:21

If possible we must work our way through this scientific climate to God. We now see a little more clearly the relationship between science and religion. Science has reference to that which can be weighed and measured, and religion to that which can be evaluated; the one has reference to the quantitative aspects of life, and the other to the qualitative.

Science comes to a mother's tear and defines it in terms of its physical structure: so much water, so much mucus, so much salt. But is that an adequate definition of a mother's tear? Hardly, says religion, for there are ideas, emotions, values, meanings using the physical structure of the tear. Religion would evaluate those imponderables. Thus it would take the answer of both science and religion to give an adequate definition of a mother's tear.

True. But the snag is this: You can verify that which can be weighed and measured; can you verify values? Why not? You can put values into life to see what life will do with them. You can test them by experiment. If the values are real, life will approve them and back them; but if they are not real, they will wither and not be able to stand up to life; the universe will not approve them. When you live by them, you will fight a losing battle; they will let you down.

Abundant Living
(Week 2, Monday)

The Five Steps of Science
Romans 2:19-20, 14:10; Galatians 6:7-9

Can we take the same steps in verifying our knowledge of God as science takes in verifying its knowledge of things that can be weighed and measured? There are five steps in the scientific method: (1) the statement of the problem; (2) pick out of the most likely hypothesis that will meet that problem; (3) experiment with that hypothesis; (4) verify the hypothesis on a wide scale; (5) simply and humbly share verified results.

Can we take this fivefold method and apply it to the realm of value? First, state the problem. The problem is how to live in a universe of this kind, and to live well. It is a moral universe, and it seems to take sides on moral questions. In this moral universe we are free to choose, but not free to choose the results of our choosing; they are in hands other than ours. This moral universe is not something that we create out of our taboos and rules; it is something we discover; it is a "given."...

Just as Newton did not pass the law of gravity, but discovered it; so we do not pass the moral laws written in the constitution of things; we discover them. And we must come to terms with these moral laws, just as we must come to terms with the law of gravity. If not, we shall be broken. We do not break these moral laws; they break us. If we run afoul of them, they will throw us back, bleeding, broken, and blighted.

Abundant Living
(Week 2, Tuesday)

God Guides through Opening Providences and the Natural Order
1 Corinthians 2:9; 12:8; 2 Corinthians 2:12; Revelation 3:8

God guides through natural law and its discoveries through science. We have a primary faith in revelation and a secondary faith in science. But in a sense, science is revelation: God speaking to us through the natural order. That natural order is God's order. It is dependable because God is dependable. God works by law and order rather than by whim and notion and fancy. There was a time when we tried to put God in the unexplained gaps in nature; we said God must be there, for these gaps are mysterious and unexplainable. But when science began to fill up these gaps, God was pushed out. To have relegated God to those gaps was a mistake, for God reveals the divine self in the very law and order and the explainable facts of nature, and not merely in the unexplainable and the mysterious. The law and order express God far more than the unexplainable and mysterious. For this very law and order is of God. God is in it, is the author of it, works through it, but is not strait-jacketed by it. For this law and order is full of surprises and of freedoms. A closed system of nature is now unscientific. God guides through science. Accept that fact.

Abundant Living
(Week 37, Friday)

God Guides through Opening Opportunities
Acts 16:9-10; 1 Corinthians 16:8-9

Perhaps you can apply the fourfold method of science in getting guidance through an opening need or providence: first, study of the problem; second, unconscious incubation; third, emergence of the solution; fourth, verification by experimentation. Study of the problem means to gather all the information possible. Unconscious incubation means that you may get guidance through the subconscious mind. "He gives his beloved sleep" (Ps 127:2) is more correctly translated, we are told, "He gives unto his beloved in sleep." God speaks through the subconscious in sleep. You awaken in the morning and all is clear. The emergence of the solution may come through conscious or subconscious processes. When it does come, try it out, verification by experiment. If life approves of it, go on with it. You will find that life will approve only what Life approves.

The Way
(Week 41, Wednesday)

The Two Approaches to Life
Colossians 1:15-17

The discoveries of science have done nothing but corroborate Christ. For his laws are written into the nature of reality, and all the discoveries of science are but the uncovering of those laws. The Christian can stand assured and watch with breathless interest the discoveries of science, knowing that those discoveries—if they go far enough—will lead us to the feet of Christ. The God of nature and the God of grace are not two Gods; they are one God, and that one God is the Father of our Lord Jesus Christ. The laws of our universe, the laws of our minds, and the laws of our bodies are turning out to be the laws of Christ.

The Way to Power and Poise
(Week 30, Sunday)

According to the Nature of Things
John 20:26-29

The more science has grown, the more the Christian faith, rightly conceived, has grown. . . .

The discovery of the laws of being, underlying nature and human nature, is revealing the fact that these laws are the same laws written in the teaching of Jesus. When Jesus finished the Sermon on the Mount, the people were astonished at his teaching, for he taught them as "one who had authority" (literally, "according to the nature of things"; Matt 7:29). He was teaching something not imposed on life, but exposed from the very heart of life. So his teaching was supernatural naturalism; it was the revealing of supernatural laws embedded in the natural. The Christian faith is therefore not an attempt to escape the natural order, or to work above that order or in spite of it; it is an attempt to work in and through the natural order and to redeem it and make it the medium of revelation.

How to Be a Transformed Person
(Week 15, Monday)

Real Science Brings Faith
Romans 15:18-21

The facts are driving us to Christ. . . . We are on the verge of a great era of faith, and that era will be brought in by deeper and deeper explorations into the material. "Raise the stone, and thou shalt find me; cleave the wood there am I" (Henry Van Dyke, "The Toiling of Felix," [1900], part 1, prelude). And yes, look into the constitution of your being; you will find my laws written there.

I am not afraid of science being too scientific; I'm afraid it won't be scientific enough. Half-baked science brings doubt; real science brings faith.

How to Be a Transformed Person
(Week 15, Thursday)

First Commandment: Love
Matthew 5:43-36

Never was love so complete in its sweep and so deep in its depths as here defined in a few swift words: "You shall love the Lord your God with all your heart, and with all your soul, and with all your mind, and with all your strength" (Mark 12:30). Note that the total person is to love God totally: "with all your heart"—the affectional nature; "with all our soul"—the volitional, deciding nature; "with all your mind"—the intellectual nature; "with all your strength"—the physical nature. The whole person is to love God wholly—no part left out.

299

Note that Jesus put in "with all your mind." It was not in the quotation from Deuteronomy 6:5. That addition was important. It annexed the whole world of science, philosophy, and psychology in a single phrase. Had that phrase been left out, Christianity would have been on the edges of the modern world looking wistfully in, but not at home. Now it is at home in the world of science and investigation. When I was told by one of the atomic scientists at Oak Ridge, Tennessee, that more people go to church in Oak Ridge than any other place in America, I asked, "Why, are you frightened?" "No," he replied, "not frightened, but reverent. We are in the presence of a great mystery. It drives us to our knees." These people knew that love must control that energy or we perish, literally perish. The word of Jesus stood authoritative at the place of the greatest discovery of the mind of humanity: atomic energy. One of those scientists at Oak Ridge became a clergyperson, having seen the necessity of the Christian faith, with its emphasis on love, as the controlling force in an age of atomic energy. "You shall love the Lord your God...with all your mind" is an up-to-the-minute imperative.

Christian Maturity
(Week 15, Monday)

"This" and Not "That"
1 John 3:16; 4:10

Philosophy is something imposed on life, rather than something exposed out of life. Science, however, is something exposed out of life; it is a revelation of the facts and laws underlying nature....It is true that there are limitations of science, but that lack will not be supplied by philosophy; it will be supplied by a revelation of the laws underlying the world of the spirit. In other words, it will be supplied by incarnation and only by incarnation.

Christian Maturity
(Week 18, Monday)

You Do Not Need Any Facts
Luke 18:10-14

Thomas Huxley reportedly once wrote to Charles Kingsley: "Science seems to me to teach in unmistakable terms the Christian conception of entire surrender to the will of God. Science says: Sit down before the facts as a little child, be prepared to give up every preconceived notion, be willing to be led wherever nature will lead you, or you will know nothing." Scientists have to be humble, or they will never be scientists. If they come to nature proud, ready to force their views on nature and bend it to their assumptions, then nature will close up....

Cesare Cremonini (1550–1631), Italian astronomer, in order to avoid admitting his error in challenging the discovery of Jupiter's moons, refused to look through a telescope throughout the last twenty-one years of his life. Pride closed the heavens to him and shut him off from accomplishing his life work. He would not receive the kingdom of fact as a little child, and so he could not enter it. The science of astronomy swept on without him and left him isolated by pride.

So Jesus and science both demand the same thing; they both demand self-surrender, one to the Person who is the truth, the other to the facts. Pride blocks access to both.

Christian Maturity
(Week 40, Wednesday)

A Sign? The Word Became Flesh
1 Corinthians 1:22-24

The intellectual climate of the world is no longer philosophical, it is scientific. India has been the home of philosophy, and yet the students are deserting courses on philosophy and turning to science. Philosophy is based on speculations; science is based on specifications. The Christian faith is based on the specific, on the Word become flesh. So it is at home in the world of science. It is its native air. It brings the spiritual out of the hazy into the happenings, out of mystery into mastery.

The Word Became Flesh
(Week 17, Thursday)

A Prescription for Health: The Nine Beatitudes
Psalm 38:3-8

We are emphasizing the will to be well. . . .

But the will to health must not be the willing of the will only; it must be the willing of the total person. There are two extremes in regard to finding of health: one to depend on science alone, the other to depend on miracle alone. Both of these bring disappointment. There is a third way, the way that obeys the laws of health on the one hand and depends on the resources of God on the other. These are the alternate beats of the healthy Christian heart.

The Word Became Flesh
(Week 42, Thursday)

FREEDOM

Our Freedom Complicates God's Game
John 4:34; 1 Corinthians 16:13; Galatians 2:21

In this freedom of ours lays God's problem and possibility. Our freedom is a problem to God. Someone has put it this way: "Here is a chessboard, and all the figures on the board, instead of being made of wood, are flesh and blood with wills of their own. The game for God would be simple if the figures would go where God desires them to go. But suppose, when God makes a move in the game against evil, that the figures balk and refuse to move, and instead move on their own, to other positions, without reference to the Player-God. That would complicate the game and mess it up badly." That has happened, and that is God's problem.

But our freedom is also God's possibility. Suppose those figures should learn that failure and mix-ups come through moves on their own and refuse to cooperate with the Player, and should thus be chastened into choosing cooperation with the Player. Then, suppose God and humanity should play the game in cooperation—and win! How much finer that would be than to win against evil with only wooden pawns to play with!

You and I can cooperate with God, can align our wills with God's will, can make God's wisdom our own, and in the end can make the victory a joint victory. What a possibility for God and us!

Abundant Living
(Week 3, Wednesday)

Evil Is a Parasite upon the Good
Genesis 18:23-32

We must spend one more day on the self-destructiveness of evil, for many have the idea that goodness is bondage and that evil is freedom. But we know that evil is freedom only to get into trouble with ourselves.

Abundant Living
(Week 50, Wednesday)

The Kingdom of God Is Totalitarian
1 Corinthians 15:24-28

The kingdom of God is a completely totalitarian order, demanding a total obedience in the total life. It was presented to the individual will; it was presented to the collective will: "The kingdom of God will be taken away from you and given to a nation producing the fruits of it" (Matt 21:43). "But," cries my reader, "we are getting rid of one totalitarianism, and you are introducing us to another, even more thoroughgoing and absolute." True. But there is this profound difference: When you obey the kingdom of God, you find perfect freedom. When you obey other totalitarianisms, you find perfect bondage, for they are not the way you are made to live. When you obey the kingdom of God, you find perfect self-fulfillment.

The Way
(Week 9, Thursday)

A Dangerous Libertinism?
Romans 6:1-6

Consider this passage: "The grace of God...schools us to renounce...and to live a life of self-mastery" (Titus 2:12 Moffatt). The grace of God schools us! Here free grace puts us to school! And the severest of schools. It disciplines the inmost thought and the outmost act and everything between. You accept the grace of God, and by that very act, you accept self-control—rather, self-control through God-control. You are free to act within God's control, which is perfect freedom.

The Way
(Week 28, Tuesday)

From Frustration to Fruitfulness
Acts 8:6-8

O God, I thank you that your dominance is my freedom. I'm free to be myself since you have me. I'm grateful, so grateful. Amen.

How to Be a Transformed Person
(Week 6, Tuesday)

Lost through Deliberate Choice
Thessalonians 5:9-10

The prodigal son was "lost" through his own deliberate choices. He decided to leave his father. Why? He was under the illusion that his father's will was bondage and his own will was freedom. The central illusion in life is this: we think our way is freedom and God's way is bondage. That is hell's cleverest twist: "No," said the serpent to the woman, "you shall not die; God knows that on the day you eat from it your eyes will be opened and you will be like gods" (Gen 3:4-5 Moffat). "Like gods"—free to do as you like! No bondage, no direction from another! Free! But from that day to this that freedom is the freedom to leave paradise, freedom to hide in fear from God and yourself, freedom to tie yourself up in knots, freedom to be a problem to yourself and others. God's will is our freedom; our will against God's will is our bondage; and there are no exceptions—none....

God's will alone is freedom. That is the deepest lesson of life. If you don't know that lesson, you don't know how to live.

How to Be a Transformed Person
(Week 16, Wednesday)

The Central Revolt
Luke 15:13-14

I am amazed beyond words that the father acceded to the request [for his son to receive his share of the father's inheritance] and "divided unto them his living" (Luke 15:12 KJV). Why didn't he refuse and thus protect the son against himself? This granting of human freedom is a mystery, but was there anything else to be done? If he had refused, the son would be revolting still, would be in the far country even while still in the father's house. For the far country is a condition before it is a place, just as hell is a condition before it is a place.

God gives us the awful power to ruin ourselves. On what condition? The condition is that God gets into the whole transaction, suffers in Godself the consequences of our wrong choices, makes them God's own and redeems us through that identification. The cross is the acute point of that identification where the continuous fact comes to light in history.

The decision once made, the son "gathered all together" (v. 13), and went into the far country; he would put outer distance between him and his father as the outer expression of the inner distance. The outer and the inner sooner or later become one. Life becomes all of a piece.

How to Be a Transformed Person
(Week 17, Monday)

The Mastery of Prejudice
2 Kings 5:10-14

"All belongs to you; Paul, Apollos, Cephas, the world, life, death, the present and the future—all belongs to you; and you belong to Christ, and Christ to God" (1 Cor 3:21-23 Moffatt). Never was there such absolute freedom to possess and appropriate. All things belong to you: all great teachers—Paul, Apollos, Cephas; all great facts—the world, life, death; all time—the present and the future; all things belong to you! What was the secret of this freedom of spirit? Strange enough, it was found in a complete narrowness: "you belong to Christ." Then belonging to him, everything belongs to you! Strange way to make us free, isn't it? Christ binds us in complete submission to him and then turns us loose! With one point of the compass resting in him, the other point could sweep as wide into truth as it could go! Sure of the center, you are free to appropriate the circumference.

Mastery
(Week 46, Sunday)

Openly and Unhindered
John 15:18-25

The thing Paul lived for was not physical freedom but freedom to preach. If the gospel was free to be uttered, he was free. The end of his life was accomplished. So this tame ending was a triumphant ending. He came through "not somehow but triumphantly."

Paul had one purpose in life. He utters it in these words:

And now...I am going to Jerusalem, bound in the Spirit, not knowing what shall befall me there; except that the Holy Spirit testifies to me in every city that imprisonment and afflictions await me. But I do not account my life of any value nor as precious to myself, if only I may accomplish my course and the ministry which I received from the Lord Jesus, to testify to the gospel of the grace of God. (20:22-24 RSV)

Mastery
(Week 48, Tuesday)

Micah 6:6-7—We Try to Restore Fellowship
Michah 6:6-7

This is a universe that is not indifferent to your virtue or your vice. It takes sides. You are free to choose, but you are not free to choose the results or the consequences of your choices. They are in hands not your own. You do not break these laws written into the nature of things; you break yourself on them. And these laws are color-blind, race-blind, and religion-blind. Break them and you get broken.

Christian Maturity
(Week 14, Monday)

"Primary Nature" and "Secondary Nature"
Romans 7:18-20

Though love is the basic urge in us, why do we do unlovely things and land in unlovely messes? We find the answer in the fact that freedom lies in the self. And that self can throw the switch, turning love toward the self and producing a self-centered person, toward the herd and producing a herd-centered person. The choice is always ours.

But the question still arises, why do we make such senseless choices and land ourselves in such senseless miseries? Can freedom of choice account for it all? Is there something within us, innate or acquired, which leans toward evil?

In a quotation by Montagu there is this suggestion:

> It is primary, and it also should be sound nature, for human beings to love one another. As it is, primary nature remains striving to love and be loved, while second nature often puts calculated restraints upon such striving and erects barriers deliberately designed to prevent its expression. All this because the true meaning of love has not been understood. (Ashley Montagu, *The Meaning of Love* [New York: Julian Press, 1953], 18)

Here he makes a distinction between "primary nature" and "second nature." Primary nature wants to love; second nature often wants to block it because it hasn't "understood."

Have we, as a human race, built up a second nature through ages of contact with and the freedom to choose evil? And does this second nature have a bent toward evil? Is there then a conflict within us between primary nature, which is agape love, and second nature, which is perverted love? Religion answers by calling this second nature "original sin." Note that it doesn't say "original nature," but "original sin." Sin is not nature; it is an alien introduction into nature. God made us in God's own image, hence good. But we, by our freedom of choice, have built up a second nature. That second nature is really not "nature"; it is an acquired, unnatural imposition on nature. It is the unnatural becoming seemingly natural.

Christian Maturity
(Week 24, Sunday)

305

Can "Second Nature" Be Wiped Out?
Romans 7:24-25

We are considering whether we can be free from this "second nature," and then become single-natured, and hence a unified person? The answer is yes! Paul, after describing the two natures in the seventh chapter of Romans, proclaims his freedom in the eighth chapter: "For the law of the Spirit of life in Christ Jesus has set me free from the law of sin and death" (8:2). The "law of sin" in his "flesh" has been canceled, and he is under a new law: "the law of the Spirit of life in Christ Jesus."

What had been built up—the second nature—had been torn down. The primary nature remained intact, but that primary nature is now controlled by "the law of the Spirit of life in Christ Jesus." The primary nature is created by God; the second nature is created by humanity. In redemption, the original abides and the imported [or secondary] goes.

Christian Maturity
(Week 24, Tuesday)

With Liberty and Justice for All
Luke 3:5-6

[Someone said]: "It is impossible to enslave a Bible-reading people." The ideas of freedom, of the dignity of a child of God, of equality before God and therefore before people, are bound to make slavery of any kind impossible. Maybe not today, not tomorrow, but the third day, Yes! "I saw thrones, and [people] sat upon them" (Rev 20:4 KJV); the people will rule, and it doesn't say which people, but just people!

Christian Maturity
(Week 30, Monday)

We Are Not Independent
Galatians 5:13-14

It is only a question of time when all people, everywhere, will be free, free to determine the course of their own national lives. And I want everyone, everywhere, to be free, since I am free only in the freedoms of all people. I am bound in the bondages of all.

Christian Maturity
(Week 31, Thursday)

Why Did God Create Us Free?
Genesis 1:26-27

We continue our meditations on the cross as the revelation of the heart of reality. I have often wondered why God dared to create us and to create us free. It was a risky business for God and the creatures created. To make us free would mean that God would have to be limited. God would have to step back and allow that free will to operate. God could not coerce it; if so the will would not be free. And the will would have to be free in both directions; it must be free to choose evil as well as good or it would not be free.

To be able to choose in one direction only is not freedom. But suppose that free will should go wrong; it would break its own heart and the heart of God too. For God would have to live alongside that straying, rebellious will as love. And it is the nature of love to insinuate itself into the sins and sorrows of the loved one and make them its own. If love stays out of the sins and sorrows of the loved one, it is no longer love. But if it gets in, it bleeds. All love has the doom of bleeding upon it as long as there is sin in the loved one.

The Word Became Flesh

(Week 14, Tuesday)

God's Totalitarianism = Freedom; Human Totalitarianism = Bondage
Romans 14:17-19

If we obey totally God's totalitarianism, we find total freedom. Bound to God, I walk the earth free; low at God's feet, I stand straight before everything else. This is an essential difference between God's totalitarianism and ours. If you obey totally human totalitarianism—Fascism, Nazism, Communism—you find total bondage. This is then its final doom, for people are inherently made for freedom and will finally revolt against chains.

The Word Became Flesh

(Week 45, Wednesday)

You Can Love and Like a Christ-Centered Self
Matthew 20:25-27

The highest freedom—the freedom to surrender yourself to God, results in the highest freedom—the freedom to know God and yourself and life and everything. You are free indeed, free to live.

The Word Became Flesh

(Week 47, Tuesday)

HEALTH

Empty Futility amid Plenty
Luke 12:22-31

Many people "spend the first half of their lives expending health to gain wealth and the second half of their lives expending wealth to gain health."

The Way
(Week 23, Saturday)

Steps to Abounding Energy
Psalms 40:1-3; 41:3; 56:12-13

The Africans have a saying, "Don't be tired tomorrow." Don't anticipate tiredness. Affirm health and adequacy. Autosuggestion? Yes, and good autosuggestion. Far better to suggest health than suggest sickness.

The Way
(Week 37, Saturday)

Acid in Her, Not in the Peaches
1 Thessalonians 4:3-8

The Spirit of God is health. When the Spirit indwells us, then life is poured into every fiber of our being. We become alive, to our finger tips. The diseased portions tend to become well; the normal portions become better; all becomes quickened. A health tendency takes possession of us. We think health; we breathe health; we are health, and we give health. When I was going through a physical crisis about thirty years ago, I heard a Spirit-filled Indian person say, "When the Spirit of God dwells in you, then you can preach five and six times a day without being tired." I wondered at it then, for I was spiritually and physically floundering, but today I do not wonder at it. It is a fact. There is a physical rejuvenation taking place constantly when we are in tune with the Spirit "so that the life of Jesus may be manifested in our mortal flesh" (2 Cor 4:11). Christian bodies are healthier and more rhythmical than any others.

The Way to Power and Poise
(Week 22, Thursday)

To Home Ourselves in God
Philippians 4:11-13

Think faith, talk faith, act faith. Someone has suggested this for a good model of suggestion to yourself: "Every day, in every way, God is giving me health." That emphasizes the fact that God is giving, and you are receiving; the source of health is in God. That relaxes you before God, opens every pore of your being to the health of God. For where God is, there is health, if we can receive it. Be on the receiving end, and you will be on the giving end.

The Way to Power and Poise
(Week 51, Saturday)

Then She Is Very Ill

Psalm 139:23; Isaiah 55:7

I do not believe that you affirm out of existence all evil and all sickness by mere affirmation. Some diseases are structural, and changing your mind about them will not change the facts. But the mind does have a tremendous influence upon the body and its health....

If you are always talking about your illnesses, you'll have a lot of illnesses to talk about. As someone has put it, "When a woman thinks she is ill when she is not, then she is very ill." If you have a mental image of yourself as ill and depressed, then you'll be made in the likeness of that "wanted" illness. But if you think health and affirm health, then you are health. I have sometimes played the game with myself—as I walk from a train carrying suitcases that are far too heavy for me to carry, and no porter in sight—of imagining myself raising those suitcases above my head and carrying them along in that triumphant fashion. The actual carrying then seems easier. Autosuggestion? Yes, of course. You're always suggesting something to yourself: victory or defeat, health or sickness. Why not suggest the constructive instead of the destructive? Your very organs will respond if you talk health to them instead of sickness. They will blush with pride, and the very blushing will send the health-giving blood coursing through them. But if you think sickness to your organs, they will blush with fear and the bloodless organs will turn sick for want of blood.

How to Be a Transformed Person
(Week 20, Friday)

Growth in Bodily Health

Exodus 15:26; 23, 25

The Christian faith is not a success cult, a happiness cult, or a healing cult. Its central purpose is to redeem humanity primarily from sin and evil; as a byproduct of that redemption, it brings true success, true happiness, and true healing. If we seek health first, we will lose it; it will evade us. But if we seek first the kingdom of God, then all these things, including health, will be added to us.

For God wills health. Disease is not the will of God. Disease of the body is no more the will of God than disease of the soul. God is out to get rid of evil in all its ugly forms. The evil of the mind is error; the evil of the emotion is suffering; the evil of the body is disease; the evil of the soul is sin. And God is out to root out all evil from all of life, including the evil of the body, disease. "However disease may be brought about and in whatever way it may be ruled for good, it is in itself an evil" (reportedly from the 1920 Lambeth Conference of the Church of England). And Jesus came to banish evil in all its forms.

Growing Spiritually
(Week 33, Sunday)

Emotions Upset the Stomach
James 5:13-16

So if you are going to be a healthy person, you cannot hold emotions of anger and resentment. The metabolism is allergic to them. They do not fit, so they fight! Our metabolism is made for love and good will, not for hate and fear. Love sets up the system, and hate upsets it. Therefore you must choose. You cannot have hate and health, or fear and fitness.

Growing Spiritually
(Week 34, Tuesday)

Self-Preoccupation Produces Ill Health
Proverbs 17:22; Isaiah 58:8

If you are to be healthy, you must give up all self-preoccupation. You must get interests outside of yourself. You must love others.

Growing Spiritually
(Week 34, Wednesday)

Overboard with a Lot of Impedimenta
John 5:5-9

Health is not a vacuum, an absence of disease; it is a something that we can have and that we can give. Jesus speaks of "a soul...breathing peace" (Luke 10:6 Moffatt), a lovely phrase! So we can be people breathing health. In breathing we take in and give out. So we can breathe in health from God and breathe out health upon others. We can be the centers of health and of health-giving influences.

Growing Spiritually
(Week 35, Sunday)

Steps to Health
John 9:1-7

We come now to the steps we can take in having and giving health. First, think health, not disease. If our thoughts penetrate to the marrow of our very bones, then let those thoughts be thoughts of health and not of disease. You can think health or think disease into your very inmost cells. So think health.

Is this autosuggestion? Yes, of course it is. We are always suggesting to ourselves something. Then let that something be health. That is not self-deception. The thinking of health opens the channels of your being to the permeation of health through your being. The thinking of disease ties up those channels through fear and blocks the permeation of health through you. The body in its inner structure is made for health, not disease.... The body was conceived by God in health, made for health, and provided with almost every contrivance possible for the warding off of disease. So when we think health, we are not moonshining; we are sunshining. We are thinking along the lines that God laid down in the structure of our beings, so we are thinking according to the grain of the facts concerned and not against them.

But when we think disease, we are thinking contrary to nature, therefore unnaturally. When we think health, we are thinking naturally; and when we think disease, we are thinking unnaturally. When you think health, you are aligning yourself with the natural, healing forces of the universe.

But when you think disease, you are alien to the natural healing forces of the universe. You are running counter to God's intention; therefore you are resistant to redemption, the redemption of the total person.

Growing Spiritually
(Week 35, Monday)

Glance at Disease, Gaze at Health
John 9:18-25

I know it is not possible always to see health, for you may be constantly confronted with disease in yourself and others. But it depends on where your gaze is fixed. Glance at disease, but gaze at health. In the office of a doctor who was constantly dealing with people who had trouble with their hearts, real or imaginary, there was a model of a healthy heart right in front of the doctor as he talked to these ailing people. He constantly reminded himself of a healthy heart instead of a diseased one. It kept his vision clear.

Growing Spiritually
(Week 35, Tuesday)

Be Receptive to Health
Matthew 9:19-22

We come now to the last step in growth in bodily health.

Learn to accept the healing grace of God through receptive faith. God heals in many ways: through the physician and the surgeon; through climate; through mental suggestion; through deliverance from underlying fears, resentments, self-preoccupation, and guilts that can produce disease. Then God heals by the direct touch of the Spirit of God upon our bodies. This is not faith healing; it is divine healing through receptive faith. The faith does not heal, but faith opens the channels so God can heal.

Growing Spiritually
(Week 35, Saturday)

The Main Emphasis on Redemption from Sin
Psalm 73:23-26

The healing of disease is a part of the application of the gospel to life. Jesus came to banish evil—all evil. The evil of the mind is error; the evil of the emotions is suffering; the evil of the body is disease; the evil of the soul is sin. Disease is not the will of God; it is an enemy to be banished.

Mastery
(Week 31, Saturday)

His Religion Is Producing Tension
Romans 7:22-25

We have seen that there is a truth in karma, the law of sowing and reaping. There is also a truth in salvation and health through affirmation, through being positive. Negative attitudes bring negative results. If you affirm disease—the negative of health—you'll probably have disease. Our lives, like the hands of a dyer, are colored by that with which we work. If the atmosphere of your mind is pessimistic, fearful, and negative; your body, mind, and spirit will be affected by it. You, as a person, will become negative.

Christian Maturity
(Week 13, Tuesday)

Bodily Health and Healing
Daniel 8:27; 10:8

[What about] the art of receiving bodily health and healing. Many are mature at the place of receiving spiritual life for their souls, but don't know how to receive physical life for their bodies. They have compartmentalized the power of their faith, confining it to the spiritual, allowing it to function only faintly in the material. Our faith should function in the total person. Jesus said to a sick man: "Wilt thou be made whole?" (John 5:6 KJV). One would have expected him to say: "Wilt thou be healed of thy sickness?" But Jesus was interested in something more than healing disease. He wanted people to be "whole," of which the healing of sickness was a part. The fact is that sickness cannot be cured unless the total person is cured. For if there is sickness in any portion of the person—in spirit, mind, emotion, or body—it will pass over to the other portions (of the body) and infect them.

Christian Maturity
(Week 47, Sunday)

Some Ideas We Must Give Up
Psalm 32:3-4

[What are the] wrong mental attitudes that we must change if we are to be healthy.…We must give up the notion that God will pass a miracle over us and heal us without our cooperation in giving up thinking and emotions that produce disease. The promising of healing to people, regardless of whether they give up wrong thinking and emotions, has left behind a lot of disillusionment and wreckage of faith.…We must give up the notion that healing can only be sudden, on-the spot healing. It does sometimes work that way, but more often it works gradually as we cooperate with God in eliminating the causes of the disease.…We must renounce the attitude that we can skip the healing of spirit and take the healing of the body.…The healing starts from the mind in letting go of wrong thinking, passes on to the spirit where wrong attitudes and emotions are changed with the change of the mind, and finally it gets to the body.…We must give up the idea of trying to deal with symptoms and go down to the disease. For instance, we are told that enough sleeping pills were sold last year [1956] in the United States to put every man, woman, and child to sleep for twenty-three days. And all those sleeping pills did not do a bit of permanent good. For underneath this sleeplessness, except in the case for the physically ill, was a conflict within that caused the inability to sleep.

If these are some examples of the wrong thinking we must let go, what are some right mental attitudes we must take on if we are to be well? Someone asked me, "What is the secret of your amazing health?" It has been amazing, for I've been speaking from two to five times a day for forty years, with no vacations except to work on a book, and yet I seem to be in perfect health. I replied, "Well, I suppose it is because I have learned the art of receptivity. I take grace not only for my spirit, but for my mind and body as well."

Christian Maturity
(Week 47, Wednesday)

Crutches
Psalm 38:5, 8, 10

The next thing I would suggest in order to maintain health is right habits of rest. In a National Preaching Mission, a prominent member of the team, after two weeks, came down to breakfast and announced that he was "across the ropes" and would have to quit and go home. Why? He would stay up until midnight talking over problems with ministers and others. At ten o'clock, I would excuse myself and go to bed. For I've found that "he who talks and runs away may live to talk another day." Right habits of rest and recuperation are necessary. Prolonged periods of rest and recuperation are not necessary if you have right thinking, right emotions, right habits that enable you to receive grace continuously. Those who know, say that if you give nature twenty-four hours of complete rest and relaxation it will balance the accounts, throwing off all fatigue toxins within that period. If, after twenty-four hours, you are still tired it is a tiredness of the mind and spirit, not of the body. Of course, if there is a structural disease the matter is different.

Christian Maturity
(Week 47, Friday)

By All the Stimulus of Christ

Here is a meaningful verse: "So if there is any encouragement in Christ, any incentive of love, any participation in the Spirit, any affection and sympathy, complete my joy by being of the same mind, having the same love, being in full accord and of one mind" (Phil 2:1-2)....

This portion, "if there is any encouragement in Christ," is translated by Moffatt, "By all the stimulus of Christ."...

A woman confronted with many diseases said to her doctor, "With all the germs and diseases around us everywhere, I don't see how we can ever be well." The wise doctor replied, "Knowing the human body as I do, I wonder why anyone should ever be sick." The resources for health are laid up in the body. In view of the stimulus of Christ, I refuse to accept my tiredness, my age, my retirement, my slow-down. In him I am well and whole. I am as strong as my strength to receive, as able as my ability to appropriate, as alive as my receptivity to his stimulus. Note [the verse] says *all* the stimulus of Christ; his "all" is sufficient for my all, and then some!

In Christ
(Week 35, Saturday)

Can the Flesh Be Redeemed?
Matthew 8:16-17

I have often imagined a convention of bodies talking about the people who inhabit them. A body stands up and says, "Oh my, the man who inhabits me doesn't know how to live. He is full of fears, resentments, self-centeredness, and guilts. He ties me in knots, and then doses me with all sorts of medicines that have no relationship with what is wrong with me. There is nothing wrong with me. He upsets my functioning. I wish he knew how to live."

Another body stands up and says, "It's wonderful to live with the woman I live with. She is rhythmical, harmonious, and adjusted. We get along famously together, and I do prodigious things for her. It's a joy to do it."

Suppose your body would stand up and speak about you; would you enjoy hearing what was said? The doctors tell us that at least 75 percent of all diseases are homegrown ills, and patients will never be well unless they change their attitudes toward life. Their life climate is wrong for health.

The Word Became Flesh
(Week 42, Sunday)

JUSTICE

The Wisdom of the Just
Psalm 72:2; Isaiah 1:27; Amos 5:24

We saw that the deepest need was to set judgment, or social justice, into human affairs. This passage concerning John the Baptist emphasizes the same: "He will...turn the hearts of the fathers to the children, and the disobedient to the wisdom of the just, to make ready for the Lord a people prepared" (Luke 1:17)....

Note that phrase,—"the wisdom of the just." It is a truism to say that what the poor and the dispossessed need is not charity but justice, but it needs to be said again and again. We have seen the unwisdom of injustice. We have built a society in which those in control have intercepted the gains brought by science and technology and have kept them from passing on to the people....

A basic, thoroughgoing justice for everybody would be social wisdom. If we will not listen to this word from the sacred Book, then we must listen to it spoken by the fiery tongues of a world in flames. For God speaks! And the wisdom of the just is God's message.

Victorious Living
(Week 26, Thursday)

Judgment unto Victory
Habakkuk 2:4-14; Matthew 15:13; Luke 10:18; Colossians 2:15

I do not say that it will cost nothing to be just. You will have to have the selfish self knocked out before you can become fundamentally just and willing to give everybody an equal opportunity. It will mean a real renunciation—a community of sharing.

Victorious Living
(Week 26, Friday)

Magnificent Obsession
Matthew 14:44-46; Acts 5:19-20; 1 Timothy 4:15

I am obsessed with the idea that poverty could end for all, for we have both the knowledge and the instruments of science to do it. We have everything to do it, everything except the collective will. The kingdom of God would mean that the collective will would be turned toward abolishing that poverty.

Victorious Living
(Week 38, Tuesday)

Working with and for Others
1 Corinthians 3:3-9; Colossians 4:11; 3 John 5-8

Just generosity produces stability. Injustice and inequality produce instability, for they are working against the kingdom; hence they break down.

Abundant Living
(Week 29, Saturday)

315

The Redemptionists
Matthew 1:18-20; Luke 1:5-7, 13-17

"The Redemptionists" [was a group movement] made up of those who were "looking for the redemption of Israel" (Luke 2:38)....

We can trace the Redemptionists in the opening chapters of Luke's gospel by the family likeness of ideas running through them all. The group may have included Zechariah and Elizabeth, Mary and Joseph, Simeon, Anna, the shepherds (see Luke 1–2). They were intensely nationalistic, and yet they were agents of a new order based on equality of opportunity to everybody. The word *just* runs like a refrain through the account of all of them. They stood for a justice that made for equality for everybody. Zechariah and Elizabeth were "both just" (Luke 1:6 Moffatt). The angels spoke to Zechariah of the "wisdom of the just" (v. 17)—a phrase that should burn itself into modern civilization; to be just is to be wise, to be unjust is to be unwise. Joseph was "a just man," but with a new kind of justice: "her husband was a just man and unwilling to disgrace her" (Matt 1:19 Moffatt). Here was a justice that was mercy, that was redemptive, and not punitive. The angels said to the shepherds, "Peace on earth, good will to men" (Luke 1:14 KJV), good will to men; not to some, but to all, apart from race and birth and color.

Abundant Living
(Week 38, Monday)

A Ladder for Mastery over Money
Psalm 62:10; Proverbs 23:4; Jeremiah 9:23-24; Mark 4:18-19; Luke 12:16-21;
1 Timothy 6:6-12, 17-19

The poor need not charity, but justice. When you give charity, you are the bountiful patron; the poor are the recipients. When you give justice, your relationships change; you become equals. It is easy to be charitable; it is difficult to be just.

Abundant Living
(Week 43, Friday)

A Ladder for Mastery over Money
Malachi 3:7-10; Mark 10:17-27; Acts 20:35; 1 Corinthians 16:2; 2 Corinthians 9:1-15

When the level of your needs has been reached, then all you earn belongs to the needs of others, not as charity, but as right and justice.

Abundant Living
(Week 43, Saturday)

Good Friday Meditation
John 15:13; 19:16-18; Romans 5:6-11

There is a justice higher than legal justice—justice in which it is right for the strong, at cost to itself, to save the weak; it is right for the holy to save the unholy. This is the law of higher justice.

Abundant Living

The Way of Transformation
Psalm 139:7-12

Life will come to us as justice and injustice, pleasure and pain, compliment and criticism. We must be ready to take hold of it as it comes and make something else out of it. In that way you face life with no subterfuges, no dodging out of difficulties, no rationalization; you face life honestly and simply and masterfully.

The Way to Power and Poise
(Week 29, Thursday)

The Kingdom Is God's Total Answer
Mathew 6:33; Acts 16:25:34

[Another life conviction is] the way to meet unmerited suffering and injustice is not to bear them, but to use them. When I saw that possibility years ago through this verse, "That will turn out an opportunity for you to bear witness" (Luke 21:13 Moffatt)—the unjust bringing you before judges and governors to be tried—an entirely new world opened before me. I had been trying to explain suffering, and now I saw that we are not to explain it, but to use it. Everything that happens to you—good, bad, or indifferent—can contribute to you if you know how to use it. Everything furthers those who follow Christ, provided they know how to set their sails. All winds blow you to your goal. It is the set of the soul that does it. When you know this secret, you are afraid of nothing, because you can use everything. That makes you march up to every human happening, with the possibility tucked away in your mind of plucking a blessing out of the heart of everything.

Growing Spiritually
(Week 51, Thursday)

MENTAL HEALTH/PSYCHOLOGY
(AS A CHALLENGE FACING SOCIETY)

The Kingdom Written Within
Jeremiah 31:33; Romans 2:14-16; 2 Corinthians 3:1-8

What does the psychologist mean when by saying, "To be frank and honest in all relations, but especially in relations with oneself, is the first law of mental hygiene." Doesn't that mean that the universe and you and I are built for truth, that the universe won't back a lie, that all lies sooner or later break themselves upon the facts of things? Since the kingdom stands for absolute truth, and our own mental make-up demands the same thing, then are not the laws of the kingdom written within us?

Again, what does the psychologist mean by, "The right thing is always the healthy thing?" Conversely, one might say that the wrong thing is always the unhealthy thing, meaning thereby that we cannot be healthy, cannot function at our best unless we discover the right and obey it.

Victorious Living
(Week 2, Thursday)

How Can We Arrive at the Goal of Inward Unity?
Matthew 6:22; Ephesians 4:1-6; James 4:8

If there is one thing that both modern psychology and the way of Christ agree on, it is this: Apart from inward unity there can be no personal happiness and no effective living.

Jesus said, "Every kingdom divided against itself is brought to desolation" (Matt 12:25 KJV). That simple statement has within it all the depths of wisdom that modern psychology has discovered from the facts of the inner life. Divided personality, inward clash, these are the things that bring desolation to human personality.

Many say to the distracted soul, "Pull yourself together." This is futile advice when there are mutually exclusive things within us. They won't be pulled together....

"Exert your will," counsels another. But suppose the will, which expresses the personality in action, is itself divided? Again futility....

So we toil in rowing, trying to get to the land of inward unity. We are tossed by many a wind and many a wave. And it gets very dark. Then Jesus quietly comes. We more easily let him in this time, for there seems no other alternative. The soul seems instinctively to feel, "The Master has come." He gathers up the inward distinctions, cleanses away the points of conflict, and unifies life around himself. We have arrived.

Victorious Living
(Week 3, Saturday)

POVERTY

An Unchristian Social Order
Psalm 1:1; Micah 2:1-2; Habakkuk 2:12-14

The psychoanalysts stress the fact that the cause of maladjustment to life is within the individual, and some schools of psychologists stress the environmental factors as responsible for maladjustment of the individual. Both assumptions are true, for the individual and the environment act and react upon each other. But if I had to choose between them, I think I should have to conclude that an unchristian social order produces more thwarted and disrupted lives than any other single cause. A dean of girls in a public school told me that the three major factors in producing problem children are "poverty, broken homes, and a lack of attendance to Sunday school or church"—all social factors.

Abundant Living
(Week 26, Sunday)

Too Little and Too Much, Alike Harmful
Proverbs 11:24; 30:8; 2 Corinthians 9:5-12

Seek first the kingdom of God! We must continue our examination of the material basis of the spiritual life. God has written into the constitution of things that too little and too much are alike, and equally, dangerous. I say "alike and equally," for the facts bear out the truth of that. We all see the devastating effects of poverty; they are manifest in sickly bodies, stunted minds, and problem souls. It is true that, here and there, a person can struggle against grinding poverty; make it sharpen the wits, determination, ability, and rise through obstruction to achievement. But where one triumphs, a dozen are broken or stunted by poverty. Let not our boasting about the achievement of the one, blind us to the devastation to the many. Poverty is wrong, for it produces wrongs to body, mind, and soul.

But if poverty is wrong, so are riches. The latter is not so easily seen, for it is covered up by refinements, by culture, by things, by the glamour of prestige and power.

Abundant Living
(Week 31, Friday)

Give Us This Day
2 Corinthians 8:15; 9:6-10

If we get the kingdom values straight, then we can pray [the Lord's Prayer] with some assurance: "Give us this day our daily bread" (Matt 6:9-13). If we seek "first the kingdom of God," all these things—food, clothing, all we need—"shall be added" (Matt 6:33 KJV). The coming of the kingdom of God would be the answer to the economic needs of humanity. For we would then pray, "Give us." Now we are saying, in an individualistic, selfish age: "Give me." If we continue to look after none but ourselves, think first of No. 1, then we ourselves will become Enemy No. 1. And we'll have to think of ourselves so much that we will become sick of ourselves, our complexes, and our obsessions. That will be our punishment. We asked for ourselves, and we got ourselves a problem. For the first time in history, humanity has become its own problem. Why? Because we has said, "Give me." Note that "Give me" was the first request that sent the prodigal to hunger amid swine. We have become a prodigal generation for the same reason. And we will get out of this alien "far country" and beyond "poverty amid plenty" only when we pray the prayer, "Give us." For to say, "Give us" would mean the following out of the opening words, "Our Father." It would mean a cooperative order instead of a ruthlessly competitive one. Nature would work with us.

The Way
(Week 29, Saturday)

Maturity in Spiritual Contagion
Acts 4:18-20

We now turn to another phase of maturity—a very important phase—maturity in spiritual contagion. Unless our maturity results in spiritual contagion it stops this side of maturity; it is immature maturity. For the end objective of life seems to be the production of life.

Franz Alexander, a psychiatrist, says:

> All energy which is not needed to maintain life can be considered as surplus energy....This surplus of energy shows itself in the mature person in generosity, the result of the strength and overflow which the individual can no longer use for further growth and which therefore can be spent productively and creatively. The mature person is no longer primarily a receiver. He receives but he also gives. His giving is not primarily subordinated to his expectation of return. It is giving for its own sake....In the light of this view, altruism, the basis of Christian morality, has a biological foundation; it is a natural, healthy expression of the state of surplus characteristic for maturity. (*Emotional Maturity* [Austin, TX: The Hogg Foundation for Mental Health, 6th ed., 1967], 4)

Mature persons are sharers of surplus by their very maturity as a mature persons. If they are not sharer they show their basic immaturity. And this works back upon itself; the more we share the more mature we become.

We can share our spiritual life in many ways: in helping to relieve poverty and in removing the cause of poverty, in various forms of church and community work, in cleaning up civic situations, in youth organizations, and in just being helpful and kind. But these are marginal ways of sharing; the central method of sharing is the sharing of the highest, Christ. The central method of sharing is winning others to him. Evangelism is the central expression of the evangel.

Christian Maturity
(Week 45, Sunday)

RACE

Another Cause of Sin—Race Prejudice
Amos 9:7; Luke 4:22-29; Acts 10:84-85; Colossians 3:11

Race prejudice is self-starvation....

[In India,] I opened the door of my heart to the people of another race and of a different color of skin, and outside of the influence of Christ. It has proved to be the most enriching experience of my life. What love, what friendships, what wisdom, what Christlikeness, what nobility have come to me during these years through that open door!

Victorious Living
(Week 23, Sunday)

Concerning Class and Race Relations
Colossians 3:10-11; Acts 10:34-35; 17:26

[Regarding] your class and race relationships. Perhaps class feeling and race feeling, not Christ, have been determining your conduct.

The Way
(Week 12, Wednesday)

Unity of All Races
Ephesians 2:11-13; Acts 10:28

Unity of all races: "All who believed were together" (Acts 2:44). If we look at the races present in that "together," we will see that the whole of that ancient world was represented: Mesopotamia, Africa and Europe (see vv. 9-11). All races and all colors were represented in that togetherness. Under the Spirit's touch, humankind felt its essential kinship and its essential oneness. They looked on people of another race, not as a problem, but as a possibility. A new sense of the worthwhileness of a person as a person had come into life.

We are now discovering that the differences between races is not inherent, but cultural. Given the same stimulus, the races will come out at about the same place. The differences are in the cultural inheritance and the response to that inheritance. There are no permanently superior races, and there are no permanently inferior races.

The Way to Power and Poise
(Week 20, Sunday)

Not Solved, but Dissolved
Acts 19:18-20

Lord, I thank you for the fellowship of those who care, care without regard to race or class. Help me to find such a fellowship, or make one, by caring beyond race and class. Amen.

The Way to Power and Poise
(Week 48, Saturday)

Are We in the Grip of Kismet?
Genesis 3:8-13

The laws of God don't listen to our attempted evasions. They are color-blind, class-blind, race-blind, religion-blind. We don't break them; we break ourselves on them.

How to Be a Transformed Person
(Week 1, Wednesday)

The We in Race Relations
Galatians 3:26-28

We continue to look at the transformation from the *they–I* relationship to the *we* relationship.

This is at the basis of our race difficulties; we are trying to live on a *they–I* basis instead of a *we* relationship. We are prepared to be kind to other races, but not to be just. To be kind keeps up the *they–I* relationship; you're the bountiful patron, and they are the recipients. To be just would put both on the same footing, set up a *we* relationship.

Even in Christian missions, this *they–I* relationship is sometimes continued. In Africa, at a tea party, the white missionaries sat on one side and the Africans on the other. I couldn't stand this *they–I* business and went over and sat with the Africans. One of them said to me afterward, "You're a white native, aren't you?" With a lump in my throat I replied, "I'd like to be."...

The race problem is no longer a problem if we inwardly say *we* instead of *they–I*. The problem then is not race, but in our attitudes toward race.

How to Be a Transformed Person
(Week 37, Saturday)

The Mastery of Race Distinctions
Matthew 23:9-10; Luke 2:28-32

The coming of the Holy Spirit dissolved the distinctions based on race. The new society that emerged was color-blind and race-blind—a new race made up of all races.

Mastery
(Week 10, Thursday)

I Believe the Bible, All Except....
Luke 13:28-30

God didn't argue the equal worth of all races before him. God did something more profound and gave to all races the same gift, the gift of the Holy Spirit. That simple fact did more to abolish race prejudices and distinctions than all the exhortations of moralists and the disquisitions of philosophers put together. It was a fact that couldn't be argued. It had to be accepted—or rejected, saying God was wrong. Some do. A friend from India was speaking in America and quoted the passage "[God] hath made of one blood all nations" (Acts 17:26 KJV). A man arose and said: "I believe the Bible—all except that verse."...

God knew what he was doing in giving the Holy Spirit equally to all, for down underneath is one basic humanity modified slightly by environment.

Mastery
(Week 10, Saturday)

The American Way of Dealing with Race
Matthew 5:21-24

America's prestige in the world will be decided by the African American's prestige in America. They will be equal.

The church must lead the way. Now it is leading verbally but not vitally. For the greatest hour of segregation in American life is eleven o'clock Sunday morning. Churches are the greatest illustration of segregation in American life. We come together in conferences and conventions, but in the basic life of individual churches segregation is in operation—with few exceptions. For years I have been pleading that every white church have at least one African American member and every African American church at least one white member. That wouldn't solve the problem, but it would be a symbol that we believe in and live in a kingdom that is class-blind and color-blind, seeing only persons—persons for whom Christ died.

Mastery
(Week 11, Monday)

A New Race Made up of All Races
Colossians 3:10-11

[Another] characteristic mark of the New Testament Church as seen in the church at Antioch...: the church was without race and class—a raceless and classless society....

This church was a church beyond race. A new race was emerging, made up of all races....

In the early church there was no division on the line of race—a person was a man, a person for whom Christ died. They had the kingdom of God, and we have the kingdom of Race.

A religion that is identified with the superiority or the supremacy of one race is a backward eddy in the stream of history where people of all races and all colors flow toward oneness in community.

Mastery
(Week 20, Tuesday)

Smarter Than I Am
Revelation 7:9-10

I asked a little girl of ten, daughter of missionaries in Malaya, whether she liked her school in which there were all races, and she replied, "Yes, I like it very much, for it gives me an opportunity to study along with Asian children and to know them." And then she added, "Some of them are very smart, smarter than I am." That child was mature in her attitudes, far more mature than many of the older generation who draw the line of fellowship with other races and narrow themselves in the process.

A white Georgia boy, when asked if he favored the coming of black children into white schools, replied, "Yes, of course. That will give us an opportunity to give them the same privileges that we have had." That boy was more mature in his attitudes than are those who see in other races problems rather than possibilities. The future belongs to that boy and what he represents.

Christian Maturity
(Week 5, Tuesday)

Fellowship with Other Christians
Luke 9:49-50

Those who are out of fellowship with God and people are immature, undeveloped human beings. The measure of our maturity can be and is measured by the breadth and depth of our capacity for fellowship. We are as mature as our fellowships. So if we cannot fellowship with other races, we reveal our immaturity. All segregation segregates into immaturity those who segregate. The payoff is in the person.

This statement holds good in regard to our capacity for fellowship with other Christians. If we can fellowship only with those who belong to our group, our denomination, or our particular set of doctrinal beliefs, then in such measure we are immature. What, then, is the basis of our fellowship? One thing and one thing only: everyone who belongs to Christ belongs to everyone who belongs to Christ. The basis of our fellowship is not around this doctrine, that doctrine, the other doctrine; or around this group, that group, or the other group. It is around Christ and only around Christ.

Christian Maturity
(Week 5, Thursday)

Christianity and Race
Luke 4:18-21

There are many people, otherwise mature, who are quite immature in regard to race. And it is a costly immaturity.

Before we examine it, let us look at our Christian faith to see what its attitudes are, for we are taking our standards on maturity from that faith.

In the time of Christ there was great tension between Jew and Gentile. But it was said by Simeon, in his inspired prophecy, that Jesus would be "a light to lighten the Gentiles" (Luke 2:32 KJV), or "a light for revelation to the Gentiles" (RSV). This light would reveal the Gentiles and their worthwhileness and their possibilities. That was the keynote struck in the very beginning; people of other races were not to be problems but possibilities.

This was followed up by Jesus, when he announced his program in the little synagogue at Nazareth: "good news to the poor"—the socially and politically disinherited, "recovering of sight to the blind"—the physically disinherited, "set at liberty those who are oppressed"—the morally and spiritually disinherited, "proclaim the acceptable year of the Lord" (Luke 4:18-19). This was a fresh world beginning,

324

based on the Jewish year of jubilee; every fifty years all slaves were freed, all debts canceled, all land redistributed. The people "wondered at the gracious words which proceeded out of his mouth" (v. 22). But Jesus went on and let them know how far he intended to go: there were many widows in Israel but the prophet was sent to a Gentile widow; there were many lepers in Israel but the prophet was sent to a Gentile leper. This program of total redemption was to go to a person as a person, apart from race. The atmosphere changed; they were all "filled with wrath" (v. 28). It was too big for their small hearts.

Christian Maturity
(Week 29, Thursday)

Some Doomed to Inferiority?
Luke 4:25-30

We are looking at the Christian attitude toward race. Paul, a narrow Pharisee, having inherited all the Jewish racial exclusiveness in an intensified form, comes into contact with Jesus and then writes this amazing sentence: "[In Jesus Christ] there is neither Greek nor Jew"—race distinction, "barbarian nor Scythian"—cultural distinction, "slave nor free"—social and economic distinction, "male nor female"—gender distinction (see Col 3:11; Gal 3:28). All these distinctions were wiped out, and a person was looked on apart from race, birth, color, position, and gender. A person was a person for whom Christ died. No greater leveling-up proposal and power has ever been presented to humankind than this. This is the authentic Christian position. Departures from it are sub-Christian and anti-Christian, even though they may be made in the name of the Christian religion. The burning of a cross in the name of race hatred is burning Jesus at the stake.

Some, in their desperation to find Scriptural support for their racism, turn to passages like the one in Genesis in which Noah cursed Canaan, son of Ham, saying: "A slave of slaves shall he be to his brothers" (9:25). And what had Canaan done to deserve this curse? His father, Ham, saw Noah drunk and uncovered in his tent and went and told his brothers, and they walked backward and covered Noah with a blanket. Noah awoke from his drunkenness and uttered this curse. God had nothing to do with it. A drunken man uttered the curse as he came out of his stupor. To get one's racial attitudes from the curse of a drunken man is to gain doubtful backing. If God would doom a whole race to slavery because of what Ham did there, then that God would be my devil.

The Christian position in regard to the person of color is this: "Symeon who was called Niger" (literally, "the Black") was a prophet or a teacher in the church at Antioch, and he laid his hands on Paul and Barnabas that they should go and preach the gospel to white Europe (Acts 13:1-3). Paul was ordained by a Black man. This is the position of Christianity; it is color-blind. Christianity sees only a person for whom Christ died.

Christian Maturity
(Week 29, Friday)

The Bell Is Tolling, the Tide Is Rolling In
Acts 10:28, 34, 43-44

We continue this week to meditate upon the text: "I saw thrones, and [people] sat upon them" (Rev 20:4 KJV).

The social revolution is on. The people as people are arising everywhere, tired of being downtrodden and exploited. The Communists did not produce that social revolution. They have betrayed it, betrayed it by turning it into channels of suppression and compulsion. We must rescue it and turn it into channels of freedom and democracy. It cannot be turned back; it can only be directed. Said a African American minister, in regard to the Supreme Court decision and the opposition to integration: "The bell is tolling, the tide is rolling in, and you can't stop it anymore than you can stop the flow of Hampton Roads [Virginia waterway] with your two hands."

I picked up my morning paper and read that the legislature of a certain state voted that "state funds shall be cut off from any integrated school." My guess is that the children, or at most the grandchildren, of the people who so voted will look back with laughter on that voting, as an un-American, undemocratic, and unchristian attempt to turn back the clock.

Christian Maturity
(Week 30, Sunday)

"These Boys Right Out of the Bush"
Acts 4:13-14

We must now face a question that lies back of the unwillingness to grant equality of opportunity to all. And the question is this: Isn't it true that there are inherently inferior races and inherently superior races and that these differences are fixed and unalterable? My experience as I have mingled with all races for many years has brought me to a different conclusion. I am convinced that there are no permanently superior races and no permanently inferior races. Given the same stimulus and the same incentive, the brain of humanity will come out about the same.

Christian Maturity
(Week 30, Wednesday)

One Blood All Nations
Amos 9:7; Acts 8:27-29

We said yesterday that there are infinite possibilities in every person, of every race; that exposed to the same stimulus and given the same incentives, the human brain will come out about the same. There is one blood in humanity: "[God] hath made of one blood all nations" (Acts 17:26 KJV). A friend from India speaking in America quoted that passage, and a member of the audience arose and said: "I believe in the whole Bible, all except that verse." But his disbelief could not turn back the facts of science. Under the microscope there is one blood. You might have a blood transfusion from a person of another race who has the same type of blood as you have, while the blood of your biological brother might be unsuitable. So you might be nearer in blood to a person of another race than to your own brother.

Christian Maturity
(Week 30, Thursday)

This Property Not for Sale
Acts 11:8-12

To be prejudiced against people because of their race and color is as sensible as the attitude of the woman who said she would not vote for a candidate because she didn't like the way he combed his hair....

The future belongs to the white Georgia boy who said, "Of course, let the Blacks attend our schools. Then they will have the same opportunity as we have and we can help to lift them." That boy is in line with the wave of the future. He is mature in his outlook and judgments. Those who stand against equal opportunity for all are immature.

When a respectable black man moved into a block of all white people in St. Louis, six signs went up on property in that block: "For Sale." Then this sign went up on the largest and finest home on the block: "This property is not for sale. We welcome to our neighborhood any person who is of good character and intends to keep up his property. We do not inquire into a man's politics, race, or religion—only his character." In a few days all the other six signs came down. That man was mature.

Christian Maturity
(Week 30, Saturday)

A Church That Cared
Acts 15:7-11

The social prejudices die hard. A man went to his pastor and said, "If you lay off your emphasis on race justice, here is a check with five numbers." The pastor left the man with his check and kept his soul. He was a Christian; he could do no other. For the Christian faith is class-blind and race-blind.

The Word Became Flesh
(Week 35, Wednesday)

WOMEN

Another Cause of Sin: Attitudes toward Women
Matthew 19:3-10; Galatians 3:28

The economic and political order is largely the result of male organizing. And in the organizing, woman has been fitted into it largely on the basis of a sex-being, and she is supposed to be treated and to act as such. Woman has, in general, accepted this false mentality and has given herself to the petty business of being attractive to the male. This has been the cause of much sin in human society....

Woman, in driving this new force called freedom, is making a wreck of many a fine reticence, many a strong trait. But we cannot stop until woman arrives at the place where Jesus placed her as a human personality and not a mere sex-being. She must be given an equal place and an equal tasks in the reconstruction of the world.

Victorious Living
(Week 24, Tuesday)

The Highest Open to Woman
Galatians 3: 27-29

The Holy Spirit makes both sexes equal. There had been a specially sacred [gender], the male [gender]. "Every male that opens the womb shall be called holy to the Lord" (Luke 2:23; see Exod 13:2). That was as far as Judaism went, but the Christian faith went beyond this; a woman as a woman received the highest gift of God—the Holy Spirit—and if this is true, then all the lesser gifts must be open to her. "All these with one accord devoted themselves to prayer, together with the women....And they were all filled with the Holy Spirit" (Acts 1:14; 2:4)....

Then something happened; the Holy Spirit came upon a woman equally with a man, and that planted the equality of woman in an experience of God. If the highest gift of God is open to a woman, then all the lesser gifts of God, must be open to her too. This outflanked all the arguments of antiquity about man's superiority, and placed man and woman on the basis of equality before God and hence in all the rest of life. No wonder Paul sums up the Christian attitude in these words: "There is neither Jew nor Greek, there is neither slave nor free, there is neither male nor female; for you are all one in Christ Jesus" (Gal 3:28). To take any other attitude was to blaspheme the Holy Spirit.

The Way to Power and Poise
(Week 13, Wednesday)

Inferior Status of Women
Luke 8:1-3; Acts 1:14

Growth in social consciousness should wipe out of our civilization all remnants of social inferiorities that are still there, sometimes consciously and sometimes subconsciously.

For instance, Paul gave the Christian position regarding the structure of a Christian society thus: "In it there is no room for Greek and Jew [social distinction], circumcised and uncircumcised [religious rite distinction], barbarian, Scythian [cultural distinction], slave, or free man [social, economic distinction]; Christ is everything and everywhere" (Col 3:11 Moffatt). And in Gal 3:28 (Moffatt), he adds: "There is no room for male and female [gender distinction]; you are all one in Christ Jesus." That is the Christian position—clear, positive, sweeping. And in Peter's speech at Pentecost, he said: "Your sons and daughters shall prophesy"—note "and daughters"—(Acts 2:17, Moffatt).

But in 1 Cor 14:34 (Moffatt), Paul enjoins something else: "Women must keep quiet at gatherings of the church. They are not to allowed to speak...as the Law enjoins." Note that he appeals to "the Law" for authority. Is he falling into the very thing he told Galatians they were doing? It seems so. Every time Paul tried to put woman in a subordinate position, he appealed to the Old Testament, not to Jesus. Note: "but woman represents the supremacy of man. (Man was not made from woman, woman was made from man; and man was not created for woman, but woman for man" (1 Cor 11:7-9 Moffatt). Here he turns back to the first creation for corroboration for his position—the first creation—not to the new creation in Jesus where "there is no room for male or female." Again in 1 Tim 2:12-14 (Moffatt), he says: "I allow no woman to teach or dictate to men, she must keep quiet. For Adam was created first, then Eve; and Adam was not deceived, it was Eve." Here he turned to the first Adam for the sustaining of his position—the first Adam—not the Second Adam, Christ. His Christianity slipped a cog. And that slipping back to the pre-Christian thought has caused much confusion. Paul says that sometimes he was not inspired; he was speaking on his own. This was one of the times. And the ages have suffered because of it.

Growing Spiritually
(Week 44, Friday)

And the Ground Was Level for the Women Too
Acts 1:12:14

But this gift of the Holy Spirit was not only open to men as men; it was open to women as women—"with the women" (Acts 1:14). Here were women taken into the very center of privilege and opportunity. Women received the highest gift of God, the Holy Spirit. That opened everything down the line. At Pentecost, women not only received the Holy Spirit on the same basis as men, but they proclaimed that gospel on the same basis as men, "your sons your your daughters shall prophesy" (Acts 2:17)....

There was equality of standing before God and equality of opportunity before persons; there was equality! And that equality of opportunity extended to Mary, the mother of Jesus. The last thing we see of Mary is that she was praying for the Holy Spirit on the same basis as the rest. She was in her place along with the rest.

The Word Became Flesh
(Week 28, Wednesday)

The Divine Illustration
Mark 1:16-20

[Jesus] did not argue the worth of womanhood and the necessity of giving women equal rights; he treated them with infinite respect, gave to them his most sublime teaching, as to the woman at the well, and when he rose from the dead he appeared first to a woman.

The Word Became Flesh
(Week 51, Tuesday)

CPSIA information can be obtained
at www.ICGtesting.com
Printed in the USA
LVHW02s0219141018
593311LV00002B/2/P